OBEDIENCE TO THE CALL OF ART

Red Jordan Arobateau

JOURNEY Volumes 6-10

Any resemblance to any person living or dead is purely coincidental.

Cover art by Red Jordan Arobateau; Student At The Golden Pot 2008; oil on canvas, 30" x 22". Artist's collection, San Francisco.

ISBN: 978-0-6152-2144-1

Published by RED JORDAN PRESS
484 Lake Park Ave. PMB 228
Oakland, CA 94610
USA

Artist! Don't be disappointed! Continue! As many of the other Greats have done before you! Each brush stroke! Each written word! Each on-point ballet step! The Great Dance Of Life must continue! Must have you! When discouraged, listen to the others who have gone up this rough, stark mountainside before!

--THE PASSION OF ART

2007-2008

Index:

COMPASSION

JOURNEY Vol. 6

2007

You shall serve one another.

Seek God while S/He is accessible; call upon Her while S/He is yet near. Let the wicked forsake their way and the iniquitous person their intentions; let them return to God who will show them compassion and to our God who forgives liberally. For My thoughts are not as your thoughts and your ways are not as My ways, says God. By the height of heaven above earth, so are My ways higher than your ways and My thoughts higher than your thoughts. For as the rain once fallen from the sky never returns there, rather shall it water the earth making it blossom and fruitful giving seed to the sower and bread to the eater. So shall be My word which proceeds from My mouth; it shall not return to Me ineffective, but will accomplish what I desire and will succeed in the mission for which I sent it. For you shall depart in joy and be led forth in singing and all the trees of the woodland shall echo with applause.

--Isaiah 55: 6-12, Holy Bible.

70.

Here is a confession: In the spirit of Compassion ---which includes
sex, naturally, very much so (sleazy sex is a vital part of the human
construct) —am going to be hip deep in pussy tonight—my own.
Meaning just had my T-shot thus am revved up on male hormones;
purchased a new toy at the store Joni Blank founded. Carol Queen
and Robert lecture Sex-Ed there; that Sex Shoppe wherein worked the
fictitious Rosa Salazar; Good Vibrations, Yeah! Which hires open
unpassable transsexual clerks of all colors, races and sizes ---and
might add my new toy is called the Purple Plunge.

I will Dress Up in fake tits. I will top myself; bottom for myself too!
I will create a fantasy scenario, loosing self in it for pure animal
pleasure.

Well, as promised, just a hint of the jerk off scene. *PS. None of this
is true!*

71.

My message first & foremost is to remind you, that--the human heart
has many chambers. Love, greed, envy, hate, fear, anger, lust. —
Choose life!

Dear World, today I shall lecture… and ramble… and reminisce…
and take into account various & sundry things. I will speak of faith,
religion; and will utter prophecies. Am empowered to do so by
authority of the biblical scriptures regarding priesthood of the
believer. PS, I am a prophet. Yes. One of the biggest brainwashing
jobs forced on the human race since time immoral—for the sake of
seizing power—is the lie that God(ess) speaks only to these or those
few persons, or special groups, races, or religions, when in fact the
opposite is true, God speaks to all who will listen! And there are
many prophets. Go into many tiny black storefront churches and you
will find a prophet(ess) ensconced on a cheap chair lovingly draped in
clean, ironed, white linen, decked out in their special robe, fancy hat,
possessing all the specialized religious paraphernalia which has
caught their eye. Among these self ordained prophet(esses) are those
truly gifted, others shams. Although I am a hustler, you must take my
words serious!

So my political analysis, it is:

> First: for education of others.
> Second: to serve as a calendar of reminders of just ways to move our tiny chess pieces over the game board of good/evil called earth.
> Third: to remain in permanence by faith, while being shown the real motives of the corrupt powers of authority, & speaking aloud to this so history will have a witness.

Whereas in previous decades of writing I portrayed spirituality, & left-wing lessons of a political nature vaguely, disguised as a story, with fascinating characters and spellbinding dialogue, now I tell openly what before was only hinted at between the lines. And type in further knowledge of spiritual matters as a religious project; & also because its my life work; and finally because to me it's a joy, and when I'm creating it, it falls under DOC's 13th rule; i.e., *The Order will have grand, clean religious fun.*

> Your journey to the Most High should be exciting; it should be fun! Plenty of Good Works, and Social Groups of Action will be involved! Food! Your lonely board of poverty has increased to Largess of the community at a banquet table.

'These are the most deepest of human thoughts.' Thought the old Transman, shuffling about his studio with his book bag. He daydreamed this: *'I will read aloud to the Children of the Revolution, great PASSAGES of high inspiration!'*

Out of the gutter of common stuff I presented LAMENTATIONS* — maybe time will prove that document a special one. Regarding World War III approaching on the backs of the four horsemen of the Apocalypse; the state of U$ military affairs, especially the Middle East; Christendom's umpteenth 'pilgrimage'.

*Lamentations For the Cool Of The Evening—Words Of The Prophet.

I'm totally uneducated, unschooled & untaught about these subjects— yet as Marx or Lenin did not march into the city of Saint Petersburg alone, nor up the Czars palace steps as a solitary soldier to render the final coup, but it was the masses of humanity, their brawny muscles, the strength of multitudes moving for justice that won the victory… So, it is not always the wise, school-educated pundits who are entitled to rite great books!

My journal continues. A kind of Dreamtime For The Every Day Revolutionary.

At his advancing age, 63, Transman contemplated how things that made so much difference once, like to have the love of ones life, or be a famous artist, made no difference now. —Yet still they do.

I want to tell you something. I'm not an extremely intelligent person, but somehow have the gift of love and of compassion. And that only to the degree that God says it is. Now this might be a small love, and a narrow compassion, but over time and exercise by works it can grow quite large. Exercise of works beginning in prayer, in empathic thoughts about any troubled situation. Plus I have a natural talent and decent mind---by which I have written these 80-some odd books.

If you've ever had an eviction notice taped to your door—you will always remember it, maybe in a flashback as you trod up your dusty-walled, worn red carpeted corridor hallway just before turning the corner, visualize waiting upon the blank white door front, that deadly message signed by the sheriff for your removal. This is the threat constantly held over the poor of this city! —In the fascist wave of landowners robbery known as condo conversion.

'Ahh…' Sighed the old Transman; thinking, *'it would be so good if the hills came to an end & there was only level ground. Then peaceful valleys. But we must keep going…on our journey.'*

Saw a futuristic movie; its backdrop; shelled out apocalyptic buildings. It was so desolate. The kind of desolation I understand. There are some who live upground in the sunshine and acclaim of their peers and others who live in the land of eternal night. Not included, never asked, remaining on the outside. Always on the outside over a lifetime, which has a heavy consequence. Thus, upon miraculously finding a good wife, one would think he would have held onto to her as the most precious thing in his existence, especially having so little else, yet she had slipped thru his fingers as a precious gold coin.

I wandered 7 years now in loneliness and depression, when I think about it, because of sin. I neglected God. I committed adultery against my beloved wife. And have suffered a consequence.

Dear Children, you have the Masters touch but you must discipline your passions!

To practice discipline no matter how feelings are raging within you is the Christ-like* path. (Buddha, Mohammad, etc.)

We have spoken of the highly alienated. Those disenfranchised from society. They live in a soundless world. Seldom permeated by the voice of human kindness.

Those who walk around with a heart split in two. We present Transman, he is like many; living an ordinary life in a small studio apartment quietly with books, their church, synagogue, or ashram, their via media lives, simple, plain, holistic, prayerful; devoted to God. A nun, or priest of a different sort.

Transman limps out of his studio apartment, down the worn red-carpeted hallway. Stains on his worn black trousers is peanut butter from a dog treat for a furry four legged red tongue tail wagging client at the animal shelter where he volunteers. (Works.) He exits out of the moldy, cool, quiet interior into the real weather of earth, air, & sun. He sees on the front entranceway that the glass in his apartment building directory is smashed. Jagged glass like sharks teeth. Drops of dark red blood, dried on the stoop. Some tenants last night fight.

I have walked, and I have walked.

Bright flashing of light cameras explode everywhere. It's tourist season.

A rare gem hiding in plain sight! Me! --- Yet undiscovered.

God reaches us *thru oceans of time...* It's the only way, love. Time bending on a light beam... to bring about bonding, gentleness... This seems so impossible amid nuclear holocausts, genocide, modern day red-hot infernos sweeping earth... but it's the only way.

Will money ever get you the things you want? Well, your life would be more convenient; you would have distractions to forget loneliness. But we've got a journey. And we must go on it.... Each soul has a journey...

Some of the obstacles to be overcome upon the destiny of a human journey:

> 1. Preoccupation with money— in any way, rich or poor.
> 2. Veering off the path to marry with some person in an arrangement, which shuts one off from community, and spiritual/religious growth.
> 3. Anger, vented in red fiery bombasts, or suppressed in black simmering rage.
> 4. Desire for fame of self, Napoleonic ego.
> 5. Gluttony of the physical senses so that mindlessness takes place, and suffering of self and of others is ignored, thus no growth is possible.

If you aren't part of the solution, then you're part of the problem. (Adage from the in-between-war years of the 1980's.) Here's one reason those High Rises are going up all over the city like ugly weeds:

An obnoxious cell phone user is on the bus—topic of her loud conversation? *Real-estate!* Condos for sale! She's wheeling & dealing houses like red/white chessboard pawns in a city where the poor can no longer find housing, not even a single room hotel occupancy in the fleabag/bedbug infested Tenderloin. Impatiently snaps the cell phone closed. Suddenly she gazes down at her hands... red splotches have appeared on them!

Bright red splotches now cover her hands and wrists! Red, wet!

"Where did this come from?" She queries, her voice addressing the air, as she holds her hands in front of her in disbelief.

"WHAT IS THIS?" She says, louder, her face turning towards the other passengers, bewildered.

Miracle! A miracle! That's what it is! ---Stigmata! It's cell phone stigmata! A miracle on the bus! Her eternal reward for devotion to using cell phone and ceaseless prayers on wireless for real estate acquisitions! She is branded & marked forever with the Blood of our Lamb!

*

We know by now what we are supposed to do. To do good. To keep evil thoughts out of our minds –least they come to fruit on the material plane. My initial reaction to people who cross my line of vision, is I see them as enemies, which slows down my process of spiritual redemption. This is probably due to my severely abused childhood, and outsider status as an adult. An idea, quite an old one; predating the Judean-Christian religions, is to look at Gods people more with love and not hate. Not judgment.

Roughly I re-quote Saint Augustine; 'my heart cries out for God. In God is my peace, and it won't be until I've gone to God that my soul will find its home.'

God said *I Am*. Always Was, and always will Be. Earth and mountains and oceans pass away, human and animal life will cease. And God still Is.

72.
Part I. The Student. Adventures Of The Spiritual Disciple. This protagonist is a person of different races, ages, and gender descriptions. Remember, each day is a journey between awareness and blindness. Chose one!

Lesson #1
The student goes out on his or her first day—the master is watching from above.

The student, being impoverished due to his principal vow—abandoning desire for material wealth-- must take public transportation. A small scene develops amid the crowd of scruffy persons at the bus stop. A dope addicted beggar tries to sell off a bus token for $1.00. The student is sick of seeing poor homeless bums hustling, smirking, thinking they are cute, thus he is already somewhat rattled, mentally off-center, when he wearily climbs up the bus steps & takes a seat.

A woman is singing, poorly, on the back of the bus, shouting and laughing with her friends.

In front, the hustling bum who has also boarded the bus peers back at the revelers, looks to see whose singing. Then she begins a tirade against her. "You'll never make it to the finals! HA! HA!" This causes the student to guffaw loudly. By laughing he has encouraged her! So, feeling she has an ally the woman shouts even louder; "Sorry but a cow ain't got nothing on you. Wide ass bitch."

 Suddenly the student snaps his head away. 'Oh shit! She is being cruel! Aw this is the test!' The student comes to his senses. Love has awakened him!

He restrains himself; averts his eye---diverting his precious soul from sin. Inwardly he engages in feverish meditation. *'Oh my Gawd! Some of the people I most love or have loved were fat. And can't sing worth shit! I must look out on the avenue with different eyes...'*

Lesson #2
The student comes to a crossing, she is ragged, hair wild, feet and legs; dust flurries stings her eyes.

Right or left. Which way shall I go? She looks at a signpost, faded old wood, split boards, she can barely make out it's words... it says---God—indicating that one of the ways leads to God. But demons have twisted the signpost, so it no longer points in the correct direction, or does it? Which path leads to God?

The student closes her eyes. She gives up her mind to pure light, of no thought. She consults the Spirit.

A golden glow appears straight ahead! That is the path, neither right nor left!

Lesson #3

The student goes on a job interview. He is black and possesses a mild gender ambiguity. The interviewer is a racist and homophobic. Also hates women, and the student is either a sissy male or a former female, now transitioned. At the close of the meeting the miscreant interviewer mentions to the student that his case is hopeless and to find work he might go up to the Castro District—which has a high concentration of queers. And makes this remark:

"They hire your kind up there."

"Thank you very much." Replies the student, then turns on his heel and walks away.

This is an example of maturity. He responded to the unkindly remark politely. He did not linger there in a place he was unwanted discussing the matter any further. He did not offer up any information as to 'which kind' he was, nor tip his hand.

The student has discharged his/her duty for the day.

Lesson #4.

The student goes out on his fourth day. The master, in spirit watches from above. The student strides down the path, then stumbles. Falls into some foolish situation. The master in spirit slaps the student gently as a means of instruction. The ordinary individual makes this same response to the foolish situation commonly, falling into rage or despair because of his failures or inability to overcome its challenge, and is thus brought down from the lofty place to the low---wounded in addition by the slap. The common person scurries back to his hiding place and sulks, but we are not common folk. After all our training. And, if struck by the master—we are not unknowing of karma, of cause & effect, divine return, etc, --- we recognize this as discipline. The student by now possessing the glimmer of realization that s/he has merely failed this particular lesson and only delayed his journey by a day, thus has hope for the future, does not consider this setback a mortal twist of fate un-repairable or irretrievable.

The 5th day the student again goes out. The master/teacher waits, watching lovingly from above, to see how far the student will progress this day. This time the student passes the first test, making it nearly to the middle of the scheduled route, but again an incident occurs, in which he stumbles badly and falls. There is still tomorrow to try once more! Each day a new lesson. Having mastered 5 lessons, the student purposefully sets out once more. This time s/he is able to go such a far distance with out falling that the lesson is complete. The journey to the first plateau has been obtained! Now it is time to go on to the next level—towards the goal of enlightenment.

> You have the Masters touch but you must discipline your passions! To practice discipline no matter how feelings are raging within you is the Christ-like path.

Apes are given tasks, to gather leaves to eat, to find water, to migrate for food in season, to raise young. We, the higher mammals—human beings have, given to us, commandments. This is our work, the work our limited human capacity can grapple with. We were given those Ten Commandments but we can't even do that!

73.
> I have 20 friends and 64 enemies.
> --Overheard at Babylon Falling Bookstore 2007.

Lesson #5:
The student trudges uphill on his way to the Benedictine Society; pulling a heavy 2-wheel cart of groceries/on-sale foods from the over-price Kapitalist Market so he is almost bent double in the effort to climb the steep upward slope of Cathedral Hill. Sweat pouring from his brow he pictures his enemies of the moment, thinking cruel revenges, then dismissing them, yet cannot stop remembering the enemy's face, fantasying nefarious tortures for each, but then putting that inside too; only moments later taking upon his soul once more that hideous conflicts of the past—and dismissing them just as fast according to the teachings of our Savior about forgiveness, all the while legs pumping, arms dragging the cart, steadily mounting the hill; and thus he recalls, lets go, remembers, dismisses, back and

forth, on & on in a tiresome tug of war of devil vs. angel—his immortal soul being the prize---digesting his remembrances, over and over and over and over running circles along the machinery of this conjunction of physical stress & turmoil in his mind; when, midway uphill his straining eyes happens to notice CAT LOST! Sign on a lamppost. A little grey kitten, sickly looking, innocent. PLEASE RETURN HIM HE NEEDS HIS MEDICATION! The student stops to pray. *What are your thoughts?'* instructs the master. At once the student realizes the benefit of not harboring dark, violent thoughts in his soul! Again, a benefit for aiming to be pure in heart, it is ---to have a clean prayer to go to God. *Things prayed for, prayers answered...*

Lesson #6:
The student sits near the front of the bus where, inadvertently he is able to witness the following transaction. A dark complexioned black male, younger, driving the bus, scowls at the road ahead. Three affluent white girl-women very well dressed go to disembark and one asks for the transfers for which they have previously paid.

Unknowing Woman Tourist: I'll take our 3 transfers now please driver.

Spiritually Stupid Driver: NO YOU KAIN'T HAVE NO TRANSFER!

Unknowing Woman Tourist: Driver I paid our fares!

Spiritually Stupid Driver: YOU 'POSE TO GET YOUR TRANSFERS AT THE TIME OF PAYMENT! THAT SIGN SAY SO! (Jabs finger at sign.)

Unknowing Woman Tourist: But I already paid for them! I paid 3 fares, for each of my friends when we got on!

Spiritually Stupid Driver: YOU KAIN'T GET NO TRANSFERS NOW! YOU 'POSE TO GET THEM WHEN YOU GET ON!

Unknowing Woman Tourist: But I didn't know that!

Spiritually Stupid Driver: NO! I KAIN'T GIVE YOU NO TRANSFERS!

Unknowing Woman Tourist: Driver I already paid 3 fares for myself, and my friends! I'm not going to pay all over again when we get on the next bus!

Spiritually Stupid Driver: I DON'T KNOW YOU PAID! YOU MIGHT HAVE SNUCK ON AT THE BACK OF THE BUS!

The Student: You must be from the 'hood man, you 'custom to them ghetto gals! These women type of women they don't' sneak on the back of busses!

Following the stubborn drivers inability to part with the 3 slips of paper, he is summarily trashed by the other passengers.

Male Passenger (To driver; disembarking bus in disgust): You'll want somebody to do you a favor sometime!

The Student (To driver; disembarking bus): What goes around comes around buddy.

Unknowing Woman Tourist (Disembarking the bus): You're ridiculous Driver!

The Master: You are venting your own anger at his ignorance. Say it in a way they can hear. —That is a lesson given in love, not hate. Are you big enough to love the un-evolved Driver who is behaving stupidly?

*

Each act of good—no matter how small, isn't as insignificant as it seems. It is a model for others, many will emulate it in their modest way, and each of these acts gives rise to other people doing more good works, and so that single act grows to immense proportions.

74.
Here are some more commentary on DOC:

There are levels of devotion among nuns and priests of DOC just like ordinary non-religious people, or non-monastic people; some take Gods Word to a higher state of mind and deeper meaning of revelation into themselves.

> Slip on vest of white or beige background with the red Maltese cross emblazoned on the front & on the back. Our uniform can easily be slipped on over any clothing of the world or habit of our DOC organization.

Eikes! In my excitement & suddenly dawned on me, Islam, Wiccan, Jew, Hindu, might find it impossible to wear our emblem the cross of the Templers ancient order, the Maltese Cross, which is an adaptation of the holy crucifix of our Savior! Gaack! What to do… Well a similar costume with a patch in red of each members own unique holy symbol then! (Star of David, Etc.) Amazing my small brain did not think of this until 4 books later!!!!!!

DOC will grow because of preaching & pandering to the peoples better instincts to try to do justice. DOC will help people mobilize their power to overturn adverse and backwards situations.

If I wasn't religious what would I do? Collect antiques? What else is there? I don't want to collect fine arts oil paintings--I'm a already a fine arts oil painter myself and have my own art.

*

--Further notes about the Order—DOC: No DOC members should be subjected to slanderous, hurtful, hateful attacking statements from priests, rabbis, mullahs, masters, etc., by any religious institution in the surrounding communities in which DOC is located and which DOC Order members are mandated to attend. And which they will support. If those institutions are purposefully anti-gay, anti Semitic, anti Islamic, racist, sexist, male supremacists, & so-forth, the members may walk out, but they must do by agreement with each other, en mass… for if one is offended, all are offended; and never more return to that institution. If no friendly institutions can be located within a reasonable distance of travel from the Order, then they will have to hold ersatz religions community ceremonies in their own House.

Regarding Rule #8, of Relationships.

> She slept with a guy she met an hour before.
> --Overheard SF Yuppie on cellphone—2007.

***

> Had I made the leap into the life of a monastic, I would rule out romance of a personal level, exchanging it for the dance of the divine.
> ---WORKS.

I see emphasized in motion today that very important statute regarding relationships, and will now reiterate what I'd said previously, based on my knowledge of the human heart. That it is very difficult to fully serve God in community and in the world as a person involved in a personal romantic/sexual relationship. Today at one of the holy places I go two esteemed group members sat quite close to each other, seemingly absorbed in some private exchange between them. That two-person relationship soon become evident to all others around. Shortly they were ignoring the entire group process and were all but billing & cooing. See again how this hampers group dynamics. The 2 now joined as one animal are bulky, taking up twice as much space, and seeming more space then did their individual selves which, independently could move more rapidly, gracefully and not get in the way. In a couple their energy is absorbed back and forth between each other with not enough to spare to dole out to the fellow members of the Order, nor the surrounding community members, much less the greater world! The erotic, romantic personal love life relationship between two people is a distraction from doing the Work, building the Order, and serving humankind!

There is much less time to ask questions of either of the twosome. Together walking or sitting repeatedly together like lovers on a park bench arouses jealousy of the more needy of the members--- and hinder the healing progress of weaker members who need to draw on the information and strengths those provide, but are too shy to interrupt them. There is less energy to give on one hand. And more room for jealousy, and the idea that one may be intruding on the couples 'private time' together, or private conversations, is defeating.

20

Would you give up family, lover, money, house, security, to follow Christ? I have heard talk of Hildegard, a 10th century visionary who wrote of Caritas—divine love.

One of the most profound, difficult decisions in life is realization that you must love God more then you love a lover, a companion.

I like being out in the world, alone, the cold concrete, the wind, rainy weather, isolation. It ex-sponges up the pain.

Well, on the worldly side of things, I know betrayal by people you once loved & depended on certainly will lead you into the arms of the Most High.

75.
So the torah scrolls roll right to left, with the turning of seasons, winter, spring, summer, fall; the month of Av-- destruction, Elul, then Tishrei, the month of joyous celebrations follows. Christians will be celebrating our Holidays not long from now. Amid all this joy, the ever-pressing form of the beggar waif pressing her nose against the frosts white icy windowpanes, on the outside looking in, looking in at what could be… wondering *how much longer?*

The hot grind-away road, on which a chorus of traffic honks— impatient drivers laying on the horn. In the din of this cacophony the musical genius hears symphonies; is motivated to go to higher worlds because of such great beauty! They hear such beautiful music, sounds no words can describe!

I will get out of my death-bed to write!

Does the poor villager who cares for the sick in an impoverished, primitive and private world win the race to divinity first, or does the monastic who, connected with a greater organized religious body, as they do good works, move upwards in that hierarchy taking various pre-established offices thus earning greater collateral that serve him to some day be judged a saint? Can this lowly village holy person be Sainted? Will great religious pundits examine their lives for the Steps towards Beautification? A great Saint is Mother Ama, who gives hugs; whose goal is to hug everybody on earth. Her Ashrams are in the US, and India. Yet she will never be recognized as a holy woman.

You can serve Me as well. They serve Me just the same.

Well I'll never be a saint—nor offered that title, because I'm not a catholic!

I feel I have been prepared, then, called by God. Wonder if I have been chosen. (I do not know. Nor do I assume.) Those 25 years spent as an atheist were not wasted. Maybe its no accident. I came back to God relatively fresh, not brainwashed, nor indoctrinated.

Red spent his teenage young adult hood and early middle age in gay bars like a torture chamber with fun. All the tired old nameless trade hunkering down on their usual barstool exchanging meaningless words; every time the front door opens letting a cold draft blowing in, their heads turn to see who it is.

Barfly until age 45, then Works Red built alone were becoming public, in the form of publishing's, --novels, anthologies, readings. And then, the second half of his days finds him searching the Spirit of miracles in & out of many sanctified houses.

@ Grace, Sunday. All the implements of spiritual warfare are assembled. The Cross is uplifted, dazzling arrayed in gold. The candle sticks lit upheld like torches, some 3 feet high, each one born by an accolade, robed in white with rope around their waist; the Deacon in her prayer shawl; Bishop with his crooked staff. The pageant flurries its skirted habits, an army of the Lord stirs, now proceeds down the aisles. The chelser, the cloister, the chalice, the censer, the incense, an ancient bible uplifted, housed in silver brocade --- the holy processional flows down, from the choir loft past the alter down towards the pews, flows like a river, riding along the banks between long rows of wooden pews twisting & turning in serpentine fashion. In moments they arrive at the communion table. It is here at the banquet table of his Savior that every week Red must deny the blood of Christ! And cross his arms before the golden chalice –of wine! Of all things! He cannot drink—because its alcohol! 'Well you can take the host.' He is informed. Yet it is the blood of Christ we plead, not the body! The blood is the most important part—even of the whole service in fact! --- Yet he can't take it! Being a reformed alcoholic, not one drop of alcohol must pass his lips! Not one!

You will do great battles against evil.

Back into the streets, after a beautiful respite in an ethereal world. Out here, the wind sweeps cold, but not as cool as the hearts of the rich, fallen-away children of Babylon. The dispossessed have lost their housing. A shabby young woman, thin, surrounded by a meager household composed of several hard wood chairs, 4 pieces of luggage, a table, stands beside the curb waiting for the moving truck to haul her away.

Haul them away to where? To hell? Who cares? Who has time! Being too busy scuffling upon the rat race wheel trying to keep their toehold here themselves.

It is all about the dollar; running from the rent everywhere I go, in one high-priced city after another.

As I look around my small 'monastic' studio apartment-some 500 square feet-- I take into account what is there. Primarily it houses 'The Work' and very little of my own personal possessions. There are great storage boxes of books, rolls of canvas, paintings, some business machines for the creation and production of books for distribution, two desks, an easel, oil paints---you get the picture. In community I would not need my own bathroom, nor kitchen; nor sitting room for friend's visits. (Here in this small space an area about 7 feet by 5 feet contain 3 chairs can be used for 'visiting with friends' ordinarily it is space used to step back and examine a canvas being painted on. One chair holds my cat by the window in a pool of sun, another to sit on for myself… The jolly parrots chortle in their cage. I go about the itemization of personal stuff and that is quite small. Some threadbare clothes, one pair of walking shoes--donated, a pair of sandals, a pair of loafers, both found atop garbage cans.

For those of you who might find interesting details of the story of the poor artists life; must remind you that the Transman like so many of his class and station was living in a dwindling housing pool in the City of Saint Francis, whose increasingly high end price driven market was pushing more and more poor people outside of its borders, to find cheaper rents; yet, often this too is a mission impossible; since the outer lying areas—the East Bay, (Oakland, Berkeley) the South Bay (San Jose, Santa Cruz) and the greater bay area are spiraling upwards into astronomic heights as well, because of their center, the core, SF becoming so high in value. There was nowhere to go but Southern California, Los Angeles or out of state, Colorado, back to the Midwest… He was paying more rent then his social security and disability checks combined—making this difference up by a combination of things which were, renters rebate, his writing sold to archivists, chiefly the Bancroft library, and book sales on line, also his art work, and money for the sparse few public performances he was invited to do. The great dragon whose fierce breath licking at the heels of the poor, was condo conversion. The latest tactic of the moneyed class who hold class leverage over those without funds. It meant at some point in time this old building which currently housed him with it's creaky boards, its windswept below-code basement, inadequate drainage system and faulty electrical, might some day change hands-- leaving that of the crusty old European woman who held the deed (as supervised by a property management company)--- to be purchased by an investor who might convert its 33 plus units to those condominiums—each put on the market for sale at the going rate of $300,000 on up. If the current tenant could not afford 300,000 they would be evicted. At this point s/he would be 'paid out' $4,500. And would be adrift in the neon city without an anchorage. (Even the position of an anchorage might seem enviable to sleeping on the cold dangerous concrete city streets, while your worldly possessions sat comfortably in a storage unit which costs a mere $200 per month.) Also his health was not good, in part due to insufficient money to create a proper diet---which would entail no more canned salty foods from the free food bank, less starches and straight out fresh meat and vegetables which are the most expensive items for a poor person to buy. If he lost this last place of refuge, he would no longer qualify for a credit check for a similar apartment—if one could be found—because his income wasn't great enough! If his ex wife refused to co sign the lease he'd be up shit creek with his bird cage of 2 parrots under one arm, and fluffy white grey cat under the other, and a truckload of books & paintings, and 2 sacks of worn out clothes.

76.
'Their making their armor off of you.' A homeless person in a dream. T. had come up to her. She was getting on the bus and held a rolling luggage cart piled with brown bread sandwiches, some substance between the bread. 'No.' I couldn't have one she shook her head, lowering her face so I could barely see. A male to female transsexual dressed in monks cowl down to the ankles, sadness creased into her face; sandals/and sox on her feet. The sick sad soul of a shy mentally ill homeless transsexual woman, large hands under her brown cowl did something strange. She produced a small bit of coins & dropped them in one of Transman's open pockets. As she prepared to board the bus, Transman asked her 'what religion are you?' 'Buddhist.' She said in a painful shy altered voice, barely audible. She kept turning away but he caught a glimpse of her large face.

She stooped down into the gutter a moment, took out a slip of red paper from amidst the effluvium there. 'Do all you can do now—to help stop this war madness--because it's a war against yourself.' Meaning our nation, Amerika.

So we are again reminded that our country has turned fascist, and that once again we are at war in a foreign land, whose peoples & customs are not familiar to us. These seem to be primitive peoples. They wear turbans on their heads. They're superstitious, ignorant & they use their women like cattle. This is who fights against them, -- we, the mightiest U$ warplanes silver streamlined modern; our gun power 10,000 times greater. This is all we are, we come against a scientifically primitive society, and we have failed. We still have not won that war. And in the meantime look at what evil we are doing to their ordinary people in the process of staging this war—which rages on their homeland.

I visit the impossible situations.

***

Turn the page
A piece of cat shit,

Brown, wrinkled
With time
A piece of thread.
Lint, & balls of dust.
Dead stuff
Which long ago
should have been thrown away.
So is your soul; your minds
arguments.
You must get rid of these
Now!

You are all sisters & brothers, all. Even the rich ones. Even the poor
ones. Even the stranger.   Every prophet has said this. Every single
minister of God!

77.

I remember being introduced by friends to Bernadette Dohrn
sometime in the late 60's or early 70's. She was on the run from the
FBI. She wore the same kneehigh boots as her WANTED! photo—
cowboy or lace-up? I can't recall--- and long curly hair to her
shoulders. She was a slight woman, young and pretty. There is no
telling how revolutionary acts alter the course of history. Of course
they never have the result you hoped they would. If it had not been
for speculations made by the authorities, by the sight of them, from
examples set by these revolutionaries, hinting to these powers above
that even the most ordinary citizen might be soon be moved to
revolutionary acts, --operating in private, alone; or in small cells of a
handful of comrades, totally undetectable by any authorities, and that
ordinary citizens might all become galvanized by such an unpopular
government, by a war nobody wanted which is increasingly draining
the resources of this nation—while enriching a few rich moguls, --
that the government might have backed off of its bent on totally
becoming a police state, totally demanding complete control over us,
and the taking away of our civil rights; all because of the realization
that those risky actions of a few revolutionaries might have inspired
ordinary citizens to do the same.

The Lord is Just.
& the Lord gives you plenty of time.
And the Lord balances.

Justice from injustice.
Rights out of wrongs.

Just a few of us have the fiber of being it takes to step so far outside of the common herd in thought, word and acts that they are branded revolutionaries and far fewer out of those who will risk everything they have to do Works which go so far outside the law that they become WANTED by the authorities!

Everybody's got their own skin to be in, their own shoes to walk in and their own Cross to bare.

*

@ Faithful Fools Saturday night, Brian showed Igmar Bergman's The Seventh Seal, a magnificent foreign film classic from the 1950's, with subtitles. The subject of the struggle with fate, playing chess with death and the outcome for the looser—who in part looses the match because of trickery. Some interesting observations of the group of 9 or so in attendance afterwards; Franciscan Sister Carmen, and Kay, a minister and former social action director of the Unitarian church; brothers Brian & Alex, me, and several others. Alex commented in his analysis; —those who try to cheat death wind up suffering more. Someone said it reminded them of Elizabeth Kubbler Ross's book on death and dying, of the stages people about to die go thru. The first is to bargain. To promise God all the things you will do if God will keep you alive. The second is to say let me live to the hilt right now in the moment—which they regret they never did before. There are those who claim the righteous ground, 'haven't I lived a good life? I've done so little wrong! Why are You doing this to me!' Others have prepared themselves for death and maybe by immersing themselves in scripture—like the movie wife, the noblewoman of the castle who waited 10 years for her husband the knight to return from the crusades prepared herself with grace---reading from her holy book (the bible). She had also illustrated great faith in waiting for her husband, the knights return—where as all the castle help and towns folk had deserted, and she had remained there alone tending the hearth fires.

Alex told how he had feared death as a teenager (remind me of my own early years petrified thinking about death, and somehow one of

27

my parents or grandparents told me not to think about it, and by Gods Grace the subject did leave my mind and did not return). In the movie the knight is approached by death—to take him-- but he argues and bides for more time by playing a game of chess—as long as the game goes on he will live. Alex suggested that the results of this waiting, this postponing, events seemed to be more terrible in the end then they might have been; for those innocently connected to him. Alex then suggested to us of how we claim as a nation we are protecting ourselves in large gas guzzling cars---which only hasten the global warming and destruction of the planet, and how we engaged in a bloody war supposedly to protect ourselves, which still has not been won—and may be failing—in the Middle East, that the number of dead in the World Trade Center building was 3,000 Americans, and we have now slaughtered over that amount of American GI's on the battlefields of Iraq and Afghanistan, over 3,000 and approaching nearly 1,000,000 (one million) Iraqis, the vast portion of those innocent women, children and innocent family men—not enemy terrorists, nor enemy soldiers. And I suggested the ultimate price of this 'protection' may well be the building of an army of hate lasting generations afterwards, of those who wish to avenge their dead family members, and themselves by waging war upon the U$. And then I had the though, about how I seek to protect myself---desiring to buy a very nice condo, or house in San Francisco—which today on the market approaches millionaire status. Where as I have long ago made the vow of semi poverty. I.e., 'Oh God, just a little condo please, and then I will return to my semi-poverty!' This, in order to 'protect myself. Ah, it is all complicated. Anyway, am glad I wrote, wrote, wrote; did my maximum, while I was able. ---The passions you felt at 20 you're not going to feel at 60---so that the story I once told in the 1950's is a of a different flavor then that same story I'm telling you right now, and am thanking God for the opportunity so when the ax man comes, steel blade upon my neck, I will not feel all of my works were left undone! One more consolation! That I have loved. That I have had a relationship, which lasted 16 years, long by anyone's standards, especially a queer, and pray to the Almighty and feel in my heart I am forgiven for the trespasses I committed during that relationship against the one I loved. Yes, that I have loved. Much. Yes. Loved. Cared for small 4-legged beasts, and a few 2-legged flying beasts (birds). And loved quite a few unknown souls whom I prayed for—their situations were so severe. This Seventh Seal was a thought provoking movie indeed, and we all went to ruminating into the corners of our souls about it, which is what a genius masterwork can do!

I'm inclined to believe it's our basic purpose in this world to get thru this life alive. And to help others to do likewise. If we are truly nothing more then those prisoners of death in the middle ages dying of the black plague—they didn't know the cause of it, ---- chained together wrist to wrist in a dance macabre, skeletons jittering, following behind the Grim Reaper, Death with his scythe, then it is our purpose to hold each other up as we march along on our moribund journey; to prevent, at all costs, *mishaps of greater falling* along the way.

We live in a horrible world, but most go thru it –*Journey*—and to accomplish this the best possible way. I.e., accomplish, to get to the end intact. Next, to live each day holistically in our approach to ourselves and to all of God's beings. Synagogue, church; holy places can ease our struggle, although it's not necessary for some who preserve themselves in a situation of outcast from community. We will not be denied entrance to the next world and its far more happier regions therein, by number of our attendances at earthly religious services.

More about Saint Hildegard who reached nirvana on earth after 29 years of severely cloistered life. By her own desire and insistence young Hildegard had herself walled-in with another nun in a tiny cell consisting of two rooms, each with a straw mat on the floor. They had one desk for writing letters. And a chamber pot for human waste. This cell had two small windows, one facing out over the cloister courtyard, and another, with lattice work across so they could look out, but not be seen, and listen to the monks reciting their scheduled prayers. Thru these windows the monks passed in a basket of food once daily and took out another basket of human waste.

When the older nun died, Hildegard chose to go out into the cloister as a teaching nun. The monks had to break down the walls of her self-chosen cloister with sledgehammers. Hidlegard then discovered Caritas--- Divine Love. She wrote and painted pictures of divine inspiration. Consisting of visions given to her. Caritas! A Love

Supreme—according to the Church of John Coletrane. At the end of her 86-year life, she spent 3 years under interdict. She and her band of nuns couldn't receive Holy Communion, also they couldn't sing. This ban was lifted 3 months before Hildegards death. That was her crowning moment of faith. What a severe monastic life! *These are the most deepest of human thoughts.*

*

Grace. A slender well-dressed Asian man is contemplating the entering point of the newly finished labyrinth set in stone inside this great cathedral.

Inside, solemn grey stone interior sits an exhibit about Darfur. A politically violated land in Central Africa. At the Darfur exhibit I was moved by the typed quote of one refugee about whom was said, 'we have nothing. No belongings.' This reality imposed from outside, along with those whose sacrifice is self-imposed, from within, the Order of St. Benedict, who give up all worldly possessions, not even owning a toothbrush of their own—and this for the love of Christ; and I felt for a moment, that I too desired to give up everything, and then I received the knowledge that God would be moved by this step of faith.

> "They live without possessions, sleep in donated tents and subsist on sorghum & beans."
> --Darfur exhibit.

I thought how this fits in so well with the vow of poverty…and thought… what if I too lived without possessions. *I would be moved.* Says God.

I leave the exhibit there as the same time as the Asian man has come to the center of the labyrinth. He kneels there, in inward searching. Has he reached the epicenter of his life? Has divine illumination broken thru his human headpiece filled with straw, into true knowledge? Has this thought of mine been heard by God, and is it what we must all do—to find the true center of our meaning here on earth?

I would be moved.

Back downhill on the windy street yuppies are scurrying helter-skelter jabbering; "Letter of the law! Estate tax! Tax shelter!!!!" -- with their pretty petty protections—plutocrat pigs!

Few more blocks descent, into the TL; see the devil walking inhabiting the bodies of wandering derelicts. Can be seen by their faces, they've lost. Some are still fighting, others have died, but continue to stumble onward going round & round, on their feet. Here among them a fallen transsexual sister poses; muscular tattooed arm in cut-a-way jersey; high-heeled silver boots. S/he accentuates the curve of her male rump in skin-tight jeans; s/he has a tiny female waist; body hair of a male, dual genders perceived, all wrapped up in a single individual.

One block lower on Market Street sat situated a small upscale hotel whose motto on a large metal color advertisement board behind glass proudly declares: 'We are in the middle of it all!" Having a background of favorable pictures of SF's downtown financial district, the world-famous Golden Gate Bridge; however this bitter-sweet sign was telling the truth—yes, they *are* in the middle of it all right--- smack dab in slum sector overflowing with winos, freaks, fallen prostitutes who approach middle age on crutches, meandering specters whose minds of dead whiskey fire burnt down poets who never wrote.

The Tenderloin is rapidly becoming the Trendy-loin... Thanks to upscale capitalist ventures further down the side of the hill. This is the amazing part, even this skid row haven is closing; hamstrung by the strings of economy, time tightening an inexorable noose. First in 1967, the demarcation line, dividing slum from affluence was Polk and Bush streets, in 40 years this has shrunk to Hyde & O'Farrell, themselves increasingly dotted ---between their grim, grey pigeon spattered tenement relics overcrowded and decayed with driven-insane inhabitants--- with fancy hotels sporting chic canopies outside, enhanced by potted palms chained to their entrance ways. How many more years can this slum-haven, for outcasts, exist, within the blueprint of change?

Greater distribution of wealth is mandated. Both for the outcasted poor of San Francisco as most of Amerikas major cities, and the entire world estate.

The lower reaches of humanity calls up to the higher to awake—we who can do something—and push the cause of global justice & equality just as the lower have done so with their prayers and groaning to the Almighty in pain; & God who is just is sending Her/His word to us thru the prophets in instruction: Are given to be included into further workings of Gods purpose—which operates mysteriously thru Smoke of the Holy Spirit but becomes openly manifest.

What must be done immediately in America is that her housing stock needs to be nationalized and each person be given a place of their own to live. The old infirm be appointed ongoing caregivers to help them in their twilight years, free of charge, to maintain their independent living in their own housing unit until death. America must step up as a government to the world table and shake hands in agreement with all the other powers as to how we will participate in a new mass global sharing and cooperation with each other to bring equal resources of food, potable water, medicine and education to all nations of earth, so that all are equal in well being, and finally, and vital-- of supreme importance--to insure that the status of women be brought up to a humane standard. Here is one of the 5 positions of the Episcopal church:

That the condition of women be raised.

This is what a revolution calls for... This is why we speak, this is why we act, this is why we fight. Not just liberation of women, but changing the foundation of the world's old basic structure.

*

It took 13 million years for the human population to reach 200 million. Another 200 million have been added in the last 3 years.

7 billion human beings inhabit earth. 1 billion of them subsist on less then $1 per day. 2-billion on $2 per day. One third of the planet is starving and in jeopardy. What are we going to do about it?

Incidentally this $2 is the price of a coffee at STARFUCKS, a Kapitalist Korporate chain, which is a treat for me to get—which I cannot afford on my limited budget. Thus the inequality of global distribution of wealth, brought home to the domestic level for illustration. Right here in our city where the rich buy up cheep housing turn it into condo's and drink many $2 coffees per day; and myself who can't afford to purchase even one $2 coffee per year; my existence from year to year, continuing only on the largess of friends, & charitable organizations—and that $2 is the days income of someone's family somewhere upon this earth.

Many years ago when I'd first arrived in this city—in 1967-- a slim young 24 year old dike, attired in bluejeans and gymshoes, carrying 2 suitcases & a guitar; as any newcomer I spent my 'internship' adventuring around the city on my poverty funds of welfare vouchers, interspersed by minimum wage jobs, mostly solitary, and very lonely, going sightseeing. One location was the SF zoo—so that I place this event I'm about to tell you fairly near then, maybe early '70's—so that's nearly 40 years ago as of this date (2007), —don't remember having gone back to the zoo since visits of those early days. An amazing thing happened. Pre-Transman was viewing monkeys in the ape house, suddenly a large black furred leathery-skin gorilla began looking out at him thru the bars of his/her cage, then, gestured with it's (his/her) uncannily human-like hand, pointing at Red's gymshoed feet! Gazing down, nearby, Transman Red saw a green comb. Hesitantly he began to bend down to examine it, and saw the gorilla continuing to point at it, with growing determination. So he picked up the green comb. Now, 40 years later I can't recall what the gorilla did next, but somehow young Red got the message—that the gorilla wanted that green comb! So he tossed the comb at him/her over some 30 feet distance. A perfect throw! The ape caught it in its primitive, powerful hand with smooth black rubbery fingers. Its gorilla face furrowed with concentration, then the next truly amazing part of the story—the ape threw the green comb back to Red! He was astounded! By the intelligence of the human/animal! By the precision of aim. It was an amazing happening! But here the story takes a strange twist, today, 40 years later, in 2007.

As we have found Dear Children, God knows not time nor place. God Was before the beginning and will Be forever after. God sees the future. God is 'I AM'. Well, this afternoon, thru the program set up at Grace, Andre had a booth on the plaza about Darfur, announcing a meeting to confer shortly, and I was compelled by conscious to attend. The fact that we'd be watching a movie and fed free food certainly prompted me in this Christian/Judaic undertaking of compassionate tikkun olam—which begins with knowledge about the subject for which care is badly needed. In this case, care is needed speedily and soon.

So here I am, in a house of prayer again, dim, lighted candles all over. It's Old Saint Mary's at the foot of the hill on California Street. (Grace being on top, and Sherith Israel being on the descent further westward.)

The movie The Devil Came On Horseback was shown. It is an excellent film, made mostly by women and staring the true life hero, an ex U$ Marine, and what he saw and information he gathered on the genocide in Darfur, a state which exists in Somalia, the capital of city being Carratoon; focusing on the refuges who have crossed the border to neighboring Chad. Near the beginning of the movie is shown the burnt-up corpses and on-fire villages of the helpless animist Africans, the suffering camp refuges, women who are subjugated to multiple rapes by paid Arabic horsemen bandits when they must go outside the frail safety of the camp to gather firewood. These Arabic soldiers are sent by the opposing government to instill terror and totally subjugate the original inhabitants of this land. These soldiers are not paid money by their employers, but instead are given license to loot, kill and rape. A native African woman is filmed amid the squalor of the camp, ebony skin, posing in a dress of beautiful reds and yellows. All her brothers, uncles, and husband have been killed. She has lost her children in the tumult of the horseback riding devil soldiers who torched her mud-thatched roof village. She has nothing, yet portrays the beauty of life amid suffering. The positive accentuated by all means! The uplifting of self, of hope! Many images are shown as the camera pans thru this unfamiliar scene of her burnt down village in this foreign land, so far from the much higher ground inhabited by Americans & Europeans, in the West. Suddenly, amid the camera footage of scattered, burnt out articles and artifacts---is a green comb.

34

The green comb has been thrown out to me over eternity by God. The challenge is returned to me, the summons is given. What am I going to do about this genocide? What are we going to do? All of us!

Later on, a multifaith gathering includes Islam, Judaic, Buddhist and Christian. I gaze up at the walls of Beautiful Old Saint Mary's. "This is My Church!" Says an acquaintance, Mary from the transex clinic. Meaning her faith—catholic.

A lofty picture inhabits the naïve. A blue and white unfurled sky, a message to the world unfolds. A winged angel with blond hair, clad in a silver helmet, light body armor, sword drawn, his symbolic foot upon the head of Satan who grips the earth ferociously. Lofty clouds/sky above.

I'm looking for light. Looking for compassion. I'm looking for life. Says the prophet Mohammad in the holy Koran.

It seems one after another these horrors unfold on earth. Eslie Wisenfals Holocaust museum is a particular voice advocating action to aright the injustice in Darfur—no wonder; he is a survivor of a holocaust of a different time, the Nazi concentration camps of World War 2. We were asleep then, back in 1945, but awakened at the end of such greet horror---7 million people poison gassed to death. Human beings burnt to ashes in the crematoriums of Dachau, Aswitch, Treblinka, Krakow. Whenever a few ruthless men who are completely evil and totally corrupt, amass other men to themselves, and rise to power, these social monstrosities will happen. The blue/white sky spreads out behind them. A message to the world has unfolded. The world is being awakened. Those capable must fight. The world must never go to sleep again.

Adolph Hitler established a Christian church, a puppet organization of corrupt clergy, which kowtowed to his ideals and turned blind eyes to his genocidal acts. Doing this to envelope in blindness the family-orientated citizens of Germany.

Suddenly one Sunday, in its magnificent nave as the acolyte douses the great candlesticks, reaching up with her long bronze wand some 4 feet in length, to extinguish the flames in perfunctory duty, all the candles burst back into flame simultaneously! Novice priests in white carrying alter cloths run shrieking into the great caverns of the cathedral; a great tide vomits up out of hell---of gibberish speaking slaves entrapped by Satan, all the prizes of hate, all the captives that evil has made; it is an awful sight!

I have heard, that to do good always requires a sacrifice. Something will be taken from you. From hence the street slang—*no good deed goes unpunished.* So I've begun to expect this, and not be indignant, nor flare up in anger over it. The food is ready on the table—but first the guest speaker goes on stage with an amazing message. So that the meal goes cold, the sparkling beverages turn flat. We sacrifice the lower—the food—in order to eat of the higher—the message. One steps out of line a moment to help an elderly women whose shopping basket has turned over. When all her belongings are gathered together once more—their place in line has moved rapidly on, and the one who helps finds they have held themselves back from their own destination. Love. Compassion. —Expect a sacrifice in the doing of it!

*

Things that were of such importance in ones life—make no difference now, like a great love for a special person. Only those fires of artistic creation continue to light my path.

Like I said before if you are on the road or making art you might be a seeker like me. You will stumble into all the pitfalls—romantic love, ego, worthless arguments & debates, deceptive lures which draw you away from your calling, like the love of money. You will postpone life being a flunky in some sealed room without windows bent over a desk, vulture-like, working for a business, which isn't yours.

There comes a time when you cannot stand by anymore. Stand by and watch it happen---even tho you wanted to live a normal life, a simple life—you must stand up and make a difference, and take a stance and interfere with the fascist drum-roll of the machinery set in place which is crushing so many.

For so long I had a writers task, having been blessed with that vision and ability to start early—age ten or twelve-- writing poetry, later

36

novellas, and continuing on, now at age 64 so that after all this time I thought life would just keep going on like this, me simply putting my ideas, my great plots for justice down on paper. You should know that one of these days will come a time to put into action the sympathies which you have held for so long, those close to the heart. Those issues you've spoken impassionedly about, discussed & ruminated over in your small study groups, concerning those situations of injustice on earth which rankles your ire to such a fiery degree!

Remember the revolution in India was accomplished without a shot fired—by peaceful means. Sit-downs, strikes, refusal to work. India remains a sovereign nation today, with borders intact. –Her revolution did not comprise her national security. She is a protected nation, self-governing.

Change. Think of it as the end to one no longer useful way, and the beginning of a brave new experiment in human advancement. This is the only way human suffering can be alleviated--when the old shoes are too tight, painful, corrupting the arch of the foot, a new pair must be found. To look about for a better style, and a stronger design. It is necessary, not superfluous. It is not a random exercise in change, nor the kind of adventuring a pirate or corporate raider does, but a thinking, planning construction of a more equitable society.

The end to privately owned for-profit housing stock must happen. Reinstate a public health care system and universal health care for all humans. Open up food banks to all under income citizens whose diets are now at the level of malnourishment, or who must sacrifice other necessities of life just in order to eat and stay alive.

The world must put an end to discrimination because of class, race, sex, gender variation, and IQ.

A time of revolution for this country---this means change!

Finally must state, concerning my patriotism to this country of my birth: we as citizens must vow to protect this country from outside invaders from foreign lands, and most especially from those forces inside, born-citizens of our nation who would rise up within the ranks to power and in conjunction with others gathered to them of a like intent lead our nation down destructive paths nationally, internationally, economically, ideologically & by manufactured laws, covering all of it in a smoke screen deluding you to think they are right, all with the true purpose of seizing power & reaping personal aggrandizement. Don't ever forget the complete fascist take-over of the legitimate government of Germany in the 1930's!

75.

My plant revitalization program continues. The old man moved among his plants. 8 of them now, found half dead in the cities gutters, replanted in likewise abandon pots—different ones then those in which those plants, yellowish to brown-green, were discovered—but all castaways, like he was. Transman wore his old black shirt & trousers, as usual. To him a tie was a long tongue which food is spilled upon. He was preparing to go out on his daily routes. While pouring water over his plants he ruminated following thought:

> Compassion does mean empathy and the seeking of inner understanding for as many beings as you are capable and this grows, like when a plant, found abandon in the gutter once yellow or brown, is watered, becomes green once more, and this watering in an ever expanding reach so that today we think for and feel for on behalf of citizens even on the other far side of the world whose lives are caught up in struggle and mayhem; and realize by some passage of time, that further compassion for these individuals will eventually necessitate actions on their behalf. Actions of some kind wither great or small to help alleviate their pain.

Fantasies amidst green plant watering. The little things of which his day was composed. It is quite apparent why some Works are given to the mentally ill or those who can still see with a child-like mind. For few normal people would go thru the discipline, hardship; and denial of adult society it takes to be an artist; to go out across vast deserts of aloneness to find strange wonderful fruits—these visions-- and bring them back to a studio, set up their easel and paint them, or rush to their desk and compose them into books—designed to give back to the world. Nor would many feel the compassions of a saint. Anyway it is not solid material but spirit, inspiration which is important. And art is close to this. For isn't it said one of the reasons God always accomplishes everything is that God lives in Spirit and always works in Spirit and the Spirit is stronger then flesh? It can be said about him that he was mentally different. The old Transman had first discovered imagery when s/he was a child back in the 1940's--- listening to classical music besides his parent's old console record player--- the 33 rpm's--imaging; *it's the best friend you have.* Visualizing and creating a world of daydreams, creating adventures to accompany this beautiful music. Far later in his life he would use this same visioning to incorporate empathy and feeling for others into his being—which became so vivid, so intense that they resulted in the necessity of doing social actions! Red had come from a severely broken home. Tortured by his mentally ill mother. *Your eyes begin to turn inward.* The thoughts he dreamed, the dreams he visioned were vital pivots of his time spent on earth. Dreams. Ideas. Thinking these with great fervor—almost too much-- for his life, on the personal level, it was so desolate. The kind of desolation few understand. Outdoors a magnificent sun blazing in the west with white light enflames the sky; engulfs the tall city skyscrapers in a white bath of blazing light illumination. However his small room was lit only by partial rays, since the sun was blocked by surrounding concrete buildings, (from which, in the small uninhabited concrete courtyard could be heard the cries of infants, the echo of great groaning of toilets.) Inside his rooms smelled green leafy, and earthy. A mixture combined from pots of dead plants, added to compost, mixed into soil of a rich blend, which when wet by a jar of water, took on a healthy dirt smell, green growing... To one wall of his small space was ceiling-high stacks of his books in cardboard boxes. To the other, on a found table, 2 bookbinding machines and a computer. Oil paintings of strange and unusual pictures, surrealistic, hung on the vacant spaces. His room reflected one whose art is their entire life and dwelling place. *My toys have become my work.* He looked into the far recess of his mind, into its dusty corners for what is missing… what is it? A lover! At least he was not entirely alone, having numerous worship services to attend. *How pleasant it is to sit in the tent of Abraham and Sara.* He still could hear Congregation Sherif Israel sing the familiar songs. Singing rises & falls. The old Transman had danced with Torah scrolls last night carried the heavy scrolls down off the bemah, -- which is quite tall in this elegant synagogue, founded by Polish Jews some 100 years ago-- a risky maneuver because of his sore foot, but inspired he had forgotten that at this special moment when called up by the female rabbi, and only marveled that he'd done so well—

39

feeling his way down the 5 red carpeted stairs from the lofty bemah gingerly groping with his better foot, which he could just catch sight of over the large bulky torah ornately dressed which he clutched in his arms like a precious baby. *The torah, undressed for you to see is a bark of wood, ancient as time, enriched with mysteries, peaceful as all the oceans of the universe; in it are the secrets of life, the recipe's for the future, the touching of God.* Transman's mind was poetic. It was filled with a clutter of recent memories, and spectacular daydreams! Sometimes the inside his brain was like the inside of a comic book character animation fantasy one image after another deluged him, most especially of doing brave deeds, talking brilliantly to audiences, speaking to multitudes, tap dancing, being victorious in situation of battle. —By which he fantasized saving the world! By great works. (Works. —A prayer set in motion.) However so few times in a persons life arises the opportunity to do truly great Works! It is instead by the millions of little Works daily that the human race continues to plod along on its dusty path. Some examples of Great Works; he now jotted down **NOTES**, which he would enter into his Journal under 'Thoughts & Ideas', entertained in thought-picture:

Some Great Works of Humanity:
Such as in 1930's and till the end of the war in 1945; Gentiles who risked their lives to hide, help escape, or otherwise aid the Jewish people to escape the death concentration camps of Nazism.

Quakers and other whites who secretly helped move escaped black slaves thru the underground railway up from the slave owning states in the South and up thru the free Northern states, on into Canada—to become free.

People who stand up for the rights and sovereignty of the environment, & the animals.

Wise people who understand and spread the message unceasingly, that in the tug between intellect, vs. the human heart, ultimately each individuals choice must be to sit in the seat of love & compassion. There in only can reside the true judge.

Transman thought of the saintly woman he'd shook hands with only days ago at Grace Cathedral; he had written down a quote from her:

> The citizens of the United States have an unsustainable lavish lifestyle. While so many of the world have unimaginable poverty. If the whole world had the lifestyle of the average American, we would need 4 new planets and we don't even have 1 new planet, just this old one.
> --Jane Goodall, 2007.

Shortly Transman would turn key in the door of that tiny room in which he stretched the limits of his imagination, go out to begin his day. Heading out for the royal road, the kings road--which is Gods solutions. Now, back here inside his dank, close little studio apartment he could not tell the whether was, was it cool or warm? Rainy or dry.

There's a cold wind blowing said the Spirit, so he took his heavy coat (a present form ex-wife some 7 years prior which had insulated him by now from many colds & flues) and went out. Going up the long red-carpeted hallway. The day was sunny, warm & passerby's wore teeshirts; were in shirt sleeves, some in jackets and coats. But sure enough, just underlying was a cool wind blowing. & he was glad he was prepared for the night ahead.

76.
So day-by-day I sat, as a faithful sentry beside the doorpost of Babylon Falling, hearing proprietor Sean's answer to the now familiar question of a customer:

> "Hey man, nice store. How long yuh been here?"

And heard his ever-changing answer in a polite Jamaican accent:

> "About 2 months."

Which soon morphed into:

> "About 3 months."

And soon it was 4.

41

He made a mental note: *Must introduce Sean to my friend God. It's overdue. All will need God, but some more then others because of the work they're doing.*

We do race talk occasionally—which is all-too familiar, being a Colored person. Sean speaks of the beautification product used commonly in Jamaica, his homeland:

> Nadanola whitening cream—is still used in the island. Please make me brown is the black woman's prayer. Please make me white, the brown woman's prayer. The white woman does not use Nadinola— she uses the tanning booth in winter, and the beach in summer—to make her skin a golden bronze!
> ---Sean, a white Jamaican.

October. The other end of which is Halloween. Entering to the holiday time. A magical season. Its calmed down after the Jewish holidays of Rosh Hashanah and Yom Kippur---the Hebrew New Year by their lunar calendar, and the days of atonement but Christians just beginning holidays all over again—so that is a fine spread of 2 months worth of festivities! Thought the old man dressed in black, mentally licking his lips as he thought of feast foods; him salivatating & gnawing upon turkeys w/dressing; hams garnished with pineapple; as meanwhile, here & now was the familiar feeling inside his stomach grinding from lack of food. *So….he mused…the groups done. The show is dead! Time to move on!* A pickup truck full of crumpled gold tinsel, wood scraps and pried-up plywood; covering it, a tarpaulin, roped down. Another stage struck. The beginning and end of deals. Back in the day, in the black ghetto, me & fine hustlers we marched thru the picture frames of the calendar in fine suits & jewelry cardboard cut out dolls of the fast life, when I was bad. Yesterday, it was this cutthroat shit on the part of my ex-group attendees. Only to be with the Spirit of God is safe—found inside holy places all over earth. No wonder so many of the populous clusters there, so often! And often receiving no miracles over their long prayer life—but that faith, in which they are sustained by the ever-quenching presence of the Most High.

As he sat there, a sole sentry beside the doorpost, the kindly young Sean played for Red-- In the words of Damian Marley:

Jesus fed the multitude with one loaf of bread;
there is something for you.
Mankind cannot afford resistance anymore
still there is something for you.
Written in the book of life we will live forever more and
there will be something for you.
2007, Pop hit, One Loaf Of Bread

Seated in his niche by the front window the oldster tapped his toe to the music, staring into space lost in fantasy. He was simply a strange and colorful person albeit dressed in nearly all black. The amazing thing about the old Transman is that he had concocted this whole elaborate plan for a religious order in his mind reminiscent of Worlds Of The Unreal by Henry Darger a mentally ill recluse (who also attended numerous Catholic masses, God being his only earthly friend)—Darger, who populated a fictitious realm with angelic baby girl soldiers and ruthless outer space marauders all in careful watercolors and hundreds of thousands of pages of prose; likewise, Transman's invention DOC, this Order complete with all the intricacies of laws, rules, restrictions, and admonitions:

Further to elaborate one point, the Order of DOC will not become of itself a church, mosque, temple, etc., on its own, but remain an Order; albeit a powerful and world wide Order, which will adventure out to worship alongside the congregations of other religious institutions or places designed for that purpose. DOC members will not attain high positions or titles in those places but may take on small roles to aid in their services; and can be called on to be helpers, as able, by a chief or head of these places.

Red dreamed this Order into being—at least drew up the architecture of its infrastructure and jotted its instructions down onto paper. While in real life he habituated churches & synagogues, just as he had cruised the old gay bars of a different dispensation.

77.
Enter now into the embrace of Grace; cold grey stone colored dank by outside's dark shadows of October, Fall; Grace with her old tapestries, cold rock walls papered in gold brocade baring the

imprimatur of the flur de leis & garlands of pink rose, green petals & vines. With tulip shape spaces in the grillwork, Islamic in design, which fence off the progress to the alter, upon which sits the communion table dividing the common from the uncommon. Her vaulting arches rise up into a dim apex; her outstretched arms in the form of a crucifix; the horizontal bar of it being the two wings of pews at either wing, and her long vertical aisle, -- which stretches from high alter--- a block long down to entrance way upon which congregants enter/exist; symbolizing the beam of the cross, once, 2,000 years ago planted into the earth amid tens of thousands of crucifixions of enemies of the Roman state, murderers and thieves hung along the Apian Way.

Regarding my Order, I must look back in history—2,000 years. Jesus on the Cross, might have entertained the thought he had failed miserably. That his teachings were fruitless and would not produce historic results; that his tiny flame had burnt out in the stubble grass of the hungry multitude; not knowing it had ignited a huge fire within the infrastructure of humankind who hears.

Beside a wall at a praying niche Transman stuck 2 candles into the sand inside a bronze vessel; many others have been placed there before, now burnt down to their wicks; stubs still imbedded in the sand, not yet gardened by the vicar. The metal collection box, affixed to a grey stonewall, with its slit that gapes in profanity at him, dull, spiritless, earth-bound. Transman bows his head, to cast up his profound most heart-felt prayer, for him and his ex-wife who is his closest friend on earth.

The collection box remained empty after Transman departed. Was he growing into a miser due to his vows of semi-poverty? He had $2, in his pocket, which he needed to buy another bottle of vinegar used for indigestion due to old age & the clogging effect in his guts from the many pills he used to keep himself alive & sane.

It is 6:00 pm. The cathedral bells are intoning. Now, as was his custom, he entered the small chapel inside the Cathedral—the one to the right. *It's time dear ladies, it's time...* He bows to the Cross ensconced in it's wooden niche serviced by 4 vestal virgins, with the golden duck squatting above. *Service.* Spoke the inaudible voice of God to him.

Later the small group of Benedictines—9 that evening--- repaired to the dining room across plaza to study, read from the Rules Of Benedict, and to eat soup, bread, and a treat. Seated at several round dining room tables; painted portraits of now dead Priests decorate the walls. After, came study. As their human heads collectively bowed over Lexico, they began. In the scripture Luke 17: 11-19 Jesus heals the ten, of which one, only the Samaritan comes back to give thanks to God. According to the Lexico notes: *The Jews regarded the Samaritans as heretics worse than pagans.* After healing the ten, Jesus says; w*here are the nine? Was no one found to return and give praise to God except this foreigner?* One phrase stuck out in Red's mind. The words leapt out of the page at him; *I am that foreigner.* He realized, 'I am that stranger'. Soon, by dim light of the dining hall he was writing a poem:

> I Am The Foreigner
>
> I travel the bombed-out land
> of reality, & of the heart.
> I go by their houses
> I look thru their heavy curtains
> of their doors.

Another thing that stood out to him was Jesus admonition, loudly, *(weren't ten cleansed? Where are the nine?)* It was almost as if he could hear the Divine Rabbi yelling off of the page! One all-important fact he carried away with him into the night, down the cold wind struck steps of the castlesque edifice, a sheet of paper from lexico:

> The word *mercy* literally means *"Sorrowful at heart."* But mercy is more then just compassion, or heartfelt sorrow at another's misfortune. While compassion empathizes with the sufferer, mercy goes further. It removes suffering. A merciful person shares in another's misfortune and suffering as if it were their own. And he will do everything in their power to dispel that misery.
> Lexico Divina @ Benedictines.

45

78.
Saw a traffic accident today, which had just transpired seconds before
he arrived on the scene. A slender woman neatly dressed in a gray
suit jauntily upon her way now lay in the street, dazed, red blood
oozing from her white skin; struck down at the corner by a car turning
the block. Thankful it is a responsible driver who appears to be
insured. His companion, a woman, ministered to the injured
pedestrian. A small crowd gathers. Several assured the injured
woman not to get up. Someone checks her neck, says it seems
allright. A black homeless man stands on the outside of the little
crowd now assembled around the victim to insure the wild speeding
traffic does not hit anyone of them. Whereupon Transman joins him
to guard them also. A female witness saw the whole thing, and
remains on the scene to aid by giving a witness report. A man calls in
the accident on his cellphone just as the old Transman had limped
down the street with his cane. The response was great, within 1 ½ to
two minutes the ambulance arrives, then 2 fire engines and a squad
car. The paramedics immediately began checking the woman. One
of them singles to the heavy lifting fire engine 'three fingers' a three
stage accident rating, so they slowly drove off, not needed. 2 fireman
climb out of the other engine to help pick up the stretcher, where the
woman lays in compresses, to carry her to the ambulance. "Surprised
your neck doesn't hurt! The way you flew over the hood of that car."
Someone says. At total 5 squad cars and a motorcycle cop stood
around. Then the ambulance speeds off; takes her to hospital, sirens
wailing.

At the bus stop the crowd of those waiting to board the outgoing
transport were unusually somber; all wore dark looks, serious,
continuing to gaze at the site of the accident where vehicle which had
struck the pedestrian still sat, 4 cops tape measuring distance, tire
skids, ---calculating speed of the driver was going, "This is the worse
area. People always getting run over." Exclaimed a Middle-Eastern
man. And Transman proposed how it was safer to negotiate that
particular corner by waiting for a group to assemble itself, then
crossing the street together.

As the black clad figure stared back downtown along the long line of
multicolor jumble of storefronts searching the distance for his bus,
there came a tempting swell in his breast of fantasy—flling the wild

46

sails of his mind--how he would have rescued the woman himself!
Been first on the scene to rush to her aid! Had he just been moments
sooner!

Thought again about Works. It is a higher thing to do; acts of mercy
towards one in need; even more then the worship of Eloheim (God).
Worship is pleasing to Me. But acts of mercy are greater in God's
eyes.

Time was slowly moving past the accident. The nagging feeling
which flitted only momentarily on his super conscious, dissipated, of
wanting to be a part of the helping of some one—even valor—saving
someone! & how he might have earned a big Works Award from the
Almighty for this valor—but he was reconciled with the thought: *I
did stand in the street with my cane as a stop to protect the others.
Me, & the black guy—we made them visible…* So he contented
himself & soon the bus came, the matter forgotten.

79.
     *On the next day the student went out and encountered the
     following situation; which must be viewed as a lesson.*

Blue Angels are in town. Navy supersonic jet planes. They travel
faster then the speed of sound. It's inspirational to see them roar
across the sky. Uncanny to see their mathematical precision fly across
the clouds; an artificial grid of such immense proportions, a black
metal construct superimposed upon the natural blue/white sky by
mathematics, put up there by science, moving not even in the variance
of a single inch off their positions as they roar by faster then the speed
of sound; so close, in tandem, but remaining apart from each other.
None of them out of line. Measured and calculated distance,
accounting for wind, for velocity, for variation; they proceed.
Descend, nose dive down, suddenly reverse, thrust up straight to
stratosphere climbing an altitude of 1,000 feet in seconds. On the
other hand, spiritually, this same vision is reduced to the level of a
warlord dragging his scimitar like a large outrageous dinosaurs tail
behind him.

It was a pleasant warm day, peaceful, blue/ white clouds, but every
few minutes came a terrific roar of the futuristic war planes which

rent the air in two, and split the sky with the unbelievable sight of their grotesque yet compelling forms.

Transman stood outside the bookstore scanning the sky; a cup of steaming Jamaican coffee in hand. Examined his soul. Specifically this troublesome swell in his spirit upon seeing the fearsome Blue Angles. Was it some atavistic thrill of the chase, the hunt, the kill; of superiority, of humans now with wings in wild, triumphant flight? It was so easy to rest in confidence upon those black metal science fiction wings. Elements within the country were getting swept along in the tide of war lust, although they should have been doing everything in their power to stop it. For this war in the Middle East was doing irreparable harm to the world and threatening the future.

Sean (proprietor of the bookstore, to Red): Those babies cost 78 million dollars apiece.

Red (To Sean): Occasionally these 78 million dollar planes crash—and not just shot down by enemies in the theater of war, but by simple stupid human error. You can see billowing columns of smoke, oily, black, rise to an altitude of 10,000 feet obscuring the sun. (Red continues) I see there have been 24 suicide car bombs across Iraq this week. You see this regularly. Seldom do you stop to think—what it means is, in each car, is a driver who set off a bomb. This was an individual who has prearranged to kill themselves. —For their cause.

In Babylon Falling you will find a lot of truth.

It's a persons innate assumption that what they read in newspapers or view on TV is correct so then we have to go upon the difficult process of undoing these beliefs, thru conscious intellectual reasoning, & by example:

> The new forms of life will take the place of the old not by preaching
> or voting but by living them! ---Emma Goldman.

Change is difficult because the ideas from which these lies are being told are still in operation. To find the truth among fragments of things, as children of the present we must pick thru the potshards & antique artifacts of evidence to uncover the lies our foremothers and fathers were raised on, and which continue to this day. These lies continue, inherited generation to generation thru the dim minds of those who don't understand; who are fearful and clutch onto to lies because of tradition, familiarity, taboo, human likes & dislikes wither truth or mistakes, as they do anything familiar. The plan is to wrest these falsities away from them like a blue security blanket, which they hold so dear. Because all of it is like a blue security blanket which ultimately destroys their souls. The soul—this is the second difficult struggle.

This is why change may be difficult, and some say all but impossible except thru the barrel of a gun. For we who have seen too many gun barrels parading across TV's screen nightly news, guns in increasing destructive power, may think twice about a violent revolution and lean more on the side of education, dissemination of thought, and social actions within the bare limits of legality. Yet that process takes forever, and the large corporations, the mighty, the powerful and the cunning are always one step ahead of truth, figuring out new plans to stay in control, to keep siphoning all the best of stuff off for themselves and as soon as one of our good edicts finally goes into enforcement, they have long ago thought up a way to wiggle out of it still preserving their unjust advantage!

Thing about Babylon Falling being here among these young people, Red was actively climbing into the arts field. A string of artist were to appear throughout the day, to stand and chat up the proprietor; touting their wares, as Red sat beside the door, book in hand. Each month was an art display or reading by some author, painter, or dancer. Books read here most centered around the topic of the spirit of revolution. *Books enlighten me.* All kinds of subjects & eras. Harriet Beacher Stowe's Uncle Toms Cabin, with annotations which explain her use of the "N" word, this revolutionary book electrified 1800rds America and was best seller for years, helping spark our Civil War with it's realization that no person should be enchained in a Christian nation. It thus helped countless black souls emancipate.

The old man recounted tall tales to the younger gentlemen; of how one living in that area formerly could walk around to bookstores that today only exist in memory. He give an account of Acorn Books whose owners lived to be a ripe old age, retired form the biz after 45 years selling off all their long accumulated stock, right down to the ceiling-high handsome stained-walnut shelves. Lifetime Books; small, jam-packed, with shelves on every available wall, plus book islands in the center; whose lady owner died young and closed after a mere half-decade. The other tiny book/novelty shop on Hyde Street, departed. —3 in a row—to make way for this modern new bookstore stocked with revolution!

Old Transman Red, a Patriarch, felt that he, (The Lion Who Sits Beside The Door) at Babylon Falling, was one of the voyagers on a ship of fools just in its last harbor on the verge of setting sail into fame & recognition, delivering great gifts to far distant shores to enlighten minds here & there…

> I see frequently on the streets lower down, in the TL, the old horrors, hags, madmen, my contemporaries. Former insane youths; who became druggies/alkies of yore, burnt themselves out in the 1960's, never recovering; or who, by circumstance of their born-affliction just went on & on being poor forever and to this sad end they have come; babbling crones in worn-over white gym shoes blackened with filth from walking the road, wearing cast off clothes… Bent double hunchback bums who dine from garbage cans. Thank God(ess) I have been given gifts, which in using them have elevated myself over this disaster course of repeatedly colliding with rotting flotsam jetsam of the universe…I was poor, I was hungry & yes I stole, but mine weren't the calculated stealings of a thief, I was too busy calculating fine arts.

How much is really known about hermits? About Henry Darger, who apparently had a low IQ, supported himself as a janitor all his life? Henry went to mass every single day, plus 5 or 6 masses on Sunday, *God is the only friend I have…* Darger, who created the crazy, beautiful, innovative, Realms Of The Unreal; where nympho boy-girls do battle with menacing, fanged adult monsters from an alien galaxy. Was he a hermit by choice? Do hermits at some time in their lives attempt to reach out, to touch others and be like other humankind—but their adventures into sociability are repulsed so vehemently & so often, discovering they are laughed at behind backs of hands, the object of cruel gossip and instead of being friends are simply the amusement of others that they finally give up and do indeed become isolated strangers; retreat into their private hermitage like old crabs? If so it is a very sad state of affairs.

Great minds are often misunderstood by the lesser; yet a kindness from a lesser mind can brighten ones course! A backstabbing from a lesser mind is depressing, and killing. Without the love of other humans to continue to exist is only a grim determination of life, one with little joy.

Well DOC & other current great healing blueprints of Orders of Spirit that people are starting which you hear about all over this globe in these evil times, might be Creators answer to world division and strife. First because it brings together diverse religions having them go above themselves to the higher God, the Spirit of Creator and unite them in worship of that deity. Second, the good that comes from the actual works of salvation they may then perform.

Oh, --God(ess) spoke this to me: I am setting up a new nation.

Regarding: DOC, safety in the streets & other places: We shall all protect each other, both male and female members. We shall take care of the smaller, weaker, or older or more physically challenged. Thus, there will be far more women protected (being smaller) so some will find this at an imbalance; i.e. a vast proportion of male brothers are called upon to escort or to protect the smaller brothers and sisters thus it will be found that far more females are escorted by males—this is currently natures construct. Furthermore this does not give more honor, nor glory to the one protecting, it is simply part of their job.

PS. Don't think winds & storms won't come, just because things have been going so well; they will; but they will not prevail over us.

So the old guy spoke to God, and continued to build— like Darger the low-IQ janitor's Castles Of The Unreal—his New Order Of Jesus Christ (oddly named) for Multi-Faith religions to co-exist as one, worshiping and performing Works of Social Action. Must be said that these were all his fantasies. He kept himself quite entertained.

*

Present in Ship Of Fools tonight at the Robert Bowen instillation of his oil paintings was Red, a young man named Gray roommate of Sir

Van Hussen (Alex), and a dog, named Blue. Red, Gray, and Blue.
How fortuitous a conjunction of souls.

Red has put aside his book with a bookmark in this page:

> If we are paid back one quarter of what we are doing in Russia &
> Poland Frau Doktor, we will suffer and we will deserve to suffer.
> --Innkeeper in the Black Forest about Nazis. From Stalingrad –1998

Party in full swing; & Shaun incessantly taking pictures. Where Red
is incessantly taking notes.

80.
5 imprisoned dogs, bored, sleeping, or wrestling with one another,
fangs pulling each others fur, or fussing over a toy in solitary, doing
time behind metal bars & locked gates. Suddenly a human appears,
standing in front of the viewing window. Simultaneously the 5
canines snap to attention, pink tongues lolling out in breathless
excitement. One stands on high legs, forepaws pushing hopefully
against the bars. Bright, wide eyes, ears open, standing up in peeks,
wait for just a word; watching to see what good comes with this
human—food? A walk? A petting? The person departs, off into an
outer office to confer with officials. Awhile later, footsteps resound
again in hallways of the animal shelter, navigating piss-puddles with
plastic yellow CAUTION! signs set over them. Inside the viewing
room, festive dogs; 2 pairs in 2 cages at play. 1 solitary. Suddenly all
stop, and look, inquisitive, then with growing jealousy; their eyes
intent thru the bars… Another dog going home! What a merry day
when a dog gets adopted at the shelter! S/he prances out on leash
behind their new guardian; heads uplifted, 4 paws lightly stepping at a
trot, eyes sparkling in joy! Sometimes they turn their furry canine
head to greet you-- who has sat with them as companions in their
cramped cage for weeks, maybe months—for just an instant—as if to
say, look at me! I'm going home with my new human! I'm free!

And now onto the completion of his week, Fools of a different work,
but who are quite similar -- just as different limbs from the same tree
all hold themselves up in Grace to the yellow sunshine --- Faithful
Fools, a Tenderloin outreach set among the hopeless & mad; it's their
movie night.

Among the crowd is an older Saint, thin, with grey hair, a priest. Wearily reclining on one of the secondhand sofas. He is on his way to be re-arrested in a different state, on the charge that he blocked a road leading to the U$ Military School of Torture, a top-secret facility that is training our military personnel to torture and obtain information from prisoners of war. This Act done in gross inhumanity, and violation of the International Treaty The Geneva Convention on Treatment of Prisoners.

There are a lot more saints then people think—and all of them are revolutionary. From Sr. Stang, the nun who was murdered by a rich South American landowner because she protested their stealing, killing and rape of native people whose land these meztitoes steal—to amass their huge capitalistic rancheros. Stang was murdered when she was on her knees praying—shot with 7 bullets by the hired goons of a rich landowner. From this Saint, an actual nun, to Jane Goodall, whose voice calmed the animals present inside Grace cathedral during the blessing of the animals. There are less dramatic Saints, equally consistent—these two women, one a nun, the other a Social Activist Minister, who run the Fools.

> People that have a conscious, I'm speaking to you!
> You have a conscious!
> When you are ready a Spartan room is prepared for you.

Brother Brian has scored another amazing victory with his movie the Harp Of Burma—a great find dug up from archives at the Public Library made by a Japanese filmmaker in 1956, set in 1945, the year WW 2 ended.

A young Japanese soldier in a battalion of men carries a harp instead of a rifle as they march thru the leafy green jungle of Burma. When he plays his harp all the war-worn soldiers stop to listen; transported to a higher ethereal realm... This is the purpose of gifts. He told his commander: "When I'm playing my harp—all kinds of people are drawn to it..."

Later, in The Harp of Burma, this harp-playing soldier, traumatized by war, is fleeing thru the jungle; he passes by piles of rotting corpses. He sees thousands upon thousands of dead Japanese soldiers; crows pecking out their eyes, pulling out strings of their blackened entrails. There on the Burmese road he learns a severe lesson. He learns the truth and he transcends.

When one finally learns these lessons—of the heart, life changes. What it means is, you will never be the same.

There will always be beside us on the path, the lower ones, belching, self-centered, ape-like, taking up space, acting violent, domineering, ignorant. Tolerance of the lower ones—that's part of it.

The highest path one can follow is to leave off all selfish desires, which most humans crave and work towards. To leave off all desires to do with fellow humans. All craving for stuff humans want. All the houses and cars, the women, the men, the fine clothes, and recreations, the sailboats and pipedreams.

To follow the path, towards Enlightenment; it is a higher calling. It is a Work – a mercy.

Would you be a spiritual person? A weighty decision —to give it all up.

   When you are ready a Spartan room is prepared for you.

Late in the movie one of the actors says: 'The meaning of life is, to help ease the suffering in the world. To have courage. To face irrationality, to face uncertainty, to face what doesn't seem real & live with it. To become peace. To be peace. To show by example'.

Later the Old Man told his friends; "I am like many of you", he said. "I heard whispers of war. Of many wars. I've heard these reports of the torture & execution chambers". (*In Stalingrad, we saw the corpses. & the crows pecked out their eyes.*)

   I bow, my hands folded. I serve the Spirit of Buddha. The sleeping Buddha. The smiling Buddha. The contemplative Buddha. My former clothes transform. They become the robes of a supplicant.

Well, anyway, I'm still part snake oil salesman, carney barker. Remember the mooch law of the telemarketer—'Asking is the easy part. Getting somebody to say yes is the problem'. -- I'm not selling pussy, cock, dope, or lucky card gambling—but politics, spirituality & fine art wrapped into one sordid package of life-long learning, enhanced by sexual innuendo.

They must not forget—there is got to be a resistance! The old guy thought of this while seated at his ledge beside the door, a paperback book open on his lap, perusing Emma Goldman. Reading the fascinating tales of Anarchists & Wobblies running from the police although they aren't crooks. This in defense of the growing labor union movement of that era, early 1900ds, which protested unfair conditions—people working 12, 16 hours a day in ill lit, un-ventilated conditions. Many labor unionists gave up their lives in a pool of crimson red blood, for our 8-hour workday.

So this is food for action, Dear Children! Go somewhere & produce revolutionary art! Join a domestic brigade! Picket! Holler! Protest! Throw their law books back in their faces!

On the spiritual level, the truth came to me just as it did to the hippies of 1967—in those long ago times of the Flower Children.

The secret is—the Lord told me, that we must work together to make this world Eden … Re-create heaven all over again. Right now, down here, where the old order still exists.

We came out of the garden so long ago, just 78 thousand years & we've been sleeping ever since.

The dead ghosts of revolutionaries are calling upon you! You who are willing to take the risk; willing to step out in front.

> To live as simply as possible & do good works unceasingly. That's good enough.
> --God to the prophet, Red.
>
> *Would you serve me? Or would you go your own way?* Christ asks, without judgment.

I said God I give you my 2 fangs. The canine incisors. Anger & Hate are their names. Now God is involved in my conscious decision to file these fangs down. Once becoming peaceful warriors, the battle starts!

We need to be in a hurry! There are wars & rumors of wars.

I repeat to you comrades, I remind you citizens; we should be fighting for our lives!

See the photographs from far distant shores; of faces across which passed the indicators of the shadow of death.

How can these foreign nations trust us when everything we take out of our briefcases is missiles, rockets, and aircraft of war dropping bombs on their people?

Not a single promise is kept!

Include our country's name with the empires of history; affix it to the Dantean inferno list of exploitive schemes, our own U$A's colonial adventures all over the earth. --- For the sake of justice? To spread freedom? No! --For the sake of money and power.

Listen I want to say something now—I wrote a book, EMPIRE! Which, tho it comes under the rubric of science fiction, is mighty fine art. Its set in year 2054, the revolution has come and gone. In place of the former decadent murderous corporate kapitalist society, the new Utopia has passed into being—via armed force—and immediately a new rule, the Unity of Utopia has been installed, and there in lies the crux of the problem. This Unity—the governing or world-centered power is corrupt too. It has taken away freedom of the press, of speech, the vote, and to study history. Even the choice to have ones own genetic children. It has obliterated all historical documents. Everyone lives to 200 years with the best healthcare in Utopia. Everyone is properly housed without a worry, and all have a job, without having to compete to get one. Yet as you can see there has been a horrific trade-off. I am saying this now Dear Children as a warning to you in the future. Let us take for distance the magnificent coup of Fidel Castro who saved the Cuban people's island from becoming a holiday resort/brothel for rich Americans, complete with legal gambling, impoverished Cuban prostitute sex-workers, subservient Cuban servants and lavish lifestyles for those who could afford a vacation. Fidel turned it into an island of independent, educated women and men who have healthcare, free education and free housing. However one may notice Fidel has remained in power 30-plus years. Instead upon his military coup winning freedom from corrupt tyrant Juan Baptista, the former dictator, afterwards, in the interval of days in which they had to run the state on a temporary basis before giving the island back to the people to self-govern by means of democratic rule, he remained supreme chief and leader. I would think that the revolution went astray in this respect! Stalin in Russia, de facto dictator of the United Soviet Socialist Republic was proved to be just another deadly ruler with absolute command and an iron fist—not unlike the royal czars-- denying freedom of speech upon whose orders were committed atrocities against millions of citizens sent off to the gulags. Mao Tse Tung misguided Cultural Revolution was responsible for the death—by starvation – of 20 million Chinese people. And these, not in the city as one might assume, where there are no fields to plough or raise livestock, but in the country! Because the soviet Bolshevik institutions quotas were overestimated and the goods were transported forcibly out of the countryside into the cities to feed the masses there, leaving those who had produced them, (the country people) without sufficient food, who subsequently starved to death—reminiscent of what Amerikkka is doing now in south America's coffee plantations and other parts of the globe which we have colonized, the modern way, via private corporations financial leverage.

81.
> Don't let the pressures of the system get upon your head.
> Poor people there is something for you!
> --Damien Marley

Listen to me Dear Children! You must back yourself up Spiritually! This is Muy Importante! You must soon go and sit in the pews of some church, synagogue; or be found in a mosque or ashram. Dance in a Pagan Circle! You must be reinforced up by the Divine, in your holy struggle for justice!

A spiritual education is like the scholastic; one has the option of going thru all the grades and continuing on into higher education, followed by post graduate work, ad infinitum—being a student for the remainder of their life. Spiritually some discover Eloheim and attend regular services one time per week or so, others must be there for 3 services at several places, at scripture studies, plus Talmudic/Biblical discourse, to drink from God's Well whenever and however possible.

The older one gets—many of us--- the more prepared for death one is. That's because they've seen death before, in loved ones, in loved pets, in acquaintances, in standard fixtures of their community whose funerals they attend. They have had enough disappointments, enough insurmountable difficulties that nothing on this earth can repair, and they have learned thru wise teachings that one day, in the divine world which awaits us, that all things are in repair, that all injustices are righted, that all broken hearts mended, all impossible gulfs are bridged. All, which had remained imperfect, is fixed. So they have a growing faith, an abiding burning strength which is spiritual and becomes stronger even as their physical bodies weaken and fail; as their good looks desert them; as the thief of time corrupts their flesh and their skin turns ghastly green; as they see great works of their hands become dated, time-worn, and losing importance—so this faith in the divine must grow. It is nourished thru belief & trust in the Almighty, fanned by the flames of worship on a regular basis in mosque, synagogue, or church. Faith, glowing, a red-hot ember which bursts into a divine flame within us, thru time, sustaining us on the journey. I must say to you now, it is of all importance, this retuvia, to return, to make our way back to the divine Creator—no matter what humans have done to you, no matter the lies of their churches their rabbis their priests their mullahs no matter what hate or exclusion their prejudiced congregations have practiced against you. There are many churches, and many holy places. Make a friend or so to accompany you in your spiritual practice if you can. If no other land is possible for you, and no other place, then get these holy books and seeking God alone. I have listed mine in all these books. Scripture is a friend. God is your great ally.

*

The old Transman dressed in black watches as the congregation "Shabbat Shalom" each other, and he is ignored.

Who do you come to see, Red?

Furrowed yellowish face in contemplation, he looked up at the alter,
high, rich mahogany wood, its top covered in rich red velvet.

> I come to see You, Hashem.
> I come to see You Allah.
> I come to see You Buddha.
> I come to see You Goddess, Mother.
> I come to see You!

Fine old synagogue, a northern wall built of rich deep mahogany
extending up to 3rd story tall; brass pipe organ tubes zoom further up
into the magnificent dome ceiling; this is what we face for barchu;
asking for blessings, praying to Eloheim, Who lays beyond. This is
why I am here. Not simply to nosh onegs.

Privately he soothed his ruffled feathers; his pale yellow hand
stealthily crept into his sack and felt the pages of a very special book.
—One, which bolstered his ego back to functioning & humming on
its energetic pace. The pages of his latest self-publishing.

For thousands of generations back into history people of earth worked
lands, fed themselves & fed their families. Lived, died, leaving no
records--- skeletal heaps of bones, archaic pots & tools. He hoped he
would leave behind something. –As witness, his 2008 book
catalogue, fresh off the press, containing 80-book titles.

This is all it is to be a human being. Fear, hell, & worry.

> When your life becomes fragments of brokenness
> which can crush the
> remainder of your soul
> like dry plaster
> between your fingers
> into antique dust
> and fall to the ground
> with such a holler;
> servant Red
> hurts have destroyed you
> then you dead.

Then you become soul-less.
Then you can be a killer,
the executioner,
the murderer,
then you become bizarre
a mistake of life
a profound
 mystery.

But he would not become so—why? For he had been given a calling,
a job, a purpose.

Whenever a great church, a cathedral, or a magnificent synagogue is
set up, by the faith and pride of the people, there's a battle going on
right on top, over its great gilded dome; a devil and angel battling it
out right above the high crucifix, right over the toppermost peek.
Satan's devils and Gods angels, both muscular, clenched in mortal
combat, turning and twisting, each taking measure for measure,
clench for clench, blow trading blow for blow, each powerful being
holding their own. And we too down underneath the vaulting arches,
us in the pews amid the sacred scrolls and holy artifacts, we too must
fight with spiritual weapons against those devils sitting right beside
us; we too have the common prayers in mass, in community in
congregation, and do battle with powers and principalities in high
places.

Some people have a conservative life. Mine is anything but. Next
week at synagogue having Jewish ethics, we will discuss gay issues,
try to get there early.

White candles burn. Keep the fires lit. Lighting the dark cool womb
chamber of the mighty cathedral. Lit by petitioners faith.

These white candles, are burning.

Why?

We're asking for help.

What?

Things for ourselves, and others.

How?

For there to be change.

Change in the heart.

Change in the heart and change for our lives!

'I want to live to be a very old man-woman.' Thought he. To awake
daily:
>Another day! Joy!
>God's feet are dancing
> with porpoises,
>Swimming in bleu green seaspaceair.

And he realized he too, would dance with God one day, and swim
with God in a swim dance among the porpoises—whom all God's
children love.

Sunday @ Grace. The joyful child self become a morose
contemplative seated in sturdy walnut pews.

>This civilization's moving very rapidly & at a colossal pace. This
>human experiment, is self-designed. This human experiment is
>moving at a tremendous pace & we better get it in control before its
>too late…. Among what Mahatma Gandhi's called the7 deadly sins,
>are beliefs without works. Politics without principal.
>--Dean Jones @ Grace, 2007.

*'Let my prayer join with any who find this society is deeply troubling
in their souls…'* Thought the elderly Transman. Beautiful singing—
angelic ranges of voices climb the grey rock walls & find the sublime.
The Virge is at parade dress, (the golden staff laying over his
shoulder, at rest). Now the Virge is off, golden staff pointing at a
diagonal angle straight ahead & the processional begins…This Grace
is a lot gayer then I thought! All those dikes in their clerical gowns,
it's a wonder to watch, those gals, in dead-pan-face, swing down the
aisles in processional along the stone corridor leading to the front of
the cathedral. The lectors (who read the scriptures) sit solemnly in the

front pew… The crucifier at Christmas… Acolytes carrying the torches… Flaming. Incense burner swings the holy purse in an arc with a cloud of smoke. The serpentine processional winds up the center aisle between two wings of pews of rich old wood burnished black/brown filled to the brim with supplicants who cry "HOSANNA! HOSANNA IN THE HIGHEST!" and proceeds, flowing snake-like up to the naive. There, the clergy bustles to & fro upon their designated tasks. Immediately upon the high alter appear the chalices the patens the lavate—water bowls-- wine & water sacramental dishes, all that silver is blinding!

The pilgrimage continues. The Way. The Journey. Some of us have spirituality, we drink deep from the well.

The old transsexual man sits near to the front in his usual station. Distance from this 2nd pew to the Cross is about 120 feet—it is this distance that is the spiritual movement—up there it stands, 8 foot high, 4 across, the Crucifix. It is to this we bow our heads in reverence as we approach the communion rail. Because of the wretched policy of alcohol only elements am forced to cross my arms in defiance of the cup—but now listen to this: All who seek God and are drawn to Christ are invited to Her table. If you wish to receive blessing instead of the bread or the wine, you are welcome, come foreword and simply cross your arms over your chest to indicate your preference! Which means I could be just another atheist making a political stance of total rejection! Revoking the Blood, the Christ, the very soul of belief! The processional of Grace still continues; now the privileged little (white) boys school choir, these future leaders of the U$A Kapitalist machinery, in which we are the bottom layer, the dirt under the soles of their boots—their rich well-heeled tiny boots-- go stomping by in their hour of glory! Within the cluster of clergy shines an upheld Crucifix! As the shining Cross bobs past, prayers form on the lips of many; for physical cures, for peace of mind, for them, for their loved ones. Here is the Transman's: *Dear Lord I wish things were better for the animals. And for ourselves.*

Later, out in the courtyard after our religious ecstasy we gather; -- back in The World, on real time. Red mentions how some of the clergy are looking gayer to him as the weeks pass by. "They don't know each other dear. They are gayer then hell—they just don't talk about it—like you and I do." Says one dear old queen with a flip of her wrist.

The entire populous of the 11am service mills around the coffee kiosk and tables laden with cookies and slices of cheese & fruit. This is an upscale, mostly straight appearing crowd as previously documented. The sun stands at mid-heaven, blithe blue/white sky, puffy clouds; slowly the sun slides down in the west, the day darkens. Gradually all the majority of the congregation has drifted away, leaving us. We stand here, 2 older queens and me, an old transsexual man; laughing our heads off like old friends even tho we've only just seen each other a few months, because we are gay and we've known each other before- lives ago, ones like us, seated at the gay bar, dank, beer hops smelling, because we had no homes to go back to, only lonely furnished hotel rooms. Laughing, laughing our heads off, because that's all we did back in the day and that's all we do now, refreshed in the cool pristine air of Grace plaza, refreshed and free as gay jay birds!

We are howling our heads off, Red gestures frantically & is pointing with his cane, red (dyed) hair Michael testifying how as a young catholic gay man he feared at every thunder storm that lighting would strike him dead, and we comment how there isn't much lightening out here in San Francisco, at which point Michael readjusts the verdict of divine punishment, and declares, how he feels any moment the earth will open up with a colossal earthquake and swallow him alive—for being gay!!!

And God, Hashem showed me there was a long white alter extending all around the earth, and millions, no, billions of people, filed up to worship and supplicate and prey both in voice or silently, or moaning in the spirit in many different tongue; as many tongues as there on are earth and Gods Spirit sat on the other side, listening to their prayers.

   There are no foreign lands.

   *

'How about the swine Jesus, you cast demons into them—and drowned them in a lake… Some people have pigs as pets these days. Pigs are intelligent and sensitive pets!'

My mercy & compassion extends to all kind.

People offended him, and he hated them for it, but by repeated supplication to God, he cast these people and their viciousness up to the high throne, saying: 'I give this to you God, take this burden from me,' and did not dwell upon the injustice, but continually cast the memory up to God. And in time it washes away.

Grace. I belong here because of Christ and my faith; I'm at home in God and Christ, but I have no friends here.

But then came the idea that he was not really alone at all.

*

Autumn, the cathedral is full of dark shadows. Gloom lit sparsely here and there lit by rich gold lights; illuminating the faces of tapestry's, red, blues & gold. In a niche, candles of supplicants burn—now deserted. Dark, sonorous, vaulting, cathedral. So few who come here, secluded; to every 20 pews or so is a dark-clothed supplicant blending into shadow, head bent in prayer. Attending, for the weekly ritual he prepares for the Benedictines; gathers blue hymn books so that it strains his frail arms as he steps over the marble floor. Behind him now stand 2 lit candles lit from a burning stub in the bronze urn; a prayer for protection for self and for ex-wife cast up.

Grace Cathedral is so gigantic it has room for 2 small chapels held under her sheltering armpits, each on one side of the huge cathedral alter. Supplicants go from one arm to another beseeching the angelic throne from all directions; so poor they can leave no alms.

He was a mystic:

I've been broken apart so many times…

I'll put you back together.

And it was shown to me that we are to be reassembled using a new genetic alphabet; letters which don't exist in the human realm.

*

Cats, dogs are comforters.
That's what they are for.
They are constant steady reminders
of earthly peace.

Mohammad & all the prophets say it. Love is everything.

The worship of God in love
The support of other humanbeings, in love.

82.
I have not abandon the revolution. With plutocrats still running over
the face of the earth. Why is it a white man goes to the Belgian
Congo and comes away with a fortune? A European fortune, yet the
Belgian Congolese are still barefoot and dying for lack of $1 per day
for the HIV/AIDS pill treatment? Unholy financial leverage is the
reason. The two continents being a galaxy apart in technological
advancement gives one superiority over the other. So from time to
time, the elderly Transman came down from his mount Olympus of
prayer and church/synagogue-devotion-going to sit among the youth
of the world—those sad ones who find themselves ensnared in the
world-wide kapitalist machinery stuck in black sticky glue of oil—
and make his strange, prophetic remarks: They must not forget—there
is going to be a resistance! Thought of this reading Emma Goldman.
Anarchists.

The new forms of life will take the place of the old not by preaching
or voting but by living them!
---Emma Goldman

Emma Goldman, she was radical. She was the true meaning of
anarchism—to rid ourselves of faulty systems and begin doing
equitable work for all people! Because of her beliefs in the truth of
betterment of humankind regardless of 'isms'

Emma Goldman was not trying to destroy America! Her speaking
and politicking concerned very basic issues—a humane labor code,
which barred 8-year olds from having to labor 12 hours a day; to a
woman's right to limit the size of her family, by using the newly mass
produced invention of Doctor Condom--- the prophylactic. This is
what she wrote on her deportation:

Dearest Hobo,
Their mad rush in getting us out of the country is the greatest proof
that I have served the cause of humanity.
--Emma Goldman.

So this is food for thought, and subsequent action. From yesteryear's
atrocities. And todays, USA Colonial adventures all over the earth.
For the sake of money and power!

By the dim bookstore light, the smallish figure in rumpled black
clothes sat. Reading—The Slave Ship—Marcus Rediker's fine book
on slavery, specifically seen thru the focus of facts about the slave
ship (slaver) itself. I see up close the internecine monstrous workings
of the slavery empire. (1600rds-1800rds). How each lynchpin, wheel
and geographical route held the whole hideous construct of human
bondage together—from feudal wars between black tribes in Mother
Africa themselves, which created the slave 'caste' to begin with, to
the oarsmen who paddled their canoes full of slaves—held in shackles
made of woven flax--- to be transferred to the more advanced Islamic
or European holders whose shackles were made of iron, then sold to
the ships captain or first mate, entering into the hold of a slave ship
small (30 slaves) to huge, (500). The Middle Passage, in which as
many as one half of these unfortunates died. Then, the destination,
Jamaica, Barbados's, Haiti/The Dominican, and Charleston, an
American port. From here to be farmed out over the American South.
So efficient was this machinery that whole cottage industries sprung
up around it. ---Those people who became efficient slave drivers,
slave chasers, slave bounty hunters. Those individuals who helped
transport captive slaves. Those blacksmith guilds who forged out
black iron shackles for the feet, wrists, and neck; creating inescapable
despair. All the peons who helped facilitate one of the most
lucrative—and the most sorry---enterprise in human history. Dear
Children, remember; like any other huge machinery it has its
loopholes… *Poor people there is something for you…*

*

We shouldn't be taking advantage of the people this way! Each
person, each creature has a dignity. Each person, each creature needs

a home. Each person, each creature must have food, drinkable water; enough of it. And be provided for & not be taken advantage of!

> There is musical hope in Jamaica
> --Sean Stewart, proprietor.

Red: All over the world people are making revolutionary poetry, books and music… it would be so ironic if the world was on the brink of a huge mass revolution.

Sean: Invention of the printing press coincided with the French Revolution because by using it, the comrades were able to disseminate information… The use of pamphlets in the American Revolution; using the press; printed John Payne's Rules of Man…. I wonder how the Internet will play out with a modern day revolution. Because so many people all over have seen so much-and in such a short time. Everybody everywhere knows about the rich, about the poorest of the poor, they know about corruption.

Red: Our nation has been forced to make public their record. Those secret government documents… today, all our world's besieging their governments to disclose them. Each country, locally, and in the international courts. All this information is out! Its available for the common person to see at last! Documents… Like the CIA and the Cameron affair, that fiendish psychiatrist/business man in his secret mental clinic who tested mind-altering drugs on helpless mental patients in the 1950's, in collusion with the U$ Army, experimenting how to reprogram undesirable people into desirable citizens. —There's the old Soviet stuff, about the gulags, everything…

Sean: What is the incubation time…

Red: How long will it take for all this information to soak into each individual mind in every part of the world before they individually dig in their heels refusing to cooperate with the powers of authority any longer, and collectivize with their neighbors and co-workers, and these small groups join up into many separate revolutionary forces which will act as a total force sweeping the world!

Yellow lights shine down upon them. Tall, slender, the young proprietor leans back in an uncomfortable chair at his station over the computer & cash register, where his destiny has been forged; to sit, vulture-like daily, doing dull business procedures & awaiting customers. A regular has stopped by—one of the artists who have begun to congregate at this spot in lower Nob Hill. Gazing into space of the tall 13-foot high clean white-painted ceiling of the store, relaxed for a moment, Sean reminisces on his favorite pastime. If he was home, back in Jamaica. Declares: "I'd be crushing weed in my hand, rolling a spliff & feeling easy in the club." Then continues with this immoral line:

> What I like about this city, there's so many marginal people, so many fringe groups. Plus you can find all this wrapped up into one person... Like Red here, for instance...
> --Sean, Proprietor, Babylon Falling; bookstore.

A trickle of customers stop by, browse; then buy or leave. Short, stalwart, ever-faithful; Transman was the Lion Who Sat By The Door. There he perched, on a display window ledge, reading Charles Darwin Theory of Natural Selection, and comparing himself to the theorems advanced within. *The strongest, hardiest of the species stand the greatest chance of survival.* Hum... I see maybe God equipped me with a hard ego—so I'd survive the blows which natural occur upon someone bound to be unsuccessful for an inordinate amount of time of their life—if not all of their life—specifically, an undiscovered artist. —If this ego did by its nature infringe upon others, I know that I did not myself create my own hard-ass ruthless selfishness when it comes to putting my art above every other thing— including food in my mouth, and also taking risks with rent money; but that this was given to me, 'naturally selected' by Hashem, so as to enable me to spread Her word of Justice & Faith no matter what!

A species re-creates itself in Mass Proliferation, to make up for great destruction later in life. So he thinks of his many, many titles, in his newly released 'Catalogue of Books, 2008.' Surely some of these will survive the test of time!

Isolation also is important in the process of natural selection. And what a lonely life he had left! (What better way then to hone the raw talents of an artist!)

As was his habit, the old guy switched from book to book, balancing the current one on his knee, while sipping courtesy coffee from a

Styrofoam cup; the unfinished books shoved under the proprietors desk.

Now, in Slave Ship see how a person is 'radically individualized' after being sold to by a succession of masters and traders, and having occupied many different countries—as commodities, loosing all familiar ties; first their family, next their country, soon all their friends and fellow slaves; loosing these ties by having to switch geographical locations, stripped of the companionship of those who can speak the same language

Also in Slave Ship, how one of the captives eventually finds he knows no ones name---reminiscent of the gay bars, such isolation amid festive crowd. And then there's the TV program Cheers, a TV serial, sit com, whose motto was; 'the place everybody knows your name'.

> I gwe bu ke—multitude is strength --
> --Igbo proverb, Slave Ship.

Grace, it is absolutely apparent that I have no friends here. But does one have friends anywhere? Is it my fault? Is it societies? In Shar' Zahav they speak of the stranger. Reading the parsha, (Torah portion) about Abraham having to burry his wife Sarah (who had lived to be 120 years old) in a strange land, thru which they were traveling...
So, it's the legacy of the stranger, those outcasted; those expelled from their human camps, to wander far abroad, those who don't belong. Are you one of those? I am. Now, a further observation: Abraham and Sarah assemble a people unto themselves. To surround them.

> I always afflict the ones I love, to make them more perfect.

> Where will you follow Me?
> There are some who live;
> and others who live in the land of eternal night.

> Sweep up your corners!
> Of the broken parts of objects you once paid so much $ for.
> Now! There! The room is bare!
> Let us leave!

'Foxes have their dens, but I have only the path. Only the engagement.' So says The Christ. So say all great prophets. These scriptures speak of exclusion & apartheid of people who are different. The outcast.

Oh, PS, am dropping out of the Benedictines; so as not to create further confusion. My voice is too loud for them, and my ideas, blurted out roughly don't seem to be accepted as well as the long drawn out sonorous contemplations of some others, more popular, and of longer standing. One casual member who attends infrequently brought a guest with him a while back who actually got up and walked out while certain persons were talking--feeling they were departing from the lofty Spirit of God, from the high and clean Spirit of God, and meandering slowly, down a different path… Anyway, they don't need me there—my style, I guess.

> All my attempts at being sociable
> are like pieces of a child's broken tea set.
> I lay this brokenness at the feet of Jesus*.
> *Hashem, Allah, Buddha, Great Mother, et al.

A brief explanation of the events, which precipitated this latest breakup and severing in his human relations: A certain woman, thin, stick-like (bad witch-like) and exceedingly soft spoken, repeatedly takes him to task about praying too impassionedly, loudly and hence offensive to her ears. Transman Red feels attacked by her personally after the 3rd or so critique, and answers her back violently and angrily- per his own unhappy upbringing. Nobody comes to his defense by mentioning the woman's Attack Mode regarding him, her continually picking on him. No one speaks on his behalf, in fact seems to favor her! He feels he is in the wrong place, and would be wise to continue his spiritual searching and service where he is more appreciated! Sadly, even if this means his own small monks studio!

Worship in community magnifies the individual persons' faith; so this is a loss by all accounts.

Another thing, I decide I must give up my condo dreams. My romantic thoughts to have a lover, a wife. Of course I'd forgotten my anger, my rage. Its easier to think of what I desire to have this security of a condo, and happiness of a wife—and giving up the

70

dream of this, then actually stop a negative behavior which has run along the course of my life.

Now I read my Torah, the Bible more you come to see the human condition—there's no getting out of it.

Even if we grow to sainthood we are still human. This is why there will always be world wars—because we are human; & although it is good to aspire to be perfect, and perfection will manifest itself yes, but that will be in a world beyond this one, in a new time and place. For now, right down on planet earth in this physical zone the goal is to do the best you can and set a fine example for the rest; to inspire the human race.

83.
Japanese tourists all with cameras shiny new dangling from their wrists snapping photos merrily; middleaged, giggling like children. Exchanging cameras, SNAP! SNAP! at each other, posing.

A horn blows. Light gay rings; an instrumental. A mad clown stands trying to gather a crowd around herself; he-she is 6'3" yellow straw hair wig on her cranium covers her own ruined bald nappy hair. She is attired in pink dress, blue rubber boots, & purple shawl. She holds a bouquet of faux flowers all her possessions have been found in various garbage cans, over time.

Mad Clown: Come gather around me children! You are Flowers of the World!

*

Day of The Dead celebration at Faithful Fools. A beautiful room placement; an alter to the dead, a platform, about 8 feet by 16, 2 feet high off ground covered with a thick rug, upon it placed stuffed animals, musical instruments and white candles surrounding. In its center a smaller table raised up higher, the alter, on which are placed photographs of loved ones, poems and tokens of remembrance. One white candle burns and one red--being the only different candle among them. Gradually the people come upstairs to the second story and take their seats in comfortable chairs or sofas. We will eat, fill our stomachs, then go around the room, introducing ourselves. We

71

will read fragments of poetry, diary pages, later we'll call out the name of our loved ones, departed. The room has subdued lighting; dreaming up a story Red sits on a sofa, his plate being full of mashed potatoes, chicken and gravy balanced on one knee, a strong cup of coffee in a mug on the floor; gazing into the candlelight the myriad of colors shapes designs on the artful table. He is surrounded by others, poor like him, this place where he doesn't have to worry if he washed his hair the night before or if his shirt smells stale from a days walking, or if his sox stink inside his shoes. He realizes his mortality.

> Take your seat.
> Sit awhile—
> then it's time to get up & leave.
> One by one they depart.
> Their indentation on a chair still marked,
> when someone else comes to fill the place. They too
> will leave at their appointed calendar date.

*

Thursday morning, November 8. *Then it will be the 9th, 10th; countdown to my birthday on the 15; will turn 64! How fortuitous to celebrate this with the issue of my milestone 80-title* **Book Catalogue, 2008!** *Glorious Technicolor painting, La Suena brightens its cover.*

Yellowish tint, hands, smallish for a man, artistic; veined, sinuous. Red turns over his 92-page book catalogue.

> Red (to God): Thank You for giving me my gift.
> God (to Red): Thanks for using it.

As he looks around his small 'monastic' studio apartment-some 500 square feet Red takes into account what is there. It houses 'The Work;' very little of his own personal possessions. Great storage boxes of books, rolls of canvas, paintings, business machines, (one found in gutter) copies for distribution, two desks, an easel, oil paints---you get the picture. ---His personal stuff is quite small. Some threadbare pants, shirts, sox, & underwear, one pair of walking shoes, a pair of sandals, a pair of loafers. The good ones donated; the other 2 pair found on top of garbage cans…

He examined his life, momentarily: So unhappy, so sad & twisted. Well, I realize I been shortchanged in the human relations and the $ department. Lucky to have immersed myself in art.

Among the hustle and clutter of the world you find things which are destined to survive; wither they are archived by wealth, or luck; even as the current stuff, effluvium of the ordinary days is swept by times broom into a dustpile. These archived scrolls, clay tablets, ornate leather bound, gem embedded volumes hand-copied by monks. Throughout 5,000 years some dry up; turn to a finite dead indecipherable dust. Before they evaporate entirely we hope to reduplicate them. In the soul of a person one gains inspiration from long ago dead masters—ones we might hate, ones we might envy, who nevertheless inspire us on our own journey, puts fire under the recalcitrant pot, gives boil to the writers stuck by writers block, gives a kick in the butt to the procrastinate so they get to work! These words of the master evaporate into our souls, turning into a fine ink upon which we draw daily—having long ago forgotten the detested masters name, but their fire urges us on still!

84.
So Shauns* instillation of art has come to confluence. David Lee's portraiture executed with master craftsmanship, montages of homeless chiefly African American creatures who inhabit the area outside, around his studio space. He snaps them with camera, then takes them back to studio to paint a true likeness, washed over with colors and framed by designs, this done on canvas, on board and on small cigar boxes which he then glues together into various geometric forms. Photographer Shaun* snapping all the while, SNAP! SNAP! Young men take turns standing on the proprietors 12-foot high ceiling ladder arranging stuff. All these young artists come/go & I've sold a GARBAGE CAN SALLY fresh off RED JORDAN PRESS, this is one of those once in a lifetime fato destinos.

Only, but a few chances in a lifetime does this kind of royal machinery roll… & I'm in the center of it, 3 blocks away! …. All young artists here in the vicinity gravitated to this place of books… & materials, which embrace the idea of revolution. They are dwelling in roommate-shares, or private studios, or in the case of the most affluent, a 1-bedroom all to themselves—thus having an actual living space with a separate room for all the junk of their trade.

There had been other 'hotspots' of creative genius in artist Red's life. Another was in 1994, brief 'heyday of lesbian publishing' that's when Richard Kasik & his NYC machinery pumped out 8 of the then 50-year olds books; then also appeared the bulk of his contributions to anthologies—this big opportunity 13 years ago. Another felix fato he could recall at the very beginning of young adulthood when, at 15, 16, found himself, a girl-boy running with a pack of black male artists in their 20's and 30s. There was Wayne and David—the mad black poet, 6'2" a cape furled around his football player shoulders; Caton, a fine arts oil painter supporting his family by legitimate work 40-hour week at the equal opportunity Post Office, snatching free times along the edges, standing with paintbrush between his brown fingers gazing intently at some artifact over which he'd paint his black complexioned people in colorful African dashikis, and African colorful designs; there was John Coltrane whom they knew, who breezed into town to toot his genius at Southside blues/jazz clubs; Joseph Jarmin just having begun his Modern Jazz Ensemble; these artists who lived in and frequented the artsy Hyde Park area of Chicago—that was 1957. We're speaking of like minds.

The rabbi speaks of balance. On the table beside the Shabbat candles are two treys of small glasses—one of wine, one of grapejuice. The challah bread stands on a silver platter covered in its blessed garment. Someone passes a trey, it tips, but does not spill; and simultaneously in a fraction of a second the level of liquid in all the 40 glasses on the trey moves as one body—simultaneously; all retaining the same identical slant as its neighbor. Why? Because all answer to a deeper authority—gravity—one of the universal laws whose pull and forces are unseen to the naked eye, but whose evidence is quite plain. And we too, spirits, answer to a deeper authority. One of freedom, of artistic wings, of beauty, of the passion to create all this!

The bookstore—a beacon of light thru a cold holiday season on lower Nob Hill—is furiously setting stride, with a jazz jam background, Shaun Roberts on top of 12-foot ladder installing a projector for a slide show of his photography about the artist—David Lee, and the artist himself busily finishing up another picture with his special tool,

a wall papering brush, applying housepaint to wood; the other Sean*
proprietor gingerly walking the tightrope edge of a book table,
reaching into space to reaffix some contraption he has strung across it
with dangling portraiture of Che Guverra. Red a yellow monkey, his
simian hands wrapped around a sheet of paper and pencil furiously
churns out more notes for COMPASSION, his latest installment.
Then, its back to plotting his great Multi-Faith Order, DOC. The
artists come and go; its cold so we wear our coats inside.
*-- Sean—proprietor, Shaun-- photographer!

They are like monkeys climbing all over the store hanging upside
down in space.

Another tall young man speaks of squatting—in order to have a place
to stay: "Is there good squatting in North Beach? (Home of dead
Kerouks.) I just got back from NYC. It's not about business, finance
NYC is about art. That's why people all come there, for the culture,
the theatre, book publishers, magazines, art galleries, museums,
music, dance; that's what people come there to see--- yet the artists
can't afford to live there anymore, they are being pushed out. Red,
your $115 high rent West Village apartment of the 1960's is now a
$800-thousand 1-bedroom condo—for sale-- no longer for rent at any
price—all the artists are being pushed out, they're being pushed out
into the river."

Speaking of the creative oeuvre, also among this esteemed crowd is a
rare breed of person who can be found in any artistic circle in any
time or geographic place. There is a genre of highly talented people,
gifted genius's who have no product to show, or accomplished skill
nor performance mastered and yet call themselves artists:

Hi, what do you do?

I'm an artist.

Oh! What kind?

Uh... I paint... and write... and dance... and I'm the lead vocalist
for this band or that... And I have a piece in the new sculpture
garden... Have you been there?

They say they paint, compose haiku, do interpretative dance, run practice scales on a borrowed golden saxophone in the park; they have true artistic sentiments---but never take any of them on to its full limits so that one could be known as 'their calling' in life. About 5 years ago, after meeting still another of these types, it finally dawned on Red, 'these are artists of a different sort.' And then he acknowledged they are artists---of this genre not yet named. Of the Multi-gifted. They paint a picture, they write a poem; they sing before an audience for a single night… and manage to get a show here or there, a small poem or short story placed in an anthology—but then abandon that talent. All the while, being truly artistic they move around the finest artists, become known by them, confidante to them, and to an outside observer become known by their juxtaposition to these artists, thus slowly begin, inadvertently or on purpose, to be written into the living history of these artistic circles, heralded on lips of critiques, gossipers, hangers-on's & gigolos, which after this circle hits its zenith and then declines into the dusty chapters of research history--- their names remain along with all the other 'working artists' of their day.

There he sat, perched on a ledge of Babylon Falling amid rows & rows of colorful books; of which one (a free read) was open on his laps; what was he doing? Gazing into space, a silly smile on his lips—as he thought to himself about his 'Order' that mad idea he informally referred to as 'DOC':

> RE: Conversion, saving of souls, etc.:
> A person who sets out to 'rehabilitate' a profligate soul must distance themselves in that they have no vested interest in that person at all other then to win over their soul for God, and setting that person's foot on higher ground. It is a mistake to marry them nor have any kind of carnal business or any other kind of human enterprise or entrapments with that person---for they themselves will only loose.

And; moments later:

> Re: My Order, DOC. It is a wise owner or founder, having the inspiration, the foresight, the courage to present a new religious sect, or to build up a gay tavern or other venue, etc., who once having established it, steps out of the limelight to remain behind the

scenes guiding, passing final judgments-- when judgment cannot be made by underlings, who appoints a manager, or prior(ess) or some other powerful person who can guide the sheep, or lead the work in the style which the founder has prewritten, but this executed by a manager who is gifted in the art of human interaction who can 'get along' with people, and not offend. Who will not slap the very noses of the sheep who come nosing around to find out what's going on, but encourage their baby footsteps on The Path! As before said, I personally am created of the wrong material to perform daily management of the Order, people would start to hate me and my ego, my ways, my dictatorship, after the first few days, better this position left for someone more gifted in the social arts.

And, in addition, for his grand finale of daydreaming:

DOC will have common gardens. Rural chapters will farm. In the order of small businesses; a family-run independent business. But as far as the capitalist, huge, mega conglomerate business corporations, don't forget these must be overthrown immediately and be collectivized by their workers!

*

The old prophet hoped he might be one of the world's great artists, or at least a minor prophet as he shuffled upon his daily routes. Heavy book sack on his shoulders going back and forth between copy centers and paper cutting shop, his home, the revolutionary bookstore and the post office—mailing off an occasional order for those dusty tomes he had authored. Every 3 or 4 (or 5) months he changed the bed linen & his pajamas.

… Acolytes carrying the torches… Flaming. Incense burns. A white robed acolyte swings the holy purse in an arc with a cloud of smoke. In his minds eye he saw them—the holy parade--Robed in white monks cowls with rope around their waists to pull them along towards the heavenly direction. Rope so tight they cannot escape! *All the implements of spiritual warfare are assembled. The Cross is uplifted, dazzling arrayed in gold. The candlesticks lit, held like torches, some 3 feet high, each one born by an accolade robed in white with the rope around their waist; the Deacon in her prayer shawl; Bishop brandishing his crooked staff. The pageant flurries its skirted habits, an army of the Lord stirs, now proceeds down the aisles; it's holy processional flows down from the choir loft past the alter down towards the pews, rushing like a*

river, riding along the banks between long rows of wooden pews twisting & turning, threatening to overflow the aisles. The chelser, the cloister, the chalice, the censer, the incense, an ancient bible uplifted, housed in lacy silver brocade!

I stand before you dressed in a gold brocaded clerical robe or a black & white tallet, over my corruptible flesh. An old man in a tumultuous season in which is the great fear of all nations of earth for their future. I come to bring hope out of sadness. I come to impart the golden rule! The one roughly used by most religions of earth. In my own words:

> Do unto others as you would have them do in all kindness and compassion to yourself—or at lest try your best.
> Love the divine Creator of the universe, Creator known by many different Names & traditions) with all possible passion; with seeking and close-following throughout your mortal years! Don't fall away! Stay on the path! Follow the Light! Hold fast to the reigns the Almighty Creator gives you!

*

Next day, sun rising, brings heartbreaking headlines, two human hands holding a dying baby duck covered in thick gooey black oil. Another oil tanker run aground; 58 million tons of oil pours out polluting every beach in the bay area. Wildlife are dying. Worse, of all times, 50,000 migrating birds had just flown from a different continent; 2,000 miles to this place to feed in the eco system of our Bay Area… 58 tones of crude oil spilled all over the whole goddamn shorefront. Listen, what's so symbolically awful it all happens within days of November 9—the 69th anniversary of Krystalnatch—the night of broken glass, when 275 Jewish synagogues all across Germany were destroyed by the Nazis fascists then rising to power, and 30,000 Jews carted off in the beginning of the slow inexorable rolling of the death trains to the concentration camps.

About this recent environmental holocaust, this has happened again in memory, the Valdez, another mega-oil tanker which spilled her bloody cargo all over the blue/green ocean. Man moves elements of earth around where they don't belong. Drills oil up from under the bottom of the sea, then pours it out into the water—where eons before the two elements were kept separate. Man pollutes everything we

78

touch. We need to get off the oil standard and use oil only in small amounts to jump-start other kinds of power—wind, solar, water-power. Minute amounts.

You love the earth, the plants, & animals. This is the first step. You want to help & do good for the earth and its people and animals. That is the second.

Its always the lesser-minded people who oppose you—they say this work is impossible! They know more—but have a smaller scope. They innumerate reasons—why being cemented in their threatened beliefs are vital, yet they labor under something that is just tradition---which time has rendered meaningless

> God is big. & all Gods bigness is love-filled.

Work while the sun is still shining! Make haste!

There was a man who rehabilitated an abandon parrot. Its problem was the parrot had been abandon—yet still caged, not set free. Indifferent hands shoved in food, water, cleaned out shitty cage liner papers, then went on their way, leaving the parrot alone for 30 years. The good hearted mans work was to salvage this tiny little soul, which he did, eventually making friends with the green parrot, whose spirit thus came back to life, and when it finally died, it died in peace, winging its way joyously to heaven.

> All souls are reconciled to God. Even dragons with their tongues lashing out, nostrils belching steam, and eyes gleaming, love God! They rest under God's Arm, in a beautiful dragon place S/He has built for them. All shall love God. (Ve'avta Adonai.)
> --Works, 2007

Animals can tell who loves them—and who can't.

> A prayer unfolds into life; a living tallet stark black and white spots, angular, so full of love. Wagging it's tail; a pink licking tongue. Holy garment, beloved pet. God made them both, gave them both to human kind.

Ours is a corrupt society. Its not unusual among nations both present and past, but I do know that what is unusual, America's position in the world is that we are the greatest, richest, gross polluter, and the only nation on earth that by such totalitarian means goes marching off into foreign lands—uninvited—destroying their culture, political machinery and traditions of lands not their own.

There's plenty of sick things that have happened in the line of power & dominance, wholesale subjection of the classes & gender of individuals—down thru time 1,000 years of foot-binding. Prostitutes to labor like ox's in the brothel field of sex. Men, to be used as cannon fodder in total war. So it is upon the foundation of the madness that we must build our lives—somehow; create beauty; attempt revolutionary acts against the corrupt powers of authority.

> One must have chaos in ones self to be able to give birth to a
> dancing star.
> --Nietzsche.

Dear Children– don't forget we deal with The Psychology. Always consider the mental-factor. Not simply economics. The rich plutocratic man (plute) buys up all the houses on the block. A small house on the next block sells to an individual buyer. "Why did we let that house slip thru our fingers?" Asks the rich plute to his cronies as they smoke cigars in their apartheid gentleman's club with luxurious red vinyl armchairs & butlers scurrying around baring drinks on treys.

The above example illustrates the fault of the putting of everything into a political realm and not considering the physiological factor. When fighting the good fight every tactic, analysis and weapon must be used. —And not discredited as 'modern day bourgeoisie hocus pocus.' It is a fact that powerful people hate to see anyone else with power. The more they have the more they must take. The sign least sign of any one acquiring even the smallest amount of power worries them terribly—on the psychological level—and they go to draconian lengths to stamp that tiny power out. It is a beneficent and well– adjusted mind that can tolerate power in others.

> 'Never give anyone the power to take away your freedom'
> --From the movie Poetry Slam.

*

Remember Dear Children, Jesus wants you to know, love is the answer to everything.

Hurry! Duties first! Prayer second! Prayer always, but when able, official prayers, orchestrated prayers, prayers in chant form in unison.

> If voices are raised long enough and loud enough in an international community, change will happen.
> --Archbishop South Africa

Pray always! And not to loose heart. And then Jesus. The cheeky little Jewish bastard who was killed time after time after time… Prey always. Jesus Christ is our last appeal!

Native Americans take lessons from their dreams. In Native American tradition the red sister or brother invokes the guardian spirit given to them; calls it up within themselves and does not turn this process over to a chief priest—but goes and seeks God in a personal fashion. It is only the white hierarchical system which must have dominants and subordinates.

*

So JOURNEY continues with COMPASSION, which will soon morph into CHARITY and then, ENLIGHTENMENT!

The will to live is a fundamental, built in human mechanism. To over ride this takes a strong will. The strong will, and desperation of the suicidal humanbeing. Little Transman awoke. Sometimes he was so lonely he all but wanted to die. Alone as usual in his rumpled bed, except for Mr. Fluffy, a magnificent cat. Was this aloneness to prepare for religious life to become a monastic? Or would he find love once again? A warm companion at his side? A family!

It should be mentioned again, he had 25 years of atheism then found the church; so when first going into it, developed his own connection with God. Thus felt not dependant on certain religious pitfalls which might be more of man then of the Divine. Possessing a clean, fresh slate, barely written on by dogma. A superior training to voice his enigmatic prophecies, and his own holy analysis.

You've heard the call, the call to service. Now, how? Where? When? It's only the 'why' that you know—why? Because you love God. At some point in the Christian Journey, and I'm sure many other faiths, you may hear the call. Under the Christian discipline I was called by Jesus Christ, him/her asking 'who would you serve?" It was quite apparent to me this meant, would I go on serving the things of the world, or would I put everything aside to follow Christ.

> 15, 16, 17th century Jews were required to wear 1finger wide, one half human palm long patch the color yellow. Further, years later Jewish men were to wear this yellow patch on their hats, and the women on their covered heads. 'This set the foundation for future wearing of a yellow Star of David in the Nazi concentration camps. --@Grace.

I see the challenge of Judaism and Christianity sharing a mutual service. If I were to bring a Jewish friend to church—the very first hymn in this service contains 10 lines of 'Christ Be Blessed' out of 15 lines! And recall the time he took feminist friend who was dead set against Christianity, being a big Wiccan, but frankly, much more agnostic; took her to a woman's service. Every Sunday for months previous I'd attended it had been women only! But and this particular Sunday 3 grizzly men sat among the small women's congregation. One a FBI secret service man, father of one of the congregants, another, someone's mild mannered brother, the 3rd a new potential to help save his soul, dragged there by a friend---a very anti social and very tall, rangy, uncouth-acting, hirsute, male with large beard. Of course my friend was immediately turned off by the overbearing presence of these 3 males, and did not give the place a chance! And never came back.

Who is the best, the furthest manifestation of Gods self? Those who proceeded the Abrahamic religions, in the first 70,000 years of humans kind? —Abraham lived only 4,000 years ago. What of the women and men who turned their faces up to heaven, wailing from their hearts over death of a favorite child?

Who is the greatest?

Both are equal.

And:

I'm giving birth to a new nation.

And, in addition:
DOC will have common gardens, rural chapters will farm. In the order of small business; a family-run independent enterprise. But as far as the kapitalist but huge mega conglomerate corporations, don't forget these must be overthrown immediately and be collectivized by their workers!

Just as a mother with 5 children knows, fears, has been made aware by seeing deaths in other families—that one or two of her precious brood may die—but out of her five some, hopefully most will live to have children of their own and complete the cycle—and then the mothers work will be done, her life fulfilled. So God in the same way has given each generation many artists, knowing that all cannot come to fruit—is God even sure? We do have free will. Some will not be able to, others may not want to.

150 years ago—there were reading clubs for illiterate European peasantry. The average small village peasant didn't even know they lived in a nation! And none of them could read or write! So, Dear Children, in this modern severely fallen-away age I must intersperse within my body of creation of fine arts, science fiction thrillers, a constant stream of spirituality—you have forgotten what it is! You are ignorant!

I will turn the sequel to Compassion into a novel! Or an adventure story, or... an illegal battle plan for underground warfare— which I myself cannot do but you can Dear Children.... The revolutionary must fight!

First I had to learn to fight. Now I have to learn to be peaceful.

6:30; Hebrew class. Oh---am learning Hebrew ---Rabbi Rueben's class, 101. He kindly let me take it for no $ since I have nun (double ha-ha), also gave me a study manual. Knowledge! Bright lights shining! We are drawn closer to God. Times the Transfellow was filling his head with learning. ---Church/ synagogue is a different kind of University.

Regarding the state of our earth—a physical plane not yet heaven. (Heaven, Paradise, Nirvana, etc.) A place of perfect peace: We shouldn't be taking advantage of the people, this way!

> Each person, each creature has a dignity. Each person, each creature needs a home. Each person, each creature must have food, drinkable water; enough. And be provided for & not be taken advantage of!

From the beginning individuals have got up before the crowds, their arms upheld, in white robes like the messiah & the people have fallen for it. They get in power---and become another petty dictator. From the beginning armed forces have swept across nations—overthrowing their own countries governments and sized control of everything & people been too afraid to resist them—until their end in which they too were overthrown. People trusted and been were disappointed; they give their arms, their service, and their lives to a cause which sold them out. Has the time come when the human race has matured enough and gained enough sophistication to ignore presidents-for-life; sun gods, divine inheritors and armed forces who set up puppet leaders—and replace them with just executors of the law & vote in and out of office their leaders by a democratic electoral process? Have we learned by any of our sad experience of previous dynasties?

> Perhaps one of the chief reasons for the present chaotic condition of things is that the world has been trying to get along with only half of itself. Everywhere we see running to waste women-force that should be utilized in making the world a more decent home for humanity. Let us see how the votes of women will help solve the problem of living wisely and well.
> --Helen Keller 1913.

If you are a woman might find the films of the day deal chiefly with men; in a motion picture with a male and female character leads, the male will be supported with 3 or 4 or more other main men, while the female is lucky if she has the backing of one other supporting female role. It is a male dominated genre. Blacks have been saying this for years about the previously almost white-only Hollywood art scene.

For a transsexual man there is next to nothing. You can stop watching films and be inventive, imaginative and resourceful and build your own culture—however if this involves more then 2 or 3 of you, you might find a community as challenged as our fledgling, besieged trans community is a challenged one, and you may well be sold out by your 'friends' and your aim to create culture, to stage a show, film a trans-motion picture, to create a trans society fall apart. Like I say, I am portraying a slice of transsexual life—seen thru the eyes of me, so remember that, with all my fine arts ramblings and high political theories and spiritual invocations—that it is a fucken' queer doing it; reminding you I come from a highly challenged world. … Must say that I had to fight my way into the conscious of America… Well maybe my words will die with me, and not be heard, but by Aloheim Her/Himself! All the revolutionary shit, all the political awareness---all written down because I'm just so fucken' angry about it all! So that I Decide to Do something….

Quoting the bible; *when I was a child I spoke as a child… I looked thru a glass darkly, now we meet face to face,* all becomes clear. All our politics, well meaning, necessary in fact, to aright the injustice of an unjust world—all our human solutions are only temporal, they will pass and a new order will have to be set up, just as fast as our 'modern solution' passes into antiquity. A time will come Dear Children, when all our politics, and energy's in sweaty human work begins to extends into the passion of the Divine. To say it another way; Compassion and Mercy must have manifestation of that love in real works, in concrete works, but a step further, now these brave works these works of courage on the human sphere, morph into divine love and divine passions.

So hard this lesson!

This is my son! Says Hashem.

It is my daughter! Says God

Creator; The Compassionate.

Me & ex-wife Jasmin went out in her & her new lovers car. Dined. Indian food—one quarter her racial background.

Paliak Gosh (spinach & lamb)
Chicken Massala
Shrimp
Rice
Nan
Mango Lasse a drink.)
Indian Tea (like coffee)

Jasmin bought herself a red & white Christmas boa, placed it around her neck and looked pretty. After their outing she dropped Red off at his studio and handed him the red and white boa:

You can have this…

No, you take it!

No you take it!

NO! It's a Christmas scarf and I'm on my way to synagogue!

Ha ha!

It's a red & white Christmas scarf like Santa Claus and they think I'm converting! They expect me to convert to Judiasm. I'm not converting, *I'm just adding on!* I'm adding on Judaism! I'm a Christian and a Jew, both. Not either one or the other! Why do they all convert? Don't anybody just add on and be both?

The golden rule is imparted between father & daughter. It carries on thru life. —When it is not broken by corruption, vice as it was between my grandfather and mother. An unbroken bond between parents and their little ones leading to what is good and remains to this day the new generations strength and their greater good today. (dor vador.)

You will be melted and tried in the fiery furnace of tempestuous temperatures and forged into gold!

I stand before you dressed in a gold interwoven with silver brocaded clerical robe, a fine black & white tallet draped over my tan-pale & hairy corruptible flesh. An old man in a tumultuous season in which there is a great fear of all nations of earth for their future.

86

Dear Children, I must leave you with some points to remember:

--Beware of bright ideas, which are soon dulled by time. Don't worship them, or fix them in your mind as a final solution, but a temporary stepping stone. We are all marching towards freedom, compassionate, care of one another without respect as to class or color or religion or type. This is our goal. Not an 'ism', of any sort.

If a prehistoric kind of person was to stumble across a cave filed with tables of stone engraved with hieroglyphics—of the law, the Word, of all great religions---given from on High,-- without a key to that 'alphabet' they would not understand what is written.

> Learn to be peaceful....
>
> *Love!*
>
> Love the people? Which ones?
>
> *All.*
>
> Love the elephants?
>
> *All.*
>
> Love everything?
>
> *All!*
>
> *All!*
>
> *All!*

The human heart has --- chambers. Love, greed; envy, hate; fear; anger; lust. —Choose life!

I cannot help but think in some world to come, a better world, people who have no place now will have their place.

There's a saying that if you no longer have something to give someone, no lesson to teach someone, then your book of life is closing. And so is this chapter.

Well right now I am still walking, talking, teaching, preaching. Luckily I have remained 'good'; not gone to jail (what a waste of time that is) and have remained 'free' thus able to scratch out the minimal paintings, tomes… store them in my studio or 1-room SRO hotel. Disseminate these 'leavings' worldwide. They say I am a sex writer, that I write erotica for money, this is not true! —Or, only in part, being mostly a dreamer, an imager, and dyadic, ranting, politico-spiritual haranguer of you, the multitude.

Well, back to the job at hand. Is not compassion too, the loving of self? … Porn film ready in the TV/VCR; soft music plays. Then a porn actors voice:

> He wants some hard dick & some fast action.

After all is said, and done, all I can do is hope some good will come of my work

God (to Red): *You have been given a work. Build!*

Red Jordan Arobateau
November 12, 2007
3:30 PM Pacific Standard Time
San Francisco, CA
USA

MERCY

JOURNEY Vol. 7

2007-2008

```
The green bird doesn't
   realize, but it is one
   of the small tentacles that
   fasten us here to earth.
Caring for it.
Loving it.
Setting its cage in a sun pool daily.
Singing back to it as it sings to us.
Using your shoulder as a perch
   to sit upon
             together, at evenings rest.
```

85.
Some humans are a complete failure in the department of romance.
—*So the Transman thought, heaving a sigh which caused the black fabric of his very worn shirt stretched over his too-fat stomach to rise & fall; illustrating a great depth, -- that heartfelt sigh speaking worlds of pain.*

Some peoples are from a linage of oppression. Unrequited evil perpetuated upon them. He thought of black slaves, his ancestry; of the poor, his inheritance; his un-fabulous career --no thanks to the straight or gay literary establishment, --and thought; *Its long overdue, justice. Not just for these things, but a great justice.*

It is theorized that in antiquity the earth had a single connected land-mass, which, as its core cooled, on the surface broke apart into the various continents we now have, spewing off the smaller islands. One day the peoples of this earth-now scattered from each other in language, and culture; in religion and temperament, will be united. One day we will truly have shalom—wholeness. Peace. A shaking of hands in agreement between ourselves.

7 billion people on earth—none of them have seen our Creator's face. None of them know Creator's name. We stare at each other suspiciously; blue eyes vs. brown. I haven't seen Creator's face, I don't know Creator's name—and neither do you!

Monai is the Greek meaning the stages upon the way inside heaven. There are many different houses within Hashem's heavenly house.

> In my Father/Mothers house
> there are many mansions.

Scripture states many are called, few are chosen---does this mean out of 7 billion humans on earth, many of that number are being called, so that's a lot who aren't even called! -- Far fewer are chosen; who are the chosen? Those who do God's Word, who are obedient to Him/Her?

> Enjoy youth now.
> Work hard as your capability.
> Time moving swiftly soon overtakes us all,
> stands in supremacy.
> Bows its head only to God.

Well there, all this good stuff is postulated in print now—to dish the dirt!

First, to clear up a trivial matter, at the Commanders bible study, we had a scripture analysis of John 17, Jesus' heartfelt speech:

These words spoke Jesus, and lifted up his eyes to heaven, and said, Father/Mother my hour is come; glorify Your child that Your child also may glorify You.

After that, followed a commentary read out of some gospel study guide which spoke to what I'd been thinking about earlier, that is dropping out of a certain group at church, (the Benedictines); this particular scripture study rambled into conjecture about a pertinent subject; saying that: **monastic life is a most narrow interpretation of Christ's love; and that within the monastic discipline, those who appear to be sacrificing so much for God, in fact might be doing the opposite—becoming detached from the world they would most better serve!** Another reason to drop out of that group!

Now these catty revelations may seem tacky and petty—but gossip is the poor persons revenge, who cannot avenge themselves otherwise nor set things straight by any other means. I should hold my tongue! Bare the brunt of injustices in stalwart silence! Wisdom, Wisdom! Says biblical midrash. None more dear to God *however* I will reveal my lack of it by the following rant—an excellent story about Mercy:

Case Study 500,874*; The Tale Of The Skinny Food Fascist Who Snatched An Extra Piece Of Ham Off Of My Plate:
*(Chapter 100,000; Verse 9,734-47.)

This recent scandal reminds me of a similar Skinny Wench (an old white émigré from Europe) denying me a sack of groceries at a long ago free food giveaway outside a church of our ghetto neighborhood in the hot sun where me & my wife Jasmin had stood waiting with throngs of others in sad, sunny, crime haunted Miss Oaktown; –this bride to San Francisco in her long holey diaphanous gown of poverty, upholding the begging cup, situated not a stones-throw across the arches of the Bay Bridge. -- Why was this Scrooge appointed to work a food line for hungry poor people? Who are these skinny white women who think they must control human lives? Are they descendants of Queen Marie Antoinette—(let them eat cake!)? Which was allegedly her famous declaration to the starving people of France. Later the people's revolution took off her head. Transman mused, further, how it was a skinny white woman who denied his ex-wife Jasmin, food at her dinner table. Having prepared only one can of soup for Jasmin, who was a ten year old at the time and her mother! And herself! The three of them dining on one can of soup, thinned out by water! You never find a black or brown person snatching food out of someone's mouth! They would never be this cheap with food! I think of the plentifulness of the Native Americans friendship table! Succotash, turkey, chicken, yams, frybread, buttered corn, green leafy salad, acorn bread; all in abundance! Think of this! Furthermore, many whitefolks tell disparaging stories of Hospitality after Catholic mass! How pitiful and gross the priests are with so little food and bad food at that. How grateful was Transman to have as his good fortune gone regularly to services in the lovely Catholic Church, Saint Mary's of the Sea, in downtown Oakland, with a large Filipino congregation who provided the Hospitality themselves! Chicken Adobe! Wit' de rice! De Lumpia!

Back to the event precipitating his racist tirade. What happened was, a kindly, and larger Sister, using a pair of tongs, dished food up on his plate & put lots of ham on it. But the skinny woman (non-clergy) comes over grabs a set of tongs reaches *over the shoulder* of the Sister into Transman's plate and takes several pieces back off! This food is important to me! The week before she had told the old guy, when he came shuffling up for a second plate of food: "GO SIT BACK DOWN YOU CAN'T HAVE ANY UNTIL ALL THE OTHERS HAVE BEEN SERVED!" Is she a jail guard? ---- There is always extra food left over at this event—and one would think the bad publicity Grace Cathedral is getting because of this skinny white woman would not be worth an extra slice of ham! Also this other woman who told me I talk too loud, and pray to long at the monastic order is skinny/white. What is it with these people? Unconscious racism! All lurking under the eves of the sturdy stone cathedral on top of the hill?

I must become rich! Rich! That is the answer! Then I too can travel to France and light candles in every cathedral as this skinny white gal has done! Then I too will be holier then thou—and maybe I no longer will give a damn about preying so loud and so long! Maybe I will no longer go to the free food line either! But dine on affluent Fill-Mo Street and linger too long over numerous café lattés, unheeding the cry of desperate dogs! A plate of food will only cost me money, which I then can spare!

There! Got that off my chest! Enough of dishing Grace! Oh did I just make a pun? Or is that BUN! A BUN WITH HAM!!!!!! And Lots Of It!

Oh by the way—this is my birthday!!!! Well the other stuff happened two weeks ago… Good and nice stuff happened. Jasmin called me two times for my birthday, and so did Doctor S., and, a new person in my life, Nicole. 'Hen' has taken me briefly under her wing to write out a list of small 'zines to which she demands I must send excerpts of my work. She is a teacher for a living, and a poet/novelist not for a monetary gain, but spiritual imperative. I will see about procuring these excerpts. So my day wound up very nicely! (PS, another dear helper at the cathedral fixed me a big take-home container of all the extra food I missed the first time!!!!!! M*E*R*C*Y!!!!)

     ***
     The War In The Middle East:
     Dark days
     Dark deeds.

Hashem sees all. All will come to Me. All are in My Heavens. @ Synagogue the Torah portion where Hashem says that S/He will give to the eunuchs and to the foreigner an inheritance greater then that of sons & daughters. Because all who obey Hashem's commandments are accepted in to Hashem's tents, into Hashem's fold! As to who is included Rabbi Ruben points out that *'All'* to some people, -- their *'all'* is a tiny little *'all'*, --leaving plenty folks outside in the cold-- whereas to others it's a large inclusive *'all'* as big and beneficent as Godself. Then brother Jonathan points out if somebody yells, FIRE! **'ALL'** OUT OF THE BUILDING they will *all* go running for their lives, regardless, suddenly being non-respecter of persons. Likewise if someone cries; MILLIONAIRE IS GIVING OUT $1,000 BILLS!' They **all** will come running! ALL!

     Shalom
      is a hello between friends
      who recognize each other
      on their daily walk.
     They of the same tribe.
     One day we will all
     recognize each other.

One of the same walk.
The same human tribe
   created by Hashem.

Shalom!

86.

The small voices raise, yelping above the din of the animal shelter, barks, whines, beseeching howls; call attention to their imprisonment!

Sometimes he felt that he himself was in jail. Dogs' barking at a tech who fills the water bowls from a green watering can; then the door slams shut. He is left inside behind bars in a cage along with dogs whose temperaments are growing better or worse in confinement, boredom, and lack of a human family to take them home.

His visit the dog shelter lasted 2 hours. As the old Transman exited into the wealthy ambience of Fillmore Street, rich smells of coffee and steak dinners wafted to his nostrils, how he dreamed for his future success! He thought: —*Soon this will be mine!*

Home, back to his table. Pondering over many a curious volume of ancient and forgotten lore…. You can't micro-manage your history for your convenience of present times—not and be an authentic voice. I am editing LEADER OF THE PACK and see much embarrassing stuff---I could micro manage it; erase it right off the page! Knowing, at the time I wrote it how gut-wrenching important it was to me—so it might be to some one else right now! So, when finished it will be the stuff raw, just as it was!

Night, running in place & jab punch, flailing arms to Hebrew songs, Jimi Hendrix & Damian Marley. Work up a sweat. Exercise— Transman feels he must keep himself alive: *because I'm a compassionate thinking person, and all of the multi-millions of us who are, must stay alive, do good work.*

All good things are coming my way…. Hashem has told me: **what you do in private I will reward openly.** God can give so much good. After all God created every desire of our body's minds and spirit—Allah knows just what we crave!

95

I can lay it on thick.
--Creator, to the Prophet.

Referring to myself as a 'prophet' might seem crazy; but goodly
prophets are needed today! —To counteract the rotten ones. As long
as there are those who set themselves up in practice for the worsening
of the human condition. There are doctors without compassion.
There are lawyers without scruples. Teachers without desire or sense
enough to instruct the young.

  *

Such a beautiful city—all the sparkling lights—affluence, education,
great foods, language, diverse cultures, art, color, multiracial. And
so-obvious gay, lez, bi, & trans have freedom to be open about
ourselves.

Traveling by bus, subway, car, and bicycle to get here. We, the
regulars of Babylon Falling are assembled, exchange idle chat &
fabulous visions of our future artworks. Scott, Fashion Designer
states the quotable:

  Today is just tomorrow's yesterdays.

Another customer questions: *"how long you been open?"* To which
an interesting Jamaican accent replies from behind the desk: *"5
months now."*

Returned to Babylon Falling; a drab but cheerful old man sits on the
display window ledge; a black hat on his head; a thick volume on his
black-trouser lap. He speaks aloud: *"Slave Ship is indeed a superior
book."* Then proceeds to write vehemently in his Journal with a
shaky yellow/tan hand:

  The sorrow of human slavery on earth
   must be stopped!

  In Creators eye is a tear.
  The tears of the people
  compose all the salty oceans
  of our planet.

96

While in the background still another customer comes and goes, stopping a moment to greet the proprietor:

How long yuh been in business?

Ah, 6 months.

Very good.

Well, Hashem says for me to speak! To tell my truths! To reach out to all the people who have an ear left to HEAR! —An ear not compromised by financial entanglements; an ear not deafened by the weight of a broken heart. This his how the human divorce from humanness begins: Proprietor Sean illustrates it most horribly: -- "Throw a frog into hot boiling water it will hop out, but put the frog in lukewarm water, and slowly turn it up by degrees, the frog's dead before it realizes it. Just as it realizes the water is boiling, it's too late! It can't escape. Because the frog has become acclimated to the water temperature slowly." How awful for all us animal rights lovers who boycott frog's legs, pâté gras, and veal! —All tortured animals! And how true of the human race. How acclimated we are to the misery around us—much less our own lives! We are all in steel traps like dogs at the shelter.

Were the Jews of Europe too acclimated to the hate which for centuries had been directed towards them from outside their small communities from the larger outside 'Christian' world—so much so that they could not see the horrific repercussions of the Evil Grandiose Fascist Empire about to roar down upon them with all its proficiency, to sweep them away to death? Native's of the Americas, who first greeted Colombo, Cortez, conquerors of that ilk—bold enslavers who, upon sight of them, labeled their fellow humans 'savages' thus concretized them inside a lowly doom. A stronger warlike human ape reigning fiery blows on a smaller one, stupidly taking on for themselves the status of gods!

This human race, its all about trying to make sense out of a chaotic swing of life. Earth looks like a good thing when times are good, food is plentiful, fruit falling from trees, water in abundance, then season shift, harsh times

come upon the land, icy winds blow unrelenting and you realize, I'm going to die! Worse, my loved ones are in danger!
---From

Thus Transman Red continues to scribble in his Journal—currently, a work called MERCY. As the cronies at the bookstore hold the following debate:

> Dudes, I think I'm loosing brain cells. I can't remember anything for shit!
>
> So what man! The same thing is happening to me! The dumber you are the more you forget every day—the more exciting life is!
>
> Yeah! Every minute is a whole new exciting experience you've never had before!

Poor sad Transman sat, scribbling, glum, for last night; in these last waning weeks of the old calendar, his SSI/ Soc. Sec. payment notification for next year had arrived in the mail; it was not as the year before as he had hoped—increased, by $30--- but only rose half that amount—in these times of growing drain of the hellish U$ Crusade in the Middle East; so that was bad news, PLUS, after the annual inexorable fascistic rent increase due to strike in 2 months his income would be actually $1 less then the previous year (2007) and this not accounting for higher grocery/ pharmaceutical costs. (Medicines, which had also been free, before our faux president launched U$ into the ill-fated war.) Furthermore his body is slowly deconstructing due to the infirmities of old age. But he keeps himself entertained with jokes, raising his head to join with the rest as they howl in glee, from time to time. The comments continue. Someone quips; *"It's why peoples with Downs Syndrome are always happy."* To which the practical Transman, having done slave labor in nursing homes over his long 37-year work history clarifies: *"Maybe they are, if they are in a happy home and not abandon and institutionalized, like they do with us old people so as to have their houses stolen from them by their relatives who they trusted."* As he had seen the human wrecks there, stacked into beds for the financial benefit pay-per-bed scam of the corporate nursing home chain.

Yellow lights drone into the night outside, thru the cold black window of the display ledge where the lonely old guy sat, jiggling his leg & thinking nasty thoughts. As the evening wears low they talk of wage slavery, of corporations, of the now-guessed-at secret identity, unmasked, of the Four Horsemen of The Apocalypse coming—upon whose arrival Babylon does indeed fall, and fall greatly. One of these Four being corporations... In an odd deje vu he sat reading about his African ancestors who came across in a slave ship's hold, crammed in; 450 black bodies packed head to toe in shackles; as portrayed this was one of mid-1700 century's Corporate Capitalist enterprises— dealing in human property. T's head was a kaleidoscope of wild jumbled thoughts, daydreams, fine ideas, art colors. Now, transporting himself back 300 years in time he fantasized leading the revolt of black slaves! Championing of underclass people everywhere!

> Oh yeah ...he kept thinking of such fanciful things... It kept his mind highly entertained...
> --Observer of Transman Red

Sean's Princess---his pretty, smart, & nice girlfriend is here helping tonight, on leave from her cruel/merciless job. The young couple is decorating. Soon there will be a string of gay holiday lights in both display windows....

He was so ashamed he couldn't pay his rent. And would have to ask his friends for help.

What people need and want in this town is a place to live. 4 walls. Ceiling, floor, walls with a door with a lock. Address for mailing. As daily passerby's in these streets, we are witness to the unending sight of cast-offs of tenants forced to move out: furniture, pots and pans, electronic equipment, TVs, computer parts, frequently the whole computer. All the furnishings you could want. Bed frames, rugs, mattresses, chairs, sofas. Vases, toasters, forks, spoons, microwave ovens, refrigerators. Books, magazines, picture frames, and bathroom accessories. But the home to put this stuff in—that is the question... and now a cartel of rich landowners, real estate brokers & their lackeys are trying to do away with Rent Control.

You can do what you want! I don't care! I'm going to write my book—I've *almost* developed at theme. I'm going to write my book and make a zillion dollars and go retire to Europe!
--Overheard in SF

Egads! These people just assume they'll write a book and be a wild success! What Am I Doing Wrong! To have written 80 of the darn things and still be a pauper!!!

*

Commentary about the prophet/author:

He had holes in his shirt so I bought him two new ones for his 64th birthday.
--Non Professor Turnip.

He spent his money on his book inventory. He spent money on his pets. He had the same set of sheets on his bed for 8 months. He used the same two towels stole from the now closed-up Trans Space, over and over. He spent money on: his website, reordering his books, a business Post Office address. His shoes were donated by his 'pretend cousin' Angelo, a size too big so he had to wear a double layer of sox to make them fit.
---Anonymous.

His nice coat was given to him 7 years ago by his ex wife. We went in my car to pick it up.
--Dr. Sam
He spent $ on paper for his books so he could fill his meager book orders. He recycled empty boxes and bubble wrap from my store.
--Sean; Proprietor at Bookstore.

I feel, undiscovered as I am, to be a highly eligible bachelor for many women & men, & institutions of this world; few of whom know the gem-rich quality of my worth.
--Words of the Prophet Red Jordan.

87.
What is real and what is unreal? See examples below:

Hollywood is a place where they'll pay you a thousand dollars for a kiss and fifty cents for your soul.
--Marylyn Monroe

I am the real thing in your heart, in your soul, in your mind, in your life.
--Jesus Christ* to the Prophet –2007
*--Goddess, Buddha, Mohammad, etc.

These ruminations he did attempt, shuffling vigorously with his cane to the bus stop making his way during the week. Heading towards the Lost Dog Shelter, a curious phenomenon jars his PASSAGE. A capitalist advertisement has been painted over the entire bus— including its windows-- constructed of tiny dots which form a scene visible to the outside observer but which still enables passengers riding inside to look out—tho only partially—blurring their vision:

Another encroachment on my freedom. So many... all these little things, are making my world a pent-up trap. Like the extra unit the greedy rent landlord added in the basement, then got a maniac to live down there in substandard conditions, who rants and rails at the other tenants above him— he is a hater, and a self hater as well evidently as he chain smokes; all the cigarette smoke blows directly up into my kitchen window which I am now attempting to seal up. This extra unit for profit stomping on the rest of the tenants even more.

Today—a bright, crisp San Francisco morning-- riding the bus Transman felt he was squeezed this way and that; he thought; *'everytime I look out the window of this bus I think I'm going crazy— because of these wretched dots!'*

While going hurrying down Fillmore street striking the pavement with his cane, he is rewarded by a conversation with God: *I have greeted Hashem with a 'hello', and in return have the vision that Hashem has given me a big red Riesh!*

Two minutes later he's seated inside a metal barred cage, a homeless dog beside him, warm, furry. A different book is on his lap:

Dear Journal:
"I hope I shall be able to confide in you completely, as I have never been able to do in anyone before, and I hope that you will be a great support and comfort to me.

I want to go on living even after my death! And therefore I am grateful to God for giving me this gift; this possibility of developing

101

myself and of writing, of expressing all that is me. I can shake off
everything if I write; my sorrows disappear; my courage is reborn."
—Diary of Anne Frank. (1929-1945)

Food cycles, as Ann Frank calls it. In their family's imprisonment in
hiding from the Nazis, surreptitiously food was given to them as
available. It's similar to this: —A poor person gets this food in
unequal abundance at various times from charitable organizations--
like a carton full of asparagus at one time; or 35 cans of tomato soup--
I have them too, here stocking my kitchen cabinets, from voyages to
the free food bank

Nights he returns to a cramped desk, upon which the daily annotations
to his JOURNEY are factored into the growing mass of computer
files; also to the slow re-working of the cyber file of that old biker
dike novel he'd once composed, which was generated in a white hot
frenzy of sexual angst, gay nightclubs, women's sex club going, and
SM workshops of that 'Golden Era' of the early 1990's.

Thoughts about LEADER OF THE PACK, which am now editing:
Here in the bookstore is a constant music background. One hears all
male musicians music, no women. There are fewer female bands.
Severe handicap to women is lack of loyalty among women. Men
stab each other in the back all the time, their partnerships dissolve at
gunpoint, but many do survive, and they do great things together.
In LEADER decided to keep on with the concept of a loyal female
gang who stuck by each other thru thick and thin (quite unlike the
demise of my ill-fated group, see WORKS). Factoid: this is one of
the very rare computer discs of my typewritten works prior to 2004—
vaguely recall who typed and 'changed' my words, but today's
laborious process is to go thru the novel line by line returning it to its
pristine glory! It is sad and amazing the kind of stuff which was
dropped! Sexual stuff, outright descriptions of simple scenery stuff;
mechanical references to these bad girls bikes omitted, colloquialisms
cleaned up into a same boring normalcy. And to think it was a
Madame of a Business of Ill Repute who scanned it! Worse, a Hells
Angles Biker Momma who edited it! Another reflection about this
book--I realize this LEADER, and my Biker Dike Series and some
others of the highly sexual novels I've written might jar the nerves of
the more mild mannered. Further, the wild lusty striving and
downward cycles of narcotics, prostitution might offend many. Listen

102

World! Red ain't an author who writes in the genre of 'The Right
Thing To Do' books, nor 'Self-Help Manuals'; great art is not always
uplifting to the human spirit, it does not always indicate the provident
road to take for the human species. Nor is that the artistic definition.
God knows our God knows our COMPASSIONS!

*

Let me dish some dirt. Any author over period of time comes to sadly
recognize the tricks their fans play. Here's one you just may run
across: If you've ever come to a bookstore which sells used books, its
not just a matter of ego nor of pride to go to the alphabetical section to
search for a title which could possibly have your name—I've gone to
the A's, just to discover to my dismay, autographed books by myself
dedicated to somebody and using their name---which they've gone
and sold! Instead of keeping for their collection! What an insult!
You have fallen out of favor! They hated the thing! Standing there,
worn book in hand, insecurities wrack the poor author! Well, people
move, they must drastically reduce the size of their household; people
get desperate for cash- if their rent is $200 short come due in a day,
and they can get 50-cents for 'your' book they will--- because that
means tomorrow they will just be $199.50 short! Which is better then
before! One bookstore found a dozen LUCY & MICKEY'S three of
which were signed, and one dedicated to the buyer—a friend! It will
happen to you!

88.
Over a year or so period of time of my fine arts scribblings,
JOURNEY has seen me make friends & loose them, and other, older,
friendships become severely weakened. Saying that must tell you
about a new budding friendship with N. Hen. A fine writer; this
pretty youngish woman is hooked up in the literary scene, friend to,
and knowledgeable of many artists, plus, The Hen is ensconced in a
fabulous old hotel with a misty historic ambience, and famous theatric
after-lives hovering around it—owned by her relatives!

To Nicole Hen
Hen had struggles.
She wrote, nevertheless.
Battled with boyfriends.
After all that she changed her hair.
She made a difference.

103

She too knows a certain tall, trashy transwoman superstar (B. Lake); and we have discussed the very real possibility this woman is very sick or incarcerated or in a straightjacket somewhere—but probably not dead as the scandal about that would have gotten out. None of us have seen her around recently and there use to be B. sightings frequently, especially in this neighborhood. This transwoman's bad behavior is an epic example of why we T's don't make friends easily and loose them fast. We all hate/love Miss Lake. We trans love her because we see ourselves all too well within her face, figure and form. We who have been oppressed know her story like the palm of our own hand. But when she turns upon us like a snake we recoil, run from her; detest her! She is not the only T in town who is or has been hated—up until the very day they died! And then enormous crowds come out to attend the funeral—because yes, we love her & oh how we dished her!

December is here, the Christmas season. And it's Tranny Tuesday at the Health Clinic. Lana waltzes in; she looks fabulous! Fabulous is the word! She doesn't look a day older then the time we first saw each other—ten years past. Strikingly pretty, vivacious. Flawless brown complexion, perfect long black hair worn to the shoulders (a Chinese wig) trim figure, very buxom. (Enhanced by cosmetic surgery.)

She is soon engaged in dramatic chit-chat with another transsister, a tall lovely, hands on hips, who banters with her flirtatiously:

I'm gonna get me some bootie! You look so luscious girl!

After which they swap tales about their 'Gentlemen Callers', Lana testifying that NYC is the place to be; *"7 limousines pulled up to the curb for me girl!"* (Pops her large well-manicured fingers, makes a big SNAP!) By comparison, here in SF, she is all but ignored. Her pet peeve, her dates don't want to be seen in the streets with her:

> "Men in this town are afraid to go out in public with a trans girl, they want to visit her in her apartment, get their rocks off, then go home, and don't want to give her any money either."

104

Dinner with another transwoman girlfriend: another larger, middle-aged girl with a pretty poignant expression; and an estrogen glow. Transman muses how he should handle any large sums of money, which eventually will start to funnel his way out of the universe—in recognition of his lezbitrans arts. *"What can I do with $20,000—if they decide to award me a prize for my work? Can't buy a house with it...not in San Francisco where condos start at $250,000. Can't put it in the bank—the SSI will seize it."*

D. Leans across the table; suggests to put extra cash away in a safety deposit box—*that's what all the other SSI recipients do*—so as to enable them to save over the allowed $2,000. The $2,000 limit is cruel! Because to move into a new rental apartment in this town you must have $2 to $3,000 alone just for the security deposit on the place—plus if you are disabled, you'll need either good friends with strong backs or more money to help you move so $2,000 just don't get it. D's got that streak of larceny in her— hope it doesn't get her into trouble—which it already has.

Most transpeople begin to show clues of their true nature very early in childhood—3 or 4 years of age—by choice of clothing, demeanor, vocabulary, and other personal traits. However some of us, more camouflaged or reserved present a neutral ground which has nothing of the effeminate, or masculine, but are extremely blah nothings—as if erasing themselves. I believe these types grow up to be very different kinds of individuals then the loud bold obvious ones who have been so conditioned to their queer, outsider status since an early age that they become large bold adult up-in-yo'-face trannys. Most of the girls & boys I know are these.

89.
SF; it was a cold rain. The drab black-clad old man raised up his line of vision for an instant; moments before he had bent, mussed short brown-hair, reading glasses, over a book. For what psychic reason he did not know. Just happened to gaze out the window. He saw a familiar face!

Rosa Salazar had come back into his life! She stood there, right outside the store window of Babylon Falling; regal, atop tall stylish high heels; beautiful, an older sexy, slimmer —Rosa had lost 40 pounds; attired in some lavender color flowing fabric, most feminine, and enticing; draped over her sturdy handsome/pretty man-woman body. In no time he had slammed his battered black hat down to a tight fit on his head and run outside to greet her! –They spoke, igniting embers of the past. Listening to him; her strong masculine hands held together a moment, pensively… Soon the two of them had walked off to la groceriteria, and there, amid the aisles of household goods, sacks of beans, las fruitas, los verduas, exchanged a few more words in a broken conversation animated by hand motions which accounted for the missing Spanish/English vocabulary both shared. Rosa purchased a small sack of black beans. Rosa was a cook muy deliciouso. They briskly went back down the street, right by the bookstore, (Red had even forgotton his cane) off around the corner to her apartment. Rosa switching fast, hips side to side; Red limping along faster, to enable himself to keep up with her.

"Rosa, I'm loosing all my Spanish since we don't see each other anymore."

"I bein' saving de paper for you from work. Everytime dey throw dese paper in de wastebasket—at de Copy a' machines, I gets eit. I tinks of you. I tink of Rojo. I gots a stack dese bieg." Rosa pinches air with a strong forefinger & thumb; nails painted glistening pink/silver.

***

I came out in a time, which straddles the old impossible days, unheard of by this modern age, un-spoken of by my generation—to the new beginning which is today; putting our shell-shocked, world-worn toes onto this new once dared dreamed for dawn inhabited by queer children who don't have a clue.

As before stated (see PASSAGE), ex prizefighter, the fabulous transsexual Rosa Salazar had the problem many T women do—she is barely passable.

Passability hits the humanbeing on many levels. Race. Class. Language. What qualities does it take to blend into a higher echelon? The estate of those passable—who can get by, unchallenged in the environment where they choose to situate themselves. This is the question. Most transmen are passable enough to go many places totally unclocked, ignored for the most part, all who see them believing them to be born male. Even in a liberal environment if the word gets out, and their dirty little secret is revealed, since they are so standard, or 'normal' looking, they thus make fewer waves and less enemies. And finally, they have had, due to their passability, better lives, thus become more socialized, and again, even more able to blend in with the common herd.

Race is factored into this equation; in fact it was the original usage of the term 'passability'. (IE the old race movies, I Passed For White, etc.) As Transman is very fair, s/he was often mistaken for white—at first—until further scrutiny revealed him otherwise. But only part of these times was he ID'd as 'black' and not just some other darker skin minority.

> My momma warned me never go down South! The plantation owners might catch me again!

Thus, a left-over slavery mentality, sits in residue over a lifetime.

> It was the common practice for everyone involved in the slave trade wither African or European to refer to the ships crew as the 'white men' or the 'white people' even when the crew was motley, a portion of it 'colored' and distinctly non white. The sailors status as a 'white man' guaranteed that he would not be sold in the slave labor market.
> --From Slave Ship

I realize it has been to my benefit to be labeled 'white' on forms, applications; and by those who viewed me. I was not white, many could tell, but I was *white enough*. Usually to my advantage.

All these 'passings' is a form of censorship. Redolent of the 1950's when immigrant parents from Italy, Poland, Greece, & South America, refused to talk their native tongue at home around their children, believing if the kids picked it up it would hurt their chances to become Full Americans. They would be thought of as lowerclass—and not part of the mainstream. Today it is with regret you hear some 3rd generation adults testify they were cheated out of being bilingual, which is a true gift.

***

Speaking of censorship, NOTE! Re: LEADER OF THE PACK! (A
lesbian biker novel.) Here are examples of the before/after editing, from
simple mistakes, probably typos, such as:

> Roast bears
> Roast **beefs.**

To purposeful changes for what reasoning I do not know. Removing
the raunch? Sanitizing it for the 'normals'? The 'edited' version is
above, my original is under it. See below:

1.

Music's strident beat pounded out of tapes.
Music's strident beat pounded out of **an amplifier system.**

2.

Beautiful blond hair
Beautiful **brunette** hair

3.

humped her hips thrusting up into the air, and all the way down to smack the
ground, yielding her hot pink pussy to her lovers hand.
humped her hips thrusting up into the air, and all the way down to smack the **dirt,**
yielding her hot pink pussy to her lovers hand.

4.

the available woman in their party. They stop to stare at Sleazy & Lady. "Guess
what guys! She's still got milk in her tits!" The butch hollers. "MILK HER GOOD
THEN!" "SAVE SOME FOR ME!" Yells the other, good-natured. "YAHO0!"
Hollers Sleazy.
the available woman in their party. They stop to stare at Sleazy &Lady. **"Yep,
she's a veteran. She's worked the trenches. GOSH!** Guess what guys! She's
still got milk in her tits!" The butch hollers. "MILK HER GOOD THEN
SLEAZE'!" "SAVE SOME FOR ME!" Yells the other, good-natured. "YAHO0!"
Hollers Sleazy.

5.

A biker knelt at the side of the van sucking a lady's toes, soon had half a foot in her
mouth, sucking it, then the whole foot disappeared inside.
A biker knelt at the side of the van sucking a lady's toes, soon had half a foot in her
mouth, sucking it, then the whole foot disappeared **into it, toes wiggling down her
throat.**

6.

with a little help from her friend, who squatted outside in the dirt, with mouth
engulfing her foot; who was too busy sucking and stroking to notice.
with a little help from her friend, who squatted outside in the dirt, with mouth
engulfing her foot; who was too busy sucking **& choking** to notice.

7.

Stryker lumbered about with a drink in her hand. Big breasted and heavy shouldered like a clumsy bear not accustom to be up on its hind legs, nor to dance either.

Stryker lumbered about with a drink in her hand. **Had had a slug of Vat 500 whiskey & mixed it with a beer—against the advice of her physician. –The pills she had to take to make her body chemistry sane. Could hear it sloshing in her belly. Whiskey, combining with beer, as she walked, SLOSH, SLOSH. Little Stryker,** big breasted and heavy shouldered like a clumsy bear not accustom to be up on its hind legs, nor to dance either.

8.

So she'd got up and danced like a dancing bear. Alone. Danced. Across the meadow somebody saw Stryker. "She's lonely." They said.

So she'd got up and danced like a dancing bear. Alone. Danced, **whirling about in blue denims, big boots clomping, tits bouncing under a teeshirt & a bottle of drink raised to the sky**. Across the meadow somebody saw Stryker. "She's lonely." They said.

9.

Now Stryker didn't realize she was alone.

Now **the fat dike didn't** realize she was alone.

10.

The companion of the pretty blond had finished stroking her to orgasm, now got on top between the blonds thighs--legs up in the air, to get off herself. The more graphic love acts the biker club members enjoyed was embarrassing to Stryker, for she'd noticed others--straight people with families also shared the park space,

The companion of the pretty **brunette** had finished stroking her to orgasm, now got on top between the **wenches** thighs--legs up in the air, to get off herself. The more graphic love acts the biker club members enjoyed was embarrassing to Stryker, **because of her middle-class upbringing**, for she'd noticed others--straight people with families also shared the park space,

11.

The blond got up, pulled a shirt over her tanned belly, zipped up her shorts, still wore motorcycle boots, and was soaking wet where her lady's fingers had been playing in her crotch. She smiled, and pointed to the blanket.

The **butch** got up, pulled a shirt over her tanned belly, zipped up her shorts, still wore motorcycle boots, and was soaking wet where her lady's fingers had been playing in her crotch. **Her own orgasm had burst between her legs moments ago.** She smiled, and pointed to the blanket.

12.

Stryker took in the sight of the other women. It turned her on. Glad she was still alive and hadn't committed suicide, even tho she was still crazy & in pain, she was managing to enjoy life. Glad she was outdoors, felt she'd been neglecting her life, holed up in a room-and-a-half painting in oils & writing poetry & in her journal. Life was so rich! So much fun romping with the dykes!

Stryker took in the sight of the other women. **It inspired her.** Glad she was still alive and hadn't committed suicide, even tho she was still crazy & in pain **in her soul,** she was managing to enjoy life. Glad she was outdoors, felt she'd been neglecting her life, holed up in a room-and-a-half **oil painting & writing poetry & talking to nobody but her journal.** Life was so rich! So much fun romping with the **dikes!**

13.

All day long, the long ride had vibrated the bike between her legs; Angel had thought of Crystal who clutched tight to her back, riding in the saddle behind. Couldn't wait to get home to her hot pussy, especially after the hot lather they'd worked up in front of the crowd of straight suburbanites in the mall.   The day was so relaxed, she thought; 'I'll do it here. Why not?'

All day long, the long ride had vibrated the bike between her legs; Angel had *envisioned* Crystal who clutched tight to her back, riding in the saddle behind**, hot crotch pressed to her ass. Couldn't wait to strip off her pants and get to her mates** hot pussy, especially after the hot lather they'd worked up **performing** in front of the crowd of straight suburbanites in the **Mall.**   The day was so relaxed, she thought; 'I'll do it here. Why not?'

14.

Bikes.
Cycles.

90.

Tertulia is the Spanish name for a small circle of friends, such as the ones painter Pablo Picasso gathered around himself. All his life Transman had drawn to himself some kind of group & he remembered those now… Was this growing band of cronies at the Bookstore becoming still another Tertulia? In the yellow light of a weeknight afternoon, amid packing cartons, bubble wrap & miscellaneous stuffing's Sean feverishly went about stocking the latest shipment of revolutionary books. T perused a new photographic collection, which has come in, by Sabastino Salgado, An Uncertain Grace. –In it an old woman, her features become a simian face, starkly reflect her wretchedness. A greater economic misery then my own—layered on top of that human misery we all share-- looks out of stark black/white pages. I think of Gods planning for us, our human species, probably thru evolution. I have seen this look at our nearest animal relatives—with whom we share a great amount of DNA chromosomes. The link is so remote, so marvelous, so thought provoking. It is like the COMPASSION an animal lover gets upon seeing a mother chimpanzee holding her infant to her black furred breast, or a wise old chimpanzee male who has seen many years; their simian structure hands, fingers, depth of gaze of their eyes, their leathery brows furrowed in thoughts, and think, one day our far future descendants -- super humans-- will look back at our 'modern' humankind, at all the struggles we had, the pains we bore, with a great sympathy, and compassion for us.

> An infant in a sling hooked to a scale. Head hung back, huge cranium on its stick body a pipestem neck, which will no longer support its weight. "Children must be weighed & measured in order to adjust their rations." Reads the title.
> --Nation of Mali

> A table moves across a field of wavy grass; a dozen peasants wrapped in rebozas, derby hats on their heads, one carries this furniture; another artifacts, another books; they are going to prayer meeting.
> --Ecuador

> Photo of a native man laid out on the ground in the spot where he slowly starved to death.
> -- Ecuador

Red points this out; with somber looks the young people examine this photo and they all compare it to here, U$A; a nation of high finance, expensive dinners, big cars; Stock Market salespersons, Realestate agents, who speed about, rushing, operating the wheels of financial leverage high on illegal cocaine blows. The contrast is so great! This man slowly starving for lack of simple leftovers on a plutocrat's plate when they dined with abundant food in their expensive restaurants—scraped off into the trash can---morsels which could have kept him alive.

It is a point of note, that Red, after growing up in the black Civil Rights movement or the early 1960's and all its subsequent 'reverse racism', its black-hating-white assumptions arisen directly from slavery, segregation & apartheid; that over time slowly he begin to grasp the realization that one could not pinpoint 'whites' as the ruling devils, as the master race guilty of total genocide, but increasingly must recognize the autocracies of other colors, the royalties of China who wreaked unspeakable suffering on their Chinese subjects; the great African kings, who concocted fake battles in order to enslave their own black brothers & sisters of other tribes, in order to sell them for profit. *All & any human kind who deal in human properties.* ---

111

All those families, clans, and individuals of all sorts of colors and religions, who amassed unimaginable wealth to themselves at the destruction of so many under them.

> The people live in squalid dens where there can be no health and no hope, but dogged discontent of their own lot & futile discontent at the wealth they see possessed by others.
> --Harold Rogers; quoted by Jack London; People Of The Abyss—1910.

Again they spoke of the level of discontent rising around the world, as the abject poor are for the first time in human history, via computer, satellite TV, able to see the affluence around the globe; see how much money and wealth is out there.

Sean, Proprietor, referring to Jamaica of his childhood, vs., today:
> People seize on anything to show status. One thing to show signs of wealth. Yesterday's status was to eat at KFC; today, it's what kind of car you drove to get to KFC.... Consider what does it take to be a successful person in this society. They get their identity from better shirts and designer gymshoes.

The rich always win because from the beginning they made the rules. Even now as fast as protest of multitudes of people is raised against them—their high priced teams of lawyers have concocted a new scheme to slip thru the noose and continue to reap gargantuan profits via a new method.

Sadly it was so true. Red's life being an illustration. That money is a reverse funnel. —He was getting just enough of it to survive. To eat, to have healthcare, to have a 'room of one's own' all in order to exercise his US Constitutional right—freedom of speech. Despite all this, his rights well used, still, while the young men ate and discussed politics, punk fashion, new books and art secretly T. thought how nice it would be to have a bowl of chili--- suddenly his mind zoomed back nearly 50 years to cold Midwestern & East Coast winters, of NYC & Chi-Town's skid rows little cheap eateries; bowls of chili 85 cents, $1.25; dime coffee, cut-rate in price. But immediately he realized--- he hadn't had the money for it back then either!

91.
AM Shabbat.

At Temple an animated Queen led the service---she davined, she cantored, she spoke great drash, she fairly danced with enthusiasm on the bemah—so much so at one point lost her balance & nearly fell off the edge, which luckily is only two steps above floor level! Managed to aright herself by flailing her arms vigorously—and was saved only by Divine Providence!

PM Faithful Fools.
A gathering of multi-faith individuals—again hear the idea, voiced by a balding middleaged man in sandals that future world religion should be drawn from many different cultures and take the best part of each. At which a lusty argument broke out, as this statement was misunderstood by several other gentlemen in attendance—each person believing the other was making chauvinist statements about the superiority of *their* own religion. Then I told them about my idea in LAMENTATIONS of just such an organization. People finding ways to worship together, and work together—on a common understanding they would discover. God(ess) being centermost. All religions—Wicca, Christian, Islam, Judaism, Hindu, Buddhist. There must be something we could agree on! Some great work we could do together! —For the betterment of this planet!

Strange how so many of us are beginning to think on the same track about this stuff! -- Due time!

A confession:
What I am has always been a problem for others, since the beginning. Born into trouble. Multiracial, too light to be fully recognized by blacks, colored enough to be shunned by prejudiced whites. Transgender—which is some uncomfortable midway between the gender norms of neither male, or female. Now, stuck between Judaism & Christian! Plus having the stigma that every word I write, my journals, sexploits etc., are controversy incarnate! Rabbis seem to shun you once they realize you are going to keep on being Christian and not convert—which seems to be the rule in most places I've been that that entails *giving up what you already are!* Its kind of like a nation which makes you choose one citizenship or another—that of birth or the new country to which you have arrived--you can't have both. However some more enlightened nations, and some with special circumstances seem to be able to have duel citizenship—

113

which is what I must have! I ain't given up Jesus Christ—and I'm spiritually drawn to Judaism, and always have been socially drawn to Jews, a 'Jewish Journey' which dates back to my childhood. *I nosed around many campfires waiting to be taken in by someone, but it did not happen.*

The un-embodied voice of the rabbi declared itself over the sound system—he was nowhere to be seen in the vast synagogue sanctuary; not among the rows of hundreds of seats; did he know he was mic'd? Again the familiar tone boomed—making final plans for the service to follow shortly. "That's the rabbi's voice, it's coming from "Goodman Hall." commented one congregant, meaning a downstairs area.

I'm looking for my place in their world---have not quite found it.

       ***

No one knows the placement of themselves on the scale of greatness or of fame. We work in a vacuum of information about our outcome! To over estimate ourselves or to underestimate can be harmful. Had Van Gough known one of his paintings alone, The Potato Eaters, would sell for 64,000,000 million dollars, 200 years after his death, and others would soon sell—when he could have still been living; that he could buy all the oil colors, canvas, food, housing—and draw a woman to him for companionship as a lifelong partner--would it have stayed his hand from suicide? Would a Napoleon or Stalin think better of their high-handed egotistical ways, under the blaring stage lighting of the evidence of history? Which mocks them all for their shortcomings, their impotent dictator inadequacies with great guffaws of humor. Little Transman often pondered his future, and his worth, by now, knowing at age 64 that fame, greatness, genius, and money do not bring about happiness. *'Will I have a great fortune to care for me in my ancient age? Will I be a pauper—even worse off then I am today because of advancing years?'* (Would he even live another day---such being the uncertainty of this state we call human kind.) Often nights, at his makeshift desk—(a dresser top removed from its dresser ((found in that long ago woebegotton hotel in Downtown Oakland)), the single, heavy long board now situated atop a file cabinet on one end, and a concoction of a bookshelf with --crammed in the space on top of it-- several books to level it at the other —a

gossipy Radcliff Hall biography and the Dictionary)—scribbling over
and over, totalizing his per month income:

$706. Social Security
184. SSI Permanent Disability
100. Total of renters rebate & regular
large book collectors IE the
Bancroft, & a few friends.
80. Estimate other book, art sales
$1,170. Grand Total

Sadly, his current rent was $996.54, and due to increase in the New
Year. So that left him exactly $173 per month to spend on busfare,
food, phone bills, website service and his business address.

When I'm too tired & I can't work it any more, what will become of
me? (No free food lines, no walking long distances to save busfare,
no hustling, no free dinners at church hospitality/synagogue onegs, or
potlucks at Native American gatherings. No haunting of great social
institutions to beg & borrow from their facilities. No petty light-
fingered-liftings from here & there... As friend Ms. D. says:

> We are just movers of the money. Perpetually moving it back and
> forth—never get to see any of it, or use it for our own gain, but after
> receiving it give it out here and there, until its gone.
> --Dominique Leslie

Not ever having been well publicized he could not plan how popular
he might be! Since he had a legitimate complaint, that the audience
he might have thought would be his, perhaps poorer, undereducated,
queers of multiracial backgrounds—the very people many of the
stories are about--may never have heard of him! Due to his shunning
by the status quo queer publishers of that day.

Why was Transman's work so excluded for so long? Throughout the
'lesbian heyday of publishing,' about the mid 1960's on, by a number
of small gay women's presses? He had often pondered this... and so
do his friends, some highly placed—who believe this to be unfair. T
had a standard response: *'its racism!'* Or, *'it's because I write too
much sex for the girls to stand.'* Or, *'it's because I didn't kiss
nobody's ass in the publishing world'*—which was a ridiculous

comment, seeing he'd never gotten close enough to any of them to reach their ass from the beginning.

An interchange of interest at the Tranny Health Clinic occurs between the black clothed artist and a slim, handsome young white gay doctoral student from UC Berkeley; a social anthropologist doing research who had ensconced himself for better or worse in one of the battered wooden or plastic chairs which do utilitarian service in a long line down the grim white tiled hall—some 2 years ago—and has remained there since. Chris speaks with seriousness, his cheerful face now somber under his white collar and proper tie; how, for a paper on transsexuality he has presented to the University, he has been told he must remove all the real names of us transfolk therein quoted, substituting fake names for them *–even people who have given permission to use their first names & have signed a release form to that purpose.* To which T has informed him he won't allow his fabulous quotes to be misrepresented by a fictitious made-up name! -- Which is what the University has told C. to do.

> "I'm proud of my work! I want credit for it!"

> "I agree, but they told me they can't use anyone's real name in this paper —for legal reasons."

> "Fuck that shit!"

> "They tell me they are trying to protect 'transpeople of the lower classes, who have systematically been victimized already'. But you know, I think this is actually just erasing them even more."

They try to erase us because we are known as an unstable population.

> There is all too little lesbian literature, to begin with. Amid the under-class there are would-be writers too discouraged to testify to their truths. Non-professional queer writers material has been ignored not simply by a bigoted straight world, but because of failure of the lesbian press, and cold shoulder avoidance of gay men's press. Further, too many are afraid to take the risk of bringing up difficult subjects
> --2007 Intro; LEADER OF THE PACK

116

One last statement about class issues—is this why many underclass are so outraged at the intelligenzia. At those Professionals who purportedly are licensed to 'help' them—while earning large salaries to do so; and thru whose hands, and channels it is impossible for the common person to access necessary services, medicines, aids, housing, permissions, channels to information, etc.; is this why the Chinese revolution murdered its intellectuals? The Russians revolution smashed its fine art? —All because it is realized to be trappings of the true rulers, the overbosses, the plutocrats, those buyers and sellers of human flesh, the dark genius inventors of wage slavery? And seeing these middle men, these professionals—doctors, lawyers, preachers, teachers, social workers in their white collars and proper ties as pawns in the game of class warfare—as the modern day overseers of the plantation, so similar to the cotton fields, the grape vineyards, the backbreaking murderous work which is province of the short-lived laborer-- a much more subtle controller?

Dear Children, have you observed how green growing plants lean towards the light? So here is another lesson for you—let the ears who can, hear it. Our good Lord(ess) created all different kind of people; and the reason S/He created them was to be of use. God created the animals; and furniture and other accoutrements—made thru human hands—what for? To be of service! So it is a waste when one goes unused. When black women/men's hands and yellow women/men's hands sit idle. When great works of poets is not unearthed, brought to light and celebrated according to its worth, when poets and artists are not heralded within the arc of their abilities!! The powers who govern us --tho technologically and intellectually far advanced over anything this earth has ever seen before--- are primitive; they go running helter-skelter onwards paying no heed to these simple lessons! As a consequence, so many of us are dying by the wayside, unused. Like so much surplus furniture created in some white-hot frenzy of mass production, gone unsold, now destined for the dumpsite. Like so many once-green living plants thwarted, who inclined themselves vainly seeking the sun, turned dry, yellow, dying, dumped out of their pots by the side of the road.

        ***

117

Here is yet another of the groups disfranchised by the infernal reign of the current powers that be. Gay man at synagogue; when I look into his face of this elderly gay man, I see the feminancy of it. I know his life like I know my life. Know it has not been easy for him, wanting another gay man. ---This world attempted to force him to be straight. The world limited him, kept pushing him out of its center, time and time again, into the outskirts, off into the dark corners, the shadows.

In addition, by time's fleshy corruption, he is no longer pretty, thus he is segregated once again; over looked by younger gay men, unwelcome at their clubs and houses.

How bad it has been for us queers! People are intemperate. Their patience is short. They loose their tempers over nothing at all. Yet ordinary life is mild compared to those dwelling under the microscopic scrutiny and terrifically compressed physical area of the transperson. Over the wear & tear of time, if the ordinary person becomes intemperate, the transperson goes quite mad.

Confined by the outer world from the start—by its stares jeers and sneers-- we turn inward to attack our own group body. Trans, we cut each other down, we pluck each other, we dish each other, clock each other, read each others beads, run the dozens on each other. It is the life-long gallows humor; the dising queers do to each other.

We're like a pack of rats caught in a trap too small, climbing over each, other backbiting, hating each other's scent, grimacing at the sight of each other; all-too-well reading ourselves mirrored in them. Yet this is the only social sphere we have. So in this way the hostile outer world compresses, confines us. Then when it is done, kicks us out of the other end of their system, which we were never in.

92.
One of Sean's great books has a photo of an abandon church with a skyscraper in background, a burnt barrio iglaise at the foot of a great skyscrapers of banks and onerous financial cogs of empire. The crumbling stucco walls of the iglase bare scrawled graffiti in Spanish: *Toro cholo Los Angelos*; from this trajectory of sediments at the bottom filament of the city arises the next class of assimilated persons loosing their language, adapting the speech of the ruling class

(English) adopting its false gods of capitalism over compassion, & community; of ruthless acquisition over mercy. Soon all nationalities become the same under the same banner--Ayn Rand's $-dollar sign. -- Their system has worked. No longer a cooperative multicultural social body; but one same, uniform, grey, whitecoller, robot labor force, blindly obeying.

Here is a short 20-line play about another group victimized because they were looked down at as 'savage, soulless, sub humans with strange gods & nasty habits.'

Have A Warm Night
A play in 10 lines by Red, a Red brother.

2008   College intern student, a middle- class Native American women, is doing researching the library stacks. She peruses the Native American section laptop computer, pen & paper in hand. She reads the following (flash back):

1780   Amherst sells smallpox blankets to Indians.

2008   Flash foreword to the University. An Indian protest, a sacred drum circle outside City Hall! In the forefront the student is waving her thesis about class warfare shouting thru a microphone. Speaking for all the voiceless masses of Red peoples suffering on the Trail Of Tears—which has been the occupied lands; the long white subjugation of the ancestors.

According to author Ward Churchill America's always carting off bodies—by the wagonfull—of its war victims, its hostile takeovers, in a pursuit of riches.

More & more the elderly Transman began to see what American supremacy and world-dominance is based on; how the tools this country uses, is terror.

Once conquered, the vanquished are shunted aside, regarded no more then garbage. In it's pursuit of atomic fuel to empower the nuclear war machinery of US Imperialism, Indian lands were raped for their uranium supplies. After decades, the mining for uranium is done, the waste products are left there, lying on the ground, on the destroyed

119

native land. Dine Indian children playing in a 'sand pile' which is mounds of tailings—radioactive residue after the process separate pure uranium out of ore into 4 pounds of yellowcake necessary the nuclear fission process, the remaining 1,996 pounds are lay to waste—called tailings. They have a half-life of 10,000 years.

The system is cruel. It takes, takes, takes away from you and unless the individual people come together as a unit; and stand up as a group---which numerically is far more powerful in muscle and infinitely larger then those on top, ---saying Enough is Enough! And make a stand, and take a claim for their rightful share then, nothing can happen. But then it will. Now for a while things are ok, but pretty soon those on top start to chip away, a bit here, some more there. Slowly, this, and that, a little at a time, then the bites grow greater and greater. Soon, once again the people loose. The rich get back their leverage, their power, and what we get back is only just enough to survive and no more.

***

The tall, powerfully built figure slips on the hooded cowl, the long crimson robe. It is Satan! --Or is it the church? From the KKK back to the Inquisition, religion has been used against humanity, because it is power.

One day, no one left on earth will be ignorant. All will see in full the great deception done. The tricks and lies. Then the evidence, so overwhelming will leave the rulers absolutely no leg left to stand on. No support. No ally. No paid lackey mercenaries.

> You can't hide from a hurricane under a beach umbrella.
> --Daily Worker, 1924.

93.
Blow baby Blow! Winds of jazz. A sunny blue day from the 1950's. Miles Davis, black master musician blows torrent of soul out of a golden horn, as for me its blow baby blow—these words into your mind.

Two white men sit together at the front of the bus and are speaking. "It's easy man, first I got a $5,000 camera, $1,200 lense, and a $500 laptop". Well-dressed, a suit, carrying all this camera equipment.

The bus rolling thru the time warp of the old black Fill-mo teaming with people from the 1960's, followed by the miles of desolation broken bricks demolition of the 1980's. "Frame by frame, eyes open, eyes closed…"*Can you remember it? The pageant? Can you still hear bluenotes of the ghosts who survived on this land once?* The young, privileged whitefolks continue. A black woman and her child, dressed in poor clothes sit also at the front of the bus, they look lost. The bus rolls on. It is simply amazing how the powers that be managed to tear down a whole tenth of a city, and displace 30,000 thousand black human souls—and barely a finger was lifted against to stop this.

Red remembers when the Fillmore was torn down and reinvented— for upper income inhabitants—called re-gentrification. Back in the day the term the city officials actually used for this process was 'redevelopment.' Vacant lots stretched for miles, rubble; black men in worn clothes, watch caps on their heads against the foggy cold San Francisco nights which now blew down openly upon them with no obstruction, looked around with dazed expressions as they walked. "Where everybody goin'to?" A shrug. To the black ghettos in Oakland, East Palo Alto? Back down South? Some went to 'Hungers Point'. —30 years later this too is being gentrified. Where is sanctuary? Can we find the niche, the stray corner? Will it be the cardboard box in a store entrance closed by night?

Late that evening, a black street man read him. It happened this way. About 10pm, downtown in the worse area, adjacent to the TL. A black man stumbles thru the street; his pants down around his knees revealing plaid boxer shorts over his firm muscular black ass; well built, but a ruined face. (Absolutely no action shakin' in front.) He shouted, jesting with some other black street men who, as bad off as they were, seemed ill at ease with this derelict, who obviously was all the way off the deep end—very high on drugs, or insane. A police cruiser trolls along right beyond the curb in the stream of silver car fishes, blue uniformed cops inside scan thru the windshield looking for somebody, and it comes back, circling the block again. Transman walked past this scene of dereliction, the black man stumbling at a distance after; who then shouted out:

"Soldier Boy! Hey soldier boy, if you wasn't so white you'd be black. Black on the inside white on the outside!"

Transman continued on, gamely with his limp, paying the man no heed, up and up the blocks. When he finally looked back at where the waters of time had closed over the Blackman, he was no more and a police siren wailed carrying him off to the po' man's hotel—the jail at 860 Bryant.

They had eyes for filled with troubles seeing no more then the past repeating over and over, rather then the future.

      ***

T belonged to a class of people whose lives didn't exactly have the warmth & security of families but whose socializing is basically framed by public bars, cafés they sit in—where people know their names and where is held informal conversations in a social galaxy, but which includes only a very few intimate friends. For the poor, half mad Transman, being religious, this informal family included the ecumenical.

It is true, he decorated his sparse life with dreams of success—like a Christmas tree. In the past many of these Christmases had passed with only his dreams for the future as gifts—to himself. And these preoccupied much of his prayer.

      Red: At the Cross of Christ, I bow.
      The Spirit: Follow!

I'm dedicated. I preserve. I've taken on dragons! Loneliness! Isolation being predominate of these. But now poverty coupled by the weakness of limb in old age is creeping up rapidly to the forefront; just when I'd begun to reconcile myself as the life of a bachelor living out my days in measured economy in a cheep hotel room!

One reason people seek supernatural support, is that they are not happy with the world, their placement within it this world, their treatment by this world, and if they are supersensitive to the plight of others this makes it the more compelling to search for an alternative to this world. But some struggle for political change---to replace one world system with a new one. Others transcend as much as possible out of grim realities, and seek a 'kingdom not of this world' as Jesus spoke of.

Transman thought how 40 years ago came to this town, blown in from Chicago, he'd left a cold room, bath down a worn carpeted hall, cheap residence, his perfumed show girl, injectable heroin; and took a risk in his frail mental state to come here to an unknown city. He certainly was glad he'd found a kinder place.

What other city of all the cities on earth could you hear a saleslady calmly give instructions for a new sex toy proclaim:

> "Do it in the missionary position, hold it this way! Or, if you're doing it doggie style, that way!"

Transman bent his head in worship of the Divine. Really thought it was a privilege to be here. This major metropolis, with great synagogues, churches, and small Holy Circles. So many places so many of such variety. As big as God is you wouldn't think God could be misplaced. But people loose God all the time. So here he came, week upon week; the synagogue likewise, to find his Maker. Before him, up on the alter, the sacrificial table is prepared, the crucifix, emblazoned by illumination, the candles in their bronze holders 6 feet tall, ablaze, all is ready, no one is yet there---the clerical procession not yet started--- from somewhere inside the guts of the cathedral, an un-embodied voice rises in a tin tone of emotional suffering: "Jesus Christ, our Lord! Make Haste To Save Us!" Is it a ghost of some long dead priest? Is it a glitch of the audio technology that wires this place? The sound system at Grace is being redone--$300,000 has been allotted, and soon, any Sunday now, we will hear more clearly. As for now the ghostly voice continues its passionate plea, quotation of some scripture said as a prayer but no one is there, no one! Premature; ahead of the mystical procession. Shifting nervously in their wooden pews 800 congregants stir in their seats, looking around, bewildered. Is the service starting without them—being held in some secret location, and piped in to them unknowing? It is the priest and clergy huddled together in a side chamber, blessing themselves before the service is to begin—not realizing their mic's have been activated!

He found himself in the tapestry of colorful music that is Grace. The stained glass windows refracting light, blues, greens red, yellows, onto at the alter table, covered. The gay, garish & magnificent pageant unfolded continuously around him. But by time for the announcements Transman's head started to nod, he was so god awful tired, his chin sank to his chest; *"all kinds of delicious goodies."* The priest is saying. *"Right after the service downstairs in the Crypt,* **will be all kinds of delicious goodies**", Transman upon hearing the words *'delicious goodies'* came to life—his head raised up in expectation! -- However, by the next split second his hopes were so dashed, that he made a gasp—audible, echoing in the looming grey stone walls of Cathedral which could be heard in the several rows of pews around; as the preacher continued *"All kinds of delicious goodies* **For Sale**... *down stairs in the crypt after the service...'*

> But with righteousness shall he judge the poor and reprove with equity for the meek of the earth; and he shall smite the earth with the rod of his mouth, and with the breath of his lips shall he slay the wicked. And righteousness shall be the girdle of his loins, and faithfulness the girdle of his reins.
>
> The wolf also shall dwell with the lamb, and the leopard shall lie down with the kid; and the calf and the young lion and the fatling together; and a little child shall lead them.
> And the cow and the bear shall feed; their young ones shall lie down together; and the lion shall eat straw like the ox.
>
> They shall not hurt nor destroy in all my holy mountain; for the earth shall be full of the knowledge of the LORD, as the waters cover the sea.
>
> And in that day there shall be a root of Jesse, which shall stand for an ensign of the people, to it shall the Gentiles seek; and his rest shall be glorious.
> -- Isaiah 11: 4-10

Again I say, Christ, keep me in your control. Keep me doing the things I must do. Keep me from those things I should not.

> & Jesus Christ said,
> Let there Be Light!
> and there was a soft candlelight.

& Jesus Christ said, Let there Be Peace!
And there was peace.
Jesus said, Let there Be Friends!
And there were friends.
Merry Christmas!

94.

A big fat grey pigeon walks in the bottom courtyard framed by his
building over the cement; finding no scraps of food; flies effortlessly
up to first floor fireescape, cocks its head looking about then turns,
ascends to 2nd story. The investigation continues. A few pecks turn
up worthless. Finally, the pigeon waddles to the edge of the grey
paint chipped fire escape gazes a moment then jumps off flying,
makes a sharp turn out into the freedom of the skies—having
descended into our little courtyard only momentarily perhaps
prompted by an ancient pigeon memory of the Good Times Transman
use to surreptitiously slip food out over his window sill --as if from
out of a jail cell--- breadcrumbs for them to dine.

> May Almighty God, by whose providence our Savior Christ
> Came among us in great humility, sanctify you with the light
> Of his blessing and set you free from all sin. Amien.

> May he whose second Coming in power and great glory we await,
> make you steadfast in faith, joyful in hope, and constant in love.
> Amien.

> May you, who rejoice in the first Advent of our Redeemer, at his
> Second Advent be rewarded with unending life. Amien.

> And the blessing of God Almighty, the Creator, the Christ, and the
> Holy Spirit, be upon you and remain with you forever. Amien.

> ***

> *I remember the day* Brenton later wrote; "the doucet bought the
> painting from Picasso, who, strange as it may seem, appeared to be
> intimidated by him and offered no resistance whatever. The price
> was set at 2,500 francs."
> --Picasso, John Richardson

In the words of many—'I remember the day.' Let me tell you a story, when I was young and came to this city in 1967, tried looking for work—going from door to door asking if they were hiring in each business downtown on Market street, while scourging the want ads. I was so poor. Living in the TL on welfare. The welfare department easily gave a per-week grant, at just one sight of me—being a transgender street dike. So when I was out of work I got two vouchers, one for $15 rent, the other for $10 food. A friend, 'Ingrid' known in some of my ROUGH TRADE or BOY'S NIGHT OUT stories had introduced me to her Chinese trick, a grocery store owner, who gave me cash for my food vouchers. With this I got typewriter ribbons, busfares and a bit of spending cash. My dad sent me $15 every week, --which arrived by check on a Monday, and it was on this I got additional food for much of the week, but the food always ran out; my money got up and gone. I was starved hungry by Saturday night. There was a small, shabby hole-in-the-wall hotdog/burger joint on Market street, which sold two hotdogs for just 25 cents (cheep even back then); I would take my last quarter and purchase these, the greasy apron cook passed them over the counter wrapped in a piece of waxed paper inside a brown paper bag. I took them to the condiment counter, loading each one up so they were dripping with free ketchup/mustard/onions & goo-gobs of piccalilli spilling abundantly over the hotdog bun onto the waxed paper —then, seated on a barstool tall chair at an against-the-wall counter top, wolfed down one hot dog ravenously, took the other home to eat later at the end of the day. This is all I would have to eat for 24 or 36 hours—until dads $15 check arrived. Hunger became my constant companion when I was a poor young artist. A gnawing stomach ran along with me, in a marriage throughout my life over many years. Not enough money to purchase food, and not well worked into the charity food bank system. I write about denial in these journals. That forced upon one; that self-enforced. (AUTUMN CHANGES, PASSAGE, JOURNEY). Flash forward to today. I realize with each pang of hunger I am loosing weight! This is the secret! To eat well, and often at regular times, — to go without others. This will be my new battleplan for longevity. My new stratagem against loosing this fat potbelly, which is giving me high blood pressure no doubt! I will embrace hunger! Eat less often! Take hunger back into my life—as if it was part of my eating routine—hunger as an actual food of sorts!

    ***

Oh la la, what gossip! Have just viewed the Internet page of a transwoman friend in a popular listing for 'social activities, meeting people & networking'. Under its categories for Job Experience she has put:

Freelanced in the adult entertainment industry.

Oh la la! She must have had a hoot & a howl concocting *that* jolly euphemism, hopefully with a friend or two to share the fun! AND, *here's* what she has put under the 'My Interests' department:

My interests include 22 karat & 24 karet solid gold ethnic jewelry, emeralds, rubies, & sapphires.

Obviously her price-- written in code so as to throw the vice-detectives off her track! So what is this girl? A tranny ho? Yes! But an educated one, hence, she is must be elevated to the status of 'sex worker.' Alas, trans; we are making the best of a bad situation. To be trans, a life-long dilemma. We felt it as children, we felt it since before puberty! It has been a handicap in so many respects! But Oh la la, the gossip! The fun! The *Drama!*

***

Times in T's life of reinforcement for his art—occurred during times of financial surplus—when he had money to spend—thus free time. The old Transman recalled:

Several periods of unemployment compensation checks.

Living on money saved from better paying jobs, for a short time. IE: 1973; in which HO STROLL, BARS ACROSS HEAVEN were created from piles of notes; and FLASH ON THE HUSTLER, HOW'S MARS? were resurrected from the past.

1976. Upon the death of his dad Transman inherited $60,000 was it? Which enabled him to write assiduously for 7, years basically interrupted by very little minimum wage work. WESTPOINT OF THE UNIVERSE, and the entire Old Collection (some 33 books.*) Plus the 15 or so chapbooks of religious poetry (Upon his conversion to Christianity from the state of unbelieving ((atheism)); CHRIST YOU'RE THE ROCK! And etcetera.

1989. Jasmin's invention-- Gardenia House Cleaning service, which she and Red worked in partnership for eleven years allowed him more free time then his regular punch-the-clock low menial work which as we know Dear Children, in a draconian fashion inscribes exactly how much of the peoples time the rich will steal—while using these people to earn big surpluses of capital for themselves, which they covert to power, power to get expensive attorneys & police forces to keep control of the labor force--while paying you back barely enough to stay alive. As their own capitalistic 'corporation' Jasmin & Red could cut back hours, tailored to their needs. The couple might bid for a 4-hour job, then complete it in 3 hours—giving an extra hour for fun! For Jasmin's Dance, and Red's Books.

2004. SSI/Soc Sec money, the standard $2,000 pay off came all at once over period of 6 months, enabled him to paw thru the green file cabinet which stored copies of his 'ancient books' collection to resurrect what he referred to as the Lulu Series—Lulu Print On Demand. --- Including THE BIG CHANGE, VENGEANCE, BARRIO BLUES.

During these times great break-thru's in his art occurred. Times in which Red gained proficiency and skill more difficult to come by when on the run between jobs; free-time snatched in spare hours.

*The works written were: my now made-public 22-volume Old Collection series, as described in his BOOK CATALOGUE, 2008; including: THE LOVE LAMENT OF PETER PAIN, WESTPOINT OF THE UNIVERSE, CAN'T GO ON ANOTHER DAY, LIGHT AT DAWN, IN THE MAELSTROM, PRISONER OF HEARTS, ELECTRO SHOCK DOKTOR, A HILLBILLY GIRL IS LIKE A BUTTERFLY, TO THE MAN WITH HIS HAT IN HIS HAND—WITH LOVE, A BLAX MAN IS NOT A WINDUP DOLL, THE MAN FROM THE BLAX GALAXY, BOOGIE NIGHTS/PARTY LIGHTS, THE BLOOD OF CHRIST AGAINST THE LIES OF BABYLON, THE BACCHANALIAS SOCIETY BASH, THE CLUBFOOT BALLERINA/THE PRIM DONA, HOW DON JUAN DIED, WHITE GIRL, BOY CENTER; The Scavenger Trilogy-- ASHCAN BETTY, FLEAMARKET MOLLY, GARBAGE CAN SALLY.

Well to end this drash on money, food, and lack of both, here is the latest entry to my journal; it is a bit complex, involving intertwined stories, so pay attention Dear Children:

Christmas dinner @ Grace.   He stood at attention, among the 3-dozen seniors waiting in the food line! He was ready! His spoon stuck in his pocket, all set for action, like a soldier carrying his bayonet-fixed gun! The dining area is festive. Gay streamers draped over the walls. Lovely place settings, delicious aromas. --The food fascist stands guard over her pots, brandishing a pitchfork-sized serving utensil— but amazing news! A lovely gentleman, David, comes up to Transman, greets him, and softly whispers a word—about that long ago society, the Benedictines—they want me back! They miss me— all of them except the one who troubled me so greatly. -- They think I was a valuable addition! Startled; Transman stood, still-empty plate in hand. His spoon rattled against his glasses! He had not expected this!

Later, a fellow traveling left-winger among the congregation confides:

> My God, I asked her if I could have a second piece of pie and she
> acted like I had come to rob the bank!

This is another bit of good news! So! Its not just *me* this Nazi persecutes! Ah ha! I must learn not to take things so personally—I must flow more with the universe. Om Shanti Om! The last few months have been working on not retaliating so viciously when offended. Buddhists call it, The Path.

It's just the yin-yang of life, that some are put on this earth in a position of privilege-- & have mercy on them. *Mercy!*

Another good thing gotten out of Senior's food day, a book, (reject from a long-past 25-cent sale); courtesy of one older gentlemen with completely white hair, beard, -- and thick reading glasses. ---Cry The Beloved Country. What a magnificent book! --- A good book—a fine book; a book to be proud of! By Allen Paton. & written 45 years before apartheid fell. Here is my vision concerning that situation, just before the walls of segregation fell, given to me, circa 1992. A black African mother is laboring over her over cooking stove—stirring a pot of beans. Her young children will never go beyond the level of a 5th or 6th grade education. They will never rise above the pot of beans, to the beef. Which sadly has somehow become the limit a poor black child can go under the white mans system---apartheid—which has possessed the African's own country!

95.
Another few hours spent at the Shelter, hearing comments of the prospective owners who come to peruse dogs:

> "Good Boy! Good Boy! Look at the way the tail goes round!"
> (Accompanied by vigorous hand twirling motion.)

In the lunchroom on break, Transman plunked both his hands, palms upturned, down on the table, sighing deeply. Felt the nails driven into his own hands—one of empathy for others, one of the sense of injustice committed against them, which sometimes was almost too great to bare. And thought: *'I feel like I'm crucified all day long... My love of the beasts; of the weaker creatures, of those to be protected; & wish no harm would come to them.'* And then thought of those, quadrupeds, terrified, wild eyes rolling in their furry heads, soon to be led to the slaughter house. So this is why he did not think about these subjects for very long, it was of a killing intensity.

God has nearly killed me with love again. A dog at the shelter Reverend Lovejoy--- the 3 legged pit bull who was found in an abandon auto wrecking yard in Oakland, owner ran off without paying back taxes; there weeks later, the pit bull was found—his hindquarters crushed by a fallen wrecked car. One rear leg had to be amputated, a clean cut right at his rump. The brave dog has learned to maneuver himself around wriggling, and exerting great muscles in his forepaws and chest. Black people named him when he was first found—giving him a loving name which would make all who saw the young pit bull care for him—and not be afraid, due to the hideous reputation of their breed—prone to violence & bloodshed from their huge mouths with fangs and inbred bad tempers. The black folks called him three wonderful words—combined: —Reverend, (a person of peace), Love, and Joy! (Simca!) Well this Reverend has truly a big mouth, as does all of his breed, a very round humanish head, and big jaws the size of his whole lower head, they all do. The

130

Reverend grabs his food dish and carries it where he will—wriggling on 3 legs—to a place better to dine (within the confines of his small 4 by 4 metal barred cage). So you get the picture of this huge mouth, red pink tongue. The Reverend has turned out to be a truly loving Pit Bull, and cuddles and cozies to all his guests—such as Transman who goes there to visit him many times per week. Well here is the picture. At the Seniors Dinner Christmas white robed figures march thru the cathedral in processional. They are to protect the laws & statues of the Most High Creator. The service is important. The *diner and free food baskets* is secondary; and to think otherwise is incorrect. These religious services held every Sunday must be attended frequently, for it is to remind us of God's Spirit, like a perpetual flame in a lighthouse summoning sailors floundering at sea; and to surround us with Her protection. The white robed clerics march to and fro, brandishing their Bible upheld, and the accoutrements of the Holy Cross, incense burner and flaming candles on giant gold sticks! I exaggerate. For this gala hoopla is the Sunday extravaganza. This weekday service, held in the small chapel, is much smaller in almost every way, but one--there on the alter between gold candlesticks, and the gold platter which hold the Host, here is a golden chalice by which we Christians take our Communion, (likewise, we Jewish say our blessings with motzie & kiddish; ((the kiddush chalice)). Today, before him Transman saw one of the biggest gold chalices he'd ever remembered! And directly, based on these things, Transman saw a brief vision—it was a fragment of God! God, bigger and powerful, also was seated at our communion table, larger then life—drinking from the golden cup which was just God's size. On Her/His head was a very human Reverend Love Joy's head, with the Reverend's big mouth, so sad, drinking carefully out of the cup along with Her/His people! God, looking so sad—bewildered. I was filled with the sense of such great beauty, which is God and God's creation, but then this killing sadness! God, with the innocence of a child, who had so lovingly created each curled toe on the foot of a parrot to perch on branches in the wilds—and on your shoulder in the city; God who had so magnificently crafted every being, every person in this universe—made all the planets, and stars in the sky, God so dismayed at how it has all gone wrong!

Now that I have seen God looking so sad —so abjectly sad at our messed-up world. I can't offend God any more then I already am

131

doing! The last few months have been working on not retaliating when offended. As the Buddhists call it, The Path. The Way. Enlightenment. I must even forgive the Food Nazi! (Forgive them for they know not what they chew!)

96.
My life—it seems like just a minute—that long journey of struggle, the whole thing. Now I'm limping down towards the finish line…

Determined, despite weariness, the Transman walked up hill towards his little studio, making his way; stride accompanied by a Tap, Tap, Tap, of the aluminum cane. Full briefcase contained stuff he'd picked up in the streets that day; first the bag itself, clean attractive, with a handle to carry or a shoulder strap found discarded at curbside months previously; a flyer for a free BBQ Beef dinner at Glide Memorial church Christmas Eve; a small mirror, a pair of dainty silver high heel cocktail pumps (ladies) which he would employ in his masturbations that evening; some cubes of granite kindly given to him from the wastepile of a Mexican construction worker who was finishing cutting with electric saw a granite slab to inlay in still another condo conversion occurring—granite cubes Transman would use to stop up holes in the bottom of the flowerpots he'd also found discarded that week—so all the soil wouldn't run out into the saucer. As he walked the streets he had been keeping an eye out for half-dead plants to save. Some pigeons were dinning by starlight overlaid with neon outside the grocery store @ Hen's Mayflower Hotel, thereupon Transman stopped, & in a briefly executed generosity, produced a crust of Challah from some previous Shabbat service @ synagogue; the pink-foot, grey feather beasts at once descended on this repast pecking hungrily with their beaks, Peck, Peck, Peck. The night is cold-blooded, as we know Dear Children, yet there is love in it. The moon was full on the variegated sky, grey/black like ripples on a sandy beach in outerspace—the whole heavenly universe, amazing!

Life to him, as it is to many others of Hashem's Saints, (quite a few alive today, right here in this metropolis), is like a little wheel of fortune hopping down the street, with him skipping along besides it. Fortune for which some conspire in greed, for wealth, and still others assiduously approached wealth with figures, calculations, studies charts and graphs; where as these other kind, these saints, some deny

132

self, and others give away all they have to those in more dire need then themselves; his approach was that he wasn't in fact following fortune it at all, simply skipping onwards in the same direction--just swimming in the sheer stream of things. Now, about this Great Fortune... Would life actually deliver to him a Great Disappointment? Would the end of his life be sort of in the manner of a person too long having before them on the table an empty cup—to which now at long last some substance has been added—poison? Or would Hashem see to it that everything worked out perfectly fine!

***

It was cold the next morning in the bookstore. The young proprietor hunched over the computer at his desk—reading COMPASSION. His icy white fingers moved under some lines; he was perplexed:

> This is so funny you spelled my name one way on this page, & another way on a different page—and they're both wrong.
> ---Sean, proprietor of Babylon Falling

***

My Hangings:
A brief resume of Red's Paintings, as shown publicly, in chronological time-frame:

> Chicago. Late 1940's; thru early 1950's. Wall on both sides of hallway of flat, in which s/he was raised as a child, is lined with his crayon and watercolor drawings on paper from school.
>
> Chicago. 1962. 20 paintings on the walls of the Old Town Pub. A nightclub at near north side in Old Town, an artist/beatnik, soon to be hippy commercial area deluged with tourists. He had left town after delivering the works, but before the show opened, having no faith whatsoever— escaping to SF. Ted, his Dad had to go there, to take the paintings down.
>
> San Francisco. Circa 1969. Two paintings, the Watermelon Eater, and La Suena were submitted to a City show outdoors in Civic Center Plaza. An old wino bum stole one of them! He was seen walking down skid row with the Watermelon

133

Eater under his arm, an alert gay man realizing the picture and the bum didn't fit together, apprehended him and got the painting back! He then notified the authorities, and Red and his friend Suzie De Young, photographer, went over to his apartment in Fox Plaza and retrieved it!   Kudos!

Berkeley. Circa 1970. Two paintings accepted to hang in a Gay Art show. Drove them over in his truck. It was an all-gay men's show, and Red was ignored. After a few hours, when no attention seemed to be paid to his work (little attention was paid to any of the paintings) he lost heart, took the works down and drove back home with them.

SF. 2006. A small gallery in the Mission run by a lady, formerly in the Sex Industry; both their names shall be omitted. Contracts were signed, but no more was heard from that lady as the show date fast approached. The hanging that wasn't. Partage of all individuals concerned!

   ***

Berishiet. The organ music grinds; it is the beginning. —The verger sails forth—staff upheld, her eyes expressionless, gazing slightly upwards, and far off, off on her divine mission, her chin bravely pointed forward like the prow of a ship. A giant ship composed of deacons, the Dean, alter tenders, ministers, priests, the Bishop, choir master; and the choir follows—the congregation begins to sing. Hail Mary Full Of Grace!

A larger-then-life alter table, clothed with silk, iridescent silver, white brocade. The clerics now bow at the waist & kiss this alter, where the Lamb will be slain again & again.

Today, in the first rows in front, fate has cast to sit together Transman and the church photographer. There they sit, two artists on their jobs. Transman scribbles. The photog snaps. He is wired for sound, electric devices in his ears, unaware that his equipment is beeping audibly; annoying to those in the surrounding pews. Do those congregants nearby the scribbling writer view his seeming preoccupation with unruly sheets of paper & hastily jotting pen to be lack of concentration on the service, do they find him annoying as well?

Following are the Transman's notes upon the subject of Religion:

> If a Christian goes to a Pagan ceremony, (Pagan which pre-dates the Christian, Islamic, and the Hebrews, and from which all religions have borrowed and adapted its ritual for themselves) and at their ceremony receives a bit of sweet herbs & incense mixed together for a marvelous smell to take home—it is of no consequence—due to their faith. But when the Pagan embraces these potents to the extent of it being their total belief, excluding God, it becomes a major hindrance to their Spiritual awakening because they worship it.

> Is the vase evil because it holds alcohol, from angry resentment of those parishioners who cannot drink even a drop of liquor--from which the communion Blood is poured out?

> Red's Plan:
> I think everyone has a way to save the human race---their own little way-- & if they all did it the world will be saved! A perfect plan given to them by God—in their heart, accessed, according to Doctor Jung, in dreams. Accessed by bible study revelations. By religious chanting. We would all do our own perfect plan, and by Creator's design it would all fit together for perfect, holistic Shalom!

> ***

Metropolis is a wonderland of architecture; bright silver lights dot towering structures in mathematical pointillism. It has no heart but the fleshy, human one beating inside each citizen's chest. But by some evil devolution, our human society has become a play life, not real life. A commercial life. Not holistic, nor Godly. Fake. The corrupt social mechanism begins to wind up---cool jazz, cold, distant as a train whistle in the night over a lonely landscape. Robot players in the mechanism are set about monitoring, censoring my life, and all others who they can perceive are alive, passionate, thinking, and *not playing the game!*

I was not drinking from the common trough--which runs across the entire earth --from which billions of humans drink—trough full of yellow vomit thick, lumpy. Nor from the smaller vase of poison— pure evil, malignant, the chalice of Hitler, Machiavelli, Korporate Moguls, rulers of vast Empire. But try to take in what is higher. And would be drinking rainbows from God.

Remember Dear Children, there will come a time of Justice. A Time when all dead begin to rise–up to the surface of the earth. The reckoning, when all evidence is revealed! –This prelude having been said, --another story:

The chump was set to arrive at the Animal Shelter at 2pm. Shortly after the stocky fat bellied man dressed in worn black clothes had got his chair and gone into a cage to sit with the 3-legged pit bull, a woman, stranger to him came into the back room. Immediately all the dogs started barking at her in a most unfriendly manner. Especially the pit bull who felt he was guarding Red. She spoke to him in a voice, which he wasn't quite sure was sincere—varying between friendliness but was that a strain of trickery also? Asking him to come and meet with her as soon as he was finished being in the cage. Here is the tail in his own words:

Day before Christmas; am called into the office by the new paid volunteer coordinator about an incident…
*(In which he had yelled back at a soft spoken employee who had berated him, used a bossy tone, tho he did not have authority to do so, and given him false information—albeit using a low tone and civilized manner.) ((This is the trickery of a sanitized, civilized hypocrite who attacks with their poison but because their demeanor conforms to this fake society he creates no public outcry.))

Of course Transman felt bad. —He felt he didn't fit in anywhere at all! Not even at a shitty homeless dog shelter! Christmas. The holidays. A volatile time. When he feels sparse. His full lips formed into a pout.

Shuffling back to his cage after the bad vibes interview, *'is this a set up to begin firing me?'* (And he had never been hired.) His mind wanders for a moment; brief musing on a spiral downwards, into abject dissolution… skid row…. Barrooms… Drugs… And those crones & bums who live it. How many dreams are doused there in the

136

TL? Walking blanket-wrapped in homeless derelicts; barflies, dopefiends, dropouts, who once tried to survive in the regular world, but were so dysfunctional they can't operate in a polite circle of society—thus unemployable. Friendless. Going nowhere but down. Times when he feels like crying—but the tears are frozen… The garish Farris Wheel of barroom music grinds on and on, but Transman has reformed. He is transcended, yes, tho not entirely— caught somewhere between the degenerate and the spiritual… In the uncomfortable position of being human.

Well now you really think I am a sad case. One after another since LAMENTATIONS, I have documented rejections, breakups from various groups, friends, and positions. This makes the third! Three strikes yer' out! So they say.

Let me say finally, in closing this chapter, that people like a strong story line. They heroize and make ballads about dead martyrs, and tell and retell the tales of Robin Hood, Joan of Arc, Geronimo, all saints, saviors & heroes—who battled against the oppressive regimes of their time. Outlaws wild as the wind!

While here, uptown, on this stage set of unreal life, the players of the game, they shake my hand, say "Yoshar kov! —You write great revolutionary poetry! More power to you, may you continue in your strength!" Or they pat me on the back, "Atta' way pal! Give 'em hell! Give 'em hell for me too while yer' at it!" People look at me and they can see I'm an outlaw. Everybody loves outlaws—but not everybody wants *to be* an outlaw.

He was like any animal & liked animal things. Eating. Being with other people like himself. —People who fitted in with him & him with them. —The name for this was family. He liked to express his sexual yearnings and fulfill his flesh in genital relations & that was one of his perpetual angst—that as a transsexual man the configuration of his body, his physicality, did not match his sexual desires. That the expression of his true sexual nature as a male, was thwarted by not having a man's genital hookup. He dreamt of Castro street; among gay men—where he couldn't get his needs met. Of that long-ago Oakland Ho Stroll and to the prostitutes who worked there, where he went as a client, and as he was not fully male, their aversion of him, many workingwomen would not service him. —And today, finally, such a challenge of meeting straight women whose every assumption justifiably is, that he is a normal man--& he isn't. How to disclose to them what he is? Should he disclose it at all, until right before the first kiss? Further, after the first few months of his transition he'd discovered a secret side of himself. A long submerged desire; physically untouched for decades, which was activated by the high-powered sex drug Testosterone. He discovered that he enjoyed being in the position of a woman in the bedroom—but only briefly. A few hot moments on his back, & would never live his life as a woman, no, (before his transition, which made being mistaken for one a physically impossibility), nor had he ever, for any period of time,-- other then what it took to get a doctors exam, or to go on a job interview.

Such confusion! Such angst! Such great art is born!

…Well—thinking about fact that I am a great artist does somewhat muffle the sadness…

> Slowly he followed the bent figure up the street, saw him nodding as he walked, saw the people turning. Would age now swiftly overtake him? Would this terrible nodding last for all his days, so that men said aloud in his presence, it is nothing, he is old and does nothing but forget? And would he nod as though he too were saying, 'Yes, it is nothing, I am old and do nothing but forget?' But who would know that he said, I do nothing but remember?
> --Alan Paton; Cry, The Beloved Country, 1944.

97.
> On grey cement
> a pigeon vainly struggles
> with a large crust.
> A bit of food—solid—impossible
> for even a strong beak to peck apart.
> The human friend approaches gently.
> Steps on the crust, hard, with his heel.
> A squish, a stomp.
> Grinds it into small morsels
> —beaksized.

138

So he went around town doing mitzvots—in his own way.

***

Mitzva—talked to a friend who really needed to talk---then, upon awakening the next day felt in a light mood, realized—it was *me* who really needed to talk!

***

Since he belonged nowhere—it is obvious to him that God created him for only this one thing----to do art, & art alone! He declared: 'Must go back to having art exclusively as my goal; to haunting libraries, bookstores & coffee shops—as a solitary student of life; and expect no other thing to be fulfilled.' And saying this then made a list; 'here is my evidence, all failed':
 1. Romantic affairs
 2. Friendships (most of them)
 3. Financial matters
 4. Personal grooming
 5. Dieting.
Contraire, my success(s):
 1. 80-literary masterpieces written & distributed.
 2. A handful of fine arts oil paintings executed with copies (in poster form) of each, sold.

Very soon now I shall say; at last! Embarked on the life of an artist! Hands on! To get dirty in the muck & mire of color, smells, substance, physical form!

The easel is set up, the paints sorted by color; primary, secondary & assembled into 3 treys. News Bulletin Alert! A great treasure was found last week! --As he moved painfully up the street with great determination, feet, legs and cane comprising a human dynamo pumping forward, Transman had seen a small cardboard box at curbside; as was his habit; he stopped, went over, glanced into it; he discovered—40 tubes of used oil paints!

 Alizarin Crimson
 Azo Red Medium
 Venetian Red
 Naphthol Red
 Cadmium Red Medium

Cadmium Red Dp Azo
Cobalt Bleu
Phthalo Blue
Ultramarine Blue
French Ultramarine
Mauve
Phthalocyanine Blue
 Dioxazine Purple
Lemon Yellow Hue (Arylide Yellow)
Azo Yellow
Cadmium Yellow Pale Hue
Azo Yellow Light
Yellow Ochre
Cadmium Orange Azo
Naples Yellow Red
Burnt Sienna
Burnt Umber
Raw Sienna
Van Dyke Brown
Viridian
Viridian Hue
Phthalocyanine Green
Payne's Grey
Lamp Black
Titanium White

Duplicates of up to 5 of each hue. &, in addition
15 unnamable Russian paints tubes –colour to be revealed upon
unscrewing cap.

There is absolutely no excuse! I must begin to paint now!

Will go thru a dry run (tomorrow) News Year Day, taking out the
treys of oils, set up brushes w/turp-linseed oil mixture beside my
easel. I who went thru 10 solid years of painting who know this
routine in my sleep! Painting in cold flats with no money or food,
painting in one-room hotels! Painting for love and nothing else!

Now he had *everything* necessary to resume his trade! Those 20-
found canvas stretchers, most pre-set & reinforced at their corners;
plus individual pre-painted-upon canvases numbering into the dozens,
found upon his journeys over the last 7-years trudging back/forth in
this city (since when he'd moved from across the Bay where there is
nothing to be found in it's poverty streets already well-picked-clean
by wandering broke black men in ragged survival clothes with lint in

their uncombed hair pushing shopping carts); tubes of oil color both bought, way back pre-1995 when Gardenia Housecleaning Service was flourishing, & now, these found. Some bad old brushes (in this department he was sorely lacking) he'd purchased at a Asian five & dime store—cheap—along with some plastic pallet knives, a sheet of glass to act as a pallet, found on Fillmore street which now sits, fitting perfectly over a cabinet—(scavenged years ago in the East Bay) -- a paper pallet pad plus 3 pre-stretched pristine canvasses, untouched, once purchased. A roll of canvas purchased 6-months ago when he'd earned that $1,000 to do that Beatnik reading @ public library courtesy of Michelle Tea. —Which cost him $105. Above all—he had time! Time at last! No longer having to work, being retired! He was ready! He was ready like Freddy! He was ready to *rock & roll!*

So one could see the steady snail, the work-horse, the craftsperson, the laborer, Transman Red had slowly been spiral-climbing towards this very time, preparing himself in all little/great ways as was possible to his circumstance.

But for now he was back at his desk, writing in his Journal: --Even now, New Years Eve, to distant sound of Union Square revelers bursting bombs, howling, screeching in the New Year—fire engine sirens wailing, deep base BOOM explosions, albeit not the frightening gunshots, and automatic fire weaponry of the ghetto—a rising & falling ocean of booming sound in the background:

Red is a dirty book writer, Critiques will always perceive, but perceive wrong because 'sex sells' and I wrote a lot of it. It was not sex, it was sexual angst I was writing about.

Then he continued to prepare LEADER OF THE PACK for Internet publication:

> "She did it! The bitch! The professional woman! She made you loose your self esteem!" Cried Debbie, shaking Dena, -- so hard their hair flounced. The two attractive women, slender as reeds, with boots hugged, and slipped in each others embrace. "Then I thought, gee, I've had such a nice time at the party tonight, maybe I should just go home and rest, like normal people do.... Or, I could shoot drugs all day long and go to the movies. If I don't get 'em from Hawk I'll buy 'em on the street. If I feel this way now, the minute I'm away from the Clubhouse and all my friends I'll get into it. I'll drown in it. I don't need to hear anything about drugs."

"She did it! The bitch! The professional woman! She made you loose your self esteem!" Cried Debbie, shaking Dena, -- so hard their hair flounced. The two attractive women, slender as reeds, **with round tits & asses, clattered their high heel boots on the littered floor; as they slipped, then hugged, trying to gain balance in each others embrace**. "Then I thought, gee, I've had such a nice time at the party tonight, maybe I should just go home and rest, like normal people do.... Or, I could shoot drugs all day long and go to the movies **and watch 'em four times**. If I don't get drugs from Hawk I'll buy 'em on the street. If I feel this way now, the minute I'm away from the Clubhouse and all my friends I'll really be depressed. I'll get into dope. I'll drown in it. I don't need to hear nothing about drugs, **or getting high or partying. I'm weak.**"

They took out all the fun & descriptiveness. Ah well for the rules & standards of the pseudo middle class professional editor! PS fuck the Chicago Elements of Style! Ugh! It's Cultural Censorship in the guise of correctness! It's brainwashing!

At home the brown dying plants he repotted had turned green, and were growing again, leaning towards the light, stretching in new directions. His few windows (2 in the studio, 1 in the kitchen) got a short amount of direct sun, and a longer period of partial light. The small footage in front of these windows was now crammed with plants. Plants in planters he'd found, discarded pots; used food cans.

98.
Here the Reverend and I sit—in lock up. Behind jail bars. Both of us having had unfortunate beginnings. Pray to God's mighty intervention for a good ending for both of us respectively.

One might ask about the confidentiality of this diary. My true stories, which indict some big institutions—why would I put this, which many believe are private matters on the Internet for sale? Well first I have no great love for this class of people; it is this class above me, who runs things, who makes the rules, or who enforces the rules. It is this same class of people who, by having the power to help or not, ignored my work for so long, thus;

A. Are limiting my income directly.

B. Have cut me off from my prospective audience who was too slow to grasp the realization that one of their own—a poor Joker-- was out there writing---and kept me from having any idea of how

142

well I would be received and by what public. IE, at age 30 if I had been decently published and the works promoted—and even then received little or no acclaim, I might have been able to see myself in the correct proportions of my worth. Known my level and reached out to that audience more specifically, instead of grabbing out, floundering in all directions. And could have judged my future income and made different plans! (Although the Transman wasn't quite sure what plans these would have been, since all these financial doors were closed to him anyway.)

Second, I need the $ money! And third, love seeing tangible results from all my scribbling—in the form of a published work! And to hell what anybody else thinks! Today, simply put my trash up for sale over the Internet; hope I might earn some money for it, and be pleased every time a sales rings up---from what distant part of the world I do not know—thinking, *wow, somebody wants my book!*

Well anyway, as before stated, a lot of rejection does cut loose the slavish chains to tradition—and if you can weather the storm and stand harsh winters in lonely places and still come out of it alright, you will discover you are a bigger person, and a liberated soul.

Stepped out into the cold winter night of San Francisco. It was a harsh, and cold city, *a harsh and cold financial trap of a city*—and he had so few friends; no lover, no family at all, yet he was elated—with energy! Coffee streaming thru his crippling body! And future dreams prompted him on!

Affluent shoppers along this shoppers/ restaurant-goers magnificent mile; cold winter on ritzy Fillmore district. All white, a few 'other'; this is upper class. The stars revolve in heaven behind a cloud of fog so they cannot be seen; silver lightbulbs netted in the trees glistening webs in the branches. *So, I'm being kicked out of here… unwanted again…*

At the doorway of the pet shelter he furled his scarf around his neck with a flourish strutted out the door and went into the street, walking emphatically, his cane striking the concrete with emphasis.

    ***

The old Transman's thirst of knowledge led him again to drink at the fountain of Babylon Falling, and after reading into a curious political book it motivated him to scribble out these notes on his sheaf of wrinkled paper; --using a stolen pen:

I do not know if we will see a rise of fascism and murder here in the United $tates as there was in post-Wimer Republic Germany of the late 1920's, with the thuggish fascist takeover. Was just reading about the mass exodus of writers, painters, cabaret singers & actors, journalists, film makers and other artists of that era; about 2,000 of them circa 1933 when Germany's National Socialist Party—the Nazis-- really pulled the cloak off of themselves, to reveal the madness they were all about, and began taking over the cultural institutions of their nation. —All those categories listed above. When soldiers began to jail clowns, acrobats, circus performers, philosophers, University Professors--those with individual thoughts—you get the picture. I have before stated my patriotism to the original views of our United States of America—per the US Constitution—and have as much true loyalty to this nation as did the average German, including Jewish Germans, Artistic Germans etc, to the Germany that they too had once known. Before its name became infamous as dispensary of horror, the Reichstag had been an honorable institution in that nation, in the capitol city of Berlin. Before the takeover by the SS and thug Brownshirts, the Chancellery had been a legitimate and democratic post; before darkening evil of Adolph Hitler stepped into its seat by force of brutality, thugery, street murders and political maneuvering—aided by multimillionaire supporters in Greater Europe who saw the chance to increase their fortunes by having such a madman and warmonger in power. I am saying that anything is possible, and that our fine country with its mostly democratic based system with representation of the people, with a once-fair court system including the Highest, its Supreme Court; with freedoms of the press, freedoms of speech, and the vote, which is for me the land of opportunity, it too can be corrupted. Don't think that these freedoms could not be taken away—as they were under Fascist Germany. And don't delude ourselves that again goon & thug Brownshirts could

144

arise in our own country, as brutal army enforcers of some unrealized new Fascist empire arising like a toadstool right here in our "Land Of The Free." Our nuclear might, our financial advantage are all mega weapons itching to be co-opted and used for the ruling class, or some fanatical fringe with an evil agenda—an agenda to seize power for their own purpose—and that is not of the American people, but some private plan of self-enrichment at the cost to 300 million common Americans. In my fine novel STAGE DOOR, I documented a fictitious 'evil puppet President' (unnamed) who dominated the US from the White House in Washington, DC, and was slowly killing the people—starting with the poorest---thru tightening of the economic noose. In that novel a revolutionary act of assassination is carried out by one of the principle players, who is uneducated and fairly non-political. I won't give the plot away—but a great act of toppling the evil powers does occur. Elsewhere in STAGE DOOR in one of it's very few politic ramblings I mentioned assassination of those on high when they become dangerous, by abrogating our freedoms & Civil Liberties. For me to make such a statement sheds light on my mental state witnessing in our country the incredible snowballing effect over the last 3 years, of the falsely elected President & his clan--dragging us into a war against the mandates of the United Nations and the consensus of the American people, not to mention the advice of all the European heads of state—thus making it impossible to call in any of them as allies, but for Great Britain, Australia; and these with only a sparse handful of troops; --nomination of right wing judges restocking the Supreme Court so it becomes a puppet court, appointing Born-Again Christian officials through the country in state positions; enactment of the Patriot Act, a fascist bill which circumvents a common citizens civil liberties, rights to trials, fair representation of lawyers, or disclosure to the public or news media. When this book mentioned assassination of those on high when they become dangerous, I was using the artistic province and doing so fueled by my disconsolate & fearful feelings at the time concerning the *government of that time* and, hopefully, *not our president to come later*, who I'm assuming will be a *Democrat* who will begin undoing some of the anti-American statutes

145

put in place by the last fake president—this election due to come next year—2008. This was a very political novel for me—and made a raw stand against what I perceived at the time as a huge infringement of our way of life, and a frightening vision into what could be a nightmare future for America, and the world. — Our once-great America becoming The Evil Empire; Amerikkka in fact and in deed! After that novel I retreated from watching the news and its horrors about a second Republican Party victory in the presidency; of Clear Channel replacing small radio stations across the landscape of our country—another dying freedom—and changed the tone of my writing. Returning to more 'art' after that fiery declaration—to merely expressing my libertinage, a variant sexual stance, parrying word-genius and portraying colorful portraiture of character; writing several plays with fabulous dialogue, yes, I abandoned those raw politics glimpsed briefly in STAGE DOOR, but then, once again returned to it with a vengeance in my futurist. Si-Fi trilogy EMPIRE, MAN GONE/STARVAX, and ACTS AGAINST THE POWERS OF AUTHORITY somewhat in the theme of a brave New World, or the radical novel 1984—where totalitarianism, world dictatorship, complete abrogation of citizens rights is addressed. Next, my book LAMENTATIONS IN THE COOL OF THE EVENING blatantly calls for dramatic changes on the part of the common people—including murder mayhem and mass demonstrations of the most drastic kind—if our future is to be saved! Now I am back to writing my mundane Journal and hope to begin painting in fine arts oil colors, and concentrating on my great passion, spiritual matters—but I, like all others of us wonder what the future will bring! Will all my rants be in vain? I hope so! I hope we elect a succession of democratic, fair presidents, who can hold this ship together and keep each citizen free—while not trespassing into foreign lands to exploit them just to feed our overstuffed greed!

Junger—found that the terrorism of the Third Reich was not at all to his liking, and retreated into what many subsequently called 'inner emigration'—like others who take this course he wrote novels without a clear contemporary setting—a good number of writers favored the Middle Ages—and even if these sometimes cautiously

146

expressed some criticism of terror dictatorship in a general sense, they were still published, distributed and reviewed so long as they did not attack the regime in an explicit way.
--Richard J. Evens, Coming Of The Third Reich; 2003

***

Here's a confidential bulletin about a certain bookstore…. A brave young man who has set sail out upon this venture has told me he will not loose gargantuan money on this place, if he begins to fail. He will cut his losses and get out quick—rather then go on and on loosing and loosing, waiting for a miraculous turnabout. He will not repeat the sad story of Cody's bookshop—a very well patronized landmark in Berkeley; that branched out with a second store *In Union Square!* — No less! One of the most-pricey neighborhoods in this city! It failed from the beginning; the owner mortgaged his house to keep up with the bills. Lastly the store had to be given up—plus he lost the Berkeley store, his original shop as well!

So, our little ship of fools might not be here forever, as it valiantly sails out into the 7 seas of ignorance night after night—carrying it's proud beacon of intelligent light.

As previously documented, 4 bookstores in this area have already closed; one, down on Van Ness thankfully was replaced by another, tho it is a chain store; the second has been replaced by a Fight Club, and two stand empty. One Art Dealer—the old beatnik Chet Helms shop had closed the previous year, to be replaced by a mundane beauty shop.

Affluent people purchase books here, also do hardscrabble poorer pushing crumbled green dollars from worn pockets to exchange for Communist Manifesto's, Skateboard Diaries, and strange, arcane Nobel price winning authors from foreign lands. (Rich people, i.e. inheritors; their hands with smooth palms; they never had to work, but have wealth. Because their forefathers were slipping & sliding around in the mud, grasping, sweating to get it; to build the foundation upon which they all stand.) They all pass that lean mean green dollar over the counter to the young proprietor. While the Transman sat on his throne upon his coat on the edge of the display window, near to the stars, reading for free.

147

Sean is explaining the difference between Cuba's poverty and Jamaica's: "Don't have a lot of the freedoms can't do what I do now in a communist or in a fascist state."

To which Red agrees: "Not sexually, or writing, or art expression, or religious study."

Often someone makes some great comment. Now Transman Red offers to the mostly young clientele who gather in this establishment, one of his occasional pearls of wisdom they cannot yet fathom:

> Being old is the pits. There's only one thing worse. Being old is better then being dead.

In Sean's bookstore, I am surrounded by media; Shaun Roberts, Odell, Matt, and others; photographers, like acrobatic birds they can be seen, poised here & there, standing on stools, in doorways, up inside the display windows in their stocking feet, outside the store, aiming thru the front glass, from behind bookcases, cameras propped up on tripods, snapping away!

8pm, 1 hour from closing. Inside the pages of the soft cover book he now scanned, suddenly the meaning of what life can become when a tyrannical, corrupt, soldier-enforced governmental take-over installs a despot:

> Pathologists in block 2 dissected some 35,000 corpses so their body was studied and then stored in various jars on shelves. Tattooed flesh was especially prized. In block 2, their skins were stripped off, tanned and stitched into lampshades and other memorabilia. Nuremberg trial judges denounced "conditions so ghastly that they defy description. The proof is overwhelming that in the administration of the concentration camps the German war machine, and first and foremost the SS, resorted to practices, which would shame the most primitive race of savage barbarians. All the instincts of human decency, which distinguished men from beasts were forgotten, and the laws of the jungle took command. If there is such a thing as a crime against humanity, here we have it repeated a million times over."
> --Edwin Black, War Against The Weak, 2003

99.

When I was young,
my mother warm and furry;
 at her breast she loved me.
Others beside me;
 Furry, small, they wriggled,
 they were soft & sleepy;
 eyes still closed.
I remember warmth
 and the smell of mothers milk.
When I was young
I thought it was a world of cats.

By Mr. Fluffy, Dec. 2007.

Animal Shelter. So strange to come in here now that his situation has changed. On the way down the street he saw a woman employee (a dyke) walking a dog who he remembered. She doesn't greet him, but turns her head away. He climbs the stairs, opens the door, goes into the Reverends cage—sits. No humans speak to him. But the 3-legged pitbull wags his tiny tail ferociously, his eyes roll with joy in his round head, huge mouth open in a toothy smile, pink tongue lolling as he dances around his cage picking up his toys, tossing them and chewing them in his frantic happiness. --Having Red, for company. They sit together half an hour. The pitbull chews himself into an oblivious slumber at the old mans feet; at which time the demolished toy drops from his huge jaws, his tight muscled small frame relaxes. Transman sat; glasses on, studiously over Aleph-Bet, scrawling the Hebrew letters from memory on a sheaf of paper, then comparing that to the official version. Painstakingly rewriting the few he had forgot or miswrote. Then onto the vowels. Ah, eh, o, oo, eye, a, e. Then to the roots:

Shalom—whole, complete.
Shabbat—rest, cease from labor, desist.
Shomar—guard, keep, preserve.
Tene---give, permit, grant.
Baracu---bless.

Without a greeting an employee comes into the cage holding a watering can—steadily addressing the dog with a smile and friendly words, totally ignoring Transman—as if he were a ghost she could not see: "Hello Reverend! Have you been a good boy and eaten your

149

dinner?" She stooped in thru the metal bar door, pushing past the Red Man to pour a stream of fresh water into the dogs water bowl, then gave the Rev a pat on his black/white furry head, turned, exiting, without a word.

I can't fit in—even in a homeless animal shelter! —However, the animals did love and appreciate me! & isn't that the purpose of it all?

> All of my mitzovs are corrupted!
> Kicked out of my own group!
> Driven out of the Benedictines!
> Dismissed from the Lost Dog Shelter!

Critiques will say: that "uh, hum… couldn't you have worked it out…" But how? Work it out with no help? Did any one come forward—the leaders of the group to try to mediate this officially? No. And Transman was not going to go back & risk still another shouting match! Him versus the polite controllers--turned into a huge shouting match!

> Don't turn from Jesus, Jesus can get you thru the most narrow of places.

Buffeted & battered by a society growing increasingly affluent, cheap, mean & discriminatory. To add to his fast-growing list of exclusions, and being backstabbed, on this next particular day T is *racially profiled!*

Went to Walgreen's to pick up a medical prescription—have done this for the last several years to the tune of thousands of dollars into their pockets—paid by my medical insurance. Am re-packing my carrying case, sticking the medicine, plus umbrella into it, when I notice a middle age, ugly Philippina woman staring at me. I look down at the pack, finish buckling it, then rise up off my chair—she's still staring at me! I walk down the aisle, here comes the ugly Philippina in her tired Walgreen's uniform militantly following me and continuing to stare!

"WHAT THE HELL ARE YOU STARING AT? HAVE YOU GOT A PROBLEM?" Hollers the Transman at the ugly woman. He

150

continues: "I'M ASKING YOU WHAT ARE YOU STARING AT BECAUSE YOU'RE STARING AT ME AND I DON'T LIKE IT!"

"I can stare at anybody I want to!" Yells the malevolent Walgreen's employee, standing there militantly, defending her stupidity.

Rather then stay, yell, and escalate this level of violence, while a thin coat of civility still remains, Transman turns and stomps out of the store. Naturally the theft alarm doesn't ring—as he has not stolen anything, nor, seldom in his long life of poverty has he resorted to shoplifting.

Striding vehemently away from the store he contemplates how he will proceed with his complaint. Should he write a letter to the newspaper like he did about that long ago bad-behaving security cop at the GLBT Center—which the whole world read, and still does read upon occasion, as these things don't die, now that we have Instant Internet Search Engine Recall which scans the underseas memory bank of all the human information networks, pulling up to light whatever it connects with, in far-flung dimensions.

As fortune would have it later that day he happens to run into a Filipino friend, who just so happens to be one of 3 people he personally knows who works for the Walgreen's chain. "I have 3 friends who work for that lousy system!" Transman stands there swinging his cane irately and loudly explaining what happened.

Then the two spent 30-minutes on street hollering good-humouredly about it.

"They suspect anybody who carries a bag. They'll tell you, we catch 'dems 30% of the time—so that justifies it for them. But that means the other 70% of the time they are wrong! And look at what the poor customer has to go thru! I hate people like her." He says. "They come to this country and instead of trying to learn the new ways, they bring that old stuff with them from the Island, and they are stupid and embarrassing to all us Filipinos."

"She needs to get a grip."

Next day went in asked for the manager—an African American lady, we will call her 'Eloise'; a knowledgeable and kindly soul, sophisticated to the ways of human kind, --and it happens that she herself is totally disgusted with the employee, whom she has ongoing problems with. "I gotta good mind to write a letter to the editor of the newspaper and embarrass this whole place!" Transman was emphatic. "I wish you wouldn't." Responded the kind Eloise. She has her hands full with these retrograde employees. She reassured Transman she would look into the matter—a matter of which she was already well aware she said. Thus the incident was resolved by the two shaking hands, soul with soul.

Who is going to be first to challenge Walgreen's de facto policy with a class action suit? Sadly tho they are not the only game in town, they are so prolific and handy that people will go to them, even at this shoddy behavior.

> Age 64. By that time I had experienced cold depravation, loneliness, heartbreak. Now I was ready for success.
> ---Red Jordan Arobateau, January 1, 2008.

One thing is for sure—I don't fit in anywhere right now & under an increasingly totalitarian society--where everybody is clear channeled, clean cut, stamped out of a pattern, inquiring nothing, being fed lies out of every media orifice they use for entertainment, who are trained from birth to do their evil deeds in soft-spoken demeanor to arouse no suspicion, I stand out more! More like a Red Flaming toreador's cape dangled in front of an irate bull, or a big red sore thumb! Well… what happened to freedom?

Silent killer… The rich like a quiet falling layer of snow have begun to engulf all the City. Up and down the rising/falling hills of pretty little houses far to the limits of sight— there is few decrepit old tenements left, that of the poor. No more old junk cars, fewer & fewer people with worn out but decent clothing of the lower class. Increasingly everyone is upper middle and above. Still more and more $ money moves in! The white-collar class drove out the blue collar and retired folks; now those even richer then them—the upper class drive out the white-collar middle. When will it end? Until the full supply of the world's billionaires and multi-millionaires have arrived here from all points of the globe, displacing everyone else, squatting on San Francisco like it was their own personal island resort, fast become domain of the Ultra Rich? On the bus, one of his last journeys to the Lost Dog Shelter to visit the 3-legged pit bull, Transman encounters A., a woman from Grace Cathedral. They chit chat; she too comments that she has seen this specter which haunts our precarious lives:

> I been here since 1972, this city has changed—you know about it. Too much all the same. When everything is all the same, formalized, it will become easier to tell us how to act, what to think, how to be. What happened to freedom? I don't like it.

Furthermore, A. sheds some light on the social status of these idiots the Transman had recently been, unknowingly associating with—for just over 1 year and several months:

> My worst suspicions confirmed! It's not just Middle Class up here in the Fillmore district—its Upper Class! No wonder I can't stand them!

There is a slow takeover in America in her most desirable cities, not one person of less then a higher income can remain here. We poor, existing on Social Security, and little less, in rent-control buildings are destined to become relics of the past with a cruel future which onslaughts daily, eating away at our tiny securities. Even the professionals must via for jobs—as so many of them in identical fields wish to relocate here! One university degree is not enough, you need 5 degrees to command the position so cherished! Where as before, in the 1980's poor flunkies lined up around the block—some 200 of them to apply for openings in restaurant work, now 2,000 applicants, job resumes in hand are lined up around the walk eager for that supervisors chair, that consultants office, that professional degreed, licensed, posh titled position.

> I had to leave home so many times.
> --Red Jordan, 2008.

100.
Every religion has a service in which there is a ritual. Often repeated, words, songs, chants; format familiar to most congregants/devotees assembled, --which like a train carries them off on an interior journey.

The singing, the phrasing of Creator's praise on their lips; this all forces them to concentrate—more then they can in a normal every day setting; the focus switches from themselves, the I, to their relationship to the divine—in which immediately the individual grows smaller, and God much larger. It can bring inner peace. It can break thru grey depression. It can indicate new directions.

At the communion rail 2 large males in bluejeans, boots and shaved nearly bald heads, —a gay male couple; there are couples of 2 women (very rare), many hetero couples, and mostly singles. When 2 gay people are at the rail we're just seeing a different configuration of the couplings God, Hashem has given us.

Bible/Torah scholars agree –that humankinds negative view on homosexuality/transsexual; its due to a cultural taboo. It is rooted, long ago in a particular tradition of their clan; that is the primary influence; it is only after that, that people go into their torah and bibles to justify their stance—however there is so little in the holy books that might or might not deal with this condition. It might not speak of it at all! What remains in the light of this understanding is, that their stone, fixed viewpoints, prejudice, & ostracisms are based, fully, on ignorance. —However that doesn't excuse the bad behavior of some gays & transfolk

First of all gays/trans must obey same edicts as do anyone else; i.e. the Ten Commandments for Judeo-Christian; we are not exempt from them!

Here is another interesting observation about religious organizations. In Christianity---and I suppose many other religion—we are told that we are put on earth to do the natural things, while remaining in obedience to Gods Will according to the commandments. Now in addition, some of us are set slightly apart, it is we who are also called to do a work for God, of some specification, and this work is often more important then church attendance! For example, it is obvious God created me to be an artist, and that this job is very important to God's Plan and that I remain on my job is vital. —Just like any other one gifted in some field. (Paul: *stay where you were when you were called.*) For years of attendance first in MCC church, and later in

Grace Cathedral, there has been a hue and cry of clerics that we should take up some job or the other for the church—including to serve the poor at free handout day, as cook, food handler, usher, newsletter editor, etc. These are noble tasks, however not one of these churches in all these years has ever had the bright idea of empowering one of its congregants who is gifted by God and struggling with a work thru which they are suppose to bring fruit—to help them on their God-sent journey, for upliftance of their soul, as well as to encourage their art intellectually and materially; so that later they can employ these gifts within the congregation, for future enrichment of the church, and empowerment of that institution!

I have let many clerics down thru the years –them thinking I was going to be a supporter of their projects—Human Laborer For the Love of Christ. Many know of my gifts and my many, many long hard years of toil at it—yet none of them ever suggested the church somehow back me up in this, and likewise I could help the church in so doing! NEVER! It is much more difficult to write a full-length novel of merit, then to dish out food at a soup kitchen! Realistically speaking, many can do the latter, few the former.

Case in point, Transman dearly wanted to attend the Commanders Bible study tomorrow, Thursday at ten AM, because he got a lot of spiritual value out of it; however more pressing need is, that yes, at long last he'd begun to paint, once more, and felt that must not be delayed any further! The black clad figure squinted his face, peering into space, as he sat down in his chair that evening, beside the now fully loaded painting desk, and makeshift easel. It had suddenly dawned on him that he'd be setting the alarm for the next day—to go to the bible study, when he'd already preplanned to set it as to rise early and paint for his scheduled 3-hour period! And he couldn't do both at once! Walking the steep incline up the cold wind-swept hill, then back down--- would consume the entire block of time. While tradition, on the other hand, and all that people say -- *to do what is the right thing*—i.e., attend a bible study, ---The Master Work called him also—and more personally. And he knew he should opt for the higher decision---to proceed out on faith, and do the wild, incalculable thing, to paint!

And so he did, next morning saw him again, beside his easel, paintbrushes in hand. *Soon I shall be writing in my Journal (MERCY) today I finished the Potato Eaters—or some such.*

The master artist painted within a square floor area of 8'x 6'.

Jazz, traveling music, brush strokes of the master. I'm moving on— not enough space on this canvas! To much squeezed into this little one 22" x 30", arms, face, hands, thighs, a house, a pen, a bronze pot, the bigger canvas is what is called for! One had been assembled before—but dismantled & put away for the sake of limited space & tidiness. So the final act of painting that day was to go to the kitchen storage loft, take back down the politely dissembled, taped-together stretchers, lug down that heavy roll of canvas; set them on the floor, ready for re-assembly Saturday after Shabbat/Torah study.

Dawn. —Sun had just begin to Rose color the windowpanes at the side of a building next door; pink & bleu/grey. He awoke & wrote:

> Have reverence for all living things.
> Have no secrets.
> Trust in God(ess) the Divine.
> Leave the earth as you found it or better,
> not worse.

That evening on his way to the bookstore, he overheard this following comment so loaded with dire shades of his own disappointment in love:

> Well then, maybe you shouldn't be in a relationship."
> --Overheard SF woman to her boyfriend.

***

@ Babylon Falling. The old man sits drinking Cambodian coffee courtesy of Shaun (Roberts, photographer) from his recent visit overseas.

What I hold in my hands today is a Zippo cigarette lighter from Viet Nam. Khe Sanh, '67-'68. Bronze with American eagle, its wings-upraised, caring a rifle in its talons. —Owned, formerly by an American GI, a Soul Brother. It is inscribed:

Black is beauty
Think black
Act black
Live black
We shall overrun.

Red is reading about the set-up for Germany's show of the nihilistic theatre pre-1929, beginning back in the 1880's, with the emergence of fascist literature, & politics.

The Wimer Republic's constitution was as democratic as any nation of the 1920's. The nations capitol city Berlin was awash with homosexuality, artists, free thinkers, dancers, painters, —all the folks Transman truly loved, all the folks he *was!* However the nation was going broke. Inflation had risen to ultra-inflation, then, by 1924, hyperinflation, and quickly pushed beyond that, so Germany was teetering on financial collapse—and soon the screeching halt to all services; mass riots, the dissolution of infrastructures. Citizens were starving. People actually *did* have to carry wheelbarrows to pick up all the money of their paychecks---which in turn was barely sufficient to pay items as minor as gas and power bills.

I like sitting in this bookstore reading. One thing I like about these guys—you never ever hear them swapping facts about baseball/ basketball scores. —Ugh.

Later Transman told Sean how he was right about Fidel being a dictator—tho he had done a great revolutionary deed in defeating the exploitive plutocrats *30 years before!* But should have immediately set the nation up with the democratic process! And got off his royal throne long ago. And T. made reference to the fact that he personally knew one of the 'undesirables' who Fidel had sent over to America on the Mariel boat-lift. A transsexual woman—we will call her Clea. In the 1960's, this Boat Lift full of Cubans legally pushed off from the shores of Cuba to sail across the Gulf to America—Florida. It was supposedly a chance for all disgruntled Cuban citizens to escape communism and go to America—but instead Comrade Fidel stocked his 'freedom boat' with handpicked passengers, kicked all the criminals—including homos and trannys out of the island. (Don't forget homosexuality/ transsexualilty are criminal in Cuba.) So the American Public got an ugly surprise, instead of disgruntled doctors, lawyers, educators, came a boatload of criminals from petty crimes up to multiple murderers and serial killers; and of course those who ply the sex trade. My people lumped in along with this. --- Friend Dominique comments how none of the Communist country have any good track record for gays.

Sean recounts to a customer how he had just got his store, and one morning he came in and saw graffiti scrawled on his building—just a little bit: "My perspective had changed over night! It was OK to see graffiti on somebody else's building! —But not mine!" Somber the wise old Transman reflects from his corner in a pool of sunlight, how time, age, and experience, are the building blocks of wisdom. And how differently we view situations depending on from what side of the fence!

A momentary disappointment at the Ohio Caucus—when Hillary Clinton looses badly to the black male candidate; vieing for the presidential nomination. Must say Hillary was missing the mark when she proclaimed women were voting for her—I could have told her, women do not support other women—no matter how much some elements of that sex would like to believe otherwise. Oh well, time will see soon if this nation is ready to elect a black man, or a white woman—or neither!

Transman heard the wild wind whipping outside, humming against his building—of a growing storm. And could only hope whoever president would stand at the nations helm would bring a better life for him, Mr. Fluffy, his parrots Ariel & Bijou, all his green flourishing plants, his dear friend Jasmin, and whoever mate Hashem might one day grace to send to lay beside him in his bed.

101.
> Infancy is the process of forgetting everything useful you knew in paradise.
> --Words to The Prophet, Red Jordan.

  ***

Big storm. Obstacle course of broken tree branches across Fillmore Street; green foliage strewn gutters, fallen tree limbs lie downed on sidewalks bare white flesh now visible; naked, under their brown bark, stripped off in jagged rips.

He visited the Reverend, petted that familiar friendly huge black & white fur head, while his small rump and tiny tail wag vigorously; then made it to shul at 6pm.

Time when Transman was beginning to read Hebrew letters off the wall of the synagogue during service, intently—his mind drifting from the drash.

Church/Temple have such a gargantuan budget just for the upkeep of a physical structure, how can they in addition afford to help the people who congregate there? All that time & money repairing it constantly, patching up their Holy Sepulcher!

God's Mighty Bricks & Mortar Temple--- is a Temple whose day has come and gone. Once the patter of hundreds of tiny feet, children of thriving community—now, all of the congregation is over age 40— even the ones who are young, their old. A new fresh breath of life is needed @ Grace, the synagogue, and as well, new blood and a new style of institution to fuel it. Did Hashem once tell me—my Temple is a temple without walls?

102.

      Am beginning Sedna. And painting; 2 miracles! Breakthrus! Time is pressing!

      ***

Transman's goal was to attain the rank & title of 'Lamb" in Jesus Christ's flock. Which brought him relentlessly to God's many Houses.

A very ugly man disrupts the service @ Grace. But God has shown me he has been wronged. —And so Red himself also, tho this ugliness was not yet apparent, as Transman was quite a handsome chap for an old guy.

My house will be called a house of prayer for all people.

We should approach Jesus Christ with full confidence. It is a sin for our feet to be in the least bit hesitant or shy about approaching Christ! And I approached Him-Her about the following matters:

1. The unjust way in which my group was appropriated (stolen) from me.
2. That matter of the Benedictines.
3. The Homeless Dog Shelter's removal of myself
4. In my housing situation, a man crammed into a basement unit, who yells crazily at everyone, chain-smoking cigarettes, pollutes the air of our small studios above him.
5. My lack of success with my work—success so long denied!

I am holding my peace about these matters-- vengeance & retribution are God's domain! —Not peoples! God knows who the snakes are!

People did not like me because saw I was breaking the rules—and I must remind you, that it is the province of an outlaw, that they are rule-breakers. Society has outcasted them from their early beginnings, so, to survive both in their ego, and spirit—as well as in flesh, they have found they must weasel everything they need to survive out of an unforgiving, relentlessly heartless-- and stony society; for it is not freely given to them—ever. And to do this they must break rules! So which comes first? The law, which has no understanding, or the law-breaker by necessity! This outlaw behavior the 'good people' seem to tolerate in those they deem *far below themselves,* —morons, low IQ, or badly educated people, & those visibly handicapped. But upon seeing me, sensing I am in some way their equal—or their superior—both in learning, and in some other quality of the self-made person, by my achievements---they crack down on the same rules which they bend for others—their *inferiors.* This inequity of course is obvious to myself, and makes me additionally angry, and rebellious.

Guru means teacher. I hope you have learned something from this— MERCY!

God sees the least. For me to go to shul/church—I am going to the Highest.

Before Red began his regular Friday night shul service, he had been faithfully attending Native American services and gathered much information, all in the course of eating full repasts (they had potlucks) and being a social animal. Finding out in greater detail the grave injustice done to the Red People. This is parallel only to the abysmal enslavement of blacks—an involuntary labor force for 200 years in our nations Southern states. Whereas the one; black slaves, was held perpetually with no escape but death, in unpaid servitude, often whipped, tortured and worse; the other, the Native Indians were systematically removed from their lands; became victims of genocide via communicable diseases common among Europeans, which to which native peoples had no immunity—all compounded by starvation when their growing and hunting lands had been appropriated by white settlers; as well as by outright murder & mayhem at the hands of white soldiers and settlers. I repeat a grave injustice done! Evidence: when only one tenth of that Red native population now remains on the continent—where upwards of 100 million natives once were here—a much more dense population of Indians, then is commonly realized...

There are many of Gods creation crying out for justice!

Weavers. 18th century. Children as young as five, working. 16-hour days. Starvation, rags, no furniture but one or two 3-legged stools--- all the rest of the household chairs, tables, beds having been sold off for necessary money. Much of their work was unpaid labor in preparing piecework, for the rich industrialist. Unbearable conditions. Oatmeal & potatoes were their staples. No meat, but every several years. No aid in childbirth. No decent clothes, parents too embarrassed to send their children to Sunday school.
--From: E. P. Thompson's Making Of The English Working Class.

For the first half century of my writing life I was caught up in a fantasy-daydream, entertained when I felt most powerless, that I'd one day be successful and achieve a Nobel laureate; this kept me pumped up; working without critique, or notice, with few book reviews or editors—perhaps I have exaggerated my own self-worth out of proportion. The Lord(ess) shows me my great masterworks might only be seen by a very few people. But that those few are as important as if it was to shown to the whole world! So I must continue on---green wreath, of the laureate placed upon my head or not!

At the end of the laborious pageant of the week… He meets God face to face at synagogue… as the congregation begins their prayers on Friday Shabbat. Looking up at the great mahogany wall of Sheriff Israel—seeing, yet not seeing, but in fact *feeling* the presence of God there. His prayers, enlightenments and revelations continue the next morning, Saturday, at Torah study @ Sh'ar Zahav, and again God & he touch at that morning Shabbat thru revelations from Torah scrolls, these intimate messages to the human race authored by Hashem (God). Now, Sunday morning, the crown of the pageant, Transman walks into Grace—an even bigger edifice. Does God somehow seem bigger, the more vast the Holy Tabernacle? This mighty cathedral seems filled with Gods Spirit. Here comes bells, incense and Crucifix, Now Jesus enters, this further revelation of Gods Spirit to the mortal human race. What a complete week!

At Grace, the priest pays tribute to the Hebrew people, from where Christianity derives. A Jewish Mary, a Jewish Jesus! Let all who have ears hear!

When Mary got pregnant with Jesus—she kept herself. That was her Work. She did not go running out into the cold, jumping up and down over rocks in dangerous places; she nurtured the child within her, kept warm, healthy, ate properly; protected herself from the elements, kept herself clean; she was supported by Joseph and her own family. We are all entrusted with the care of that Work given to us. God gifts us with this Work, this gift—for better or for worse. It is a great trust on the Creators part, knowing that some will squander their gift, others will deny it, many more set it aside—until its no longer possible to achieve fruition of it. My own work, wither great or small—is art created by God---and I do the work of materializing it. Shape it, express it, craft it, sweat over it; strain to get it all right. All of us are suppose to do something with these gifts given by Creator. —To do so, life will be fulfilled. To not do so, will leave one empty, in doubt, and the nagging ghost of wonder, *what if? What if I had gone all the way!*

Two people sit beside each other in a pew. One studies the program for that days' service from front cover to back in the few preparatory moments as the rabbi/priests assemble by the bemah/alter; the other gazes into space meditatively, ignoring the program for now. For some must know what will happen next in their lives, --looking ahead when at all possible. Others prefer to set back and watch; to let it unfold, a mysterious drama, not knowing which songs will come, nor what prayers shall be chanted.

***

Here is a good reason to think of other humans as children because that's what we are—all of us. See them with gentle compassion & in this way many of us can have a greater understanding.

Again I say, Christ, keep me in your control. Keep me doing the things I must do. Keep me from those things I should not.

> In those days came John the Baptist, preaching in the wilderness of Judea, And saying, Repent ye, for the kingdom of heaven is at hand. --Mathew 3; 1-2

***

Stepped out into the cold winter night of San Francisco. It was a harsh, and cold city, a harsh and cold financial trap of a city—and he had so few friends; no lover, no family at all, yet he was elated—with energy! Coffee streaming thru his crippling body! And future dreams prompted him on!

Affluent shoppers along the street, cold winter in this ritzy Fillmore district. All white, and few others. All upperclass. The stars revolve in heaven behind a cloud of fog so they could not be seen; silver lightbulbs netted in the trees glistening in web of branches.

At the doorway of the pet shelter he furled his scarf around his neck with a flourish strutted out the door and went into the street, walking emphatically, his cane striking the concrete, with emphasis.

I walk out into the night. I am free!

Red Jordan Arobateau
January 8, 2008
 4:00 AM Pacific Standard Time
San Francisco, CA
USA

OBEDIENCE TO THE CALL OF ART/GOD

JOURNEY Vol. 8

2008

Very soon now I shall say; at last,
embarked on the life of an artist!
Hands on! To get dirty in the muck
& mire of color, smells, substance;
physical form!

103.
Notes: New Years day, January 1, 2008, put paintbrush to canvas.
Beginning the construction of a painting—don't know its title yet.
Here is a pen, a schoolhouse, a reflective face, hands, a garden; a
golden pot from which the pen is refreshed.

Each day for a week Red had been going thru the motions—setting up
treys of paint tubes, brushes, music to play while working, etc., then
the official date! Today is Tuesday, the 8$^{th.}$ Had painted on all of his
designated days –the weekdays only so far --and the system's bugs &
glitches in setting up/breaking down the painters space are ironed out.
Here is his format—(It takes ten minutes.):

1. Put on 'painting clothes' (old teeshirt, pants, shirt & shoes).
2. Be mindful of clock—1 hour to 3 hours for painting, before the
   remainder of the days' necessary routine must transpire.
3. Remove light tripod setup from corner.
4. Open up window, place fan for ventilation, then close curtain for
   privacy—all but for the birds portion so their beady eyes can gaze
   outside for entertainment and a bit of winter sun.
5. Switch on all 3-lights; aim two at easel.
6. Unfold TV-table to hold paint tube treys.
7. Turn cabinet sideways to better access easel.

8. Take out of cabinet the 3 open treys full of tubes of paint, divided by color, Red-Yellow/Green. Blue-Purple/Orange. White-Black, Payne's Grey, Browns; Umbers; Ochre's. Place them on table and a ledge, respectively.
9. Retrieve canvas currently being worked from kitchen & set it on homemade easel.
10. Wash dirty brushes & pallet knives, which have been bathing in turpentine solution overnight, & set in open cabinet drawer with other brushes, ready to go to work.
11. Switch on background music. (Jazz—Miles Davis Blue Moods courtesy of Sean.)
12. Remove lids & covers from pre-set pallet (the sheet of glass on top of cabinet) off of turp/ linseed oil tins, and squeezed out dabs of color.
13. Drink coffee! --While scooting chairs around to face canvas—one for self, and a second for cat who will inevitably sit in one intended for self.
14. Begin!

104.

Enter Babylon Falling, there, the young owner, surrounded by 8 large cardboard boxes of new books, packing paper, bubble wrap, & miscellany all over the floor, a miasma of colorful confusion. Sean mutters something about: *"goddamn books"* as he delves into the cartons, emerging with large handfuls, to stock his shelves. —A very humorous statement, being this *is* a bookstore! And it *is* the profession he has chosen! There are no customers this particular day—after Christmas/New Years consumer spending, plus its' raining outdoors. However, moments before T's arrival, Sean sold several Hemmingway's to The Hen.

Checking his e-mail on the computer there, which service the young proprietor has kindly allowed his friends, including the elderly artist, T discovers a notice of an emergency meeting to: PLAN ACTIONS TO DEFEND RENT CONTROL LAW! In reaction to the horrible new landlords bill up for vote on the June ballot —to overturn the rent control law. That law which protects Transman's studio apartment! Hence his survival in this city.

> "IF THIS LAW PASSES: it will mean hundreds of thousands of SF renters would loose their homes and the face of SF would be changed forever."

167

Today on the way here saw several very well dressed males, young, white; tall—over 6'6"-- impeccable expensive suits, ties, long formal overcoats—very chic—feet in costly dress shoes, one debarking from a cab with several pieces of expensive luggage, the other hosting a companion down the street. These terrifying young straight *riche* spell the death of us po' folks. More and more of them are to be seen—the upper class. For decades this has been a dressed-down city of daily workers, and, back in the original days before the hippy influx, just ordinary friendly folk.

This is what is meant by economic aggression; by selfish economic leverages set against those without capital (riches) unable to defend themselves. Transman discovers a gem among many upon a shelf: -- EP Thompson's ; Rise Of The English Working Class describes a time so poor, in 1700rds England, for a particular laboring group—the Weavers—whose lifestyle has devolved, due to the industrialization of their craft, by the overbosses who hire them. For the sake of Profit & Progress, humanity was forgotten. It speaks of:

> Children's burial clubs where each Sunday school pupil contributed 1. per week towards his own or a fellow pupils funeral. Where there was dissemination and serious discussion of a pamphlet (by Marcus) advocating infanticide.

Conditions had devolved so badly regarding the weavers, those cloth makers of that long ago century.

Mournfully, sad for the dead children of long-ago exploited England, Transman let the book fall out of his hands, and stared into space. He was only one small person, what could he do about this exploitation? He could pray—and promptly did so:

> Hashem is good. The kind/loving & understanding Mohammad. This is the winter of all living. Life here is growing more difficult. Increasingly the cold-blooded iron hearted rulers of San Francisco encroach upon all spaces of our habitat. I can pray—according to your Will only—for me to get a gainfully acquired down deposit for a condo—thru my efforts in art, and not by some horrible damage—and thus

drop an anchor here in this changing city, of my choice.
Security! Hashem! For my old age!

Hillary Clinton has taken New Hampshire! Wow! Our first woman
President? Transman Red had been going about the town declaring
that this election was so important to his survival—as things had got
so bad under the Republicans—them trying to change drastically
Social Security, which was his mainstay of income, 80% of it, that it
was vital to him and the poor everywhere that a Democrat must be
elected—more often they do justly for the people—and his first vote
would not be his heart's choice—for the first woman president, on
some kind of gamble, but for the BEST DEMOCRATIC
CANDIDATE ABLE TO WIN THE PRESIDENCY! He would
dearly love to believe a better president would somehow insure a safer
and happier future for his old age!

Leave Sean cussing mildly at his ownself books, which he has
ordered!
      --Fucken' books! Goddamn shit!

It has taken him all day to shelve these, and to remove non-sellers for
returns--$15,000 worth! Yes! Oh the sorrow of the distributor, and
later, the publishers, when they receive back these no-sellers!

Transman leaves to go about his rounds—grocery shopping with a
few crumpled dollars, which remain after payment of rent. From a
clear view @ the Supermarket parking lot the sun is a blazing hole of
light puncturing the grey sky; sun gold white-silver blurry blazing
blurred in the fog set down in the amphitheatre of heaven above the
planet where he stood now, marveling, on this cold winters day.

Well it remains, I don't know where to place myself on the spectrum
of art. Everyone wants to know where they belong. Is it possible to
'place' oneself on its ever-changing stream?

     Am I great, good, mediocre? What? At last! I have blasted open
     the long-closed door of a grey, dark, colorless world of form & lines
     of sentences; now it inches open; a blazing fire licks out; it rages
     beyond; a Technicolor world of colors, sea-green, red, yellow, blue,
     turquoise, violet; a paradise! All from a child's paint set!

169

--January 10, 2008.

Re: the new painting: needs perspective! To turn and twist that torso, in motion pointing backwards, indicating forewords! Need to shade the depth of the golden pot!

Next view of his life shifts to the inside of a metal cage. Scene from the Reverend's jail cell: a loud grumble builds; rumbles inside his thick neck, reverberates up from his huge chest; yells out of his pink tongue/toothy mouth fairly raising him by all 3 paws leaving the floor simultaneously for a split second! —**Grrrrrrrrrrrrr… Grrrrrrrrr… WOOF! WOOOF! WOOOOOOF!** Transman could not help but let his mind drift back to the details of this messy situation at the Lost Dog Shelter where he has been allowed to sit with one last inmate—the furry black & white Reverend—who is waiting for adoption, and then his time here will be done. ---How the argument arose had a great deal to do with the major disorganization here in the Shelter; with as many as 5 different people all giving orders—and each order varying from what their co-workers were saying! Wither right or wrong or a little of both, this most recent bout had added to his small list of *hell.*

　　　　5 failures in 3 years! I am doomed!

It has been foolish of me to try to live the life of a normal person. I am not a normal person. For most effectiveness as this odd creature God has constructed, I must simply do all the work cut out for my hands. Go to all the limits I can push! First, naturally, it is assumed I must try to be a good creature—and not evil—good! & from there on the sky's the limit!

One of the lessons I have learned & have to constantly be reminded of, from episode to episode in my long life, is, don't spread myself too thin. Don't do so many minor miscellaneous things that I no longer get a great concentration of energy in one spot needed to do a great work! So in a way the loss of my group, the church Order, and now the animal shelter—is only freeing up my time, for greater benefit!

Ever since the first amoeba put up its walls, saying: *this is myself!* So community says, this is ourself, against others; this is ourself to be contained from intrusion of the stranger, to be protected from the interloper with foreign ideas. To preserve self!

So, the Transman slowly changed his schedule-to fit in his painting. Those 3 places he'd no longer went actually had taken time away from the gift granted to him by Hashem—our Holy One. So tho he'd thought he was having fun at his group, and tho he'd learned religious instruction in the Order, and garnered the mitzvah of sitting with unwanted dogs (plus enjoyed petting their furry bodies) —he was now, most righteously beginning to chug along on the specific Path set out for him.

*

None so beautiful as these... black crows; raven blue/black circling in the grey white air between tenement buildings upon which a line of pigeons sits on cornice & ledges of brown/ grey stone to 6th story; the great winged blackblue ravens wing in circles; one spirals down the block then flies midway back, the other follows, then midway back but again circles deeper down into the next block and the other follows making concentric circles startling this mornings air. The line of pigeons seeing him, hesitant, watching to distance from the sidewalk now swoop down from the top of the 'mountain'—6th floor roof—as the poor old Transman gazes in raptures at the flight of ravens! This first bird, which flies down towards him now—its wingspread not as impressive; smaller, these pigeon—and he has no food! But wait! An old health food candy bar in his rolling luggage case! It crumbles hurriedly between fingers and feeds his flock! He then turns, mounts the steep hill towards the Senior Lunch at Grace.

*

Back in front of my easel! A turn of my head, glancing around at the walls, I take instructions from my other paintings of the past. A pink wash is the sky, a straight line—brown indicates a horizon. Thus the figure, centermost, is placed.

The painting can be titled Adore Vador. — (Those Who Came Before And Those Who Come After.) Different layers of meaning; for it also illustrates; and can be called, The Student. --- The face of the greater one who leads the way, and the others behind, following, studying; learning. Transman again approached his easel, brush in

171

hand; at its tip, red/orange/yellow umber paint mixed on pallet—an idea in mind. Volia! The separate pen & brush of an Artist—both drawing from the same gold pot!

105.

Notes: Wednesday AM January 16

Encounter an Asian trans sister while walking down Mason Street towards the subway train, which carries me to the East Bay:

Sister: Well how've you been?

Red: I been busy.

Sister (thoughtful, pondering): Its good to be busy.

A hug then we depart. Yes it is good to be busy. Such is the life of an artist. Work, work, work around the clock! Inspired!

Train breaks surface in the East Bay. Bleak grey Oak Town landscape. The coach rushes; overlooks a railroad yard and the small well-kept one and two story wood houses of West Oakland—in the process of renewal… and black removal… The white upper class man sets up the rules and the game. His rules & his game. & when others fail at it he puts them in jail. Never accounting for their rules or the games they have learned. Then when the whole world starts to disintegrate before his eyes he wonders why! Blacks all gone!

Train halts, momentarily after pulling out of the West Oakland station, before submerging underground again, into the tunnel under Oakland's downtown district. Sun blazing platinum silver wide casting beams which spread out on the horizon sideways. Blue/grey sky with a line of pink; a pink tinge along the low western horizon. To the East he saw a glimpse of a grey frieze of hotel; grey stone cornice and curlicue of exterior masonry of the upper floors (6th floor) where Jasmin moved them to save them—either callous, or desperate, knowing how Transman was fearful of heights! Then again, did she have some dark nefarious purpose to fling herself out of the window when the going got too rough?

172

As a train pulls out of the station, which retreats further and further away—so does the memory of that hotel—fade further in distance, memory, and place of his last warm loving relationship.

Headed towards the Bancroft Library. A genre of fish people debark train, flood up the escalator filling the trough temporarily with a jumble of humans of all colors, sizes, ages, races, and types; fish people swimming for their lives! Turning the treadmill of their smaller wheel which is interlaced with medium size wheels which, together, constitute one large wheel which fits in to something unnamable; grinding them all to death within its mechanism of an infinitely evil kapitalist factory.

Bancroft. Sold $430 worth of crap! --$300 for the infamous film of that lone staged reading of INHABITANTS OF A GHETTOIZED POPULATION. Jasmin finally rescued it from her video cam—a treasure! Not professionally made (sound too faint—camera focusing on empty corners where some action is supposed to transpire, but doesn't—laughing of Jasmin herself behind the camera audible on it, etc. Plus she ran out of tape after 2 hours so didn't capture the final moments!) A proper stage; a limited audience —of 4 or 5 amid seating for 90. Why? Because of no publicity! Shortchanged by the powers that be! (See PASSAGE 8!). Myself in black with hat in front row present throughout. This will pay the extra rent I never have, and maybe for something nice, but damnit, then am thinking that the infernal business address mailbox is coming due in this New Year for the annual fee.

My wish list & a song:

> Oh how I would love to walk down the avenue and spend my money! —
> On ribbed condoms!
> On Denatured Turpentine!
> On fine brushes!
> ---Especially a small short stiff one for detail in blue/brown line!
> Perhaps on food!

In my grandmother house was a figurine which always puzzled the Transchild; it was of 3 monkeys; one has its hands over its ears, the second, hands over his eyes, the third, hands over his mouth. The inscription on the 3-ape statue was: *Hear no evil, see no evil, speak no evil.* At age 7 or 8 he didn't entirely yet grasp the meaning. At the bookstore saw a Frank Kosik book which presents a poster on the backdrop of an American Flag, in which 3 skeleton heads declare: *I still see! I still speak! I still hear!* Today, while returning to San Francisco in the subway station a mentally ill young man twirls in circles. Dark glasses over his eyes, earphones over his ears, heavy jacket obscuring his body; he whirls & tugs luggage bag on wheels which contains all his worldly possessions, by the handle; hearing nothing, seeing nothing, silent; lost in his own private world.

Finally, debarking train, see a saw a young friend of mine, a singer-guitarist, we speak awhile. He talks about the songs: "I just do familiar ones that people recognize, I don't do my own stuff, not down here." As Transman exited the subway station the deep bass voice of Johnny Cash booms out of subway exit/entrance. Here is one artist who has not yet been silenced.

106.
Periodically thru his long battle for survival in the white winter of Kapitalism which has over run Amerikkka the old Transman had had to get up *early* in the AM to get to some slave job. It was the same wellspring of extraordinary energies he now employed to get to torah & Shabbat service on 9am Saturday, bible study at 10 am Thursdays, and Sunday Eucharist service at 11.

Transman slid on seat of his worn black pants into a vacant spot in one of the first pews. After climbing up hill, worn out. Well now am here! Waiting for Jesus to make His/Her; appearance. Visible light beams stream into the Southern stainglass windows down from heaven at a diagonal slant. All is holy.

>   Spirit moved over the water in creation.
>   Water.

A parade of small children, escorted by parents, file to the back of the gargantuan cathedral to encircle the font. Today is baptismal day, and it is filled with water. Mumbled instructions to the children are audible over the entire congregation thanks to this new perfected

$150,000-dollar sound system. The children clumsily repeat their baptism vows. *"Do you renounce all who rebel against God?"*

Clouds of incense; which are reminiscent of an explosion of war. Familiar voice of one of my favorite deacons: *Oh my there we go sweetie!* Whispered instructions of the priest: *Good Boy! Now, go on my other side! I'm right handed!* This sound system is excellent.... Too excellent. At last the invocation; *I baptize you. You are sealed and marked by Christ forever!*

*

Guess I got to tie this all together; COMPASSION, MERCY, and the births to follow, its labyrinth of days/memories as I write this votive to the muse; this flaming offering to God, itself set on the stage of my own ego.

PASSION is a nice title for another Journal Book. I believe this next 'rondo'—(5 books –as first described in PASSAGE), the completion of next 5 JOURNEY'S shall be called by the title of this one, OBEDIENCE TO THE CALL OF ART/GOD. It might prove de rigueur reading to art painters of the present & future age.

If I ever get a condo, then any Journey book reporting those particular times will be called A Room Of Ones Own, a tribute to Virginia Wolf; (More specifically, Red Jordan Arobateau's A ROOM OF ONE'S OWN; a la, Red Jordan Arobateau's, THE MAIDS, after Gene Genets play of the same name.)

Oh, must clarify this point (again) that I have interjected much of my poetry, imagery, and prophecies into this Journal, which are usually indicated by small case type and put in an indented format—sometimes using my name in accreditation after it, but more often, since this is *my* Journal—not putting my name after it; where as quotes from others have a name of course. But people are beginning to read these poetic utterances then look up from the book with a puzzled expression to ask me "did you write this?" Meaning the unacknowledged quote, which is mine!

Oh, did I mention? Am studying Hebrew. Know the entire aleph bet now (not cursive yet) and the vowels (dots!) and a handful of roots, and vocabulary.

*

The Lord(ess) Almighty Hashem created a wonderful world with everything we need in it, every animal friend, every plant and vegetable for food; climate, habitat, clear running streams for water, fruit falling abundantly off trees. And God created everything S/He wanted too—which was to give humans free will. To chose Her/Him or not. So, God also set down the tree, which bares the fruit of the knowledge of good and evil—and this was the fall of humankind. *Choose life! Choose life! I can not tell you this enough Dear Children!* Thus the old Transman wrote in his Journal. Maybe he was trying to convince himself...

So little to eat today, both from diet and the fact that his refrigerator is bare! White metal interior; spots of red sauce, stains, bread crumbs; there are empty saucers, a water jar... Then, a reprieve from poverty! Money! A secret stash found in checking account from an Internet sale he'd forgot to process! $38.43 extra dollars! Sausage, chicken, cabbage, beats; yams! All cooked up together in a big pot! He dined! His belly full there he lay in a quiet contentment & joyous peace of the fed. No wonder Transman cut such a Bella Figuea around town— eating was most important to him.

Note, shortly after he also earned a $10 food voucher at the new Trans Center, for an intake report:

> Cheap trick, $10! Last year it was $20! Whadda cheap fucken' po' spenden' John! In all my days I ain't seen sech! All because that hideous green toad squattin' in the White House, that slimy faux-elected pseudo president is cuttin' budgets to finance his illegal war waged upon the impoverished women, children, animals, and those men who are innocent, in the Middle East! —And I didn't vote for him!

Any queer in this city can have participated in dozens and dozens and dozens of surveys, reports, census, questioners etc. about their lives, sexual habits, economics, health, etc., and earn money for it!

176

Transman Red had done just that since his very first survey 'on homosexuality' ($75?) done in long-ago 1969.

*

Here are some interesting facts about the much-touted Industrial Revolution—which began in industry & manufacturing in England during the 1800rds. It is not spoken of—more being braggadocio about how it was such a 'great breakthroughs in manufacturing, & industry', and what is labeled 'human progress' or 'future-reaching', but the consequence of this industrialization to that class of what had formerly been small individual entrepreneurs; or cottage industries, was their devastating tailspin into poverty. Weavers of the 18rds were the largest single group of industrial workers in England. During the Industrial Revolution the average worker saw wealth rise in Britain—partly on the strength of her/his labor—while her/his own standard of living fell, drastically.

> The use of the potato did, in fact, enable the workers to survive on
> the lowest possible wage. It may be that in this way the potato
> prolonged and encouraged, for another hundred years, the
> impoverishment, and degradation of the English masses, but what
> was the alternative? Surely nothing but bloody revolution!
> Chorus:
> You tyrants of England, your race may soon be run.
> You may be brought into account for what you have done!
> --EP Thompson: RISE OF THE ENGLISH WORKING CLASS.

The subject of how callously the profit-driven businessperson treats other humans; gives T rise to personal reflection. At odd times, most thinking, compassionate persons muse over their state of being, and he was one of these. The Transman pondered: What will I say, when I look down the long ladder of my life… Looking back at it all, will I wish that I had more MERCY?

Well, am stuck in this building where my health and survival vie for supremacy. There is an unhealthy smoker ensconced in the basement. This mans particular poison seeps up thru the cracks in the walls from downstairs. And, inundates my kitchen with non-stop clouds of smoke. Hate this monster! As well as poison the air he yells at babies, birds, and everybody else! He makes life miserable upon occasion. The true revenge is, when one realizes that he is doing the

same thing to himself. An anti-life monster in the basement yet I
can't escape! Can't afford to leave this place—surrounded by ever
increasing condo conversions. Transman can't afford: down deposit,
nor moving fees to get another place—plus although he had been told
he had a perfect record with the management company, they also
informed him they didn't feel secure about letting him take apartment
just on the strength of his small pension alone, and that he needed a
co-signer. And, finally, as accustom to his neighborhood as he was,
with it's resources, including friendships, any move out of the city
would be devastating.

Have just heard from a trans sister in her building, that Rosa Salazar
is being condo-converted. All of them are—23 units. Ellis Acted
Out. This monstrous kapitalist konstuct in which we are struggling to
exist. What will I do when they come for me? Wheels of process
move slowly at first, in barely unperceivable increments, but then go
faster & faster—will soon overtake us!

Hence, the canary in the mines; Jews on the eve of the holocaust in
Germany. It is hard to make plans to escape when we're so poor.

Most certainly we should be in Hashem's hand, what place will
She/He lead us? May the Lord part the Red Seas of fate & give me a
condo/housing in SF!

Little & dark with thoughts, he hunched over table, brooding over so
many injustices, both those rained down upon his own person, and
that of the multitudes of others he'd heard about rained down on
others. He thinks: *'So many injustices...'*

Well for now, the only power I have against this fascist economic
machinery is to scream my head off on the printed page! To
assassinate character in literary construction! One should never,
never, never mess with a writer! Unlike an ordinary person without
this facility at their command, a person who vents their ire thru
scourging remarks, evil gossip, at most they only influence their
generation; but a writer leaves their evidence in print, which could
last 1,000 years. Even it if it's not out of malice, & even if it's
embarrassing to myself in the future—it's just what I *do*! Writing!
Like a rat must chew forever grinding its mandibles or the teeth grow

178

back into its head and kill its brain! I am not necessarily spewing out a projectile of hostile acid against them but just writing it all down… the ordinary course of events of a person's life. Art is recording this—some of us meticulously document whatever transpires in their daily life—how they see it in their eyes, with their unique interpretation.

*

Missed church this AM. Tired, and just at tail end of fighting off a cold, which thankfully haven't come down with. Must renew my soul. Maybe will read from my Jesus-Speaks-in the red-letter edition of the bible later today.

> A person dies from the interior
> little by little.
> Because of the shocks of living.
>
> Her substance, his fiber,
> taken away
> day by day, until
> there is nothing left inside
> to hold her here.
>
> The attendance of a religious temple fills back the cup
> that the drain of days has emptied away.

Often we are so disappointed with the holy place, but with what else do we replenish ourselves? We have to fill ourselves somehow. The human organism is fired from within, but obtained its original spark from a greater Source —God ignites them from outside the organism; we each feed off of an energy source & this is what going to a synagogue, church, or ashram, is all about. It is why so many go there so often—it couldn't be the community with it's inner circles, gossip tellers, stabbers-in-the-back; not the community whose embrace is weak & whose love seldom enters into its transactions. Whose handclasp slides away—it is God! God! And God's love and Gods embrace that is the reason we return again and again!

Most important thing is for us to do the work given us. There are always causes, which will come and try to superimpose themselves on our minds, it is of these enticing lures, bright ideas, fascinating, and

179

new (but often old, very old and seen long before) things of which an artist should beware. Beware of it tho it may be wrapped up in glittering gold.

Good News Sunday AM—a ring on the phone, a knock on the door, a supply of goods courtesy Dalora*, plentiful amount of *cat litter*! Sack full of tiny canned catfoods. A box of vitamin C sizzling powders pour moi; a jumbo 24-roll pack of toilet paper! Plus, a package of turkey. Today must procure vegetables—turnips, sweet potatoes, cabbage; beets if possible, and 4 sausages to pop into the cook pot— meat already provided! PS, Jasmin cautioned Transman: *"Red it would be better to bake the Turkey, not boil it."* (January 21, 2008)
*--Dalora: Morphing of Jasmin & her lover Laura's name. (This is *supposed* to be a secret.)

PM. Dined with Hugo at small Polk Street eatery. This kind friend bought me a new black shirt for my birthday, (which passed 2 months ago). Everyone is bringing me gifts! Ah the life of a hustler!

T. did not attend Grace that morning, because of fatigue. Praying about this matter in advance, he decided he might at least read from scripture later, as a replacement, and then seemed to feel the gentle presence of Jesus who 'spoke' to him: *I'll come to you.* So, Transman did not attend, as his usual habit, the Sunday 11 service, but had promised Jesus to pray—which he did, out of the Bible, at 3am late that night. Before this however, he had awoken out of a nap, after a successful & lusty masturbation), and was troubled by an unusually sharp pang of depression: *is it seeing Jasmin, then her leaving, driving away in their car—because she lives with someone else, not me? Is it my advancing age & illnesses? Is it 'that time of the month' (every two weeks)--that I'm low on testosterone? Due for my shot? Ah! It's because I didn't drink from the well of Christ this morning!*

His short 5-minute bible study fixed that good! Jesus had indeed come to him. Because the first scripture he turned to was Mathew where Mary Magdalene is in the garden to attend to the murdered Jesus' corpse—when suddenly he appears, gently reassuring her, that he is not dead, but alive again! Here is also a scripture Transman read, in addition to Mary Magdalene seeing the resurrected Christ at the gravesite, which may prove vital to you too Dear Children, during the coming storm:

> Put on the whole armor of God, that you may be able to stand against the tricks of the devil.
> For we wrestle not against flesh and blood, but against principalities, against powers, against the rulers of the darkness of this world, against spiritual wickedness in high places.
> So put on all the whole armor of God, that you may be able to withstand in the evil day, and having done all, to stand,
> stand therefore, having your loins wrapped about with truth, and having on the breastplate of righteousness;
> And your feet shod with the preparation of the gospel of peace;
> Above all, taking the shield of faith, wherewith you shall be able to stop all the fiery darts of the wicked.
> And take the helmet of salvation, and the sword of the Spirit, which is the word of God.
> --Ephesians 6:11-17

107.

The world is blind. It sits on a vast unrest. Rumbling beneath the surface, quaking under the soles of our feet. There is little security, and the only thing constant is change.

Spoke unceasingly about Negro Removal to others over the last several days—I use this old terminology for African Americans; for that's from the era when it began, with the exodus out of Fillmo' circa 1960's—'80's. Quote a kingly black man w/grey beard on bus who speaks in an Othello-like voice built for opera:

> 30,000 black people leaving The City from Hungers Point—and nobody says anything about it! Like it's not wrong!

And gossiping with friend J. over the phone, and with Hugo over coffee's about the ever-tighten net of plutocrats here holding The City like a purse with a closing neck. —Their own personal purse.

> Pol Poi's infamous 'depopulation' of Phonom Phen. Whole city blocks disappear in a matter of days, the populations loaded into trucks & forcibly relocated to new townships that the government has established on rice fields outside the major cities. Urban cities were replaced by projects like the new Rangoon golf courses aimed

181

at western tourists and Japanese businessmen. The generals moved a community that had been on the site for 40 years. Those who resisted were either arrested or forcibly removed to a settlement 15 miles away."
-- Planet Of Slums by Mike Davis 2006.

*

AM. Painted briefly. The 'Golden Pot' picture progresses.
Deepening violets, browns of background. Adding golden yellow to grass in forefront. Sean helped him download MERCY to the print-on-demand Lulu; and, noticing his misspelled name **attempted to change it to the correct spelling!!!!** Upon which mild holy hell broke forth from the old Transman who began ranting about:

> Freedom Of Speech! Censorship! You are violating your very code of ethics, which this bookstore is supposed to represent! Etc.

Needless to say, the manuscript remains misspelled!!!!!! —It better be! (Fixed it for this manuscript, but the five chapbooks which compose this remain in the original.) Well, got TRANNY BIKER from Lulu today to send to Amazon who sold a copy this month. With all this shifting around of books from hand to hand, there is precious little left for the author—after purchasing his/her own book from printer and paying TWO mailing fees, first to get the book, second to send the book where it is wanted. If I was hooked up with the Special $50 Link complete with ISBN, they would handle all this middleman step for me—but at such a cost that I'd be making LESS then when I process all the shit myself—however, it is utterly painless. Work free. Only tap a finger on computer to download sale profits into my bank account, to be withdrawn at a Coffee Shop, Yum Yum!

> Of course if the Transman ordered his books from the print-on-demand in **volume**, he would save tremendously. But, he could not afford the outlay of **capital** to do so—hundreds of dollars, when the landlord was gouging him, plus him having such a small pension! This was his dilemma. **Thus, he could never get ahead of the game.** So it is obvious that Kapitalism Sucks The Big One!

PS, read thru THE BIG CHANGE, which arrived with that latest mini-shipment. Damn fine book if I say so myself! Thought the old chap.

PM. Tranny Tuesday @ Tom Waddell Clinic. Horrible tests given, of which the needle prick for blood draw was the *least*. Yes, the infamous P Test! Which all Transmen should have regularly (except those who have had lower surgeries). After, Dr. Sam picked me up and we dined on Mediterranean food on Fillmo' street. Fun. Raconteuring. Gossip.

Wednesday night January 23
Painted this AM; vibrated the pastel wash colors of 'The Student' ('The Golden Pot'?) with deep purples, browns, blues & blue/Greens. Delineated a finger. Added yellow to the Sun!

Babylon Falling. Today had privilege of meeting Emory Douglass— illustrator of the long ago departed Black Panther Party newspaper. All shook hands, exchanged a few words, then must leave, duty calls. Later that evening, his rounds about the vicinity complete, the old Transman Red reappeared. He made himself unnoticeable; quiet, hunching back down into his coat, poured silently over a book—while Sean made a sale. Not wanting to scare off the buyers.

Sean is reading some book in the history department which speaks of castles, fortresses, cathedrals, pyramids, mighty edifices and says it is wrong for people to criticize them as status symbols of the rich—no these mighty architectures are a credit to the people who built them— the common people. And the Transman told the young proprietor how a portion of his daily Journal contains reflections on Grace Cathedral, a mighty edifice indeed.

Day is done. Am broke. Tomorrow is free food day Senior's @ Grace, thank God--and some kind of Trans Health Fair at the State Building Friday, free food advertised. Must save last 6 dollars for:

> Turpentine
> Batteries for sex toys
> Carfare in Oakland when go to pick up mail—might be checks just waiting!
> Food!

Tonight, going home with furrowed brows, Transman thinks; *'upperclass! That's all that lives around here now—outside of the homeless. The streets are spotless! Not a speck of castoff food to be seen'.*

Back at home. Noise, shouting, & confusion in the next door studio apartment. An uncertain future awaits this building, and this city. On his floor he sees a roll of bare white canvas waiting to be cut to size. All the tools are here. God thank you for giving me my dream.

> Monseigneur, one of the great lords in power at the Court, held his fortnightly reception in his grand hotel in Paris. Monsegneur was in his inner room, his sanctuary of sanctuaries, the Holiest of Holiest to the crowd of worshippers in the suit of rooms without. Monseigneur was about to take his chocolate. Monseigneur could swallow a great many things with ease, and was by some few sullen minds supposed to be rather rapidly swallowing France; but, his morning's chocolate could not so much as get into the throat of Monseigneur, without the aid of four strong men beside the Cook.
>
> Yes, it took four men, all four able with gorgeous decoration, and the Chief of them unable to exist with fewer than two gold watches in his pocket, emulative of the noble and chaste fashion set by Monseigneur, to conduct the happy chocolate to Monseigneurs's lips. One lackey carried the chocolate-pot into the sacred presence; a second, milled and frothed the chocolate with the little instrument he bore for that function; a third, presented the favorured napkin; a fourth (he of the two gold watches), poured the chocolate out. It was impossible for Monseigneur to dispense with one of these attendants on the chocolate and hold his high place under the admiring heavens. Deep would have been the blot upon his escutcheon if his chocolate had been ignobly waited on by only three men; he must have died of two.
> --Charles Dickens; A Tale Of Two Cities. 1848.

These fabulous, funny lines written by that nascent Socialist Charles Dickens uncannily herald our present age—in which the rich grow richer exponentially—the poor sinking backwards into an abject poverty not seen for generations. —An American serfdom, from far out in forsaken rural areas with overrun yards of rusty unworkable cars, to inner city slums, adrift with drug peddlers; no jobs nor education; no opportunity —but to serve as foot soldiers in the Amerikkkan Kapitalist war machine, the Military-Industrial Complex; both male and now female GI's; their red blood spilled out on foreign soil.

Does that writer of 2 centuries ago suggest our coming situation here? Where a fabulously wealthy tycoon controls unfathomable amounts of wealth—piles of it? With no heed to reality of what life truly means, or a heart for compassion, nor sensitivity for the needs of other humans? -- All the dead people on a plutocrat's plate.

Oh, on the news some asshole in France stole 2 million from a French Bank, which is now costing that nation 10 billion dollars—to bail themselves out of financial crisis! *Billions!*

> Red: The devil is good. Good at what he does. I hate him. I can't hate him enough.
>
> Holy Spirit: Keep working, no matter what, that is your victory. God honors a good fight.

Addendum; speaking of censorship here's a good one. Back at home, the laborious correction continues, page-by-page, night-by-night, little bit at a time. Censored version of LEADER OF THE PACK:

> After this came the checkpoint in which the biker was handed a trick towel and a sack of safesex stuff. Condoms for dildos; latex gloves, latex dams, lube. There, a second slave wiped off the boots of the bikers with a towel before she walked onto the lush carpet surrounding the pit. Later, when they reached their cubical, the slave would humble herself by removing her dike masters' boots-a sign of submission.

Uncensored version:

> After this came the checkpoint in which the biker was handed a trick towel and a sack of safesex stuff. Condoms for dildos **which might be inserted into the ass of a slave, then into her vagina, thus needing a fresh condom as a protection from bacteria, as well as using the dildo on different women.** Latex gloves **for penetration, including finger fucking & fisting.** Latex **dams for licking & sucking cunt. & sheets of saran wrap (a clear plastic wrap, cheap which unrolled off a tube0, for cunt on cunt screwing.** Lube. **Both non-oxidal 9 germicidal variety and plain.** There, **at the second checkpoint, another** slave wiped off the boots of the bikers with a towel before she walked onto the lush carpet surrounding the pit **filled with screaming, nude female flesh.** Later, when **the biker & her purchase** reached their cubical, the slave would humble herself by removing her dike master's boots-a sign of submission.

108.

Seniors @ Grace—a meatless lunch, how disappointing. Can't eat it, because it's rice—Europeans can stay skinny on it, and Asians, but not Colored people like me and Jasmin (and Laura who is white). Another complaint about the food fascists—one of the gals snatched the tablecloth out from under the very plate where this gentleman, a 45-year long membership congregant was dining, and while he turned to stare at her in amazement, the other had come up upon him from the other side and snatched the soupspoon out of his mouth! Irate gentleman, red-faced, lambastes the devilish duo @ men's room. I steal a bunch of yogurts, eggs, tangerines, tunafish, and bananas in addition to those given. Jasmin showed me a trick—rinse the salt out of the tunafish in a strainer—that helps—because of my high blood pressure.

Movie night at Senior's, Steve chose Amazing Grace— about Wilberforce of England. Scene where a horse is being whipped brings me to pray! Jasmin had already warned me not to walk out after seeing that—its' in the beginning—and glad she said not to. After the show, Steve leads group in discussion about the Christian Call to social action.

> I don't pray for myself, but for the animals.
> --Red

> The principals of Christianity lead to action, not just meditation
> --Wilberforce.

> Am I called to the pain of prophecy?
> --Ideas from a movie about Wilberforce

Wonder, is all this art of mine armament, -- tools of battle---for what I must say & do in the future? I sit reading Kemperers' War Year diaries (1933-1945) a German Jew in Nazi Germany—married to a Christian German woman, Kemperer survived. He'd kept a diary since age 17, and left with it from Dresden escaping Nazi Gestapo and from the Allied bombs fire raging, to tell his tale. Beginning 1933— daily encroachments of fascism—moving much more speedily, then one might have expected. There was no mystery to the Jews of Germany who saw their Civil Rights rapidly being stripped from them; its escalation on a daily basis.

Shaun R. —master photographer—sits with a glorious copy of Black Like Us; anthology containing Red Jordan Arobateau's piece Suzie-Q, --in the company of Langston Hughes, James Baldwin, et al., whose faces jump off its multicolor glossy cover for a split second of deje vu to stare out into Babylon Falling. While Sean Steward—proprietor—plays back an audio interview with Emory Douglas, from the Black Panther Party of the 1960's. (BPP) All this great stuff happening simultaneously. History!

They have made this tape in anticipation for the bookstores upcoming Black History month party February 8th, in which the artwork will be originals of the BPP newspaper illustrations Emory Douglas did—weekly for their revolutionary newspaper.

So revolution is in the air everywhere! On all fronts! Past, Present, Future.

Late that night, while entering into his Journal; the Transman reflected how the spiritual center of this day had come while leaning on the communion at the Seniors Chapel service 12 noon. When, just after received the host (while denying the blood---since its *alcohol!!!!*) -- he looked over at the communion dishes and chalices, and felt Jesus was telling him he was close to Him/Her—you're right up here next to me!

Friday night January 25
This happened once before. –Transman Red had reported in his diary only the day before—(Thursday), how the young men of Babylon Falling discussed the French Bank employee who had somehow swindled the French bank of 7 m*illion* dollars. He was now wandering around loose somewhere with practically none of the money himself, soon to be apprehended. This fiasco is costing the French Bank 10 billion dollars to bail themselves out of trouble, to make good the debts etc. A case of Grand Larceny, Mega-theft on thievery highest degree! Well, today, attempted to cash a 2-party check made out to me, and Jasmin, and our bank refused it. I'll recount what happened. –In a roundabout way.

Must go back to Oaktown to get mail from perpetual mailbox.

Now I see site of an old car lot on Broadway and Macarthur Blvd where the bus turns carrying us up Macarthur to Grand. A Mexican girl brightly inquires if she can walk to Highland Hospital from the busstop—she wants to become a volunteer there! So there's hope in the world!

The acres windswept of the now demolished car lot has also engulfed a few other tore-down businesses at its periphery. It is a huge property, having eaten some other stores farther up right up to the edge of the pet hospital at its west edge, where once Husky and Coriander (Jasmin's dog) were held in dog jail because our hotel wouldn't take them; and is being constructed into some gigantic construct of future totalitarianism thru whose rules, windings, incantations, we, the workers must try to figure out our path. It also borders at the north on a motel, the Capri where ho's dashed in and out its balconies, slanging loud voices like an aria from Carmen and dawdled in the streets hooking. Hos' with bejeweled silk rumps/tits hustling love; did all their efforts account for anything substantial? Did they build anything? Not even a house with their name on the deed. Maybe in the name of some pimp who sold them out. Not a property here—in increasingly white mans (and Asians) land, and no blax. They were outlaw workers—not even paying into the Social Security system to put up a tiny poverty future for themselves, like me, a minimum wage flunky for 37 years. See the blax neighborhoods, being tore up & raised down—poor peoples home snatched up by the city machinations under city hall dome, in eminent domain.

—In hindsight BPP—is society better or worse after them? Their images of art; strong words they used—now held up to scrutiny of our modern knowledge. Embarrassing? False? Too True? Inflammatory? Necessary? --For change to happen? Or a luxury the floundering blax community could not afford. Well the popularized revolution didn't exactly happen—not then. And my own work, how will it stand up to the future light?

Transman bailed out a handful of mail—from the son of the Chinese owner of the store, a pleasant enough youth who informed him the box was 2 months overdue—as he'd mixed up the yearly due date— and next time there would be a $10 charge. Cost $50 for 3-months which he was not prepared to pay. Scrapes his last pennies out of checking account. Will replenish it with the refund money. He headed home. Not a check nor correspondence about his books in the box.

Day gray. Sky meets sea—constant gray background—gray/white, limitless, fog, atmosphere—trucks, busses, cars, travel along at a low rate of speed over the Bay Bridge. Fog, grey white, surrounds; wind; nothing but the road ahead.

Now the stately gigantus sitting on the toe of SF loom into being—soaring, skyscrapers, tremendously tall—at rippling waters edge. Back on SF soil. Bridge span meets land @ the other end. Was actually a production, which got me moved in here—6 carloads of my crap, from 4 friends, numerous trips, and one rental truck. 7 friends evolved--& I don't want to move again! GASP! A chilling frightening worrying thought!

Idealistically, and somewhat piously, T was thinking this, as he headed towards the bank to cash the check:

> It's not enough to work for individual rights, we must work for human rights as well, I am convinced. And there is a place for moderate voices too, not just radical ones.

Little did he realize the minor skirmish he was soon to have! To put all his high-minded philosophies to the test!

Slight battle in bank—caught me unawares—them refusing to cash my check—with my & Jasmin's name on it together. She has an account with this bank also. Me raising voice, calling them 'clowns' berating them for pettiness, castigating them for being 'part of the system!' This has been my modus apparatus for a lifetime. Volatile, angry, lashing out at the affronts—the injustices-of the world. Coming across like a wild man—controllers of petty wealth, status seekers, lackeys of the System identified me with trouble—so they immediately turned their backs on me, gave me the cold shoulder; avoided me for ever after. It helped keep me pure. I never sold out because I never had any *offers*.

So today have witnessed the hideous face of the monstrous Korporate Kapitalism in which we live!

> Sean: —"the money flows out."

A worn out Transman recounted to the ear of Sean who wanted to know what he'd done that day:

> I missed two delicious free dinners having to deal with this bullshit. Two! I'm so sick of my own cooking and I don't have enough money for food! My schedule was all set up—a free dinner at 2, then oneg at services at Temple! I missed them both! Had to call Jasmin on the phone, she left work early to meet me at bank and fix this check business! Was out in the rain, taking busses back and forth everywhere! No money in my mailbox, only bullish—after 3 months---and a notice the mailbox fee was overdue! Shit! Missed the 2 o'clock free meal and was so whipped and exhausted, just didn't have energy to get to Temple, plus my shirt stinks from all this running around, I can't go in there stinken' that's an upscale Temple!

And there he sat hunched over, wet, dripping from rain on his ledge in the window of Babylon Falling.

> I could cry salty tears.
> Where have you been
> all these years?

Tonight we watched a video about the oppression by police CIA and FBI personal of the Black Panther Party. Interwoven in this film was the assassination of 4 great leaders—BANG! One after the other; the Kennedy's; John, & Bobby. Martin, and Malcolm. A connection is drawn between them all—an indictment of the superstructure, the rich; powers who rule Amerikkka like their own private estate, comparative to intrigue of Queens & Kings of medieval Europe.

Got home, and lay down for a cold winters nap.

Wind is whipping outside---suddenly a huge knock on a door fills the sanctity of the quiet hallway POLICE! OPEN THE DOOR! POLICE DEPARTMENT! OPEN THE DOOR! Laying in bed under the blue blanket with his fluffy cat under one arm, Transman gasps wide eyed—*it can't be my door they are knocking at! What have I done wrong? That incident at the bank?* Sitting bolt upright, listens some more as the pounding continues, then, leaping out of bed, on stocking feet he pads to the door and stands, listening. Sure enough the sanctity of his door is intact! The loud noises are coming from nearby.

LET'S BREAK DOWN THE DOOR!

Then comes a mighty **CRASH!**

PUT YOUR HANDS UP! PUT THOSE FUCKEN' HANDS UP!

Transman cracks open his door, sees 4 policemen charging into the apartment across the hall—5 feet from where he stands, guns drawn, then another pair of cops, one with his gun drawn then 2 more after that—a phalanx of eight or ten, a sea of blue uniforms go pouring thru the hole in the wall where the door was, into the apartment.

A trembling old Transman stands there with his furry cat; after seeing the films of police brutality and injustice against the long-ago Black Panthers he was very nervous! *Will they be coming for me next to drag me out in the hall in my pajamas?*

It was a domestic altercation—between the two gay men who shared the domicile. T was relived, but still upset. Having been out in the rain all the previous day doing battle with Kapitalism, he was more exhausted mentally, physically, & spiritually then he realized. He missed Temple the following morning too.

One last comment is this, referenced to the asshole who embezzled 7 million dollars from the French Bank. While an honest $89 of your own money is impossible to get. But those who know how can shake down the mighty for tremendous sums. Am glad I cussed out those flonkies at the first bank—PS, I said, as I ranted loudly under the florescent lights of the sacrosanct bank, while stuffing ID cards, proof of address, Jasmin's bank number, etc., back into my wallet: "you know some real thief will come in here and steal you blind, but an honest check like this one, $89 stinken' dollars, you give me a hard

191

time over it! Yer' flonkies for the system!" They are like the conductors of the Nazi years, the engineers of Germany who prided themselves on keeping the trains to Dachau running on schedule!

I said this was the second time something like this has happened when my tiny messed up financial record is juxtaposed in history by something much more awful and earth shaking—here is the first. It was pre-2001; you can look up the date in history files. I was trying desperately to move back to SF from Oakland after the departure of Jasmin, but was told by a particular rental agency that my bad credit reference was a problem! And that this was a shameful thing! — When I got home to my dismal, now-lonely hotel room, switching on the TV for companionship, —I saw the Enron banking CEO thief being led away to prison in handcuffs for his part in a billion dollar swindle—of the bank trusts of old pensioners, Social Security recipients and other small people who depended on those stocks from his corporation—Enron—for their future old age comfort. SHAME! SHAME! He has crushed hundreds of thousands of little human dreams! *Which of us is worse?*

Tuesday morning January 28
Here are some hot lines from Mathew 4, 16. I won't read them all, but this one in particular resonated inside my soul:

> The people which sat in darkness saw a great light; and to them which sat in the region and shadow of death light is sprung up.

Monday PM January 28
I continue to paint every day, (weekdays only). The set-up works fine. 5-minutes to set up, 5 to take down. Pull out treys of paints, move chairs around my small space, bring out the tripod light, set ventilation fan in window (despite bitter cold.) Wash brushes which have sat in turpentine all night. My current painting shall be called: The Student And His/Her Golden Pot.

Transman Red was one of the genre of artists who use inspiration to construct their painting. He did not draw out a sketch in advance. Nor did he have any idea in particular beforehand which he wished to express, but that it would be an *expression.* A twisting of passion from out of his soul, refined thru his mental facilities, combined with passions and energies from the region of his heart, all of it drawing

192

from that deeper mystery, the soul, and present it on canvas to awaken a like sensation within the viewer who may one day see his work!

Definitely abstract—but human. —Quite obvious a hand was a hand, a nose, eye, ear, arm, a foot upon occasion—quite plain to be seen in blues, yellows, reds, greens—very colorful! Bursting with pigment, many of them!

Sky lightened/darkened/lightened in his little garden windows, as the flaming golden orb passed behind clouds emitted a pale yellow steam of light, to reemerge full blast of bright golden silver warm sun. There were now 15 pots, most with a found plant in each; the garlic's had sprouted long vine-stems, which bent and snaked thru the foliage of the other plants. Two beady eyed parrots in their cage sat amidst this jungle.

Sat upon his toilet daydreaming technicolor fantasies. He thought about Sean's electrified toilet @ Babylon Falling, the toilet is not bolted to the tile floor, so it rocks back and forth at the slightest touch. Not that Transman ever dared sit on it—the owner has forbid anyone to take a shit there, only piss! So he pisses standing up, as he was able to do. Furthermore, one would naturally turn on the light switch, and thus was liable to be electrocuted because when it is raining, water leaked into the bathroom from the roof, directly thru the *light fixture* in the ceiling. There were pools of water forming on the floor---where some water missed the 3 buckets the young owner had stationed under the leaks. Sadly he pays, like many, an exorbitant rent for the store!

A lesson in Socialism 101:

> Transman has run out of solvent. Thus, a new can of turpentine is necessary for the artist to continue to paint. To mix pigments. To clean brushes—of their oily residue. The older gentleman hobbles into the Art supply store, filled with the usual affluent students; locating the aisle he speaks to a figure who he assumes to be an employee for she is bent there; industriously packing up a huge basket full of supplies; the kind young woman hands him a large can, when he asks the cost:

How big a can do you want?

It's not the size, it's the *price*. What's the cheapest one?

Well... here's a little one for $8.00, but you'll get a lot more for the next largest size, its only $11! But if you just need it for a one-time project at school, the small ones ok.

I'll take that small one please. Thankuw. OHHHH I thought you were an employee! Transman says. Amazed at all the supplies a single person is able to afford.

The small can of turpentine reads $7.99 on shelf of the art supply store. The large one is $10.99. An ***outlay of capital*** which registers in having twice as much turpentine—where as the price is not twice as great, only 1/3rd less. He is loosing money to buy the small can. Alas! Transman has only $11.00 left in the bank, and must buy sausages for dinner to go with those vegetables in his soup pot. He must have some kind of meat! He buys the small can. ***Having an ever-ready outlay of capital,*** is the difference between rich and poor!

109.
Wednesday AM January 30
The proprietor is gearing up for his Black History month show at Babylon Falling, of which the star attraction will be Emory Douglas, former illustrator for the revolutionary Black Panther Party newspaper.

> All I just want to have a simple life.
> --Sean Stewart

Not that hanging out with members of the former Black Panther Party is simple... All the next week, Sean is nervous—his computer goes down at 6pm exactly each evening. He thinks its the FBI or CIA hacking it.

He fears the FBI followed him over to Douglass's house and took photos of his license plate!

> Everything on this earth is crumbling. There* it is perfect.
> *Paradise, Heaven, Nirvana, etc.

Outside the store window comes a strange figure—with problems worse then ours. Ragged; strings/hems of his worn coat hanging down to brush the sidewalk, barefeet in sandals despite the ice cold rain, a madman walks the street doing penance for this biter earth. He, and he alone; a prayer without words; a prayer of breath pushed out with each step; locked up inside his brain. His face perpetually reflects the same expression, haggard, mournful, unseeing.

*

Sunday Church. He thought; *There is only God for our champion!* Transman sat in the first pew, fortuitously there was a spot left for him—just him and no more—for back at his studio he had tarried @ desk working JOURNEY (Vol. 8, Obedience To The Call Of Art/God). And now sat, rumpled, hair on end, beard scraggly, tie disturbed, waiting for a divine revelation—which always came. And here it came! He saw before him—7 feet distance over the cold grey granite floor-- the base of one of the mighty support columns which upholds the Cathedral—about 8 feet in diameter. It was grey. Slowly it morphed into a new state of being which reminded him of an elephant's foot. An 8-foot diameter elephant's foot, and the other similar support columns were Her other Feet. And he felt safe, guarded, there beside the great Elephant Feet of God Almighty, sensing God was standing right there over him—his protectoress; safe as a small elephant is beside its mighty Mother!

Ready to do battle—spiritual warfare—soldiers of the Army of Our Lord(ess) are assembled! The service begins! In perfect precision, 75 clerics stream down from the High Alter in contingent. Out of the North arm comes the choir, the 3rd contingent convening in the right arm of the nave is now set in motion, coordinated with the left arm moments later, so all three converge, one right after the other, synchronized, in a long magnificent river of acolytes, deacons, preachers, priests, bishops, choir members, dance masters, deans, ministers, prophetesses, and feeders of the poor—divided by 5 vergers—they stream down into the congregation blasting them with holy water, clouds of incense and magnificent prayer in song with great jubilation.

*

195

When I was young I formulated a lot of my thoughts about writing & painting, what it takes to manufacture expressions which should be found in a novel, in painting, how to go about it, etc. Age 15, 16, 17, 18, those beginning years; this in the middle of adolescent confusion, fighting for my mental stability—when now, at this much older age, the mental haze has all cleared up, and I see the simplicity of all of it. Back then; 50 years ago, I was fighting my way thru a maize.

Art is your friend, as has been said before. Humans have been given physical gifts—eating, sleep, sex—all of which can be done alone, if necessary, tho each is more fun with a companion. In addition to these, which all humans are given, the artist, s/he has the gift of art. The debater can go down to the tavern or bookstore and enjoy conversation. So can the artist. But if the debater goes to the tavern and there are none to debate, he is dissatisfied. While the artist, finding no one to debate with calmly pulls out a notepad and begins to use his gift---to write poetry, or to sketch pictures. It is an additional gift, along with the physical ones. Your art is your companion for a lifetime—even in the face of loss, when loved ones have to leave, when your community is shattered, when the dreams split apart—you still have the art, this gift to do, to be busy, to accompany you, it is a friend.

Wednesday morning January 30
You set up for the day. Lights set up shine on the easel; chairs pulled out, surrounding to sit in for perspective, and next to easel when working sitting down; paints set up, brushes washed. Then the canvas taken down from a shelf and placed on easel. You are ready to begin. You turn; across the studio The Work stares at you in the face. Somber thoughts crossed his mind.

This world increasingly encroaches on the average struggling citizen. A lot of little people in a lot of little departments, all demanding something from you... Will I survive the coming storm?

Babylon Falling. Night has fallen too. What amazes me about Klemperer's diary is how loyally German he was! Would not think of leaving his country, Germany. He actually disparaged Jews who left to Haifa (Israel.) He was first and foremost German! How that nation betrayed him and his German wife!

196

Klemperer's diary has many similarities to mine, here is one, *lists*:

> Events of the year:
> Eva's very poor state of health & mind.
> The desperate struggle of the house
> The disappearance of any possibility of publication
> The isolation.
> --I Will Bare Witness a diary of the Nazi years 1933-1941 by Victor Klemperer

Another interesting quote:
> Our 2 little tomcats are always a comfort and support for us. I ask myself a thousand times in all seriousness; what is the state of their immortal souls?

Ironic, for this is one thing I'm sure of—the eternal existence of our cats—they and other pets and animals go on, just like we do!

Sean "is doing a black history makeover" as he puts it, of his store. Rearranging the location of all his black books, from sitting on the shelves in relative obscurity, to bold, face up on the center table, and, in the front windows facing out into the street on display. These books are featured for 30 days of the black history month of February. Then they will be returned to their niche on the shelves.

Sean as usual curses his product—wearily--- as he has to fairly churn about, a human dynamo all day long arms & legs flying about the store taking books down off shelves, putting them on table, putting books already on table into a holding pile, rearranging the huge gaps left on shelves, replacing the books in holding pile into different spots where they belong, and thus having to rearrange each shelf.

I've seen dozen displays come and go. The banned book display. Now, this Black History display.

> Sean: Lousy books! I hate this shit! Hate it! (Racing back and forth with a stack of books under each arm.) Hate these fucken' books!
>
> Red: That's your livelihood! (Aside) And he makes this statement! (Red found it very humorous indeed!)

197

Sean: Certain things I don't like about this business! (pant, pant, running around after more books) I'm sick of this shit! Too many books!

Red: It's your business! You don't hear a dentist say too many teeth!

Sean: I bet they say it all the time!

Red: Yeah, maybe huh… They go home and dream about friggen' teeth!

Sean: This is such a fucken' pain in the *ass!* Such a fucken' *headache* to me man!

Meanwhile the old guy had limped over to the uncomfortable computer chair to search the net. Red saw his book Lamentations In the Cool Of the Evening listed under Christian Books & Music web page for sale. He imagined inside his fantastic brain, and then spoke aloud:

Red: I can just see a tour bus full of Christian Bible College students pull up outside Babylon Falling---a tourist bus…

Sean: —On pilgrimage, to Babylon Falling. "Where Brother Arobateau got his inspiration!"

Red: Then they'll see what's actually in the store—Oh No! Anarchism! Socialism! Atheism! Emma Goldman! Arrrruggh! Then they'll have a Christian prayer service in front of your store— right out on the sidewalk there, in front to pray for the soul of Brother Arobateau—on his way to hell!

Interesting—all these little nuances one picks up from reading a personal diary. –Hitler was completely against university and scholarship:

They don't want anyone to study: intellect, scholarship are the enemies.
--Victor Klempterer

It is a commentary about this book—that its every day's annotations about the abject state of existence in Nazi Germany collaborates in

198

odd ways what I'd heard from other Germans who lived thru the war years. It's deju vu to read them again formally in his diary, --what I already knew from off hand remarks from others. Here's one; the 'Up In Heaven (after its all over) jokes. From Klemperer:

> Up in Heaven what does Hitler say to Moses? "Ache Herr Moses, I bet you set that bush on fire yourself!"

Here's a joke the Old German woman, Frau Reiger from my story MEIN THEORY told me:

> Up In Heaven people noticed how Gott never got up off His/Her throne, so one day, somebody asked; Gott, why don't you ever get up off your throne? And Gott replies, "Because Hitler might try to sit in it."
> (Referenced in Meine Theory; STORIES FROM THE DANCE OF LIFE Vol. 1).

110.
My life... where is it going?
That pregnant pause—before the curtain goes up. The anticipation, jittering in their seats, the audience, transpires before the show...

Have I exaggerated my self-worth? Living in his dusty studio--- particles of dust flickered on the light shafts thru the windows.

Day. ---Sun sailed in the sky. The sun blazed brilliantly into Transman Red's studio; a deep yellow flood—yet in less then 2 hours it passed permanently for that day behind a building; there its direct light ceased, & only a dull grey partial light shone.

My shrink but not my friends is nudging me towards idea of government housing for which me, a senior and disabled am qualified ---only problem, many don't allow pets, most allow just one 'service animal' they have a 2 pet limit. Well Hashem has bestowed me with 2 parrots—long-living beasts that fly on wings—and always a cat, plus one day would like a second cat, and/or a dog. All of them old, and not needing much space to run around. That would be my natural pet-limit in a small apartment like this.

Such a miserable life. Man in basement non-stop smoking when he is home (about 4 in afternoon to 12 night or so when he goes to sleep.) Somehow this smoke is finding its way into my kitchen! Spent 2 hours today—sick with another cold in part from having to blow gales of cold air into my studio to cleanse it from his poisonness cigarette smoke—taping a canvas up to window to see if that would block out the horrible smoke. Devised a curtain across doorway to kitchen several days past, thankfully it cuts off smoke from the rest of the house! I can't use the kitchen until he stops smoking? And I pay $1,000 for this shit? Talked to the property manager once before, she never got back to me. Am writing down her number to try again. I can't move because of reasons already mentioned in this diary—can't qualify without a co-signer and Jasmin isn't happy about being on this lease as it is! Don't earn enough money to qualify on my own. I'd love to think of this place as my little home—my palace--- he's polluting it, and the man is garbage, sheer shit. Yells at other tenants, repeatedly calling various building inspectors to come out and cite this building for various violations—which means we all now have to take our garbage down to the basement, instead of using the very convenient garbage chute! All because his call to a building inspector resulted in a violation—and all the chutes on every floor were closed. How about the tenants who live on the 5h floor? They got to walk their garbage down the stairs, or take the untrusty elevator! This creep is a winner! The real winner of the fools and atrocity awards are the greedy landlord/property management co., who decided to gouge a little extra profit out of this place—and opened up the lousy basement unit to begin with—about 3 years ago. Then the creep moved in—because of its cheep rent. They got their money s worth allright—all these fines and violations the creep has caused them! Tens of thousands of dollars! All to gouge a little $600 extra dollars a month out of this crummy place! Serves them right!

More and more crowding into this apartment building, into this city. We are like rats crawling over each other.

> ...because the majority of the people are so thick-skinned are not really touched by the disgrace of the spirit.
> --Victor Klemeperer.

Reverend Love Joy destroys his plush toys daily! Chews them to bits! Two per day. As many as are given to him. He does this to keep himself from going stir-crazy.

Sean @ Bookstore shows Red an article about a test done of rats confined in a too-small space, how they fall upon each other in new ingenious dominance games, hoarding; tailbiting…   things ordinarily below the dignity of a rat!

So there you have it; overcrowding, humans forced into situations seeming in which they have less & less control. The hate. The hatred we have for each other! Those too close! Tail biting like rats in a laboratory test.

The hate! The hate! That is the worst of it! These daily infringements upon the human spirit push it up the only avenue apparent—to turn upon the others with rage---visceral, apparent, fist shaking, or silently, in secret, harboring, black and brooding forever. The hate!

Sunday AM February 3

> I'm busy in heaven.
> Making things whole.
> Making people well.
> Healing hate.
> --Jesus Christ

Hate, overcrowding—and strange—loneliness! How can it be? All us humans crowded together, yet we are alone?

Thought of the song, Eleanor Rigby, that old lady who when she died, nobody came to her funeral; and that Priest, Father Mackenzie darning his own holy poor sox in the night…. *'All the lonely people where do they all come from? All the lonely people, where do they all belong?'* When it came out it was a drug song---to me in my drug years; alcoholic years; my teens, a young adult pre-20's, describing the loneliness I felt inside. The Beatles were hardy guys, each from a family to back them up, untouched, not that I know of, by the mental illness which destroyed my own childhood family. I wonder at the observations behind the song---it was apropos. Did Paul McCartney

201

(the writer?) see these 'lonely people', maybe their obituaries in the London News? Did he stumble across them—then frame them in a song, as one does portraiture in color? Or did he plumb the depth of the same pain as theirs within his own soul? None of us want to die like Eleanor Rigby, an old woman who no one remembers or cares enough to attend her funeral; nor to live like Father Mackenzie, with holes in his sox, commanding a drafty old church; alone at his station on the battlefield of Our Lord(ess). Well these sad two, connected by a Priests duty to his flock—and by a lonely woman loyally attending church until her last dying days---in a sad spinster/bachelor marriage of sorts, commentary on the destruction of family in this modern age, the isolation of people living so close to each other, yet eternally separated—our Savior comes to me with this:

> My compassion is great—it extends to all people.
> --Jesus Christ to the Prophet, Red.

Yes, Our Savior comes, even to Eleanor Rigby's of the world.

Synagogue, at oneg, sharing the table with me, Yetta, a very old woman from St. Peters. Says the name of her birth city in low voice. She is Russian. From St. Petersburg—St. Peters--- she calls it. Now a city by a different name, it has gone thru quick evolutions, flipped on and off repeatedly in fast-forward time—Originally St. Petersburg, then the Soviet's re-named it something else---- and now its that once again. Is she lonely? Yes, or she would not say so often how she loves that faroff place, that long ago wonderland, better then San Francisco where she's lived now 20 years—with family. Then my friend J turns up—she was upset by the drash Rabbi L. gave (it was a good one) involving loyalty/love between siblings—of course I transposed that to make it 'between friends' having no family of my own. And thought again about the long dead groups and venues in which I have put forth my free volunteer labor, only to be disappointed. Like Essau and Jacob, Cane and Able, Joseph in the Coat-Of-Many-Colors, & his brothers, I cannot get along.

I don't know if families and loved ones, and companionship is fiction—and only the love of God is real.

202

Note: one week later Transman discovered the smoke-leak, broken plaster and gaping holes around the water pipes & drain under the kitchen sink; whose opening lead directly into the basement which the anti-social smoker fills nightly with noxious fumes. Simple duct tape repair, the air is now clear!

111.
The next book of JOURNEY my long-extended Journal is to be THE PASSION OF ART, and the last book in the rondo (I.E., rondo: groups of five as laid out in the predeceasing Journal PASSAGE) will be JOY/SIMCA. (Simca, is joy in the Hebrew.)

Talked to Grey today about art supplies and toxicity. Grey just started working in an art supply store several weeks back. He says there's a hella-sale going on, on turp 75% discount. "Did you hear about the artist who got sick using that turpenoid—its toxic man, its as bad as turpentine! ---He had to have a blood transfusion!" This young curly head man leans against the doorpost, and says, philosophically, "It's a shame the art we do is killing us." We discuss Aqua-oil-- a new product (out about 10 years) which is the same as oil colors but with a water base; supposedly acts the same, works the same, texture, results etc., Red asks him about the toxicity of acrylics—are they worse then the aqua oil? Grey isn't sure. Must research this. The next big money I get will start switching over to some less toxic media. I continue to paint.

Each canvas should tell a story.

Sunday AM February 3
Transman sat at his desk; one bird upon each shoulder; Bijou the white female Cockatoo on her side—his left-- and Ariel, the smaller green male Conure on the right, in his accustomed perch. He was taking a break from studiously compiling his Journal for the evening, adding the days snippets, & continuing to enter LEADER OF THE PACK into its edited, final form; having just completed an anal fisting scene between two lesbians on stage of the Outlaws Club at one of their wild, raunchy social events. —A study in female empowerment and group bonding, which in real life is sorely missing. To take a break he turned away from the luminescent computer screen and had picked up a daily newspaper—it was a mistake. News of normal people, chiefly bio straight men. He soon threw it down in disgust.

203

'It's not my world! It just makes me mad! I should have known better! He never should have picked up that paper! And much preferred his own small queer slice of life, and his new counter-culture friends at the bookstore. The next page of the newspaper proved more fortuitous—showing a map of northern California. The landmass and sea, which belongs to all, not just some privileged white (and increasingly Asian) boys club. He looked over the green, brown and blue map full of jagged lines contrasted by straight ones—the delineations of Gods rivers, and shore lines, and those of man mapped out on an architects blueprint. His eyes traveled to the smallest furthest part of the map—right on the Pacific Ocean, San Francisco beside its narrow sliver of water, the bay. So, by bus & train he had come in to the city, with 2 suitcases and a guitar in a brown cloth carrying case; after traveling across half the continent, from Chicago thru so many states, past so many marks on a map, so many lines, and mileages and altitudes, temperatures, gulf streams, weather, charts, rivers, small lakes... *I was so afraid.* He thought. *But I came. I was afraid! Can you believe it? I came here, and here I am.*

Ve ahav ta Adonai.
You shall love God.

This great book is entitled JOURNEY. I'm on my way. On The Road by Jack Kerouak. La Strada. Don Quixote on his pilgrimage of Christendom.
---INFINITE LOVE, 2007

> You see… that all the stuff of the past laments; injustices done to you, injustices we have done, stuff hard to get past, you will not have to go over it diary page by diary page repenting each last detail to God, each mistake—God is ready for you to move on! To take a giant leap forward—you see! Already you see The Road, & in your heart of hearts you sense The Path, all your fragments of Teachings connect, you see…. Open your eyes!
>
> *
>
> Sunlit. The tired, hot, sunbaked road.
> I feel I'm harnessed into The Path. Locked into the universal turning wheels of The Way.
>
> *
>
> Monday AM February 4

Sean says, he's living now with one foot housed, the other in the road. He lives precariously, one rent in front of displacement—like me, like so many of us. My disability check and Social Security checks arrive on the 1st and 3rd of the month; must have the additional $126 in the bank which it don't cover, then go to the property management company with a complete rent by the 5th. That's 2 days leeway. If for any reason any of these 3 sums of money aren't deposited into my account by the 5th then begins the long slide down into the road. The road awaits us all…

Let there be no doubt the hatred I have for the capitalistic system— their cheapness in dealing with people--- for profit. Every last petty thing, they try to gain advantage. From the low watt lightbulbs installed in your rental unit—in hopes you'll use less energy, hence greater savings to them—to the lack of plaster to patch up holes under my sink, causing me 2 weeks of agony in a smoke-filled apartment; the little petty ways in which their business practices twist a human soul.

Monday PM.
Oh well, another fiasco—no more for me @ Faithful Fools; one brouhaha too many with some of the less-together mental/drug addict people who attend the place, who apparently are these noble Sisters 'Work'. I will not dis Kay & Carmen at all because they have great love, are devoted human beings in the Service of the Most High, and are fine human beings. However, one less resource pour moi! The Red Jordan Arobateau machine chugs onwards nonetheless!

PS, also lost semi-friend J., because of this mess!

Have I a big huge placement in this world? Big as a Walt Whitman, a TS Eliot, an Ayn Rand? Or a little place-like Joe Somebody Or Another Few Have Heard About? It would be nice to know! I stand before the Lord(ess) High Creator and Tell Her/Him now---that I will be happy wherever upon the scale that place of mine truly rests! I will be happy with it, not resentful it is not greater, and not fearful of how grand it might be. Until then I continue to work! Work towards the day of our Great Salvation!

There is a vague type or category into which special persons fall—persons such as myself, whose problems although great, can comport themselves within a 'normal' society—offending no innocents in their wake and doing a tremendous amount of good works themselves---while operating on little resources. We of this type don't get the benefit of the bestowers of goods & resources because we don't seem challenged enough, sick or sorry or fallen low enough, yet we labor under many of the same sad circumstances. I think this is the root of some of the conflict between me and institutions who serve the poor, like those mentioned above.

Well anyway... Our standard of living is way beyond finest of the queens and kings of medieval Europe. Longevity, education, hygiene; ease of travel & global communication. I will do the best I can with my ability in accordance with my situation—as has been the plan since my teenage years.

So; the flipping over of calendar pages, *Tishrei, Cheshvan, Kislev, Tevet. Shevat, Adar...Sukkot, Rosh Chodesh, Chanukah, Christmas, Palm Sunday; Easter...* Sitting in church learning over and over the same assortments of bible/torah studies revolving through the ecumenical calendar, the same storytelling's, stumbling around and around over them like a child learning its alphabets.

Listening to priests & rabbis tell stories of faith again & again, year upon year, decade upon decade, through a lifetime. Our Lord hearing our prayers, and answering them. This is why I envisioned DOC.

A Dragon! It's Chinese New Years! An exuberant Dragon roars down the center aisle. Dancing and drumming accompany. Flailing and churning the ferocious dragon attains center stage, turns and bows before the alter! The dragon dips and bows and dances off down the aisles! That's what I meant when I said, 'Even the Dragons praise God!'

Transman took communion then made a short trip across the plaza to restroom while the remaining rows of congregants filed up to the rail, knelt, and drank from the golden chalice; and in the windswept cold winter plaza which is surrounded on 3 sides by three story ivy covered monastic walls, the looming Mothership of the Cathedral herself being the 3rd; he envisioned future compounds of DOC! A humane habitat full of food, friendships, and praise of God with service to God within the community at large to include all souls, and thought, *'we will celebrate regular festivals!'*

Well, on the subject of faith and belief in God---an invisible God, not human-- and this combined with the subject of church divided from state, here is the following, from Victor Klemperer. (Oh, the Catholics had trouble with this one):

> On Wednesday November 14, (1934) the swearing of the oath. "Loyalty to the Fuehrer and Chancellor of the Third Reich Adolph Hitler. About 100 people in the 2nd group. I was 'not present' at the first oath taken during the holidays in the hope of perhaps avoiding it altogether. It was not to be. The ceremony was held cold, formal as possible. Lasted less then two minutes. We spoke the words in chorus after the Rector, who had first of all reeled off; "you swear eternal loyalty; I am duty-bound to draw your attention to the sanctity of this oath"; and afterwards; "you must put your signatures to the oath on a printed form" and concluded with triple Sieg Heil. ---VK. I Will Bare Witness.

Let all free spirits hear! Let all those artists, thinkers, sex deviants from the norm, worshipers of God -- not Man, pay attention to what fascism means; beneath all the stunning formations of parade uniforms, the infectious drum rolls, the pomp and pride, the adrenalin rush which inflates the mind—it means bowing low to kiss the steel toe boot of the strongest man. You must beware of entrapments, Dear Children, and weary of political doctrines, which lead to death!

The painting continues. When The Student And The Golden Pot is done, I will switch from oils to either acrylic or aqua-oil; which is water-based and supposedly not as toxic. Will keep all the oil tubes, and the newly purchased can of turp; maybe switch back to painting in oil from time to time—until all the pigment is gone. Plan never to purchase any more oil colors, just use up what I've got. The roll of canvas, and the lousy brushes will suffice for the future—all I need is the new, less toxic medium. Waiting for Bancroft money!

112.
AM Wednesday Morning February 6th.

@ Babylon Falling, Red saw Mister Oto, lets call him this, for anonymity purpose. Mr. Oto, the industrious photographer. The perfectionist photographer. Red observed: He is touched and cursed by art. Art is a fascist master. It is not good or evil; it is great. It is genius, it can be used for good, for evil, or be of a neutral declaration—but it is powerful no matter what. Asserting itself into the conscious of the viewer, just as it has asserted itself in the life of artist themselves—who must bow, obey, follow the muse—because ultimately art is a gift from God.

As far as this particular photographer, he will continue with his craft, his love; and hopefully will not sell out to money, at which point art becomes corrupted because of the influences of others, to whom the artist must pay heed—as they are in their pay. Hope he will not become a twisted soul, rejected by women, bad childhood or something of that kind—which is my story, too.

And on the subject of injuries in the past—mental damage, etc; the shit by my mother, Jasmin leaving me, my dad dying… So all this horrible thing that happened, it's up there killing me in my mind, until it passes away, become a thing remembered on occasion, but anesthetized from that murderous pain by distance and time.

The Internet-ready edition of LEADER proceeds:

> And Cookie, well that's a joke. She tells me she loves me, & then I catch her with Lou, whispering the same thing. I think her mind is so burnt out from liquor she can't remember who she loves from day to day.' The hotel room was small. Walls covered with gay paintings of sunburst color. The dike wore her best black pants, blackshirt & a buckskin jacket with fringe on the sleeves, & black boots. A scent of men's aftershave. She winced to see herself in the mirror, all dressed up with nowhere to go.
> And Cookie, well that's a joke. She tells me she loves me, & then I catch her with Lou, whispering the same thing. I think her mind is so burnt out from liquor **& pills** she can't remember who she loves from day to day.' The hotel room was small. **A few strides in any direction met with a wall. Covered with gay paintings of sunburst color that few other human eyes had seen, and for which few had given her credit… The little dike was confused. Night after night two years she'd made a beeline for Oils. Biker events had been her destination. Suddenly she saw how dependant on them she was. —Literally didn't know where else to go for fun that evening.** She wore her best black pants, blackshirt, & a buckskin jacket with fringe on the sleeves, & black boots. A scent of

men's aftershave. Now in the mirror **against a drab wall** she winced to
see herself all dressed up with nowhere to go.

Furthermore:

> Many gay people are separated from their families due to the problem of
> their homosexuality.
> Many gay people are separated from their families due to the **problems
> their homosexuality causes.**

    *

I believe that God has—in soul/spirit, as Her human construction
created each of us into physical being thru the high placement and
office of women (who are usually more spiritually advanced), to
become living human beings on earth—and those of us who are given
a gift or a Work cut out for them by the Creators plan on earth—a
Work as great as the following of the Ten Commandments and living
a halectic life—then this gift is paramount, and if a person in the
course of their days, busily engaged in their particular gift-doing their
Work finds some other pursuits aren't so successful, they must keep
in mind the Divine Purpose, and realize the Divine Overview, and
realize the Supreme Intent—which is that their Work become
manifest thru them is being fulfilled, wither or not they are
completely happy with their life—wither or not they have a wife/
husband, family, close friends, high position in society, material
goods, etc., and furthermore that each brushstroke done in an ill-
ventilated studio, each sentence scrawled out on failing computer,
they are one step further to the achievement of their Life Work, of
their God-Given goal, so they should have faith in this, despite the
barrenness, and have confidence that She, Creator will bless them
with all other things which they need, which all humans need for fun,
joy, and whole-living.—Abundance. In the interim, if you are really
busy in creating this Work that God has given, then everything else
must stand down.

Everyday day pull that painting table out and paint! Paint one-hour
minimum during the morning—then at night, my First Love. --Am
pleased the way the words flow for JOURNEY, my on-going daily
diary, (currently (Obedience to the Call of Art/God, Journey 9.) Must be
because I paid the dues for so long, of hard, enforced labor scrawling

on tiny little desks made of boards in cheap hotel rooms and
condemned buildings.

Hope these Journals will be an inspiration, and a table book for
struggling artists/writers/dancers/actors everywhere—as it regards the
labor of the love of their respective crafts!

PM Thursday February 7
I must add, the day before, was Super Monday—the football playoffs
which transfix fully one half of the American population. (Male,
mostly.) I walk past a thousand doorways of taverns down the strip—
each turned to the *football* station, with avid patrons staring into the
tube, anxiously waiting a field goal, a pass, interception, touchdown
or such... I feel blessed to sit in a bookstore where among the young,
straight men none has mentioned this wretched super bowl at all!
And, neither has any single one of my friends! (But Jasmin's lover
watched it on TV).

                    *

I look down at my life now—from the top of the ladder, not staring up
bewildered from the bottom. It's been a 64 year climb. God has given
me what I asked—to create art—80 books I have in this BOOKS
CATALOGUE 2008, and I thank Her.

My mother left-a long time ago-from this bitter earth. It was she who
encouraged my art, a child at her knee, showing me Picasso prints;
pale blue & pink, in bound folios checked out from the excellent
Chicago Public Library, and got me started on the reading of fine
literature.

With the Call of Art pushing me—even over the compelling health
reasons that those pigments, oil based tubes sitting in boxes can
destroy one later. Especially since already have damage liver from
shooting heroin in my early 20's; had a clean bill of health since, will
continue, as said!

Well, have stated before, the crux of 'the thing' is to follow your true
desire—sit down at the painting table even if there seems to be no
hope; if an awful painter works long enough, s/he will become at least
good. If a good painter works long enough, s/he will become very

good—even great. What is great, genius? Does that too kick in at some point never anticipated early in life (but thru the interest, the desire, but by no previous indication of any talent, not even a drop of skill apparent) does this genius kick in at some point and the artist find that they had it in them all along? The genius? Greatness? Sheer hard work! No substitute for this!

He was busy to finish the process of living, and went out for the evening, just as he had all of his teenage thru adult life—to mix with others, at least several hours of the day... For decades it was the bars; straight & gay in his youth, later gay ones exclusively, even later, taverns replaced by group meetings & political movement events; and now, the bookstore. Every so often Shaun would turn in his vulture-chair, make some arcane hand symbols at the window, to some passing crony outside—God knows what these gesticulations meant, they weren't harmful, something of youth, of the current age.

A lady storeowner from down the block—Ransack—and S., discuss their relationships with their stores, how they'd like to get away but can't, how they're tied to their stores in a way never anticipated. Likewise, Transman's mind drifted into interior thoughts;, since he'd begun to self-publish as far back as 1971 to duplicate his poetry manuscripts, in a crude pamphlet form he devised (later known as the chapbook) to make available to the public one day; about how he too had to share his time with additional chores—Photocopy today, another day editing, still another buying stocks from office supplies store—book spines, paper, mailing tape, et al. Time spent accumulating mailing boxes from curbs at midnight, currently gathering up discarded bubble wrap at Babylon Falling, etc., time researching places to send his holy shit---enough creative time siphoned away from him in which new works are tapped from the well spring—(from the Golden Pot) and furthermore, just as the store owners couldn't release themselves from the hold of their stores, so he could not get away from his book business, his boxes of stock, his paints, his canvasses, which occupied now, the majority part of his living space, the small studio.

The artist should hold in mind the following analysis in its simplicity; time, money—is equal. The things one does for convenience buys more time for art, but drains the budget drastically! How much easier in the throes of creativity to take that $20 just sent by a kindly friend in the mail (Eli W.) or that $25 from sales of book (N. Hen ((for STREET OF DREAMS)) at BF no fees extracted courtesy of S) and rush to the nearest deli purchasing ready-to-eat food, expensive sausages to boil later in the eternal pot, cream for coffee, thus depleting the small savings tres rapidemente—when a longer and more *time consuming* trip to a supermarket would be practical, and money saving! Yet the time taken to walk that distance eats into ART! However, when ones cash runs out, and one is hungry, it becomes difficult to muster the energy needed to sit down at desk and write, or to stand/sit sit/stand ever adjusting ones position, (for perspective of the painting) over and over all day painting---stomach gnawing with hunger!!!!!!

The lovely and wonderful thing about art painting is that it can be a child's playground! Everything does not have to be in anatomical perfection, or photographic duplication of it's 'reality.' I don't worry about an extra finger on a hand, or a foreshortened body with a too large head. The child dreams! Paint your vision!

Feb 5th.
The rent is due! I cannot pay the rent! Look around me, our cozy home; animals safe, birds chirping in cages, cat purring on bed, art works safe, books stacked neatly in cartons waiting for orders, all the paraphernalia of publishing and creativity and photographed art posters. MUST Save this Home! Vow to save every penny of next months Bancroft, of next years Renters Rebate, of moneys from book/art sales! Blah, blah. Blah. A last minute reprieve from friends! Home is saved! Then! An art supply sale looms! Must switch over from toxic oils to acrylic! —An order comes in-- must purchase a new discount photocopy card! A sex toy breaks, post haste to the Sex Shoppe for a replacement! The money comes in, out the money flies! Again, another month! The rent day fast approaches! Wringing of hands and gnashing of teeth!

> Aw shit, my room rents due! Whad yuh mean there's no money?
> There's always money!
> --INHABITANTS GHETTOIZED POPULATION.

*

212

The spirit of revolution has just sailed into port! Black Panther Party posters adorn the store, revolutionary artwork, new paintings with political themes. The Party paid in blood; they were murdered by police (pigs in their terminology). This artwork, the struggle, the memories inflames his soul.

Then, an interesting conversation, most humorous and a commentary on ordinary class distinctions took place under the florescent 15-foot high ceilings of the bookstore:

Red: You mean those photos Shaun took when Emory Douglas was painting in his studio…

Sean: (Yelling) **Painting in his garage!**

Red: Aw, studio is too bougie, huh…

Red: (Singing along with the old 1968 Party Revolutionary do-wop group, The Lumpin): Free Angela! Free Huey! Death to the fabulous pigs!

Sean: (Yelling louder.) **Death to the *fascist* pigs!**

Red: Aw shit, I'm just bougie! Aw dude! We know the world would be better off if *everybody* had a bourgeoisie standard of living! I'm bourgeoisie! (The little guy yells, words spilling out of his mouth, hands jammed in his pockets, head upturned to the ceiling): I wanna be bourgeoisie too! I wanna get a condo so I can stay on this god-forsaken island! (Actually SF is a peninsula.)

*

After visiting the 3-legged pit bull he wrapped himself up well in many clothes, all of which were donated:
1. Trousers—LA, Spouse of Jasmin
2. Coat—bought new, Jasmin
3. Shirt—bought new, Hugo
4. Scarf—a gift from?
5. Necktie—found in freebox
6. Sweater—gift sewn by Rosa Salazar
7. Shoes—his used, Carlos
8. Hat—bought used, Hugo

Stepped in a coffee store to get warm, admiring the little sandwiches, which he could not afford, displayed so perfectly behind glass, on a cold winters eve, while he waited for the bus. This is what he was thinking:

> The way this system is, for a poor person, its one step away from being in a prison. You are judged by middleclass professionals; you are shunted in this door out that one; your life stays stuck no matter how hard you try. One false move or misstep—you are accused, and found guilty by unanimous verdict! To be tossed out into the cold, with no resource!

PM AM Friday morning February 8
PS, have been sick consistently since began painting in oils.

Regarding this matter of the toxicity of oils, the bookstore computer is working once more---due to the efforts of a burly uniformed serviceman busily digging into the sidewalk, outside, beside a mountain of broken concrete, yanking up wires & cables by their roots. No, the CIA wasn't jamming the line, it was a cross wiring mistake whereas some ordinary citizen returning home promptly at 6pm each evening switched on the sports channel, thus jamming the bookstore's line—Googled info on Internet mili-second fast data banks, and found studies which all say acrylic is much healthier to use—with window fan ventilation. God has told me, during a brief prayer, that the finishing of my first oil painting in 33 plus years, will coincide with the arrival of the Bancroft funds and a quick sale stock of Liquitex color is required! To start again!

Is said you can lead a horse to water---etc., for years have in back of mind been cognizant of my neglected painting, tried to jump start it up again on 3 occasions, but failed—first noticed about 4 years ago that I was right in an epicenter of so many art galleries, also arms & branches of the tarantula-like commercial art college including it's student housing, which surrounds me, as it appropriates more & more buildings in The City. Now, being in this bookstore have come to know many young art students, right up face-to face--all this encourages my art.

Saturday February 9
The Black Panther redux show is gearing up; everybody is here.

214

The sweet, quiet, pretty young woman seated behind the counter today—in the nefarious Vulture Chair--- is the mate of the proprietor. With a solemn expression she informs the Transman: Kensey Lamb wants to be in my book. (She already was, but not by name.) Some will call it a nefarious book, others a radical, free thinking book which seeks to shake the world and wring justice out of it! Others might comb thru it searching for a list of traitors to the old order which is now struggling to keep power; control over us poor, average citizens of our nation, also with an iron boot set directly on the poor globally—thus for ones name to be found in my book may be problematic. I'm sure the angels on High will approve however, and we must not hesitate in the goal of Tikkun Olam --setting the world right. In a future age we who are labeled seditious today, may be seen in the Light as heroes. Now Kensey Lamb is immortalized in JOURNEY, despite the fact she is the archenemy of wild writers because, to earn a living she is an *editor.*

Oh, here's an informal quote from Emory Douglas at his talk:

> If you leave earth and look back, after a while, the planet looks like a dollar size. Further distance, it shrinks down to the size of a nickel, then a dime, and the further you go the planet is just a speck, and its surrounded by all this space with no time, no beginning, or no end, all this meaningless space and time---and to think, on this one tiny speck is all this war and killing and hatred! On just one tiny speck surrounded by meaninglessness!

It seems to me Mr. Emory Douglas as a young man began his career as an artist, just beginning to study illustration commercially at City College, this at the same time as the rise of the Black Panther Party, all of which was part of the radicalism of those time which inflamed the hearts and spirits of many kinds, and races of people from many walks of life, all hungry for justice, seeking change from the crippling old social structure left over from segregated 1950's. The Party informed his art in a political sense-- so an intersection between the two was made and his art transformed into political art—which it might not have done had not the two arrived at the same point in time simultaneously.

There are some who have a political cause behind their art—Diego Rivera's revolutionary art of the people, likewise Emory Douglas.

215

Some work of Frieda Kahlo does so too. There are certain emotions/ drives also that put fire behind the artists work. Sexuality is one of these. In some of my selections this can be seen: (AUTUMN CHANGES, STREET OF DREAMS, LESBIAN CUM STORES WITH FEELING & MEANING, and others of this genre within my body of writing.) Picasso for instance:

> The unpalatable truth is that machismo—a specifically Andalusian term—made for some of Picasso's most powerful work.
> --John Richardson A Life Of Picasso Vol. I.

More notes on being an artist—don't know how a creative artist can be great, and truly creative if they abide by the status quo! The very root meaning of creativity is to make something fresh, and new shooting up in a spot where it did not exist previously. Following all the others, only for a time, --*while learning*; --then straying from that ---*to create!* You don't create something new out of somebody else's plan!

You ever get lonely, so lonely that you're out of your mind?

On his way home that evening after the party, Transman Red grumpily kicked an empty brown paper bag on the sidewalk to see if it contained anything of value, he thought: '*One day I too will have a wedding.*' Upon reflection of the several young couples present in the bookstore that evening especially for the event, some snapping photos. Yet a love life isn't all Roses as he knew; and as proof, here down the very street where he was traveling came an angrily strident young woman screaming into her cell phone: "YOU LIED TO MY FACE YOU TOLD ME YOU WOULDN'T!" People with cell phones are always having these monstrous conversations—about their love life, or realestate deals—or in the case of black folks—about they Momma.

     *

Bought my first acrylic set today—first time since painted in that medium briefly some 40 years ago. $16.00 including tax. (Will give the tiny case/easel to Jasmin to do her watercolors.) Contents:

3 brushes
2 pallet knives
1 charcoal pencil
Tiny plastic water cleanse pallet

Minuet canvas
The case; can be used as a laptop easel
6 tubes of color:
> Cadmium Yellow Medium hue
> Naphthol Crimson
> Ultramarine Blue
> Phtalalocyainne Green
> Mars Black
> Titanium White.

Big plan to switch over when this painting is done. Put the oils away.

Down Polk Strassa at Market Street, fabulous architecture looms—40 stories tall, in distance white stone, clean sweeping planes giant multi-million ton art planted everywhere—this city like children's giant toys with humans inside.

Pigeons chased small fudge balls the Transman surreptitiously tossed for them into the gutter outside a corner coffee store; they trundled around after the morsels like a football of fudge; broken from an ample size piece he had found clean, re-plated in cellophane atop a public garbage can; he has resisted sugar 3 months; weight continues to creep down the scale, a sliver of ounces at a time.

Observe at this street corner the women of Fillmore; wealthy, stylish who cultivate a fashion models elegance, who are agent provocateur of power beauty—or the aurora of ultra high-class whores. (While real whores struggle to look as normal as possible in order to ply their trade over a greater radius, not attracting attention of the cops.)

Regarding my Journal, and now Victor Klemperer's diary; what makes peoples life interesting of course—is the struggle. Many of us are suffering artists, and sad souls—a compelling theme. However, it goes deeper then this. Where a person is set down in time makes a vast difference in the material they present. For instance Klemperer in the War Years. He was at the epicenter of an insane dictator takeover of his nation; lived thru it with long-suffering wife, (reminiscent of Jasmin) and wrote about what he saw daily, finally carrying his diary across the flaming battleground into a free world. I hope the children of this time and the future will find interest in my JOURNEY, and my instruction—and hope.

A majority of the people is content; a small group accepts Hitler as the lesser evil, no one really wants to be rid of him, all see in him the liberator in foreign affairs, fear Russian conditions as a child fears the bogyman, believe in so far as they are not honestly carried away, that it is inopportune in terms of real politix to be outraged at such details as the suspension of civil liberties, the persecution of the Jews, the falsification of all scholarly truth, the systematic destruction of all morality. And all are afraid for their livelihoods, their life; all are such terrible cowards.
--VK, War Years 1936

PM Sunday February 10
What kind of people are we? What kind of people do we know? How will our friends prove to be under growing oppression and tyranny? —Which is the path down which our nation seems to be headed. Will they betray us? Or risk themselves on our behalf? Will they be false or true, or, most likely, something inbetween? Which of them will betray, disappoint—and thus aid in the destruction of a person, both wittingly and unwittingly? —We don't even know what fabric we ourselves are made of! How will I stand up, against the coming storm?

Reading pre-fascist era material about the 1890's, seeing how the stage was set for the holocaust, seeing these cyclical dramas in history—tyranny, then revolt, repeating itself, can't help but wonder, 'will that happen here?' Everybody is saying so. In addition no matter how bad things might seem to be today, we all agree it would be truly a horror, if, in 2 years, 5 years, even 10 years, we were to look back at these days of 2007-2008, as 'the good old times' because things in the future might fall to be so unimaginably worse.

There are different levels of marginalization of any human soul within a society; one of the worse is the treatment of queers. This destruction, the neglect by a greater population to this lesser. If that ostracized group doesn't provide for or care for or lobby on behalf of its own people then each individual in its group is reduced to a great poverty—and this not simply economic, but mentally, emotionally and spirituality. No wonder the higher rate of alcoholism, cigarette smoking, suicide, —all things destructive to the holistic longevity of a

human being —are found within our ranks. Over and over he had
heard this:

> I found that as a Native American, a female, and on top of this, a
> lesbian, I had practically eliminated all my chances for success as a
> writer.
> -- Informal quote of Crystos, Native American poet.

It was to this marginalized population, that Transman belonged. By
race, by gender, by queer, by God! He had seen it, heard of it, and
lived it. —Apartheid.

And here is the antidote—simply, it is a Word from On High: The
Bible, Torah, Koran and other Holy Scriptures are instruction
manuals. If a person buys a car, or a washing machine, that product
comes with a manual of instructions how to operate it. The best care
for optimum results. The manual is calibrated to the fine-tuning of
the machine. Human beings too come with an operator's manual—
these Holy Books are what God has given us for the better working of
ourselves. The deeper, darker essence is what these Holy Scriptures
tell us—to follow the Ten Commandments to the *utmost degree!* For
each degree is closer to God!

To care for a lonely old sick guy—give him a warm sofa to spend a
cold night; a hot bath, and a plate of food; 8 full hours rest, respite
from the cruel cold heartless world --this is the Compassion of
Christ—not all the hoopla on the lectern of churches, nor the showy
parade of acolytes, priests and smoke and holy bells chiming.

I was born on a lonely planet. And this you've seen by my Journal.
Many of we citizens of this lonely planet wish Christ was right here
by our side—so we would have a friend; and a powerful friend at that,
who could bring our situation to peace, to wholeness but S/He is
gone. Christ currently resides On High; but also exists in fragments
and little pieces of Christ in each human heart. Transman decided
he'd go out and look for Christ among them. Duefully placing on all
the donated clothes upon his body against the howling cold; trousers,
shoes, shirt, tie, sweater, coat & hat, and a donated backpack (Hugo,
found; blue w/silver clasps) on his shoulders and the silver cane free
from the Public Health department, with, one last glance in at his
beady eyed parrots who sat in their cage surveying their jungle-world
of found plants @ windows, and a pat upon the furry lump at repose

under a blanket—Mr. Fluffy-- with a swirl of his coat, out he went—
to look for Christ among the multitude.

113.

> Build your dream!
> Cement it in!
> Cement it in!
> Or it will wash away
> like mud.
> It will be pounded away
> in bits by the feet
> of thoughtless people.
> Art must stand!

Pick up brushes and oil treys after the weekend break. Must finish
this in oils, but still not over this sickness; is the toxic oils making it
worse?

Oh, must talk of Picasso in regards to political art. Pablo Picasso was
one of the greatest artists of the world—vast artistic scope, evolution
of style, and technical mastery. However, he lasted thru 2 World
Wars without comment.

At Emory Douglas show met Ika Hauffman, radical photog for the
Grapeworkers strike, Black Panthers, and others around that era. She
snapped photos of Cesar Chavez; he unionized the low-wage,
powerless migrant workers who picked grapes, tomatoes, cucumbers,
lettuce, etc., in Salinas Valley. Said she was going to set up her
darkroom tomorrow and this made me think…

Of course many modern day photographers have the option of using
digital camera—thus there is no toxic chemical bath involved in the
process, not for them at least. ---Just for some unknown developer
down the line, if they print. They share the same dilemma as the oils
vs. acrylics people. Shaun R. says how he loves the rich tones of film
which digital cannot duplicate. Likewise some painters say oils give
a deeper richer more brilliant color then acrylics. I know acrylics dry
fast, and for someone like me who works and reworks their vision on
canvas this can be a problem.

RE: The setting up of dark rooms, writing desks; building makeshift easels, setting up painting spaces, dance studios et al. Dance studios I have known—in concert with Jasmin. The lean-to darkroom of Suzanne de Young. A brief offering from my memory about these various disciplines.

Topics to be covered:
  I.   Writing Desks.
  II.   Make-Shifts Easels & Paint Set-Up
  III.   Photographic Dark Rooms
  IV.   Dance Studios/Rehearsal Spaces

This brief essay is written from the perspective of the *poor* artist, who must 'make do' to obtain the necessary accoutrements of their discipline.

Writing Desks:
From my earliest childhood I recall a fondness for desks upon which I did my homework, which later grew to an enticement to write on my own, this prior to age 13, when was still living at the 'family compound' that 2-flat building of unspoken abuse and dark nightmarish shadows. First of all, adjacent to my writing space in my bedroom growing up, was a library—it stretched from floor to ceiling and occupied two walls, a window taking up the 3rd, and the stairwell from the ground floor the 4th. Many great black writers could be found there, Richard Wright, Langston Hughes—this was the era before Baldwin—and a strange pink/blue page Gertrude Stein book which made absolutely no sense to a child; on its back cover, a photo of Stein herself, a suspiciously man-appearing Jewish woman who lived in Europe.

I developed a crush on a new 3 by 3 foot size top, normal height table at the church parish house where we brown, tan & black kids had classes. It was brand new; one could see the grain of the wood top. I coveted this desk. This is one of the first inclinations of an incipient writer—passions for pens, pencils, zipper briefcases, pencil boxes, erasers, and tablets of paper, blue-lined with punched holes. This, and reading prolifically.

That was around ten or eleven. Since then was an office desk in my new room in the small apartment my father and I fled to after leaving my snake haired, insane nightmare witch-clutching schizophrenic mother and my financially well-established, lawyer-enhanced blind to reality hi'-yella grandmother who fought my exodus. A desk with a lightstand on it which turned off and on by a chain. The next house was a converted garage, we moved to from further west, to further east, off of State Street, on Calumet Ave., an area just turning black/brown flooding into the housing abandon in white flight; there was a smaller desk proper again, which changed its position inside my small room once facing north, the last place I recall it was facing south, with a modern lamp on it, typewriter—old fashion manual Remington, soon replaced by my dad with my first new Smith Corona. It went out of my room to travel to the Near North Side where I adventured out to try to be around gay environment—which was tragic in the late 1950's early '60s in Chicago. Once while working in an office I met in my apartment building a Scotsman who had worked a sojourn in America and was headed back overseas, he sold off his few worldly possessions and young Red got a nice little desk for next to nothing. Very cute, and compelling to a writer. He wrote on this awhile. Poetry, and a few gay novels, his first.

There was a flurry of days, drugs, criminal girlfriends who worked in the stripper/sex world; writing here and there on kitchen tables, real desks. Then flight to San Francisco to save his soul. There were hotel dresser top desks, and tables. Finally in the condemned building where he landed, with dog Brown, on the ghetto fringe, in throes of demolition, a desk made of a door laid lengthwise upon wooden crates or antique tables, or something I can't remember. His first small file cabinet was purchased around that time, from a flea market—a single olive green drawer. He filled in half of it with manuscripts typed on onion skin paper dad purloined from his job, and mailed cross-country to him.

Taking him up to the year 1972, were some constructions of desks—boards, or doors atop of stuff, typewriter, sheaf of paper and lamps situated on top. In 1975, he first owned house. With wood from the lumber yard, built a table/desk which traveled with him for a while, later moving from prominence as his sole writing desk, to just a work table for assemblage of notes for various books.

In warehouse apartment, it was several assemblages of boards/ material from old sink top in kitchen of the now foreclosed house he'd ripped out, upon leaving; file cabinets to support it, and an ironworkers table; this construction stretched ten feet across the side of the massive warehouse. In a huge gap jump from the 3 year later evicted space to a single hotel room bath down the hall, the desk shrunk to an amazing 3 foot by 2 & ½ foot top table desk with room only for the electric typewriter and a pile of papers constituting AUTUMN CHANGES. Nothing more; files, papers and paraphernalia assigned to a storage locker 10 blocks, in distance towards the west towards where the sun set behind the railroad tracks. One and one half years later after the millennium turned in 2000, a larger walk-in closet in a different room in the same hotel, the desk sprouted out again to the length of the ripped out board from the foreclosed sink to about 5 feet wide.

Today, 2008, it is the same construction as when arrived at this studio 7 years ago, the top of a dresser savaged from that old hotel across the water; plastic milk cartons full of supplies, and now, computer.

Make-Shifts Easels & Paint Set-Up:
At age 15, 16, 17 there was an aluminum easel, which lasted all thru my Chicago painting years. Paint tubes carried in a brown attaché case much stained with oils. In San Francisco, no painting was done until the setup in the condemned building, in which great works became manifest, both oil & acrylic; on a lumberyard wood-built easel.—On wheels. The paints & brushes laid out on several stands— a TV trey, a chair. After eviction, again no painting of consequence until this date—a large 8' x 4' wood panel, structured by a wood 'stretchers' 2" x 2", gessoed and a painting begun on it—this found abandon in streets and dragged in. Leaning, tilted back against boxes of unused notes & other writers miscellany, a bar clamped across its middle upon which the canvas rests; 3 lights trained on it. TV trey and cabinet hold the colors & brushes.

Photographic Dark Rooms:
1957. My own bedroom in dad's house in that small converted garage off State Street, blax Chicago South Side, when I was 15. Treys of chemical baths. Developed my own photos—a brief 3 week-long episode, abandon. 1968. Suzanne De Young, the Texas

photographer asked me to come downstairs in the condemned building and help her construct her darkroom, which I had already sketched up and told her what to buy. —4 simple beams of lumber and some black plasticine tarp. (Same lumber-yard which afforded his easel & stretcher bars for self stretched canvasses, and masonite to be gessoed.) Nimble bluejean clad Transman climbed up like a monkey on tables, chairs, nailed the wood into the side of her kitchen wall, nailed it to supporting beams, cross beams and hung the black tarp over it. Suzie was amazed, and a bit disappointed he secretly thought, that her darkroom wasn't more elaborate.

Dance Studios/Rehearsal Spaces:
Jasmin's first studio with Transman Red was the room he 'built' on their soon-to-be-foreclosed house in Oaktown. The diligent ersatz carpenter had previously knocked out the lovely glass French doors to the room, and cross-beamed it, forming a large permanent entrance from the hall (he'd previously built) which enlarged the room somewhat, then knocked out the 2 windows which had once faced the street and replaced them with a sliding glass door. A real carpenter had enclosed the porch with a door across its open entrance, thus visually, the room was expanded; it had hardwood floors. Intrepid Transman also had enclosed the entrance to the bathroom, which was adjacent, with a kind of make-shift closet. It was here the poor couple decided to create Jasmins Dance Studio. They advertised it in a neighborhood newspaper and actually got 2 students—both at separate times. This endeavor was el Projecto Grand Fiasco. Their next try at studios was their living space in the warehouse in North Oakland. The nascent carpenter had already built a wall across the huge space dividing it into two sectors, and the existing floor was a convenient linoleum.

At first this wall was ¾ of the way down the space, carving out a tiny living space at one end (adjacent to the kitchen) and the tremendous other part for the cat colony, which had been foisted on him by two seemingly kindly little old ladies. –That grew to 27 felines under their diligent, soft-spoken coaxing & bribery. This wall was to move its position two more times—in a laborious effort. During the 'Dance Studio' era, it was a good size—in the front part (cats) who were barred from the area for the class. Transman swept and mopped and Lysoled the linoleum, removed all the cat dishes and several cat boxes, and cat water dishes, so that no trace of the felines was visible, in preparation for the great event, while Jasmin prepared herself donning costume, doing stretch exercise warm ups. Bellydance music began to play… Several students had called. A sign was set up outside in Great Expectation. One student arrived. She asked, curiously "Do you have cats?" And they couple replied, in unison; **"Oh no we don't!"** She changed clothes in the bathroom. Midway thru the class a big fat orange cat (which the couple had attempted to hide) sauntered thru, gazed at them from his blue eyes, preened a bit, while Transman tried to shoo him away, then disappeared with a grand jette out the window. In a while the lone student excused herself and fled to the bathroom. There she threw up then left.

114.
Obedience To The Call Of Art! --Fast visit to the Reverend. He is preoccupied by chewing a rawhide strip, so that Transman is ignored, his breakfast—meal in a bowl, sits untouched; the rawhide strip must be devoured. Forgot to mention, last time I was here, a horrible thing—a red string hanging from the Reverend arsehole—where he's eaten up one of his plush toys and it's coming out the other end! So today its rawhide; perfectly suited for the canine digestive tract. From there its off to the supermarket—the artist must have food—fuel upon which the human body runs; Transman feared one reason he'd been sick for a whole month was not simply the toxicity of oil, but his diet, by which he'd lost 5 more pounds, but didn't have enough to eat— partly because of money worries, and for time issues (to go shopping/ cooking) then the Bancroft had come in like a ship returned from the high sees containing bounty. Off to the supermarket! —But first Art store! Acrylic paints! More are needed to compliment the 6 primaries in the starter kit. Won't replace broken sex toy—money is running out thru my fingers like silver fish in water! Transman contemplated also winding up his Monday at Borders Book Store Kapitalist chain, in a comfortable chair reading—maybe they even had Klemperer—like he had done before Babylon Falling opened its doors back in June '07, but was too tired. He still had his weights to lift that night.

I want to live a long time and produce a lot of great work. The price for this is the sorrow, for one will see everything, hear everything, & know of practically every evil on earth by living a long life. Maybe my words will be a torch in the wilderness to encourage the hearts of others to keep on The Path! Reminding them of all the reasons we have to live—even if it's just for them to immerse themselves in this lousy diary of my crummy life!

Hashem, I have one more prayer:

> I pray for the soul of mankind —that it doesn't go mad.

A witness to Transman Red:
> He was so poor he'd notice in the street one of those tiny little packets of mustard or ketchup they give away with sacks of fast food, & he'd grab it and take it home with him. First he'd push his cane on top to see if it squished flat (which showed it was already opened and used) if it stayed plump, he'd get it shove it into his jacket pocket and use it to flavor his homecooked meals.

> T changed the sheets on his bed, which had sat there 6 months, also, after a long procrastination, in which his hair was growing out into a girl's hair, cut it with buzz clippers to ¼ inch off his scalp, trimmed his beard and toenails—all in one week. Most ambitious.

Being Old. That would be a good title for a book.

If you in America, or anywhere on planet earth reading this Journal find it surprising, Transman's constant comparison between his times and those just before WW 2, of the fascist avalanche impending; hovering over the European nations of Germany, France, Russia, Belgin, Holland, Italy --must know that this is how he and some of his constituents truly felt—that they already might be doomed.

115.
Monday
Setting up the work site, dealing with what medium is the greater toxicity, safety, room rent—that's all part of the struggle of an artist— to make way for the creative flood of pure gold.

Since I'm still sick, have decided to start immediately in Acrylic, put the oil painting on hold till I'm well—finish it then, and go back to acrylic.

Idea for a painting… Will call it Niche Of The Easily Pleased
Prostitutes—the theme being 2 old queens, (one an FTM transsexual)
who, being so poor, as well as aged, must set up shop advertising their
services in a coffee shop, as they have become to weary to stroll the
avenues—they'll submit themselves for the price of a delicious cup of
coffee! What services do they render—well *Ear Service* of course!
They will listen to your tired banter for a measure of time—all for a
cuppa! … Actually that sounds more like the theme of a short story
then a painting…

Work on LEADER continues. In the future hope that it will provide a
sweet, eternal revenue per month, via the Global Print-On-Demand
deposited directly into my checking account. At $3.50 apiece, selling
several, that's $5, -$15?

> Stryker went into the cubical with her slave, a not very attractive girl,
> much older then her own age of 25. The slave helped her off with her
> jacket, sliding her hands up over her fat shoulders and back. They sat
> down on the mat together. "What do you want to do?" The girl asked in a
> musical tone. "Oh I dunnoe." Stryker sez. "Can you spread your legs and
> let me lick you, and then you lick me--at the same time?"
> Stryker went into the cubical with her slave, a not very attractive girl,
> much older then her own age of 25. The slave helped her off with her
> **heavy** jacket, **rattling its chains & zippers & studs;** sliding her hands up
> over her fat shoulders and back. They sat down on the mat together.
> "What do you want to do?" The girl asked in a musical tone. "Oh, I
> dunnoe" Stryker sez. "Uh… Can yuh spread **yer** legs and let me lick you
> **there,** and then you lick me—at the same time?"

Ah, this one's even better!

> As if a rattlesnake had bitten her in the side and injected a lethal dose of
> poison, and somehow she'd acclimated to it, Hawk raced down the road on
> her bike, spike hair of green/pink bristling like a porcupine. A punk held
> tight to her midsection--a hutch, black leather chaps, head shaved and a
> black bikers cap. Another punk drove a foreign made bike in tandem
> beside them. Life was not wine and roses. They rode their bikes to Oils
> with a vengeance. The rattlesnake had bit her side long ago, she'd pulled it
> out of her by the tail, fangs dripping venom.
> As if a rattlesnake had bitten her in the side and injected a lethal dose of
> poison, and somehow she'd acclimated to it, Hawk raced down the road on
> her **cycle,** spike hair of green/pink bristling like **an angry** porcupine. A
> punk held tight to her midsection--a **butch,** dressed in a black leather **vest**
> **&** chaps, head shaved **bald &** a black bikers cap **sitting on it.** Another
> punk drove a foreign made bike in tandem beside them. Life was not wine

and roses. **It was mean & nasty, and the spirit of vengeance rode along.** They rode their motorcycles to Oils **on a supernatural power of hate**. The rattlesnake had bit her long ago. She'd pulled it out of her by the tail, fangs dripping venom, **& wielded it as a weapon ever since.**

There is another reason Transman Red wants to get LEADER up on line fairly soon; the young proprietor of the bookstore has kindly aided him in his last entries to the Print-On-Demand company; (POD), Lulu, and it's Global Account is more difficult to set up, so Red will definitely need help, plus, the novel is so long he'd had to break it in half, & put it on 2 floppy discs, which now must be combined on one of those silver disc—DVD things? Whatever—and then that submitted to the POD; all procedures which are very expensive to perform at the hideous KKK which charges 35 cents per minute to access their Internet; so he must hurry and do this before Sean decides to close up shop and leave the area! ---Which he has mentioned he might do more then once. The cronies in that ship of fools are counting on the store to run at least to its full year-until June.

> --How many books do you have in this store do you know?
> --I have... 3,000 titles. 4,000 books.

I am convinced most of the worlds great literature goes unwritten-is only spoken between friends, associates in coffee shops, taverns and other artistic circles. The great debates on world politic, which last until dawn, the theorizing over java in student lounges; in this informal *tertulia* @ Babylon Falling bookstore at which I now find myself, many great & wise observations have flown freely. For example:

> Sean, proprietor is leaning beside a shelf of books, in rumpled bluejeans, an AK Press hoody, and spiffy gymshoes. He, points to his feet.

> Sean: These fucken' Nike shoes everybody's going crazy over; their lined up down at Huff around the block waiting for the store to open so they can be the first to buy a pair. What I want to know is, what is the effect of advertising to make us want to buy this crap? In Jamaica it was the shoes. If you had brand name shoes you could get a girl. I get up to the states, I think, I'm here in America now, I'm older I don't have to buy that crap! It's the advertising that makes you want to do it! And those shoes are so fucken' politically

bad. The shoes! They pay kids to make those shoes—7 cents an hour! Kids work 15-hour days!

Shivo: But at least they have jobs! They're getting paid! They have school, and housing and food. Other people in their country don't have jobs at all! They're begging for a chance to work at the factory—for 7 cents an hour!

Sean: Child labor in the US in the 1800rds, the Supreme Court turned down the child labor laws because they said it violated corporate rights for free enterprise in a free capitalist system. It wasn't 'till few years later the high courts finally began to deal with impact on workers, humane working conditions, and such.

Shivo: That's why we've got to have redistribution of wealth!

Suddenly, the door opens, stage center, Alex, Mr. Van Hussen, arrives, right on cue. —Carrying 2 shopping bags full of $150.00 worth of new clothes! Shirts, sweater, new jeans; and several teeshirts. Including a pair of Nike shoes—a most unpolitical brand!

Alex: Hey guys!

The next 20 minutes is spent discussing brand name clothes; the global trade bargaining, etc.

February 14, 2008
Red learned a new phrase out of the Picasso book—or was that Klemperer? *Mala de imaginaire,* as he sat reading. Sure does suit some people he has known.

--You been here a long time?
--Oh, just about eight months...

Picasso does not seem to have made more than a marginal sum out of the Suerrurier exhibition—barely enough to keep him in materials, rent and food over the next few months---for he was penniless by June. If at this time he earned a reputation for cadging off friends, he can hardly be blamed. He knew his worth and was in no doubt as to where his first duty lay: to himself. His progress could not be allowed to falter for want of a few francs. That the world owed him a living became an article of faith.
--A Life Of Picasso, John Richardson

Likewise, Red thought nothing of demanding his friends treat him to dinners, coffee's, even loan/give him the missing portion of his rent from time to time of distress. —For he knew he was laboring for the Higher Good. Dinner courtesy of Dr. Sam. Fun. Expecting a dinner with Hugo soon… Faithfully, J. supplies missing $60 rent monies for February.

Then suddenly, a miracle occurs…

Once again am scraping the bottom of the middle class--$7,160.71 has come in! Back pay from Social Security—disability! Deposit from the US Treasury Department!

Should I hate art---because its keeping me poor? And upon my first sales turn away from art; like a bitter hurt lover whose been dragged thru the mud, but now avenged? My first level of prosperity damming the flow of angst-energy, that crazed energy of living in uncertain conditions, which is driving me to produce more, more— then stability comes, and I turn angrily to my slave master—**Leave Me Alone! Let me enjoy my life! Let me have Peace—in doing nothing!**

116.
In the past he rarely talks about his earliest art efforts--- water colors of a child, lining the halls of his first earthly residence; drawings done on frantic teen energy, while captive in the seats of high school classrooms, —given that he had done so much discourse regarding his writing—but seeing that this is Obedience to the Call of Art, we will reiterate it. Drawing incessantly in early teens in a professional art book from the art supply store; he always purchased one of the spiral bound 14 x 17 inch size with hard cardboard cover and 100 sheets of manila drawing paper; which the crazy kid filled with fragments of people chiefly faces, hands, feet a few whole bodies.

Monday PM; Presidents Day (semi-holiday) February 18
3 bare surfaces stare at me—the bare surface of the cabinet, upon which once was the glass sheet used as pallet on which oil pigments had been squeezed out of their tubes in an array of colors; and linseed oil; turp tins---now awaiting a fresh pallet; one large canvas, a new one, on the easel, untouched, facing out into the room, beside it a tiny canvas which came with the acrylic oils kit also bare, still wrapped in

plastic. What a tragedy it is to waste ones art! My idea is to paint, paint, paint; let the canvasses dry, then have them professionally photographed---print out the discs into different size posters of each painting for buyer demand.

For now am setting up for arrival of new computer—hopefully tomorrow. Went for coffee and eggs w/cheese & spinach w/Hugo (Non-Professor Turnip)—ever-generous friend, who is pouring cash, labor & love into his cabin in New Mexico (and fixing his 4 motor vehicles), while engaged at job in continuous battle with the mad hissy fit sissy queen male gay head of his department a/UC Berkeley library. Unfair discrimination against the Non-Professor, which cannot quite be proved, thus he can't sue. It is the paradigm of situations. A gay discriminating against another queer in the worse way! Hugo is protected by law as a tranny, the only other person who has floated free thru the department nearly 20 years is protected as a black—she's put all her kids thru college; and the woman they've sent against Hugo is a Jew plus a senior citizen; --two protected categories! They have become friends, but there's just so much intervention she can do! All these protected classes—its' like a chess game! Great debate, furious reckoning, before a single move can be made. The head sissy fit queen's prejudice against Hugo— paramount-- has an impact The Turnips future income in his/her old age; simply, he is doing the work of a Class 5 but is only a Class 3. He should by rights, at least have been promoted to a 4 (hence greater salary, greater retirement) but the queen opposes this on the grounds of hatred! Let me quote myself:

> Notes Sunday PM February 17
> It is possible to kill someone thru limiting their ability to make money, to limit their social sphere, so that their free exchange of ideas dies, limits their growth in segregated, shut off venues. So what you get is a very close knit little reactionary band of homosexuals, lesbians, transgender people.

I digress. Am setting up electrical cords to be ready for the installation of my second functioning computer—with printer-- mannana. After that, the nightly Masturbation, ---then, into the bathroom goes Mr. Fluffy & out come the winged beasts, screeching & flapping— the parrots keep me company @ computer, composing, documenting this JOURNEY, continuing to copy LEADER, re-edited onto disc, and miscellaneous putterings. Oh, tonight read more of VK's diary at the Korporate Borders—committing adultery against Babylon Falling, which is closed (still on vacation). Since the Koprorate Whore did not have Part 1 in stock of I Bare Witness, had to pick up Part 2 (beginning randomly in its first quarter). Have covered quite a bit sitting there on a ledge by the window beside a lovely view of Union Square, basically undisturbed—as in Babylon there is always a commotion of friends to chat with; arriving, Great Debates, bickering, Internet surfing, ad nauseaum, then departing.

Good title for one of the JOURNEY sections (books) A Life.

Note of interest regarding the 2nd WW; in the 1930's inhabitants of Europe referred to that previous war—in 1915—as *'the world war'* for they not yet realized that currently they were at the beginning of another world war—soon to be called, *'the second world war'*. From that infamous day after the Allies entered into world theatre against the Axis powers, they would become WW 1 and 2. Would it be horrible if now, I am keeping my diary on the verge of WW 3? Many believe it is.

My long erstwhile work history on the kaptialist korporate laborforce, a memory: Doing inventory for a soup company, in it's computer room—that is, in the 1960's, *one whole room* devoted to a single computer---and all its various memory storage chambers; 7 or 8 gargantuan monoliths each 6 feet tall, four feet wide & deep, weighing 800 pounds—completely unbelievable by today's youth, which due fact that the memory banks have been reduced one million times down to the size of—yes a chip. The microchip. Technological discovery which has made its inventor a multi-billionaire.

In the day by day struggle of his existence, VK comments about technology which has gone into use during his lifetime. He has seen the advent of radio, airplane, movies with sound---yet human ignorance still rages; greed, violence are still with us.

> Please Hashem, cleanse our minds so we are not so blind, so
> unreachable, unborn, dense of soul.
> *
> Day after day insults of the world wash over us, with an ugly film,
> which blinds the eye of the soul gradually.

232

Disappointments break us down.
But God will be our bridge.

Tuesday PM, February 19
People in different ages of human progress can be racist, or sexist—
exclusionary in some way to others—and set in their time/place of
ignorance, are unaware of how much damage they do to these—
'others' these who they by matter-a-fact exclude from their
mainstream, their standard of acceptability. Jews, Native Populations
of invaded continents, Catholics, Artists, Gypsies… Have mentioned
my mother was a victim of this—segregation for her being Colored, a
woman of African blood. Why did my father have to hide the fact
from neighbors that he worked for a white (Jewish) business on the
North side—would this news have destroyed him if overheard by
someone of an evil mind, who might have informed that company of
my dad's 'black status' and caused him to loose his position? Why
these killing secrets, tight lipped kept over a lifetime! Damaging to
the human spirit!

Well, anyway, I do not harbor for one second the allusion that what
great horror happened in Germany from 1934 to 1945, could not
happen here! All the Civil Rights queers, blacks, & women have
gotten—upon these new path stones we assumptively walk on in
victory—how easily they can be revoked! Each paving stone of
freedom pulled out from under our feet on some pretext or another. I
have seen anger seething under the polite masks! Given several great
catastrophic events to strike our country at the same moment---our
great nation brought to its knees economically, under siege of some
unknown entity, the strongest could easily turn against the weakest as
some kind of blood ritual under the guise of 'expedience for national
security' 'safe guards against terrorism' 'economic necessity' or some
other rotten paltry excuse—for the sewage of raw hatred to come
spilling up out of the depths of the collective human body.

At distance on the foggy street a grocer stands outside his market
puffing cigarette smoke. For now, all is quiet on the western front.
Biding time. But for a wandering tourist, a student, or two, the night
streets deserted. Some, the most unlucky, —their circumference is
only a sleeping tarp made of plastic covering them, a water-logged
duffel pack at their head; a pad of cardboard on which they lay; all
compact; 5'long x 3'wide; x 3' high, on the concrete… Ahead of him
233

on the foggy street a grocer disappears in a cloud of cigarette smoke. Transman entertained this thought:

> I may not be that special a person—but do know I am a test. —It is people like me—how we are treated, by the majority of the world—will they be fair or unjust. Understanding, or misanthropic?

117.
Felt a little blue as the oil painting was derailed by sickness, now am recovered this windfall of money is somewhat—depressing! — Because it's a break in the sameness of my routine. Soon hope the geyser of inspiration will well back up as I switch over to acrylics. The new brushes are assembled, will sort out the new paint tubes today, have constructed one trey (for blues and purples) out of cardboard box top, temporarily the easel/carrying box the acrylics kit came in will do for the 2nd, reds, yellows, oranges and must find a 3rd—blacks, whites, browns, grey, silver & gold.

The canvas stares out into the room, blank. Waiting. Ready.

I enter the silent world of painting.

A person who is inspired is a very lucky person. I am inspired. Of course it comes and goes—dependent on external circumstances, bouts of depression, but generally speaking it is self-renewing. Has gushered up thru my lifetime, always saving me from the absolute nadir of living and pushed me into art again and again.

How special I am! I am an artist! A person inspired! Ego rants! Me, me; me! I, I, I, --all of it! Me tooting my own horn!

Vanitatum vanitas. Because of the Picasso & VK's War Years Diary, am now using mo' bigger words! Also-soon will be able to research as I compose via Goggle Search Engine via Internet! Such an outpouring of information! Technology progresses—but the soul of this world still mired in mud. The mud of ignorance of a different kind…

Wednesday PM February 21

Beginning to discern—from other peoples mention, and own opinion, that to find your own voice artistically, is worth more then technical mastery. Ones own voice. Some artists who have mastered perfect technique have unfortunately mastered someone else's concepts in the process, and do not have a voice of their own, so they tinker with bizarre themes as a substitute. Individuality: this is something Transman Red took for granted—always having had a unique voice and a personal statement. Was it from his very queer inception as a bi, no tri-racial individual, growing up with gender disphoria--- qualities out, traversing the world, in a new enhanced edition?

After day's chores walking on foot between shops & stores… Enter again the surreal world of Babylon Falling. Sean is busy stacking shelves, reorganizing. He says:

> I've been doing this since you left this afternoon; 5 hours!

> Geeze…

> It's a race against time!

Bluejeans have slid down around his hips, hang there precariously in the black prison gang 'baggy pants' style first made popular in the 1990s ghetto. He rushes from table to shelf, carrying handfuls of books. He comments franticly:

> Time's running out!

Pm Thursday:
No longer an involuntary student trapped in the classroom doing dead prison time, desperately slashing pencil strokes across paper. 53 years has elapsed! These days when he went into a waiting room, carries a book to read (one of his own perhaps) or a found New York Times, which is quite well written, highbrow, literate, global-informative. Back then, as a teen Red took a drawing pad into his sweat-drenched, nerve wracking prison classes, just having come out of childhood where he had done so much intense reading of many a curious volume, and as a young pre-twenties adult haunting the Chicago Public Library, one of its specter, (by Hashem's grace not destined to grow into a more wretched, permanently mad, ragged, homeless gaunt phantom of the insane who populate many of the

chairs of metropolitan libraries of the world, shunted so far off the spur rail of the human railroad, they are so lost, off in wilderness doing jailtime of the soul among the book stacks) back then teetering on mental illness & subsequent alcohol/drug addiction young Transteen made bold slashes of pencil over paper which was necessary for the mending of a hurt soul. So today, he would not do this. His tension had been mastered. It did not threaten his sanity any longer. So he'd bring a book, a newspaper. Recently, his Hebrew studies—(aleph-bet, vowels, roots). No drawing but what is necessary to plot a design for the canvas. (Or to doodle floorplans of the expectant condo of his dreams…)

Thursday AM February 21

> The world to come
> It is a perfect world
> And we fit in it perfectly.

Sunday AM early February 24

Another sickness. All my life I've gotten sick in winter from colds/the flu. No flu so far—thanks to flu shot the last 15 or so years, just tired. Chills. Alone. Now is time one needs a friend.

I am in the sea of abandonment & belong nowhere.

Well it is no wonder recluses i.e. Henry Darger went to mass 5 times on Sunday… Can't make it up the hill tomorrow, am sure. Did make it to Shabat Friday & Sunday at different scholes—first time in several weeks.

Must say anyone who has written about practices & lifestyles that I have, i.g., drugs, criminal underworlds, skidrow madness—of this, mostly my life was poverty of deprivation and loneliness—and was not running with the wild herd or I would not have attained this age of 64 years.

We are the product of our environment. Many don't use the freedoms they have, don't realize what they are; are fearful of stepping out. & I guess people need to be taught what freedom means, and learn how they can be free. I stand by my awful prose! It illustrates my freedom!

236

Monday early AM February 25

Meanwhile in his increasingly fascist-controlled German homeland, Jewish Professor Klemerer, now Klemperer *Israel;* his condition is fast going from terrible to horrible, however he believes that survival in his severely commuted world can go on. *On ad infinitum—*

At first opening of his diary the reader (some 50 years later) sees the important details of daily living; the slow German blood letting being described in atrocities, the secret military build up, later, as the greedy Third Reich begins to expand itself, acquisitions of all nations around itself, —France, Poland, Belgium, Czechoslovakia. VK's effort to get monies, and to retain strength to write his literary papers. Battling depression. But this isn't the darkest times—they are coming. Now, it is here. In this diary implied that he must get rid of their little tomcat Muscal. To put this healthy fun-loving little cat to sleep. And he is the joy of VK, and Eva's life. As a Jew he and his Aryan wife cannot own their house any longer, nor live in it. They are being removed. To Jew quarters. So it is in the times of our lives when glacial conditions sweep down over us, conditions we cannot fight, when the few small things we love are being taken from us. The half mad grief struck dike who moves into a strange town a with 4 cats, and can find no lodgings, who is told to abandon her pets; times when you get old, sick, no longer have physical strength, when stronger people officials, authorities, relatives so-called friends demand you be removed—removed to the horrors of a nursing home, so they will be free of your burden. Now the diary steps into the blackest times. --- Well at least their little Muscal will miss the worst blackest time, the starvation, the concentration camps, firestorms of the Alllies bombs, the blackened smoldering ruins of Dresden (once the jewel of Europe)—he will die of a painless lethal injection and immediately go to heaven, to play and rest; his full furry belly turned up to the sun, lounging in a paradise of unnamable beauty—of Gods Peace.

118.
Ha! At the anarchist book fair, sellers could not bring certain books… no Mao, no Chea, no Trot shit… No communist shit. Even the non-political Jasmin had a laugh over that.

Good ideas in BF—

"The next revolution will be precipitated by disruptive technology. Not dangerous, nuclear explosive type technology. It will do what the Internet did—but greater."
--A French artist, visitor to SF.

Hunched over the store computer in his most severe Vulture pose, working on some business lunacy, Sean utters a long low hound dog moan.

You don't understand the *pain* I feel doing this bullshit! This shit should not be happening!

*

Disaster has struck! Someone has been thrown out of synagogue! --- **NO! It is not Transman!** —No! Someone *else!* Sadly, of a Person of Color persuasion. A Mexican-Catholic-Jew. A questionable person, —like Red. Allegedly for threatening violence.

Transman is secretly relived. Ah! So he is not the only one to get the boot out of established places—(even ones he himself has established, like his long-lost group). Privately he has concerns however, was it true violence, which was threatened, or is this an example of a severe culture clash misunderstood? One nationality against the other, both blind, locked into the customs of their own heritage, both misreading each other's intent?

Monday PM February 25
VK speaks of human dignity—how sure he was of his, -- up until the holocaust, when each last human decency is stripped from him and his Aryan wife Eva. And this makes me think how it applies to myself, as being, IE:
A Tranny
Mixed race
Semi-insane/eccentric
Artist.

Never know if they are coming to get us… Everybody says to get my Passport now or it will be impossible as a Tranny to get a Male passport after the National ID law goes into effect. Was too poor to

238

afford it at first. Now am too exhausted and terrified of red tape to try, but I should since have this terrific windfall of money.

VK was a Jew and first & foremost a German National. A total patriot. He did not think of himself as: A. an Israeli (*perish the thought*) or: B. a Jewish outsider, but a *German* in a long 100-year old line of Germans who just happened to also be Jewish. He thought division between Jew & German was a fictitious construct. Furthermore he thought other divisions were worse, those between catholic & protestant, between Communist & capitalist.

Vision at 6am Monday May 25
I see the black empty hood of death hanging like a cloak over a yellow mental news rack. -----What will the news bring us?

Meanwhile Hillary Clinton the woman candidate for President, and Obama, a black man, are struggling in the trenches, pelting each other with mud—which stinks like shit. This whole mess is sorrowful to myself. Vox populi communis opinio: everyone I meet & all the newspapers text, no one accredits the need for equality in having a woman president—i.e. role model for girls and women-- but do greatly & constantly accredit the necessity of having a black for president, as assurance to African Americans; (not Hispanics, who are against him). So am disappointed. See this whole political campaign being fought on a down deep subliminal woman-hatred base, especially observe this in my young straight male friends (whites). Also, an exotic crush on the black forbidden fruit by many young middle class white women, including lesbians who seem to love Obama to a frenzy—shades of Elvis Presley fans who swooned when he wiggled his pelvis on stage, and tear the garments off rockstars if they can catch them. Is that the kind of fight it is? Well the Republicans play dirty and they are sitting back having a big hardy Hee Haw at this cat & dog battle—they might have orchestrated the whole mess themselves.

*

Work on LEADER proceeds, with two parrots accompanying; green Arial on one shoulder, chortling; white, bigger Bijou, peaceful, silent, on the other. Frieda Kahlo could have painted a picture of this excellently.

239

Oh, after 2 days of trepidation, after wiring the Beast together, finally pushed button on the computer—it started! Now to get Jasmin to come over and set up the WORD program, which I don't understand how to do, also to get Internet hookup. RED JORDAN PRESS IS ROLLING!

Oh, when starting the Beast, after humming, and flashing lights at me, it began to go thru its changes, and soon demanded that I name it! — So I have called the Beast Red Junior. Actually, since Red Junior demanded one single string of characters with no break—*RedJunior*. So this is the Beasts legal name. I hope to communicate to the world via Internet directly from my own home soon, instead of having to beg, borrow and steal computer time throughout venues in the city as poverty has necessitated the last 5 years. No porn will be watched ever on this site! Made that stupid mistake with the last computer (not my composing one donated 2 years ago by Delora). It had a dial-up connection, and stupid Transman jerked off to fleeting glimpses of raunchy porn on it—much to his dismay when it infected the whole machine and had to be thoroughly fire-cleansed with a complete deletion of everything. (Thank God nothing important was on it.)

Tuesday AM February 26
In keeping with his re photocopy series which he saved from oblivion tucked inside a green file cabinet; 22 ancient volumes of quick novels written in the late 1970's Transman has begun upgrading BOY CENTER (which has sold 3 copies in its life) and so his surprise found he enjoys reading this himself! A fascinating account: Last night I read over BOY CENTER, and several times today had to pick it up. It's interesting! Every few pages bring back memories of the political, social clime of 1970's gay life. Things forgotten, now remembered. My stuff is worth it for this historic reason as well as its characters who begin to appear in the first few pages, one after another, and are quite entertaining. A good addition to my male books, which sadly aren't as many as the female/dike/FTM trans genome ones. Equal time!

Feel sick. Sicker off and on now more then I've ever been any winter recently--is it old age? Is it just this weird flu? Reports from others that they haven't been this sick since they were children. Nothing

240

Hashem can't fix-if S/He Will. I see in a dream (about Daughters Of Courage ((Yes have not forgotten my dreams of DOC)) that the most important thing in building a religious movement is to strengthen the human circle. The human links. That is the original purpose of our human race—since the cave people days, nothing new about it! When human beings sit around in a circle together to tighten bonds, to make family --and DOC is a family of strangers drawn together from all parts of the world, and all walks of life-- their human hearts united in a boundless love of God. Their minds agreed on with the laws of God.

The home of an artist. Colorful. 2 & ½ main rooms—the 14 x 16 'studio.' A narrow kitchen 4 feet wide at one end, 3'6" at the other, 11 feet long; it is here most of his stuff is made into books, & miscellany is stored; the opposite end from the stove/refrigerator/sink/ microwave, kitchen combo, has the loft he built, the book binding machines, page cutter, stacks of unmade books printed free at different facilities in better years—still not cut & bound; that drying oil painting, still unfinished, and at the window by the sink, shelving (found) stacked with little plants, a bucket on cinder blocks containing a found spider plant which now thrives. The big room, which is the studio section has gay colored paintings hung on three walls, against one wall entirely covered are stacks of books for sale, and boxes of old manuscripts not yet done. A row of empty shipping boxes and bubble wrap sits on top at 7' feet, light weight materials extending from one end of the room to the other, and a lone oil painting atop that. The other wall has windows and here sit the parrots in their cage---overlooking a forest of plants clustered in buckets, cans, pots, against the window and seated on the floor beside it. The makeshift easel, holding a canvas leans against the racks of boxes; rectangle; glaringly untouched, sparse, white. 5 unused TVs sit here & there gathering dust. Then, the walk-in closet, 4'6" x 6' 7"; in which sits his composing computer and the new Beast, --*RedJordan;*-- stacks of cardboard boxes containing print masters of 3/4ths of his 80 books, (those not on the POD) and other miscellany. A cat completes the ensemble, sleeping peacefully on Red's bed, a medium size mattress elevated so as to utilize space underneath--weight lifting set/bench; in the entrance way he has built himself a cloths rack to hold much of his sparse wardrobe. Bathroom adjoining with a gay shower curtain bequeathed from Delora, and nefarious, tho attractive sky-blue cat box.

Soon I will say... Due to long sickness, flu, toxic reaction—have begun painting again after 3 weeks absence—acrylics.

AM Wednesday morning February 27
From Kemperer:

> The situation is made infinitely more difficult by the unsuspecting tomcat who we keep alive with almost the whole of our meat rations and for when our moving out will be a death sentence. Eva is passionately fond of the poor creature, which is basically better off then we are. At—they had crayfish in tins at 1.20m we rationed for awhile, I feed the cat with that when there is no more meat. Reserve 14 tins; how long will they last?
> --January 1940.

Transman Red awoke with wonderful words, and wrote in his Journal:

> So beautiful
> So wonderful
> Every kindness will be there.

--Meaning paradise.

119.
Vile vile birds! They have shit on this master copy of OBEDIENCE TO THE CALL OF ART! A tiny green turd; liquidy. One guilty culprit, beady orange/black eyes, preens itself calmly on my shoulder, then turns its head to stare blankly, as if to ask; 'C'est moi?'

Must recount a memory from me and Jasmin's long ago days as housecleaners. Several times we worked for gay men who were then falling victim to the HIV virus. They never discussed their disease, or even that they were sick, I suppose because this was too painful. But you could see the truth by the medical equipment in their house. Pills, AIDS-specific in their medicine cabinets. One particular place, we had only been told his 'roommate' was in hospital. Several cleanings later we returned, and in the upstairs bedroom encountered a strange man lying in the couple's bed, unconscious... T didn't recognize

242

him, because his body had become so bloated, so distorted, dying of HIV. And thought in his ignorance they'd substituted some other sick patient—of a different nationality-- that it was someone else. The partner had told us nothing. Nothing at all.

I am now thinking about migrant workers, and how they make the terrific trek up from lower South America into more affluent Mexico to then undergo border crossing into the U$. Danger, murder, beatings, robbery; rape—even rape of men—happens depending upon who befalls their path. They work up here for much less wages then the average white American or established person of Color, and far less benefits—all for opportunity. And think how my Cuban (?) Honduran grandmother brought my dad up here from Honduras on a fruit barge when he was 5, to live in Chicago doing washing and ironing to support them. And how privileged I am, to be sitting here before my new Beast, soon to be connected to Internet, with a small apartment, and enough to survive—tho it gets tough frequently—and most, to have been educated enough to bring you these words of my JOURNEY!

Wednesday PM February 27
With all this talk of VK and his impending fate under the evil fascist empire, you readers of this Journal may be wondering, at times—what will be the outcome of that strange Transman, who dressed in white exclusively for a decade, upon which he began to dress in black, and still is, for 18 years (whose black hat was so commented on by passerby's, yet scorned by Delora), what would be his fate? If he would became famous? Depending on the year they read it, they might already know the outcome, but lacking the day-by-day details would read it avidly, hungry for the gruesome horrors of an outcasts' life.

Oh, here are some of the comments made to him regarding his hat:

Hope I'm not intruding, but I really like your hat.

Great hat buddy, really like your hat.

Like the hat!

Near the end of WESTPOINT OF THE UNIVERSE, in a tavern frequented by the employees of the nefarious telemarketing office B. S. Fine, a criminal black man, a homophobic hustler of gay men who the theatric Irishwoman has invited to join them at the bar, snatches the hat off Transman's head, Transman responded loudly; 'HEY YOU CAN'T DO THAT!" To which the criminal explodes, howls, going after him—for no other reason that he was jealous while being high on some substance. Transman fled from the bar, and ran into an unoccupied booth, the insane criminal after him. Transman sat quietly in the booth, head bowed—an open knife secreted beside him hidden under the table, tensed, ready to spring out, plunge the knife into the face & chest of the attacker. He did not raise his eyes in confrontation, but kept the criminal's every motion fixed in corner of his peripheral vision. Waiting. He would recoil like a spring! The black man towered over the table, all 6'2" 250 pounds of him howling, cursing—but did not approach any further because he wasn't sure what Transman held. From that day forth while working in the vicinity T carried a 38. caliber revolver, ready to blow the nigger to bits if any further attack was attempted, but ironically, it turned out later, via information from some his ex-trade, a queen who knew this prison convict well, whose own momma testified was 'no-good' wasn't particularly afraid of guns, but terrified of knives, for some deep seated psychological reason, had so much horror of them, he was afraid to go into the kitchen when the queen was cooking. Transman Red had held him off with the slim 3" silver blade—the *threat* of whatever weapon he held under the table.

The remembrance of this horror reminds him of how rough life has been, him walking on the wild side, and how in older age he just craves peace, security.

Today at BF heard from where the expression 'Mad As A Hatter' derived. Back in the day Mercury was used to cure the strip of cloth inside a hatband; this pressed to the scalp in combination with the bodies own secretions allowed mercury to seep into the brain— driving the hat-wearer mad.

Finally, in addition to these hat stories, Transman has been shunned by Delora—because of his battered old black hat! This hat has lost its shape after being *used*. Now isn't that a purpose of a chapeau? Well in the windy/rainy/cold season he shoves the hat down firmly over the hood of his jacket, on top of his head, thereby warming his head, and ears. This stretches the hat out of shape. Now the social-conscious mate of Jasmin does not want to be seen out in public with him—and this hat!

Mentioning our dismal days together in the soon-to-be foreclosed house on Lyon Avenue to those assembled, a patron at the bookstore queries, 'Did you write about that anywhere?' Well here it is. For several months —4 or 5? After being severely underemployed, Red & his then-wife Jasmin, having exhausted several fictitious names on their PGE bill, suddenly found themselves without service. No lights. No electricity. —The stove was electric. However the hot water heater remained, affording the couple a nice hot bath inside the frigid house. At first the resourceful tan, round and beautiful wife stationed candles in saucers about---very 'elegant' and they began to heat the bedroom using its fireplace—and cooked in it too, in a cast iron soup pot placed on top of the log rack! -- But practical Transman allotted monies from their housecleaning jobs and began purchasing a number of accouterments. A propane stove to cook with—its place on the now-dead stove. 5 battery powered lanterns, one for each room. Flashlights by whose beam guided them from room to room. They continued bringing home scrap wood to burn in the fireplace for heat. He typed these daily 'notes' on a battery-powered typewriter. Just a small sliver of life!

Here's a quote from BOY CENTER, in which one of the male protagonists draws in pen, slashes of lines on bar napkins; an example of how a writer interjects fragments from their own life:

> He sat there making violent motions with pen upon a flimsy napkin. Wayne had learned to draw under the fierce pressure of adolescence. Back in highschool. He was uptight. This was release for nervous tension. Seated in the classroom, not hearing. Drawing pen slashes down an immense sketchbook—boy, growing, his ears and feet bigger then the rest of him, in worn clothes the best his too-large family could afford, in the very last seat of the aisle furthest from the teacher, nearly out of sight of the blackboard & close to the window.

Sounds of summer in his ears, drawing. He fled thru the open window in imagination, he fled thru sketches, preoccupied... then teenage, he fled in reality. Never returned to the red brick school, adolescent; cast his fate to the winds. Hung out in the street.

As a youth he got into the street and street got into his blood. — Life was too exciting for him—he abandon everything to pursue it—he stopped his art, which needs discipline to perfect, and so it remained only a rudimentary talent which he would carry to his grave—like a seed that never break out of it's shell.

AM Friday February 29
I wish to share this with all beginning & longtime artists. Overcoming drugs/alcohol was hard way back in those times—even more difficult this overcoming inertia and procrastination to drive myself deeper up the great heights of inspired creation—to not stop, to keep working. But how many artists never took up the pen or brush, the musical instrument, or the stage and are living ordinary lives—when they could be living extra-ordinary lives!

Friday February 29
Ever since infancy, opened my eyes, and saw this earth, I've been on my JOURNEY—tho I didn't realize it as such.

Has San Francisco been kind to me? No, but it let me live. It's not been cruel. Some return from cities in a coffin. Some come back insane. None of this has happened for 40-years in this place. No, San Francisco has not been kind. It simply ignored me, as I skitted around its perimeter picking up stuff I could use—recyclables, minimum wage jobs, cheap hotel rooms—and notes. Notes! These infernal *notes* jotted down in dim lit bars full of cigarette smoke by which were composed a dozens and dozens of queer novels—pieced together from *notes!*

God located me quite well here;—inspired while in a death blue depression in a repressive Midwestern city by a message blasting across the continent of Hippies philosophy proclaiming love was out here! LOVE! I came... Drawn over 1,000-mile journey to find love, finding freedom instead. A long cold hard freedom; and yes, love too.

I close with the words from an African American woman in our Seniors group—she said it twice:

Animals kill for survival, but people for greed, hate, anger, power

*

I was born on a lonely planet. And this you've seen by my Journal. Many of we citizens of this lonely planet wish Christ was right here by our side—so we would have a friend; and a powerful friend at that, who could bring our situation to peace, to wholeness but S/He is gone. Christ currently resides up On High; but also exists in fragments and little pieces of Christ in each human heart. Transman decided he'd go out and look for Christ among them. -- With a swirl of his coat, out he went—to look for Christ among the multitude.

A brown tan-yellow, full lips and nose, curly yellow gold hair like a sheep's curls; blue green eyes like water and the sky. The Lamb is here! The Lamb will wipe away every tear from their eyes!

This is a Holy Book. Not one of the pages of this book shall be lost, nor any of its words shall be removed, because it has been given to me by God.

--DAUGHTERS OF COURAGE

The light still shines in the darkness.
The darkness has not overtaken it.
--John 1-5

And let the people say, AMIEN!

Red Jordan Arobateau
March 1, 2008
1:00 PM Pacific Standard Time

San Francisco, CA
USA

The Passion of Art

JOURNEY Vol. 9

2008

I see in a dream (about Daughters Of Courage) that the most important thing in building a religious movement is to strengthen the human circle. The human links. That is the original purpose of our mortal race—since the cave people days, nothing new about it! When people sit around in a circle together to tighten bonds, to make family.

120.
Today started first acrylic painting in 34 years!

Some young, poor, artists in this town live in one room, in a shared flat with others, and must paint in the same room they will sleep, eat, and breath as the work. Poison. Transman's painting system was now worked out. On his sudden windfall of money he had substituted all new acrylics for the old found/bought oils. Drying pictures had a placement outside the room he slept in—in the kitchen. A thick sky blue curtain hung from the frame over empty space missing a door to the floor, dividing them. He decided he would go back to oils 3 times per year, enough to complete 3 oil paintings. (Not in winter when cold air blasting in for ventilation would make him deathly sick as it had this just-past, first year.)

AM Wednesday March 5
A layer of golden sun along the horizon. White fog, then vast bright blue sky. Parrot's small green head against my chest, its fiery ego, insulted, feathers ruffled; his birds were little tiny fiery egos darting about. His home for dead & dying plants which he had restored. He sat in his little room being pruned by a green bird, while a white bird tugs off his hat, throws it to the floor again & again.

Oh, Jasmin has taken a look at the Student At The Golden Pot and commented---"This painting is painting."

This world is like a prison sentence—thought old Transman. However there are amenities—at night the fluffy white/beige cat sat next to him in bed. Their 2 hearts beat beside each other.

Well, it is said: It is not who wins, its how they run the race.

> And after Mrs. Behn we turn a very important corner on the road; we leave behind, shut up in their parks among their folios, those solitary great ladies who wrote without audience or criticism, for their own delight alone. We come to town and rub shoulders with ordinary people in the streets....
> --A Room Of Ones Own, Virginia Wolf; 1913.

> *

This is a hot day. Suddenly the wind picks up, the cities speak to each other—Chicago speaks on the winds voice to San Francesco; 'Frisco returns its wind message to New York. The wind picked him up and slid him across the checkerboard maps of towns, which comprise a continent of earth and put him there; then as it had pulled him out to the East Coast, picked him up again and sent him here, to the West Coast after a time. The old city, Chi-Town & all those freezing

251

winters with ice on the Lake is just a memory away. The wind is whispering. Where will it send him now?

Jamaican Sean tells about an immigrant woman from Trinidad, who lived in Manhattan; nobody had seen her around their tenement building for a long time, finally upon citizens concerns, the police broke into her apartment and discovered she'd been dead for a year. Nothing but bones left.

Will I say it came to nothing? My life's work? Will I live—housed, -- as Hashem has promised-- in a small room or studio somewhere, with no sales of my books nor mentions of them for decades & decades passing, until such point I finally give up the ghost and stop being?

People want. They want the bus to come. They want their loved ones to live. We want. We most often don't get.

Sunday AM March 9
My life has been a bad life & I don't attribute that to being purposefully a bad person, but due to exterior circumstances. — Being the world of segregation into which I was born and the situation of myself on the front line of transexualism ---a pioneer— experiencing all the hardships a pioneer must undergo to pave the way for the next generation; the fact that our large community of trannys is sweeping over earth in a new wave heretofore unseen in so many numbers—a world not yet prepared for us—and isolation is the norm. The lack of social outlets. Loneliness. Denial of service. Having to struggle for much of what we do get (which in an earlier generation was impossible).

I am an extremely valuable person, because I am a fighter. I don't just think the thoughts of other people, but my own. I go on my own course; too few will follow theirs.

He had well instituted himself in various pews of several religions… Hashem kept him company!

So the seasons washed over him & some of the verbiage stuck. Unfamiliar words, phrases, in conjunction with songs stuck. Slowly a

252

new language formed in his mind. Rudimentary things. —Hebrew melodies; the smattering of vocabulary; a strange language adhering to his mind.

As far as living in this world goes; God has more or less written us the ticket carte-blanche;

Do what you want too—you know My rules.

Just to let us play it out, the whole drama on this godforsaken planet, using our free choice for better or worse. If we don't follow God's Golden Rules however, destruction lays ahead in this world and maybe in the next. But God is not standing above us cracking the whip like a jail warden, maybe this is because S/He wants to see what we do with our free will. And we are forever reminded of the original truth—those Ten Commandments written into Judeo-Christianity, and many if not all the worlds other great religions. We don't have a choice at all! We have the constant day-to-day choice to obey the truth, or to disobey. Step by step, to stay on The Path, or to fall by the wayside.

Work on LEADER OF THE PACK, with all its sex scenes, aberrations & raunchy biker lezzies gang violence continues, soon it will be ready to go up on the Global Marketplace via Print On Demand (POD).

RE: Sex Writing; I recall while perusing the stacks in a used bookstore with Hugo, finding a slim tome, out of print, by a certain beatnik author who had depicted an episode of 1 or 2 years duration, in which many now-famous names are dropped, and the intricate sexual relationships amongst them, pairs, orgies, etc., is graphically depicted. The story behind this particular book supposedly is that it was written, semi-diary like, and submitted to the publisher, with the sex suggested in a simple few words here and there. For instance: "Kerouk, Ginsberg and I were in bed, drunk on wine & high on drugs, over the weekend", and let it go at that—but the publisher had written back that if the author wanted *'to be paid, and a contract signed, then they must spice up the novel with a more in depth detail of what was done in the bed during that time, etc.'* So this is the progression. A suggestive passage, only hinted at, expanded into several sentences, which thus becomes provocative, fringing on the prurient. And this, which expanded into a few paragraphs dropped throughout out the book, makes it a gem schoolkids will secretly search for on the stacks of the library during the humdrum world of research for their homework. Now if you drag that sex scene out for 4 or 5 pages, *then* you're getting into the world of pornography. So this is what I did with some of my own writing, only, I was the editor speaking to myself. In the 1990s, my own body heat demanding to me that I should further illustrate what I had been hinting at in an earlier style of the 1960s and 70s.

121.
Long lean in bluejeans Sean leaping about like a cat busily pasting photos of Le Bijoutier's art photos of graffiti upon his bookstore. — Deje vu! Art photos of graffiti scrawled on building walls, now hung on pristine white walls in an art showing!

> Bullets on the wall, already fired; streaks, wheat paste, tags.
> —le Bijoutier.

Le Bijou is having a baby, his wife has become the queen, as most pregnant women; hormonal surges inside her body—which carries their young—gives her mood swings; first she wants to do this, then changes her mind and wants to do that. If I was to tell young parents some wisdom to give to their young it is, to have faith, trust—not in people so much, not in this biological world, but in the Maker. *Don't forget that we are loved by an unending love...*

> **We are loved by an unending love.**
> **We are encompassed by everlasting arms.**
> **We are a soul entrusted to the Most High,**
> **from beginning to end.**
> **We are not alone on even the most solitary of journeys.**
> **We are loved by an unending love.**

Made my first purchase at Babylon Falling bookstore! Ten dollah. (Courtesy discount from kindly Proprietor.) Hebrew Language discs. The receipt says this in patios:

> One day, one day, Babylon they will be falling.

More reading. Comparisons to 1930's times, and today's. WW 2 rations. SF poor free food line. Run here, & there, all over town for enough supplies for the day, for the week. That's how it was then, that's how it is now---if you are poor, desperate and want to eat. Yet this isn't fascism?

Why are we born into such an unstable world? Nothing is permanent—not housing, not our lives! We are like jellyfish. What is the purpose of having such a life? Transman kept working despite this fretful vision.

Well! Kemperer was financially dependant on his family! Along with the best and brightest! The baby of the nest—who takes longer to mature—their brains being so engaged in higher investigations. The gestation and weaning of the chimpanzee, human beings closest animal relative; the long-memory elephant; all the higher ones, the most brilliant! (Ahem…)

122.
Well, as for me, I have not forgot the color of my skin, or my beginnings in this life…

Because I know my tribe and know my people, and tho they may make no difference to any body but us, these flashes are of especial importance to me, so will portray them.

Have spoken before of the violence in the community from which I arose. Today finally must venture back to old Oaktown, pay the yearly mailbox dues. Awful busride.

Sadly, a fight broke out between some black youths.

Every time Transman came to Oaktown—about every 2-3 months he was privy to see leaps of change in the architectural landscape; buildings up to 8th floor iron construction beams, whereas 3 months ago it was a vacant lot. These changes are more dramatic being the length of time inbetween visits. With mild interest he perused these philosophical thoughts, when he became aware of hell.

Black man chanting rap music in a violent loud explosion of hate:

> We gonna take over West Oakland, we gonna shit on yo' flo' we gonna piss on yo' rug! Black Oakland! Black Oakland!

After an interval of this, a fight breaks out—between the black youths themselves. As the bus goes rocking & rolling thru space, over the freeway overpass trying to get somewhere, but eventually it comes to a stop. The black rapper jumps off of the bus.

A small brown girl, wild, evil sparks in her eyes, teeshirt, baggy pants, gangsta style—female, a dike—does she confess this? Leaps up on the back of a bus seat, jerks open the small vent window, sticks her head out it, yells at the black youth. To retaliate he bangs the side of the bus with his fists punching it, making horrible lound CLANGS! Leaps up and grabs hold of the open window vent, chinning himself up, screaming; immediately his nappy head and part of his shoulder emerge inside the bus; evil face yelling at her broiling rage.

"YO' KAIN'T FIT THRU THERE NIGGA!" She hollers, laughing hate, jumps back down off the back of the seat, dancing in the aisles pointing her fingers at him   Her loud violent implosion, she screams. "COME UP TO 45TH STREET NIGGA! COME UP TO 45TH STREET!" (Where her gang awaits to stomp the shit out of him.) "AH LIVES ON 45TH MOTHAFUCKAH!"

Personally, Transman thought: I don't have the strength to fight any more. This shit. These black people, my cousins—distant cousins, — and growing more distant with passing time.

Then I was a stranger, uninvolved in it, just as the Asians who sat there staring straight ahead; as the middle aged black women with disgust etched into their brown African faces; the young whites grim-lipped, not turning to look at the scene; tho I was a stranger far removed, the hate and violence still lingers on my brain.

1860: Back in slave times—on the threshold before freedom—the last slaves generation who worked the fields from dawn to dusk reaping no benefit for themselves, nor share nor fraction of the worth they produced for their own control and self determination, saw the master—not the overseer, who actually worked hard at his whip-cracking, but owner--- ride around in fine clothes on a fine horse at his leisure doing very little work but decision making, going town and gambling and drinking—the lady of the plantation had little say, and was not in final control; she could not ride into town alone, nor wheel and deal with the big boys, nor travel without an escort those long distances between plantations and was to some effect a prisoner herself—the slaves saw this man who did no work; no hoeing the field rows, no lifting the cotton bale, no picking, no stooping, no bending down, but who dressed in the finest array, dined on gourmet foods and had the easiest life. This was the role model the slaves saw from generation to generation as they stooped to work their fields as their ancestors before them stooped and worked the rows all seeing the master ride about in leisure and finery & comfort. When emancipation came, the freed slaves rejoiced, but soon became bewildered---no one had taught them how to get what the rich had, someone, somewhere in that gentleman owners' linage had had to work and to work hard. To do back-breaking labor. To study, to learn. Now for the first time they could keep the produce of their work—but no one had schooled them how to attain these goals! They had no training. No skills. And above all, many had incorporated the image of the effete, leisure master as a goal, instead of the hard working climber, builder. This according to WEB Dubois.

2008: Past today's street corners, young blax man hobbled by trousers around his knees; blank eyed, hip hopped wondering whaddup? Meaning of their life's already lost and not yet 20.

Sunday PM March 9
What has happened in the tranny department is similar to what happened in the black department, —there's all these people getting by best they can. Working the very lowest paid jobs—if they can find employment at all—or stealing, or living way below poverty level, on welfare ('relief is what they called it in black Southside Chicago in the 50's), maintained at the very lowest fringes of society by being poorly paid or reciepient of welfare system charity handouts—if at all, suddenly the greater society realizes, 'we have this fringe group of people in our midst' so it begins to study us, take note of us, representatives from these communities are appointed— often not the

wisest nor best qualified, but those hustlers who can work their way up to the front of the pack quickly. Fueled by Societies *fear* largely – in the case of transsexual community, of HIV/AIDS, and, in blacks, of their crime spreading out of their ghettos over into the general populus; riots and greater social disruption. Soon you have a class of well-positioned 'pok chop' blacks, and 'elite' trannys who have government appointments, or granted positions, titles, and big $80,000 year salaries, while the rest of their population is bought off by occasional free testimony dinners, barbeque fetes, some minor awards and such. Hardly anything is done by these fake figureheads—it is the seething power of the people behind them, the masses and their muscle from whom these great changes come about; —and in fact sometimes these very representatives serve to keep a lid on things, to hamper true social progress of the people they represent. Transman had seen this in the blax community since he was a little boy-girl, and now saw it in trans world, and was sick of it, having dropped out almost entirely from all their social programs, just as he'd left the black world decades upon decades ago.

What does this racism, this sexism, this classism—mean? It means one group of society –the dominant one--is able to climb up, be empowered, enriched, and accredited in the annals of history; the other continue to slide down, builds little, and is eventually obliterated.

Another case in point is the lesbian community to which Transman Red once belonged or is a category at least he was lumped into and spent time in those cold illegal bars harassed by vice cop raids of the 1950's and 60's—of many of many years duration. This he documented in many of his curious volumes of semi-forgotten lore. But this labor of love has brought him little fame, and less money. No security. And possibly, no future.

Just reading thru Chester Himes Lonely Crusade—in which in an episode incidental to the plot a black union man rapes his wife. From the male born perspective this might not be so bad but from the FTM perspective it is. Well, I myself am writing a different kind of book.

Wednesday AM March 5

On TV election primaries Hillary Clinton is on an upswing comeback; surprising! One of the born again Christians drops out; in doing so quotes the apostle Paul which nauseates me—which seems a strange reaction for a Prophet of the Lord. I react so virulently ssince hearing religion, especially my own, on the lips of those high in power is frightening because it has become synonymous with hate, prejudice, leading to murder in the streets done by thugs who assume empowerment because of by the messages they hear from higher offices—the church, politicians, those leaders on top.

Do you think everybody has a prison? I do, and so do you--- maybe a few of them. One of Transman's prison was his gender disphoria, which he was never sure if he was hidden or not—that is if he could be 'read' or, most likely someone had told them secretly of his female-to-male status, or that they had stumbled across this wry fact in reading his books, or publicity about him in the public sphere. So, he was loath to tell people about his writing, or to offer up his fine 80-selection book catalogue, something of which he was tremendously proud—because he realized it would out him instantly, to the perceptive reader.

PM March 3
At first when one ventures out into the trans-community, which at surface look is new, enticing, fabulous, rich in its tapestry of gender array beheld in the showcase of a larger watering hole like SF, you are interested in other transpeoople, including trannys of the opposite gender from yourself, until some become so damaged by the world this is no longer possible.

Trans Center has reopened again---at half the size as the original; a welcome addition to my resources—had a fabulous delicious dinner there prepared by the gal's efficiency cooking class. Black MTF cook, Miss N. and 5 or 6 onlookers. The leader briskly whisked about with her few pots and pans and sparse appliances. —This class in most practicality focuses on cooking excellent meals on small appliances such as portable ovens, min-refrigerators, hotplates & microwaves ovens—all designed for the low-income transsexual person, who often must live in SRO hotel rooms (with no kitchen, and only a small sink). A handful of girls was in attendance, Transman, photocopying in the next room and was invited. Fried chicken, mashed potatoes, corn, and green beans. Who needs desert with food this good!

All my life, all my life! I've seen damaged, deranged girl/boy transsexuals dressed in half woman, half man clothes pieced together; man clothes re-done to be effeminate thru the addition of ruffles, garters, higher heels, pedal pushers; and the men-women in semi drag, men's too large clothes appearing in the corners of metropolitan cities.

So we come & go. Witnessed by the breathless voices of transwoman:

> I don't see Leonard anymore.

> Were not friends any more. I bet you think I'm foolen'. No, we were best friends too!

>   *

Shelter. Where the dogs, bored, patient waiting out their time until they get a home. The Reverend is still here—my 3-legged pitbull friend. Thru two sets of glass doors, and 100 feet of space he sees me and frantically begins waging his short thin string of a tail, his powerful chest bull neck and head dancing about on 3 legs excited at his visitor, approaching.

We've all been touched by the dragon's breath at some point in our lives…. Childhood, those abused… adulthood… Some their whole lives licked by its evil flame—like slavery time. Some, a brief horrific intensity, like WW 2 holocaust survivors… The Reverend when 8,000 ton rusted car, axel fell on his hindquarters shattering his leg; crushing him into the dirt where he lay pinned, trapped, unattended for a week, until neighbors heard his pitiful howls & finally police were sent over the fence to investigate—and rescued him. The cruel owner had abandon the lot, cars, dogs and all, in flight-failure to avoid paying property taxes.

Friday March 7
3 of Mother Teresa's clan mount the subway stairs—blue scarves headdress white skirts to the floor, sandals and blue socks. One holds

260

a picture of Jesus. I wonder how long they will be able to keep that up—the lifestyle. Must keep up my Jesus.

Mother Teresa & Henry Darger have extremity; severe, even harsh lives in common, dedicated to a single cause, and neither one of them sold out. That great passion and their love of Catholic mass.

Transman was temporarily rich from his windfall of cash, yet old habits born in poverty were hard to curb. He spied a glint of silver in the newsrack coin return slot. Retuvia. Repayment for honestly depositing 50-cents to board the bus, being instead of faking it, offering up a wrong, or expired transfer as the destitute poor & street bums do, or the cheep/stingy over-worked Asian women.

I quote VK: Nil inultum remanebit (Latin.) Nothing will go unpunished.

Sunday March 9
Summer compels… bustling activity in the streets—even if I know no one to talk to. Procrastinating art's beginning. Please Dear Lord let me begin! -- Idea! Set a 1-hour goal! Only 1 hour! —Nothing to be wary of. A snails pace, that way 'the thing' will be accomplished. Accoarding to the AA code— One Step At A Time.

False starts:
    1971. When moved in with another Jewish girlfriend circa 1973, she had a balcony on her roomy studio apartment. On it stored junk, such as dusty window screens, a dead vacuum cleaner. It was shared (divided by a half wall) with obnoxious black next-door neighbors who later were the cause of the entire 8-unit building emptying out of every former tenant including the manager. A brief art struggle resulting in Nothing.
1996. Driveway of warehouse (which Transman had fenced in, for the protection of his dogs) resulting in dot-dash spots of color, outline of a Negroid head/self portrait—just begun.

2008. First try here in my studio, with oils—result, one almost finished work, Student And The Golden Pot.

AM Monday March 10

261

I must say that I treated my Art like a stepchild. Put it aside in favor of other things. For some it is the yen to travel the world. For others having a good solid job on the common marketplace takes precedence. I love the word. I love writing the word. That took precedents over presentation of color images.

So Transman went to bed; he was so tired felt he could sleep for 1,000 years; & tucked himself in with his little cat.

AM Tuesday, March 11
During daily life I see human features, or animal —a dogs nostrils— study it until its etched on the lense of the eye. Note: blue & white brushstroke-swept sky of horizon… Am living the fine arts painters vision!

Painted the second day, in acrylics, child bright blues, reds, yellows— The Blue Dog—takes shape on a typical Arobateau size canvas 36" x 24".

AM Tuesday March 11
1 o'clock, past noon, still in bed—no energy, cat lays across my stomach, warm belly. When you get old the fires burn low. Don't have determination you once had. —But a cup of coffee helps!

I want to talk about passion, -- and drive. As you see I have much drive—80 titles in my book catalogue. A tremendous energy I could summon, pushed myself along the years like a sailboat, blowing and gusting perpetually; the human mechanism winds down, tires. Yes it is true, no longer have the raw carnal red-blooded passion flowing thru me. But the memory of it, and my ideals—and my goals are substituted instead. Only paint a few hours a day and write a few. Not even 8 hours daily! I didn't think this would happen. In the old days it was 12, 16!

> Gather ye rosebuds while ye may
> Time is a passing….
> --Percy Blythe Shelly

Ideas & plans slip away…

Dear Lord—thank you for the time.

Art painting being physical, while, in contrast, writing being sedentary, its all one must do is to a pull chair up to their computer sit in one space typing—and Journaling is the easiest discipline there is—much more difficult to construct the plot of a novel. As regards to painting, there is physical activity of the brushstroke; the walking back and forth for perspective. The constant changing of colors, brushes; getting up to wipe areas of canvas of paint with vigor to start over, or as an effect—a hazy back wash—meanwhile the writer has sat right there in one spot only wiggling their fingers on the keyboard while the giant dome of their human brain spins out some fantastic trash into sentences on a page!

The paint treys are assembled, chairs, tripod pulled out to their proper positions… The clean damp brushes await in the open drawer on a chair… Wearily, his steps drag… he had walked 20 blocks up and down Fillmore street searching for M. a shopgirl there who had said he should come visit her —but couldn't find the place, having forgotten its name. Then had gone shopping on Polk and walked home with a heavy load… ahem. Also that productive Monday had swept and mopped his floors & sunk picture hangers. Jerked off. Then slept 2 hours. Then typed until 5am. He had exhausted his 64-year old body. Now it was Tuesday… worn out… wanted to just sit down, go back to sleep. Then he thought this:

The Blue Dog grins out at me. I must continue!

The Blue Dog progresses magnificently! A green foot! 2 human fingers extended in a surreptitious blessing. A blue paw—instead of a human hand—a great blue dog centerstage! BARK! BARK! BARK!
Baruch!
Baruch atah Adonai Eloheinu melech haolam!
(Bless us! Praise Adonai! Ruler of the universe!)

Push a little poop of color onto pallet-for mid-sky; Blue Dog emerges splendidly out of the subconscious ethos, into reality on canvas. I wanted a bright orange color—for the mid-landscape of The Blue Dog—God told me:

You want the colors of heaven.

Hashem had showed me, long ago in a dream I was joyously painting
a show poster 8 feet by 6 done in the most brilliant, free colors; —
they are not found on earth.

> Amen, Amen, Amen!
> It is the service of the Lord
> Who has carried him this far!
> & his own grungy efforts.

Lost Dog Shelter: The Reverend has set sail! Sailor cap upon his
furry head! Off to a proper dog home—a foster care. Transman had
begun The Blue Dog that Monday, unknowing that when he arrived at
the shelter the Reverend had already shipped out! He is off on a new
adventure in a dog's life. —Something to recant to his cronies up in
dog paradise, in the Great Hereafter. His placement is a foster care,
don't know if it will be permanent, or if he will return to the shelter. I
hope and pray the best for this fine sailor of life.

Taking blood pressure medicine. Exercise, watching his diet—slowly
loosing pounds. He'd lost 25 pounds over the last 3 years.
This, and worrying, plus condo-daydreaming his incessant mantra
about:
> Living spaces—never content; long for permanency, long for change.
> The restless spirit of an artist.

123.
Your demons always come back to bite you. If it takes a lifetime—
they will come back. Because the devil has eternity —minus one day.
That last day is Gods Day. Judgment Day. Until then, unless dealt
with, your deamons can wait and dream up the perfect time to destroy
their host. So get with the God Program Dear Children—in addition
to our radical politics—for it is truly God who will save us in the Last
Days. Believe on Her-Him!

> Put your trust in me, sayeth the Lord.
> --Holy Scripture.

> Praise the Lord and pass the ammunition.
> --Mother Jones

This area where he lived is increasingly deluged in art students; the mogul who owns the art college is fighting over money—a land grab. 3 percent of all the real-estate in the city is owned by her, thru her fucken' college.

A few black remnants stand around pissing in the streets—a few anything 'po.

All the talk of residents of SF, (us poor) is rent control, and most are very curious to see the outcome of the June election in which the fate of rent control will be tested by the public vote for the first time. All fear the day it may be overturned. A disaster for people with incomes under $50,000 per year. Sean comments how the ordinary person is just scuffling to get by on a daily basis, weary they return from work and collapse in front of the TV, chill out; do nothing the remainder of their evening. But the rich have so much time on their hands; leisure, in which to plot the latest way to seize even more money from those under them. All the talk of international travelers is rising rents in all cities of the globe. Paris, Marseilles. All the big and medium size cities of America. Transman's reouccurrent day-dream was to have permanent housing—in SF, a condo, a tiny condo, but something which would lawfully anchor him here, where he could live out his old age in security. A lovely place with a balcony, a No Smokers building! Quiet! Safe! Centrally located!

All of $35 spent at art store—must spend down this $7,000 other then that $2,000 which can be legally saved, and now am on the last $500. Thinking about how precious this $35 is, for necessary supplies, and suddenly outside in the street, as he whirled out in coat, cane, carrying packages, saw a dope addict he knew (a former MTF, reverted to boy-mode because of street life necessity) who did not meet his eyes but went stumbling along on some mission and thought, now that is a waste. To blow $20, to snort up $10 to shoot up $30, to sniff $10, to smoke $5; and it is not giving anything back to the world at all.

AM Wednesday March 12
Habit, the doer of anything must learn—not just art—to get into the swing of it—to form a habit of it, pays off well! Most certainly in the doing of art.

Thursday PM March 13

How the painters *long* for heaven, the colors will be so vibrant there!

Tuesday PM March 11
Fewer trips to the Fillmore—now that the Revered has set sail. @ Babylon Falling. Voices from outside:

Hey! Is this a bookstore?

Bookstore confluence—Shaun snaps photos of Red as he scribbles notes. Sean S. hangs pictures of John Felix Arnold, David Chung Lee, & Billy X's historic archive of Emery Douglass. What an illustrious list of names. Meanwhile, in a past—not far--the end of poor tomcat Muscal draws closer. It is so cruel.

Then Alex bounces in; a slender young man in excellent clothes. Red gives his apologia for semi-trashing him in his drash about consumerism, and promises to write something nice as a counterbalance. Queries, "Alex, what can I say about you which is good?" To which he replies:

I brighten your day up, cheer you up, make you laugh.
--Alex. (Mr. Van Hussan.)

And this is true.

Friday AM March 14
They worshipped at the alter of perpetual coffee Hashem had provided. A cuppa AM, or a terrible blueish mood permeates his day. Wake up Artist!

You must be what Hashem created you to be! Artist! Triumph!

You must take the same fascistic zeal as madmen have used---take this energy—take your art, your passion to the highest degree—then use it for good, for productivity, always weighed against the checks & balances set up by Hashem, (Our God By Many Different Names) and give this gift to the human race, to the universe!

Time... It sweeps on, fast, it trickles steadily each grain in a sand dial; time is a most precious entity.

All this denial, this not-belonging my given status of being an out-cast from the system which reigns, is what gives me my dark edge. Well—isn't every edge dark? It certainly is not of the Light---this world is not of The Light, so it needs a Prophet like me.

The soul of an artist is very sensitive--at least in some respects. Often you must not give a damn about responsibility—your first and foremost allegiance being to The Gift; this can have dire consequences in your economic future, in your romance future, in your future standing as a human being in the world; but--- at least they will say, '*he/she was a Great artist.*'

Transman thought; I will become rich and then won't they be amazed! ---A hoard of supervisors, managers, bosses, themselves lackeys— who he'd worked for over his long job history. Not to mention priests, rabbis, and leaders of the various communities his life touched upon.

Artists, & street dwellers inhabit a different zone. We eschew ordinary kinds of status, cool fashion, stylish cars, money for money sake—not the actual bread, room rents it will afford--- or tubes of colors and sheets of paper--- we are not caught up in it, believing fully our great/small gifts will eventually 'pay off big' at the end, big indeed! Ha! Many go to a paupers cremation, our ashes not even romantically tossed into the sea, but buried in some unmarked poor folks mass ash grave...

You know the saying--- money can't buy love, the same is true for art... money can't buy it; a, poor person must squeeze out the time to do it, yet, for those who have the time because of possessing wealth, money is no guarantee the artist will have drive, talent necessary to push them over that fine bar into quality.

Sunday PM March 16

A surprise trip to gambling casino on Indian land; (Pomo), with Jasmin & L. who comprise the duo- 'Dalora'. And the woman who helped raise L., J. Three of us senior citizens now (56, 74, and me, 64.) Jasmin is the baby at 44.

J. has paid tribute to the gambling gods for so many years she won. J says, "I sit there and don't let go of the machine, I tell it it's gotta win—I stare it down. And play until it gives me my money. Then, when it goes cold, I stop playing." And she came home with $300. *Reds, blue, yellows lights flashing...*

This strange miasma of humanity en mass causes Transman to think... stirring his meditative soul in the face of his loss of $100; I think of all the good our modern societies could be doing with all the luxuries, the things we have, the technologies. *Black, silver, chrome, red, blue, orange, yellow, purple flashing lights of the gambling casino...*

River of sound. Flashing bulbs, lights, think of what this human race is doing to itself... *An ocean of bells clanging, wheels spinning, time racing, lights flashing...*

In restaurant none of the food was up to the par of Dalora's new diet—chiefly raw vegetables, fruits and nuts. Soy milk. They had none of this. Everyone in the place was overweight. Red saw them as they trundled out of the buffet area with laden plates, processed foods, sloppy, spilling over the sides of their bowls. Plates with mountains of beef, lavish sauces & dips; all livestock/dairy from tortured cows and bulls. Eggs from cruelly treated chickens. They came past in wheel chairs, using canes, crutches; majority of them were big as bulls themselves. Thick necks, triple rolls of fat on distended bellies. Surrounding us, the casino: *gold, silver, red emergency flashing lights...* Jasmin had very little choice so she decided, after taking a tour of the salad bar. Dalora & Red ordered salads & vegetarian burgers. J. eats like a bird. There were no other raw foods—no nuts, vegetables, no soy. She taught us our diet the whole time. In a few short hours we have become Holistic.

The four drove home from the casino in silence. We drain the last drop of fellowship out of the day, and we parted.

Our human family; we have the knowledge about holistic living, about wind & sun energy, water power, but we continue to pollute the earth gouging gargantuan amounts of oil. We know holistic, but we deny everything we've been given. The beef we eat is from tortured animals, the poultry, from unhappy chickens, the fish farms over-stocked with unsanitary, crowded, sad fish. And the advanced human race? —We walk about with a variety of unnecessary diseases. We kill. We hate. We die early.

River of sound. Flashing bulbs, lights, think of this human race; the genocide it is doing to itself… *Ocean of bells clanging, wheels spinning, time racing lights flashing*….

And what have you got to fight this evil machine? Your work! Your works! Your work stands after you!

124.
If I had my life to live over I wouldn't change anything---yes I would! I wouldn't be as lonely, I wouldn't be as sad, I wouldn't be as desperate, I wouldn't be as afraid! —But, then, I wouldn't have as much art!

I love my work, thus I continue.

Monday March 17
Fiery sunburst corona of raw creation! There is nothing to replace it! First colors blazing off the pallet! Magnificent reds, eye-shattering yellows; oranges! Vibrant green/blues! Raw! Fresh, the dawn of infant art—done by hands touched by the Master.

Week 2 of painting in acrylics. Cannot match the urgency of oils – ancient 35-year old painting which gazes at me down over my bed (the unstretched Arab). Awake to its wild yellows, reds, orange, turquoise… Acrylics doesn't get this close. Will finish The Blue Dog, do another or two in Acrylic—then switch back to at least two oils in succession (one of which is to finish up Student At The Golden Pot.)

Dominique L. calls, to invite me to go to a poetry reading with her, ends her phonecall as usual with this—with it I may well end this work:
> Peace to you and all living creatures.
> --Wiccian invocation.

I would like this book to become a 'coffee table' book for artists—especially beginners or those recalcitrant, to draw inspiration from—such as does the student at his/her golden pot. To return to this reference work for artists at such time their spirits flag low, or for sheer entertainment. Will say again—if you're given a gift you must use it! It is a Prime Directive! Written into the genetic fiber of your physical & mental being; set up like a canvas on the easel of your soul! It comes from before the beginning—and will continue after demise of your physical body! Don't let your Works go undone!!!!

T- Red had started the new raw food diet as proscribed by Jasmin on their gambling spree on Pomo Indian land, River Creek casino. The $100 he'd dropped from his windfall of $7,100+ had been well spent—having been exposed to the true in and outs and fine details of The Diet and its fine nuances on the 9 hours the 4 of them were together. Especially in the restaurant, where the foursome had loved to dine in previous sprees, in which the showdown occurred. The bill came to $45 (Red paid for one of the few times, *cause celebre*) but very little food was consumed. They had watched as heavy people, sick, people, bent, crippled, people aged-too fast, listless people lumbered in and out of the eat-all-you can buffet, with piles of crap on plates, which was now verboten to them. They order salads, vegetarian burgers, etc., Jasmin & Red fastidiously avoiding the ham in their Cobb Salad—greasy pork, the worst part of it—until the end when, weakened they both mixed a little ham into the good part—the green lettuce/ tomatoes -- and devoured the salty pig guiltily… Red had come away from the spree $140 lighter in his pockets (including picking up tab for the meal) but *inspired.*

At a suburban mall we spied poorer citizens feasting their eyes in shop window at an aluminum pot & pan set—the poisonous alloy in which metal leaches out with each cooking into the food, to be intaken by the human digestive tract. And why do they lust for these poison pots? Like dogs they smell the scent where other dogs have pissed there, --running with the common herd; to beady eyed birds, the pots are bright & shiny!

When he returned to his small studio he promptly hid all his pots and pans; placed a cutting board over the burners on the stove and converted it into a juice mixing area/cutting board for slicing up the raw vegetables he would now subsist on. He wasn't going all the way with this—still allowed himself decaf coffee and regular, with cream or milk. Had several years back abandon all sugars, sweaters both real & artificial & brown, and honey, and as of the last 4 months had ceased eating deserts.

> L: The human digestive track was not designed to eat meat. Have you seen how the human intestine winds and goes lilke this—zig and zag—well the intestine of a carnivore, a predator, goes like this! (Illustrates by making a short straight line.)

PM March 17
For years I testified in the common streets how having struggled for 5 years to give up alcohol—finally succeeded; also my struggle to break in two, toss away, destroy and stop buying cigarettes and finally after 2 major attempts was able to give up smoking cigarettes for good; but that loosing weight was a different matter altogether; for once one gives up drinking liquor one can live without taking a single drop of it, smoking the same, having overcome its use for a week or two, the desire passes, never to be reminded of smoking again; but one can not give up eating food—and thus we have our appetite constantly tempted. Now I see—ten years later. The secret is *to give up the wrong foods.* When I gave up sugar the first time, this lasted about 5 years. Now, for the second time so far I have not had any desire to eat ice-cream, pies, candies, etc., —because I got it out of my system. If one gives up certain poisonous types of food, the yen for them will soon pass off the immediate desire of their pallet. It is possible to reorientate your tastebuds and mind and body to a different kind of holistic diet so that raw nuts, shakes made of greens, (chopped finely), bananas and filtered water taste great. I have done this all day today—now to see if I have sufficient energy! Oh, the diet is not absolute-- had a cup of coffee, 3 slices of cheese and a can of sardines!

LEADER bumps & grinds slowly forward down the home stretch. These couldn't all be computer scanner errors! Looks more like the tight-lip blue pencil of censorship to me!

> As if drawn back to the reality of having two women, Angel pulled out of Saundra's pussy, and turned, laying down on the pillow and pulled Crystal over her. Expert hands undid the black negligee, and her beautiful alabaster body was bare, a sweet sight. The butch felt her clit grow hot. It

271

was swollen from having rubbed against Saundra's thighs. Now Crystal was pulling her jockey shorts off down her legs. Angel straightened up; athletic body moved like a panther, she pulled her teeshirt off over her head, a pair of full breasts bounced out. Saundra leaned over her, brown skin against white, and began kissing her breasts, and Angel felt, simultaneously, her woman Crystal's mouth hot on her sex. Curly blond head between her legs, her own knees raised up; a pink tongue licking in the fuzzy nest of her sex, probing her cunt lips, sucking the nectar of her womanly flower.

As if drawn back to the reality of having two women, Angel pulled out of Saundra's pussy, **fingers sticky and flavored by pussyjuice**, and turned, laying down on the pillow and pulled Crystal over her. Expert hands undid the black negligee, so her beautiful alabaster body was bare. A sweet sight. The butch felt her clit grow hot. It was swollen from having rubbed against Saundra's **thigh.** Now Crystal was pulling Angel's jockey shorts off down her legs. Angel straightened up; athletic body moved like a panther. **Muscles of iron flexed in her thighs.** She pulled her teeshirt off over her head, a pair of full breasts bounced out. **Saundra moaned at the sight; leaned over the sexy butch,** brown skin against white, and began kissing her breasts **in long circular sucks & licks of her full mouth.** And Angel felt, simultaneously, her woman Crystal's **lips, red hot** on her sex. Curly blond head between her legs; as her own knees raised up, **opening her pussy,** a pink tongue licking in the fuzzy nest; probing her cunt lips, sucking the nectar of her womanly flower.

PM Tuesday March 18

Shadows are falling on Babylon Falling… He used the toilet in a hurry, which resulted in wrong positioning of disc, & he pissed on himself. *Feel the piss dripping down my leg.* Evening, and the Transman had deep thoughts in his niche at the window seat, which he proceeded to scribble down furiously on the crumpled pad of paper he always carried in his shirt pocket:

Down deep under the skin that's where treasure begins.

That's a good title for a book— DISAPPOINTMENT. Have planned for my last book in this rondo to be JOY/SIMCA –but must speak to this negative issue soon, because of seeing it in the faces of so many people (as have read it in myself). DISAPPOINTMENT. From the black young men speaking patios of the doomed future who say:z

'Yo dawg, waddup?

Nuthin dawg, dis ain't shit. Ah see 'Benzes & 'Jags & shit, Ah gotta get me one! You don't know man! How bad Ah gotta get me one of 'dem rides!

From the lowest street joker to myself with my condo dreams, to the much more upscale Dalora and their wild spending. They possess both car & condo, but still want *more!* All these low-down desires will kill a muthafucka! Consumerism! The desire of money for money sake and all the trappings of money—which is not a real product. Consumerism is a false god!

Notes AM/PM Wednesday March 19
The winds are blowing—the winds of change. Am preparing: SMALL RETROSPECT OF MY ART PAINTINGS, a coffee table book for the artist.

Frieda Kahlo stares down at me from under those thick black eyebrows which join across middle of her forehead over bridge of her nose, a faint feathery moustache, with two giant grey Cockatiels perched on her arm.

Here is the problem. Society tells us to be the status quo, the norm. To follow the middle of the road upon a secure life course. But most of the worlds great saints, the worlds great artists, and, pioneers, were innovators!

Thousands of peace demonstrators flood downtown San Francisco— protest the 5th year of this war. Transman had been near the end of his working career doing telemarketing for a newspaper outfit, when fiery headlines and full picture spreads thru the first 5 pages of the Daily News proclaimed our arrival in Afghanistan, (or Iraq?). The old guy sold newspapers very well back then—but minute America's invasion was over his papers sales dropped off and the beautiful, cruel female office boss berated Red for lack of sales & he was summarily fired. Today—5 years later, after 37 years on the job market, with all that lost time working meaningless jobs--- he had not worked for any boss; and because of it created an awful lot of books, plus begin painting again, and was pleased... The artistic discipline one imposes on themselves is far less stressful then a real job.

Tonight outside the windows of bookstore can be seen groups of well-dressed people debarking cabs carrying peace demonstration posters. Traipse, trailing past, headed home, tiredly after the long march, with anti-war signs.

VK's nazi war diary is getting grim:

> According to the Judeo ban of dogs, cats and birds.
> --VK, recounting the holocaust re: being forced to give up their pets.

Back in world of art supply's after 30 years a writer; an art store I remember. Under the El tracks in Chicago's Loop —on Wabash Avenue. Going home with giant tubes of color, some brushes, long wood canvas stretchers; courtesy of my father.

These stores were places of paints, brushes, easels, pallets, pre-stretched canvasses, canvas rolls, stretcher bars, pallet knives. Today at the shop on Van Ness Avenue, a huge thick picture book—2,000 years of human made art. From cave-drawings to Egyptian pottery, to commissioned portraiture of kings & queens of Europe, to modern cubism, surrealism, abstract. Art thru the ages of humankind…

I *am* entertainment! You are entertainment! The artist is the one creating all this entertainment! Writers, screenwriters, movie stars, ballet dancers, symphony conductors, musicians, painters; all artists!

LEADER pounds down to the finish, wearily rectifying its enraging censorship:

> The slender blond felt she was on an exciting adventure. Arose from her side of the bed, climbed ever the snoring body of Angel, and, as Saundra moved to make room for her, slid her naked body in between the brown woman and Angel. They touched each other, and kissed, tongues swirling into each other's mouths.
> The slender blond felt she was on an exciting adventure. Arose from her side of the bed, climbed ever the snoring body of Angel, and, as Saundra moved to make room for her, slid her naked body in between the **curvaceous dark skinned female** and her butch. Their **probing fingers** touched each other, as they kissed, tongues swirling into each other's mouths.

And, on a more social justice theme, this following omission:

274

Night was cold outside, frost. Homeless huddled in doorways; if the black woman had been at her home across the city, there'd be no heat, she'd spend the night in a chill under layers and layers of blankets and quilts. She would have been alone. Tonight, with friends it was good. Comfort. Fun. Peace. But in the back of her mind she longed for a woman of her own, just like the couple had.

Night was cold outside, frost. Homeless huddled in doorways. **100 of them would freeze to death over that long winter in the streets of the eternal city**. If the black woman had been at her home across town, there'd be no heat. She'd spend the night in a **restless** chill under layers and layers of blankets and quilts. She would have been alone. **The building she was in wasn't safe, tenants inside had fallen prey to criminals; and she slept with a butcher knife under her pillow.** Tonight, with friends it was good. Comfort. **Safety**. Fun. Peace. **Sexual satisfaction**. But in the back of her mind she longed for a woman of her own. Just like the couple had.

125.

AM Friday March 21

A SMALL RETROSPECT OF MY ART PAINTINGS has emerged from the ethers! With support from techno-wiz Sean @ bookstore, and using the 8 photos of my paintings circa 1969, laboriously snapped by Richard Politowski, Red was setting up his 'artists coffee table book' which presents all 13 of his paintings which he is able to find, or gather up from the world—another 20 or so exist(ed) somewhere in some stray corners of earth—or are gone. When climbing monkey-like up to the top of his 5'6" loft to pull down the last stored, yet unphotographed ancient paintings, he discovers there are in fact 3 paintings, not the 2 he assumed, (The Pool Shooters, The Madman) but also a third—Flash On The Hustler! Whose visage resembles Red himself in a chocolate brown hue, and also uncannily looks like the hero of that novel, Alexander D'Oro, a teenhood friend--fellow sissy, cum actor/painter; whose art was abstract, ala Pollack.

Hashem's hand is obviously upon this project as it is rolling well. Sean frets & growls over his computer typing in mathematical dimensions, specifications from the POD who will publish the book, etc., and it slowly emerges coincidental to the sun rising in the east, then setting in the west in a grand arc of light/color over Babylon Falling as simultaneously a parade of young men drop by to give their confessionals—one struggles with the bottle, another, an artist fired from shit job @ art store is fleeing into the wilds of Mexico with backpack, sketchbook, another has created his momentary exit from reality by purchasing $100 of clothes—for one shirt! *One shirt! One hundred dollars!* With a designer label—that is Alex; Mr. Van Hussen who's snaps Red's photo with expensive digital camera; his services may be called upon to do The Artist At Work in his studio and/or a back cover photo of Red for RETROSPECT, (this in lieu of Mr. Oto; Master Photographer, who seems who have slipped mysteriously thru the cracks of Babylon Falling and disappeared down into the drains of this unholy neon city).* --The Master Photographer soon turned up once more and is now slated to do the studio shot. Prices going up in The City, Rent Control vote day approaching amid much hoopla of rent control parties, organizing events etc., and the artist plods on, temporary excited by the issuing of his new coffee table book. I will be so pleased to have this book, to encourage all my subsequent fine arts paintings. A Head start!

> I think you are very lucky you have this library full of radical
> literature right up the street from your house.
> --Hugo (Non-Professor Turnip)

Outside his window seat T. spy a hag across the way, sadly, a degenerate TS woman. S/he was thrown out of our apartment building 2 years ago, for drugs; plus her evil trade terrorizing the building, friends crashing in the hallways. Well, the drugs—its always there.

Scrutinizing the hangers-on who pass thru this bookstore I perceive that a certain young man whom I have grown close to has a wild emptiness inside. —Dark eyes. Without. Bottomless pits. Wells of anger, fire, potential evil, basically hurt. He must be helped. Patience is key. I can imagine how some of these young men may be, when they reach middleage. One can occasionally pause from them, here is their present to imagine the end of their lives; the idea today is to engineer end days coming so as to have few regrets for things not done.

When I think about the excitement I had—the eagerness to which retuned to my work every day—I see the root of my 80-book catalogue, and the painting.

276

Alex had just walked in, proudly showed us the shirt he bought--
$100—after standing in line for an hour waiting to get in an upscale,
trendy, fashionable *name* store. A wonderful plaid shirt—whose
brethren quite similar, are being purchased in the 2nd hand thrift store
for *two dollars and fifty cents*. The crowning glory is when you turn
around, this shirt has the name of the fancy store written over its back
in huge letters from right shoulder to left—in a cross stitch hatch
which stand up from the fabric of the shirt, in a gaudy 3-dimensional
living advertisement, walking around town on the backs of all the kids
who slavishly buy them. Sean is mad; he believes this materialism is
indicative of a deeper problem:

> What gets me is these kids standing in line for an hour waiting to
> receive their personality—for a small fee.
> --Proprietor, Babylon Falling.

THE PAINTINGS OF RED JORDAN AROBATEAU. –2nd
Retrospect. For a 2nd retrospect art book— should have 16 to 20 new
ones. Plus use tiny snapshots of all of the first retrospect's 13
paintings—explaining them. In this sequel book the text would be
much more about explaining the pictures. Use snapshot details of
new one's also, explaining what items in the picture mean. IE HO'S
BATH. One can see the 'ho in her bathtub, setting a wig upon her
head; also a large yellow boot superimposed—her shoes set for
walking the streets tonight! Background scenes of the street, a neon
light etc. A masterwork!

The young woman who owns Ransack, a clothes/art boutique down
Leavenworth steps up the street to visit with the Proprietor. They
begin to exchange shop-owner fantasies.

> Her: I want to go back home to the East Coast, and open up a
> shop—for fashion jewelry art, food.

> Him: I want to go back to Jamaica and retire to the beach and have a
> small restaurant.

They both want to do food shops next time… seems like more fun.
Maybe during their dull daily tasks they daydream about customer's
frolicking w/food.

I am an industrial child, sooty, smog in my lungs. Loaded with vaccines, whose toxic side effect was to give me life long allergy— just as they gave me longer life free of past, conquered diseases. Part of my soul and body now contain the clamor and hammer of big cities, traffic; crowds of these strange little beings called people.

Hashem has figured out our birth just as She has situated each star in heaven. God has given the world artists and their job is to be pioneers, innovators, to say what needs to be said, to be inspirational, to be innovative. They bring something uncommon.

>   Red, the Prophet: I love You God. I love You because You give me stuff.

>   God: I give you words.

Monday PM March 24
An interesting thing has happened. For the RETROSPECT have designated all of my available paintings—including the two recent ones from this year, yet unfinished. These two must be added because I have so few. Sean has worked on the book dedicatedly (for no money) and I see its magnificence unfolding—a tribute to Hashem's gifts. Picture after picture jumps out at the viewer in vibrant color—interspersed with a thick amount of text all pertinent to the creative arts. In a while Richard has said to bring the un-photographed paintings by his store, after hours, he'll photo them and put them onto disc—so we can plop them into awaiting niches in the book. However the two recent paintings aren't completely *done,* thus suddenly am put in the position of being under stress of a *deadline* similar to an overboss glaring down at me at my bench in a factory, or office desk. The artistic discipline one imposes on themself is far less stressful then a real job—usually, but not always!

Picasso, in the Taschen retrospect of his work referred to him working 'in the laboratory of art.' This is a good phrase. The artist is in school—wither it is formally in a scholastic setting, or simply their own studies and in constant practice at the easel with paintbrush in hand. You have now graduated from 'the laboratory of art'. You've gone the distance. You are established in your work—to self, even if only faintly yet to the public. You have found your place. Now all that remains is to grind them out.

In this Taschen retrospect Walther describes Picasso's approach to his art as having a mulish persistence.

Music, dance, painting, sculpture, literature are gifts from God. Human negotiations we have to do on earth regarding price, distribution, exposure of the work are our responsibility, and it is a royal pain!

He sat back & seemed to melt into the window seat. As the text of the nazi war years book Transman was reading grinds on:

> According to the Judeo ban of dogs, cats, and birds.---Frau K—must hand over her canary in a pet shop, way, way out on Bautzener Strasse, on foot, good, that our Muschel rests in peace.
> ----VK, recounting the holocaust.

Remember Dear Children the political struggles of the past & what it means to you here today!

Dear Children, as you may already realize most of a cultures major basic laws, ethical & moral decisions are derived from those original laws handed down over generations, and from these all the smaller ones spring like tributaries from the mother river; what was handed down over generations back into dim antiquity; first written down in Torah, on stone tablets from the flaming hand of God; and further back many more of these laws can be found in other religious and ceremonial paintings in ancient oils on walls of caves, written on papyrus, carved into tablets of stone, depicted on shards of pottery; all this, accumulating, tracing back still further from eons of oral tradition alone. Right & wrong are not an easy matter. Uneasy is the head who sits in the judgment seat, or is a ruler of multitudes, who must assess all decisions and push to the fine line of reason any decision or litigation according to interpretations of the Law. This is politics. And we, on a small minor level must weight in checks and balances our own private life, and morality. —Least we fall into the fiery traps, which lay in wait in the negative regions of this world!

Jesus the son of God let us hold fast our profession.

For we have not a high priest which cannot be touched with the feeling of our infirmities; but was in all points tempted like as we are, yet without sin.
Let us therefore come boldly unto the throne of grace; that we may obtain mercy, and find grace to help in time of need.
---Hebrews 14-16

Sunday March 23
There is only God. The light that shines thru the eyes of the living. A nor talmid, the Light beyond.

Bare feet stamp over the jungle soil, arms upraised brandish clubs carved from large animal bones, and limbs of trees upraised; menacing faces, unshaven echoes of humankinds distant past. The drum beats of this savage earth pound onward.

Futuristic News Flash—2030ACE: The Old Prophet, Transman Red Jordan—The Lion Who Sits Beside The Door--- went on to recognition of his lifelong work, thus justifying its Herculean struggle. He reaped the highest honors, the top awards.

I knew that to be successful I wanted to reach as many people as I'm suppose to reach—to melt down all possible barriers within my power to & emit the free flow of my work to all the souls which are meant to hear; wither this be a great or small number—the souls to whom my work will have meaning.

Still another tale of people displaced, young man comments how he worked on the construction crew in Austin Texas, their job was to demolish black peoples homes to form the new highway and the fancy new upscale development.

I got to this city 40 years ago on the human hand 4 fingers in November, exactly, it is now July. The timeclock of God moves steady, surely, without a pause. The Almighty knows what came before, what will come. It is all written. Her timing is exact.

Fillmore Street is today full of long legged whites. Not a black ghetto anymore. Only 1 black person. This is 2007. The changeover is complete. 1970's teeming with blacks laughing, angry, dangerous, musical. Gentrification—a mild form of

genocide—that is cultural suicide. In which the former residences of a peoples are razed, and new structures priced way beyond their means to obtain are built and sold off to an alien peoples with far more capital.
--WORKS, Journey Vol. 5

It is always black people, poor people. Chi-town, South Side, demolished; 'Frisco—the Fillmore. Texas. New Orleans after hurricane Katrina. Singapore….

126.

> Members of the gang were with her continuously, or she'd have had to go into a nursing home for the duration. The Indian, Comancho told her of the plans to move her & some homeless members in together. To set up a house for them, that the club would rent, maybe even purchase, with pooled resources.
>
> Members of the gang were with her continuously, or she'd have had to go into a **convalescent** home for the duration. –**A depressing grey barracks populated by ancient dying elder humanbeings who society has all but forgotten and shoved away under a blanket, out of sight.** The Indian, Comancho sat by her bed and told her of the plans to move her & some homeless members in **to a commune** together. To set up a house for them, that the club would rent, maybe even purchase, with pooled resources.

AM March 25
Continue Art! Pens, pencils scribble, brushes paint! I storm the gates of heaven!

Something hideous. Delora has gone to a '50's swing band party—heeterosexual. The day after Jasmin complains in a grumpy voice how she was upset at having to sit on the sidelines and watch the dancers all evening—she, a dancer herself! —Because of her & L. being lesbians and everybody else straight! When will this world grow up! When will it stop having classes of privilege while others having to watch on in jealousy and dissatisfaction!!! The fires of revolution are beginning to stir in America.

> The people must raise up!
> The people must stand strong!
> The people must fight back!
> Fists upraised!

Viva la Revolucion!

BABYLON FALLING: Its owner states: The book biz is known as the 2% business when you consider payables, operation expenses— it's a silly business. It's a labor of love. Only a fool would do. And he looks directly at Transman as he says this. I guess I am a fool— and so he—for being in this lousy business! *Such a Business!* (Yiddish.)

All an artist has is their intellectual property. They may have no muscles, bad health, be overweight, a looser—but they have this stuff they've dreamed up in their own imitable way, that only they can create.

The Blue Dog; you look at this quasi-human face, you want it to say something to you; it is strange, almost bizarre---but it is not the face, it is the dog. Specifically it is the upheld left paw of the dog—giving the benediction —that is key to this painting! A Holy Work!

Art is pure. Riches complicate the whole affair. 1 sketch on a restaurant napkin by Basquette pays for the tres expensive meal of his entire party—the waiter puts this napkin goes up for sale on E-bay Internet trading the following day, to be instantly sold for $5,000. 1 painting by Picasso buys a mansion in Paris… Andy Warhol's $24 million dollar ordinary Campbell's soup can …   Some call it high art, some call it big money.

AM Thursday March 27

Transman is hit by allergies, bad ones. Dust. Cat dander, ever-present, but now, all escalated by *Spring*; blooming pollen-producing plants/trees/flowers. He must take medication, which acts as a hyper stimulate. Wired up. Even faint sounds make him jump. Tonight: jerk off; let the birds out. Hurry, hurry! Sleep, so as to be ready to paint in AM. Transman felt he was making up for lost time—34 years not putting brush to canvas at all!

Unusual sounds make him fly out of his skin. He flinches at slightest noise; is super-aware of minor details, things out of place. Ghosts seem to glide around the periphery of his eyes. Transman is wired. He thought to himself; *music runs around & around inside my head— at least its religious music.* Adoni, Eloheim!

During these terrible trials T continued his new raw food diet—tho it had by now sunk to a 60-40% raw food diet—which was still far better then previously. Vastly reduced the amount of red meat. Less cooked foods. Ate raw greens, nuts, raisins, cabbage, spinach, apples, bananas & oranges daily. Luxury is to eat a quantity of cheese, and put milk in his coffee. Want to go the distance—Picasso's age and beyond!

Babylon Falling. The young proprietor sits vainly trying to convert computer computations and making noises like a difficult lover trying to reach orgasm—"I'm almost there… almost had it! I won't be long now!"

Sitting in the proprietors chair @ computer, I see what gives the young man such a vulture-like pose—it is the shape of the chair, its awkward sideways positioning at the desk (to accommodate the knees) plus distance from the beast which forces one to stretch, crane, and finally flatten oneself down nearly horizontal to the desk top like a lizard and from there to glare expectantly at its screen. I must say here that this young man has helped me with many things during our short acquaintance/friendship. Further, if he was not here helping me, the RETROSPECT would not be happening. Thank you Sean, and thank you Hashem!

Transman came from a long line of Colored people—documented of African descent, yet, he was a stranger among his own, due to his very light skin and European-like features, plus a mostly white English speaking dialect. For this reason he had a secret sympathy with Sean, a white man raised in a black country—Jamaica—where the vast majority of that nations poor are black. The higher stratum is brown—still visibly black-- and only 2% of the nation is white, like him, those whites ranging from poorer to middle class and not necessarily rich. As he says racism is less in that country involving strife between white, or some other non-black race, and black, as it is in America & parts of Europe. The social divide can be often seen, color wise, between brown and black people, but that is still both of the African heritage. I am hoping for his sake that he and his loved ones in Jamaica do not ever experience a growing racism and hatred towards them because they are white—in this black land—as racism is a terrible infection growing in many places, even as it seems to wane in others. A black hatred of white—this being reverse racism to

283

the long pageant of white enslavement/denigration of black. None of his family has ever been involved in the slave trades of the ancient past, or were masters of vast sugar cane plantations, nor can this be assumed about any whites there. I have experienced racism in my life from both white people and my own black people. It is a poison set loose on our earth! It drives people from the neighborhoods of their birth, from the countries and lands of their heritage! We must always seek new shores, new frontiers it seems!

Soon must set up JOY. Well, what better way to begin this fifth book completion of the rondo called JOY!/SIMCA then a passage titled DISAPPOINTMENT. Spoke earlier of the disappointment of consumerism/materialism. Well there are other kids of regrets, sadness—those imposed, seemingly, from outside oneself. The loss of a loved one because of their death, or alienation, as in the severe mental illness of a companion which drives them away from all they loved and all who loved them before. There is elation over a new work, a new book, a new friend, then the let down when this fails to materialize, or the bonds of the relationship disintegrate. I beleaguer my point of saying how faith—a powerful faith in the Supreme God, the Divine Power will help see us thru this trial. Keeping focused on something so far above us, which is solid love—pure love—agape, not the small romantic kind of this earth, is a helpmate of Spirit, which is our companion also, and One Whom we shall not neglect! —All for our own betterment!

Friday AM March 27
You have to realize when I wrote these things I was writing, nobody was reading my stuff, I had no sales, no one was reading it, nobody knew anything about it, I was like somebody jerking off in the dark.

PM Thursday March 27
These idiots! They say, with some resentment, not hidden, in fact indignant—"well I too could have been a writer!" (Painter, musician, etc.) –Well, they did not. It takes more then talent to be artistic, it takes persistence, the frankness to reveal ones self, to run the risk of making mistakes in public, it takes time, devotion, the forfeiture of other pursuits—some of them necessity, like family matters. So much goes into being an artist it is no wonder there are so few of us! But how lucky we few are—having the retreat of art to return to from the

downward tug of the earthly world; a source of inspiration, childlike joy, and mighty hope for the future!

So he sat in the window seat of Babylon Falling as shadows of evening fell…

Often be seen in the city streets pulling his shopping cart, marching with cane, suddenly he'd come to a halt in some fortuitous spot, (out of the pedestrian traffic, or out of the rain under an awning if it was stormy, in a spot of shade if the sun was blazing) whip a sheaf of paper & pen out of his breast pocket and furiously scribble; he'd stop and write awhile as if by energy renewed by each step, as thoughts flowed to him.

Transman's wallet was almost flat again-- he paused a moment, in the dying sun, outside a branch of a huge financial corporation, lending/acquisitions holding multi-millions of dollars & there rested, leaning on his cane, while beside him is a heavily laden Chinese loudsinging, dragging behind him an immense push cart full of recyclables, akin to his forefathers in feudal China, coolies caring 100 pound sacks of rice thru muddy dirt in bare feet. All the poor people of earth are still pushing carts these days—carts of senior shoppers who can't afford a car, or taxi to/fro supermarket; the homeless packing all their worldly belongings in purloined shopping carts, the ever-present recyclers of glass bottles and aluminum cans, small-time operators for pennies & nickels.

T recalled when the facility which later was to become known as Trans Center first emerged—nobody knew what it was—a study? A census? A population under siege? Being examined by the government via the arm of a Top Ten University? A drop-in-center for transsexuals? By its true definition it was contrary to what people wanted—which was a center for resources for homeless, poverty stricken outcasts; a place to eat free, relax in a safe envronmnet, get free showers, clothes. The centers funding depended on gathering information about the transsexual demi monde specifically the issues of illegal drug use, sexual activity and the spread of the HIV virus—a deadly disease. That was the beginning project, which died, not having achieved its goal, due to mismanagement and inter-office intrigue. Now the project has been revived, funded by a new sponsor, and the support of the trans community continues, but on a far smaller scale then before, and with less money to give out for individuals taking surveys. Gone are the 50$ days, the 100$ days, the 20$ days—to be replaced by the occasional $10 food voucher… *Cheep trick….*

He'd tuck challa from the motzi/kiddish after services at synagogue, or from the Seniors lunch at Grace away, & everywhere he would pull these bread scraps out of his pocket—now stale---crush them under his foot to feed the pigeons. This was his job.

Transman thought it was the funniest sight in the world to see 2 grey/black pigeons standing inside a deli, --having glided smoothly thru the doorway on winged flight to come to rest, like any customer, over by some racks of fast food treats, waiting to be bestowed with food.

For readers who wonder what the hell this collection called Obedience is, I shall put this near the end: *This diary, this journal of days; a collection of random thoughts.*

He dragged his metal cart laden w/art; passing the mosque, its closed doors behind which now worshipers are bowing, facing East before Allah; passing by the Cathedral behind whose 12-foot iron doors the congregation are worshiping God, past all synagogues of the universe:

> I Hear! Says the Lord!

By now, all of you realize we are on a Journey—you are mature enough, for this to have dawned to you; only a child still believes in an earthly permanence. Much of this worlds best music, opera, symphonies, tell of this, and all of its poets sing about it in verse; about traveling, change, & the necessity of faith, throughout our long/or short earthly adventure.

AM March 28

> One day at a time Red,
>   put a blank canvas up.
> It turns to a mirror,
> Print what God sends you
>   from the mirror of your soul.
> A sheet of paper from the computer;
>   write what I send you.
> Artist—

Create!

*

God is the true lover of our soul.
Hold each other.
Comfort each other
 Until the real
Thing comes along.

I have written dirty things.
Raw & gritty stuff.
The prurient—
But try not to have evil stuff.
Seal yourself in Christ!
Some people don't weed out
 The evil.
    Weed it out!
      Yank it out by its roots!

*

We start with a clean slate;
A clean mug---then flecks of
 Stains on the rim become apparent.
The evil---residue of the day
Encrusted thick, ugly crude at life's end.
    Drink from your cup.

127.
AM Saturday March 29

When the artist sits in front of the canvas s/he says, 'I can do anything I want to!' Tho parents, preacher, censors, friends, associates, bosses tell him otherwise, the painting calls out—he/she changes the work according to his vision—then tells them so! I had to do it! The work spoke this to me!' Thus unlike a normal workday worlds employment where one must answer to superiors, the artist is free! S/he answers only to the call of God!

2pm The Blue Dog is Done! Fini! Now the Grand Paint Down begins, whereas all unused brushes for this session are put back into drawer, drawer put away, paint tube treys set back in cabinet, the finished hiliactic work—Blue Dog-- set to dry in kitchen and a blank canvas, fresh, substituted in its place on easel; now pigment laden brushes, and blobs of color left on pallet are used up in a grand flourish of creativity, making the structure of a new painting!

Later this small canvas will be put aside and the following day, the oil treys exhumed from their substratum at bottom of cabinet under the acrylics, and Student With The Golden Pot is readied to finish—then off to photo w/Richard, (still wet in places) and the RETROSPECT'S foundation will be complete! —Oh by the way Dear Children, if riches, fame, and subsequent *power* come to me by the execution of these Works, let it all be towards doing a work of JUSTICE! And let the people say, Amien!

Coffee a la Hugo—(Non-Professor Turnip) drops by. To pick up Red's favorite sex video tape to make him copy, and have a quick coffee. The stocky, potbelly Red hands it over undistinguished in a plain brown paper bag, per La Hugo's instruction. This, since the old tape is wearing out. Hugo will perform this feat of modern technology on his nefarious 2-recording machine hook up; a contraption by which he has illicitly copied many old German films plus tranny shit. Documents for himself and friends, plus his students when he was still a Professor. On way to coffee shop the two stop at second hand store, where for $2 he buys a corbel. Then they dwaddle at the stores used book section. Hugo, corbel in hand, spies a book by Tom Somebody Or Another, grabs it with his tan librarian/auto mechanics fingers and spits spitefully at it: *"The perverse man! —In love with the corporate world!"* Then jams it rudely back onto the shelf, fuming grim-lipped. Over coffee, Red shows The Hugo his working copy of on-going THE PASSION OF ART, where upon the Non-Professor innocently asks:

Hugo: Who is this Hashem?

Red: Hashem is God! Allah! Yahweh!—It's all the same God.

The two have a gabfest in the sunny day—Hugo, being a thin lizard prefers the sunny side of the street always.

Tonight Hashem decided to paint the sky pink, crimson; yellow blazing orb at sunset—true beauty—for all those humans who cared to turn, face the horizon & watch, and there are many of us! So take heart Christians (Jews, Muslims, Wiccans, Buddhists etc.)

I call my people night & day!
I call them on the mountaintop.
I call them in the streets
 where they are walking.

I call them in the bar room, the restaurant,
 the café.
I call them in their sleep.
I call them when they first awake.
I Call!

Addendum: Since that painting was still damp in places we didn't
wrap it in plastic like the others, but carried it gingerly on top. One of
the ancient 38-year old paintings—The Poolshooters flecking its
massive stretches of blue terribly. Must photoshop for
RETROSPECT.

AM Sunday March 30
I will do a video, will call it, THE SYMBOLISM OF 13 IMAGES, in
which the artist explains the symbolism in each of his extant
paintings. I'd include the 5 un-photographed works. Who will shoot,
direct, edit this video—who will be the videotographer/filmmaker?
Delora? One of the talented guys at Babylon Falling? Time is a
mystery yet to unfold.

AM Monday March 31
I want the awards. I want to win. I want the beauty. I want to do art!
@ bookstore. Shaun's on telephone; one-way conversation:

   --John Felix Arnold?

   --Pieces of an old refrigerator?

   --Where is the refrigerator?

   --3rd and Howard? I'll let him know.

John Felix is an artist who paints/draws on old, found pieces of
civilization. —Ancient windows w/cracked panes, in their rotten
wooden frames is his specialty. Any sightings of really ancient
fragments of our modern civilization, crumbling, --washing machines
from another era, 100-year old rusted sinks, replete w/red-brown rust
scars, and the like he is to be notified, so he can commandeer a truck,
swoop down, pick up the remains, cart them back to studio and work
them into an art assemblage.

My children. —My restless children.
—Hashem

128.
Here are some notes on gender divisions among us queers: When transitioning I spent a lot of time with my sister transwoman, having wild 'adolescent fun' exploring our new gender and the crazy feelings we now had on unfamiliar hormones; going thru the TL streets on adventures; and can say I was one of the few FTM's who hung out with my sisters, here in this city although this may be different in other cities where the TG/TS population is less, for people tend to pull together when their watering hole is smaller; this being the case with gays and lesbians of small towns. I was one of the few FTMs who associated with those often crazy and raunchy gals, some of this was class differences. Many girls were driven here to SF--chiefly to the TL—as a Mecca; because of harsh, even murderous discrimination in their birth towns, whereas FTM's who came here, frequently were just passing thru town to get much needed top-surgery from one of the most knowledgeable doctors in the field, or hormone therapy, and were decently situated in the places they arrived from---and returned to.

They come from broken homes; they come from dysfunctional homes. The mother is troubled, the son or daughter grows up with only one parent, troubled; the son runs wild, he goes into a juvenile correctional facility/in and out of youth lockup, s/he returns to find his or her mother's gone into a mental institution, s/he roams the streets, s/he is picked up again; this time as a young adult is sent to prison for 8 months. His mother is released, now homeless, cast into the streets herself, and then, desperate, travels to another city to a distant family member trying to gain stability; the child gets out of prison—his mother is gone. Where? The child roams the streets knowing somewhere they have a mother. In a distant city the mother, put out by heartless relatives, struggles between facilities for the mentally ill and church refuges, telling people she has a son—where? Somewhere, she doesn't know. This is the finally broken family, it cannot fall apart any further. A lot of resources, comforting and backup is lost for the person with no family!

My own story was not as severe—having the constant thread of my father, a loyal parent, stable, hardworking, who hung thru it all without deserting me. Dad died when I was 34, and I lost my best friend in the world. —And that is when I found Jesus. And God. And the religions which have sustained me since. Then Jasmin came into my life—so you see she is family to me.

Back to the Trans Center and those wild trannygirls. (Few boys pass thru, only Transman was sort of a fixture.) Very sociable people will find from time to time upon their interactions with a diversity of others, a story—when which retold out of their own mouths becomes a lie. A story appropriated from someone else. A great excuse that they can adopt. Physical symptoms of this other person, which can be used as a cover-up for themselves. A mental state of another, which discerned, studied, then copied, is appropriated by them to fool friends & acquaintences. Down even to the words the unwitting person used. IE:

> I met this man honey, he gave me $500, but when he got up to my place turned out he'd put drugs in my drink. He raped me, and when I woke up he'd stole all my clothes, took the 500 back, and I still have dizzy spells. Ohhhh I feel dizzy now!

Soon these crazy girls were all parroting the same story—because it had sounded so good, they had all appropriated it! The very best of stories! They must be congratulated on their good taste—but not on their honesty! PS, each time this fictitious tale was retold, the amount of money increased ($700. $1,000. $2,000.) So each girl could outdo the other—and be clever.

I had not had so much fun since the sex club in the early 1990's, --- even going so far to court the elusive, elegant transwoman Rosa Salazar with bouquet of flowers, and begging the deranged A., highly intelligent, middle-age glam gal, sinuous, shorter-stature, blond A., who secretly held a $100,000 portfolio of stocks & bonds earned while still a man; begged her for a mercy fuck

Here are some more notes about gays:

Lesbians are afraid so they are lost to the world. Men have harassed them since they were boys and girls. They stick their heads into shells like turtles and don't come out.

There was once a time when we were gay women and gay men, but at one point the women's movement, late1960's, took back the word 'lesbian' from history and just abdicated the term 'gay women', leaving it totally to the boys. Gay men, who did not care to call themselves 'pederasts' kept Gay exclusively. Back in the day there also were no bisexuals, just 'ac-dc's, or switch hitters.

On a shop window of the gay district see a poster of a black woman surrounded by 4 children asking for money to help fund HIV for a single daily pill to keep her alive, cost, $1 in Africa, which is a fortune there; and next to it advertisement; $20 for an eyelash tint. What juxtaposition!

Heterosexuals have their restaurants, bars, brothels all set up for hetro males. Lesbian society picks up along the edges. Now adrift in tranny life, the gender divide remains, with pitifully few services for FTM's, and all the hoopla being over our sisters—the MTF's. Funding, services etc. Well, they need it more—being for a greater part unpassable, and more damaged as children. Yet, the conundrum still remains—female born takes the second place, has less!

Tuesday April 1

     Art; it is a Love.

As I do art, and live life, I always try to keep my mind wrapped around the Golden Rule—what as my father use to put it, what it says in the Good Book. The Ten Commandments. At any instant, I might forget—trespass—but my mind is always wrapped around that focus … keep struggling with it, then, I See! Whoops! Messed up! — Back to the drawing board of human flesh.

PM Tuesday April 1
Usually conversation at the bookstore is quite literary, political, highbrow; but today it dwelled on hideous sights of SF:
     One young man going to retrieve his car saw some attendants at the parking garage awestruck at some sight. As he drew near he turned

to see what was holding their interest. Across the street a woman, 30 or so, black, not bad looking, was being plied with drugs by two homeless men; she wore a pink jacket—and pink pants, which she had pulled down to her ankles so her lower extremities were stark naked. She stood there awhile, --20 minutes or so—cars just driving by, pedestrans strolling past; totally ignoring the sight; when no customers approached, wearily she pulled her pink pants back up along her legs, fitting into them again.

One young man and his lady companion were walking up the street and saw a homeless man, black, with a crack pipe in his mouth, trousers down around his knees; naked, his genitalia erect; with his ankles wide apart to keep his pants from falling down; he held a rolled up newspaper; he calmly lit the end of the newspaper with a cigarette lighter, immediately there shot out of it a one foot long flame, with this torch he was lighting a crack pipe and puffing, while he masturbated himself with the other. Upon seeing the peaceful couple, he turned his back, embarrassed but continued to jerk off, hand pumping vigorously, & fire up & smoke his crack pipe, with grandiose gestures.

One young man, new to town, near the infamous Hibernia bank rotunda off Market Street in the heart of the Tenderloin, no longer a bank—home to squads of pigeons, with white-splattered bird shit everywhere; also, a branch of the vice cops; a department with prisoner holding cells to the side. He spotted a homeless man in a wheelchair getting a blowjob from a white hag, down on her knees on the sidewalk vigorously servicing him, disregarding the work-day traffic speeding by.

After this was said, Transman commented:
Those white hags really know how to work it. The are the best hustlers--those ugly white ancient hags—they get out there in their mini skirts with no ass, pipestem legs, and hag-faces and pose like movie stars! They get first prize in the hustling department, those white hags!

.

Sean & Red both agreed, privately, that they were A Child Of Privilege. Both having arisen from middle-class backgrounds, being educated, for Transman this had ended earlier—but the little he got made a difference!

*

He was tiered & nearly out of breath from walking constantly to & from the health clinic. And thought: *The next street goes one-way left, the next one after, is one-way right. Just follow; let the streets carry me home.* Pulling his cart behind him, w/backpack attached by bungee cords, & a tube of prints of his fine arts posters for everlasting sale.

Oh! Did I say; the good news—finally—after several years, got prints of my fine arts oil paintings done! Replenished my storage of posters and postcards—Set up fee, a $200 price tag. This bill included two discs with the files of the paintings plus their captions already set up—to enable me to print anywhere! The visual art is rolling! The next good news that in the first week I sold $100 worth—5 posters!

Addendum: Went to 'The General' as it is known in the vernacular— SF General Hospital, for PT on his left shoulder. The doctor wanted to see what was in the tube (his arts paintings). While he was looking at Red's colorful prints another doctor comes over, looks over his shoulder and both bought one! (Ho's Bath—of course—and The Howl). PS: The Mexican doctor told how that poster reminded him of when he'd seen Giseburg read The Howl in Mexico City years back— in Spanish, so he bought it for his living room.

A crone cranes her head out of a 2nd story tenement window, & w/a look of cunning tosses a morsel of food to a seagull, white, plump on 2 orange-colored stalk legs, and gangly webbed feet, her co-conspiritor, who awaits on the roof of a two-story business right outside. Quickly the window slams. The woman disappears. It is illegal subterfuge feeding the birds---bird feeding is disallowed in SF. The crone earns big points in heaven! The seagull chortles/squawks in pleasure.

Wednesday PM April 2

> Ohhhhaaaahhhhhuurrrrhhhhgggggh! Another day of this *bull*shit!
> --Sean, Proprietor.

Clerk & Red @ Art Supply:

Clerk: That's funny, I hear most young people say how they prefer to use oils—and the older people say how it feels toxic to them.

Red: When I was young I painted for 10 years in oils and didn't notice the toxicity. The minute I started back in oils, now that I'm older I felt it right away.

That night, after drinking a raw diet health shake, Transman noticed the foul taste of metal in his mouth—he wonders, was it the toxic oxides, leads & other metals from the oil paints exuding out of his system?

Handsome, not quite young fag drops politely into bookstore; very well dressed—upper class plutocrat gay-- he cracks off-color jokes rapid fire, one after another, all aimed at the young proprietor: 'If my monkey was bad would you spank my monkey? If I was a farmer and my chicken was bad would you choke my chicken? —That's Military jokes." Plays with a great wad of money in his wallet, fingering thru a sheaf of $20, $50', & 100rds finally settling on a 20 bill to pay for an item. Final flourish in his stream of innuendos something about 'shoot' somebody or something. Sean is non-plussed, rings up the register and returns to stare down computer with a vulture glare. "I've had worse then that." He replies, after the cock-happy customer departs. Such a business! Such peddling we must do in the trades—ooops! That's the book trades honey!

The proprietor says something funny later:

"The happiest days of my life, was when the man was holding me down, and I complained about it all the time. But now I'm the boss. I'm wholly responsible for myself and, every day is an aggravation! I remember we'd have so much fun talking about how one day we'd win 100 million dollars on the lottery and what we'd do with it. This being in charge of your life is a headache, a constant pain.

Thursday AM April 3
Today's Details: Shaun, photog, is coming over @ 3—shoot for RETROSPECT; need a picture of me at work in studio. Also need one for back cover, but Dalora may snap that later, they are due over circa 5, to pick up me, & 5 paintings to take over to Richards lab to be shot to complete the book.

Today's a red-letter day! 2-photo shoots back to back—and carrying 5 works lab to be photographed for my book! Maybe followed by coffee or dinner with Dalora after our mission is complete. An artist has red-letter days—followed by barren ones, weary ones, non-rewarding ones, no inspiration whatsoever, except for their on-going dream, their hope of the future. Valleys & crests. Highs/lo's.

Minutiae: Red wore black always. Black trousers & shirt, which made the greatest impact of his wardrobe upon the eye. A variance of color sox, an of-color teeshirt, or white (not black), a tie which he had found in the free box which could have been dark blue, or black & his new shoes were a pleasant medium brown, but his old ones sent long distance from play cousin Angelo were black. This is his going out in outfit. However, to paint, he wore old cast-off clothes of other people, found/donated. So as his daily work costume @ home before the easel was of color. For the photo shoot he is thus colorfully arrayed.

Student At The Golden Pot is complete, so now the old oil attempted in 1998 (which bares that date plus letter A.) set upon easel to do the 'paint down' of last oils left on the pallet. At this point the toxic oils will be packaged up & set aside, the painting propped up in kitchen to dry; and, before the acrylics are reused on a fresh new canvas (or on the last acrylic 'paint down' canvas) will try Aqua Oil. This is a new product touted as non-toxic, having properties of oil, but the ease in clean up, etc. of acrylic. Some opinions are that you can get the effects of a watercolor! There is nothing like oils to work with on canvas, so Red would attempt to work with his new purchased Aqua Oil set—it needs no turpentine, only a water-based linseed oil. This is the benefits of having $ money to be able to experiment. Have spent hundreds and hundreds of dollars to outfit himself with new, excellent brushes which could be used for both oil/acrylic, all basic tubes of paint necessary for the acrylic, and a few aqua oils; having fortuitously already possessed all the oil colors needed.

One odd note about The Raiment Of Love the old oil attempted in 1998 (which bares the date plus letter A.) now it has the longest signature of many of my works—1998A.–08. Signifying it was begun in the old millennium and will be finished in this, new one. It has become the back cover of the RETROSPECT.

I have around my studio at least 20 canvas set ups of used canvasses, stretched, found in my travels traversing this City—abandon by an art student, or amateur; and naked finely constructed stretcher bars, nailed mathematically in right angles, plus reinforced, waiting for a canvass to be stretched on them, a great find at an artist exhibit at Hunters Point. The roll of canvas ($100) purchased from that last windfall of money --$1,000 from the Beatniks reading 8 months ago. Am rumbling along down the painters track!

Moment of truth. The painter turns to face a canvas awaiting on easel. Now s/he remembers what he's here to do. What this whole studio is for; this art set-up. Taking brush to hand, preparing to dab into the appropriate pigment, he searches his soul & mind --Now to hit the heights of inspiration!

Maybe a bit of Coltrane, Miles Davis, Damanda Galas.... *notes like birds released from horns...*

The artist studies his picture... so far, a face askew, startled, purple and Caucasian/Colored flesh tones... the heart, bleeding crimson over a multi-colored coat; the dagger, a fist upraised—murder by the persons own hand? What is this rosy crucifixion? The Raiment Of Love? Yes! The poets answer to a painter's struggle in picture naming!

On the easel; a face, hands suspended in space; the picture poses, hesitated in time.

Now the visionary must See! S/he gazes closely at the canvas... Yes, it is a serpent, a hand, and a spear...

Notes scrawled in drawing-notebook:

> Picture on easel The Raiment Of Love; use checkerboards on painting. Use the words anger, vengeance written subtly into top hair of person in 'Raiment'.

Well, LEADER is finished, Lulu-POD'd and a copy sits on my desk! This newly written preface to the heavy tome speaks all there is to say:

> Many under-class writers, too discouraged to testify to their truths. Non-professional queer writers material has been ignored not simply by a bigoted straight world, but because of failure of the lesbian press, and cold shoulder avoidance of gay men's press. Further, too many are afraid to take the risk of bringing up difficult subjects. After witnessing suicide of acquaintances; and those murdered in degraded circumstances of illegal survival hustling, the accounting of their lives never seeing the light of day, this author feels he has little left to loose but to tell their stories. The Higher Calling would not have us keep silent, but to reach out—to those unspoken too and discounted previously. -- So, here is that 2nd biker novel. For the sake of real-life characters who will never be able to write because of lack of materials, because of shame, or fear. It is a novel patterned after the authors limited motorcycle experience and involvement with the leather community of the 1990's. A lot of the biker women's experiences were the authors, in his own voice. --Red is 64 years of age, of mixed-race heritage. His education ended after 2 semesters in Art College. He studies and worships in the Christian & Jewish tradition. And continues doing oil painting, novels, short stores, poetry, plays—plus spiritual focused Journals. His newly released **'CATALOGUE OF BOOKS, 2008',** lists 80-titles. He was not stopped by the world!

When my colored momma had to teach at Burke elementary school in the worser ghetto of the South Side Negro Chicago, she had to take me to work with her two weeks out of each semester, in lieu of a babysitter because my private school education semester was weeks shorter then the public system—I got out earlier in May and went back later in September. My job was to discipline the kids; I was about 5 or 6; and already drawing pictures that meant things, on a small tablet of paper with colored pencils. I was instructed to walk down the aisle of the 40-black-brown student class carrying a ruler in my hand and slap each child on the back of their hand with it—as punishment for them making so much noise they distracted their class. Odd feelings filled me, marching down those aisles—guilt, exhilaration, sadistic power, shame, embarrassment, a sense it was wrong—all mixed up at once! It was a feeling difficult to process, a rough moment walking up and down the rows of wood desks on black iron stands bolted into floor, striking each small child with a wooden ruler, and I wished she hadn't had me do it. Another of my crazy mom's tortures.

AM Friday April 4

I'm free. I was born free, in a free country. Mother was mentally ill, my father permissive; so I got to run free thru the alleys and neighborhoods at play. I did what I wanted to with my life—it was not very happy, most often—but it was free, to dream of greatness, to create night and day and only a fraction of my time in exchange for work for somebody else for cash.

Thursday, Seniors Day @ Church.

He was forgotten again. Transman asked to show his art pictures, and was told to wait until the end of the program—then they never called on him. The best way to feed Gods sheep is to empower them! Yet time and time again the church grinds right over its members—taking what it wants from them in petty ways, ignoring the genius among them whom they might better cultivate, who then upon world-recognition could turn to bestow their benefactor, the church. One escapes the church in their beginning path to world recognition! One leaves the safe warm bosom of church positions, titles, responsibilities, —for it hampers their art in the long run. They will be called to prostitute their art in order to do church posters and handouts of a benign nature—nothing too controversial please! They will be called upon to organize meaningless committees, sit in tired promissory groups who do nothing to help the larger community and seldom the world, but mainly serve to strengthen the church body— to which the artist by now feels they no longer belong.

Red wanders wearily out of the church dinner into the wind-struck courtyard; cold grey stone surrounds. He saw in parting by grace a Name emerge! Jesus walks out of the stonewalls, upsetting the solemnity of her/his communion as a priest intones the sacraments. Then a Deacon gives a brief sermon, and he thinks on her words:

> If I was the only person on earth Christ would have died for me!
> --Margaret Deeths, Deacon Grace Cathedral, 2008.

Sunday AM April 6

Goddamn these people, I'm so sick of their lying cheating money and stealing! This kapitalist system!

Was thinking about going to religious service this morning/not going—and realizing how swamped I am in my painting newly added to the schedule since January…. To do Gods work is a form of worship. Continued my work and did not attend Sunday service. However had made it to Saturday Shabat in which Torah service davaned this: When Adam & Eve in the Garden of Eden first sinned, and fell away from God, at first they were divided only by a skin of light, --from God, as well as from each other; but this has ever been increasing down thru the ages of humankind; secretions of hate, barriers between each of us, and between us and God.

A sweet sight on roof of a single story building which houses Adobe Books, two pigeons bill & coo between opposing glaring hawks 3 feet tall designed to frighten away their pigeon population. On the sun streaked tar roof the pair of love pigeons strut, beaking, cooing carrying on their romance. One pressed its sleek feather grey green body against the other, busily pecking with its beak grooming its mate.

> No matter how much you know
> or what plans you make
>   you can't defeat the Lord.
> Even if your army has horses
> ready for battle,
> the Lord will always win.
> --Proverbs 21:30,31

Tuesday AM April 8
Another incident! @ Art Store on Van Ness! The elderly Transman proceeds into said shop pulling his metal cart outfitted with its backpack & cane—according to doctors orders at the General, not to carry heavy packs on his shoulders. Immediately a young plutocratic girl rushes out from behind the counter and accosts him:

YOU CANT BRING THAT IN HERE! PUT IT BEHIND THE COUNTER!

most rudely, as if he were a shoplifter she was intending to apprehend *before the act!* Transman Red turned about in a fury and waved his fist in the air in indignity!

2am Tuesday April 8

It is so terrible, the influx of greed, which devours San Francisco—
increasingly the wealthy pour into this city, driving out smaller
people. If the rent control bill on the ballot was somehow—by a
fluke—defeated in the upcoming June election, it is the end of
housing for us poor. For those low-income seniors who worked their
whole lives here and built community, friends, a life here. This is
devastating to us. But the wealthy pour into the city and don't give a
shit. Maybe God will destroy them! Ha! *One good shake and it
would all come tumbling down...* More and more upscale
shopkeepers cast a baleful eye on anybody poor, down at the heel,
because of dealing primarily now with the upper crust they're getting
spoiled—which makes life an even more bitter pill!

Occasionally you'll see them—remnants of the old city, slouched in a
doorway for shelter against the wind, in old, faded, worn, but warm
jackets, and frayed kakis; new white tennis shoes—second hand—
from the Seniors Services—lighting a forbidden cigarette, grey haired
old; not yet removed by price increase, hanging on by the last thread
to this city, as to life itself.

After awhile you feel like a hunted animal. No $ to go in a store,
when you do have $ and go in a store some young upperclass
salespeople have a bad attitude towards you. These 'officials'—petty
managers with little power, and what they have has gone to their
heads like a narcotic making them do stupid things.

I see their world closing in on me. What was once a city of refuge is
now become hostile. Where will people like us go? Who have had as
our oasis in a neon desert Amerikkka of redneck hatred of queers, this
city of compassionate Saint Francis, where we have been tolerated
since the 1960's. This is how we are loosing our freedom—because
of the Almighty Dollar! We found freedom here, much less prejudice
from these western freedom minded Californians, we were accepted
here, along with the Hippies, that was the beginning—we lobbied and
picketed here; fought for our human rights and dignity, for jobs as
queers, housing, proper medical treatment. We did not get driven out
from here by lynching, nor by hate, or firebombs, but it is the pricetag
to this city which is killing us!

As Jesus was leaving the temple,

one of his disciples said to him,
"Teacher, look at these beautiful stones
and wonderful buildings!"
Jesus replied, "Do you see these
huge buildings? They will certainly
be torn down! Not one stone will be left
in place.
--Mark 13: 1-2.

The marks of an artist. The painter has streaks of old paint across their shirt, pants & tie—from carrying a not-yet dry oils, while wearing his-her best clothes.

It is the great love of my art which keeps me getting up out of my comfortable bed in the early-brites (12 noon) to continue computer-scribbling my JOURNEY and my paintings.

*

I think it will be extremely hard for people of DOC to become both Jewish & Christian; those who attempt this-- because few can wrap their minds around the concept of leaving a synagogue fresh from davaning during an in-depth Torah study and the comfort of barcu in the religious service; to then pass by a Christian church whose stained glass windows depict a Holy pageant & realize this is the extent of the same Hashem, God; this is a place as true to the Word as the first place. God standing outside of time; on an equal level, it is the same Hashem Who truly loves Her/His congregants in both institutions; it is the differing arms of the same body!

My understanding is great.
My peace & charity I give
  to all nations.
--Hashem, The Eternal

*

What a Hillary-Obama mess; think she is faring the worse because of being an older woman, then if she was an older man. An older vs. younger man would not be as bad in peoples mind, ---the unconscious eye. See how this election & in fact life all thru the world plays out into these elemental grammar school sexist underpinnings. See how being female–born; not indoctrinated into the male cult at a very early age; bi racial, not connected to society, but somewhat of a loner—

302

this has made my life very difficult—if not all but destroyed me. While on the other hand, spiritually one is raised up by these very conditions—God always sets a balance; that is nature. Wither it be in a personal life, or the dynastic rise & fall of nations.

People like myself in this great America, we who lead an institutional life----not a family life—would be so much better off surrounded by a loving family—but can't make it happen for ourselves—so we have entered a world where social outlets are synagogue, church, free food giveaways, drop-in rap groups, public libraries, coffee shop's—alone—from political organizing; to senior center movie night, chatting in queues for free food; in lieu of the private sphere of a happy home.

God has given me a lot of energy—had a lot of energy to have this vision I have, -- because I was poor. I had to walk, and had to carry. I had to wait.

If you are fortunate to have had a proper upbringing—from your very beginning, -- as a child, you were trained to get up in the morning, and go to school. Mommy & Daddy are going to work. And, after awhile it's all about being somewhere. You always have to be someplace to punch a clock for your pay. You subsist in this manner 50, 60 years. Ingrained in you that you have to be somewhere! Up in the morning! The suns shining! After Transman retired that feeling still haunts him. Have to keep reminding himself, --I'm free!

So one of his outside—'homes' ---these days was the bookstore; today his feet had carried him here, where he fit perfectly into the windowseat, VK's diary on his lap, with a small pile of Art books to accompany. (Several Frieda Kahlos, Picasso.)

> People meet each other at different times in their personal development. You might meet a person and think, 'boy this guy is lame; he's nowhere!' But in a few years you come back and find he has surpassed you—because of something which happened in their life; an awakened vision of God, a moment of truth, the dark night of the soul...

The guys at the bookstore. Including Red concocted this above conversation, and its perfect for the Sci-Fi novel, 4th in the Unity of Utopia series. Yep, still taking notes for SEDNA!

One important thing is to avoid being consumed by fire genius. I pray God will provide the balance for my life—and keep me in Her/His Will, and not run helter-skelter on the winds of my own imagination without a guide.

Now you've been shown, Dear Children, God(ess) is the author of all things!

Tuesday PM April 8

The Weights Of Love. ---Oh no! Reverend is back in his cage at the homeless dog shelter! His foster-care came to an end. Red must sacrifice precious time to go & sit with the beast! Obedience is more then sacrifice? Obedience To The Call Of Art; sacrifice for love? Matisse abandons his family for adventure in the South Sea Islands to paint? Aw shit! If I were *edjamakated* I'd say—Je rein de rien, or C'est la vie, or some Latin phrase but aw shit will have to do!

@ bookstore, arrives a big white guy, 6'6" young, cheerful, having all the tools of the top patriarchy society, money for tuitions, photographic equipment; he goes armed on his spiritual Journey—I look at them, see such privilege. So many people of the world are smashed by people like these. And these young students don't know it. And they are making art. Maybe they should be repairing the world instead. Maybe I should be. With my sliver of privilege still infinitely freer then a great percent of the population of this un-whole earth.

All day long the young proprietor hunches over his desk, doing shitwork; ordering books, paying bills to distributors, sending out e-mails, then surfing the net for political news. Sitting at computer watching scandals break out one after another. Another day brings another news headlines. See what this human race is doing to itself.

> I Am dismayed.
> --Hashem, The Eternal.

Saturday PM April 12

--Just now saw your store. Don't usually take this street. How long you been in business?

--Ten, eleven months now...

Sean is making his business prospective for the future—up to December of '08. What will happen after this, & to our small assemblage here is up to fate.

La fata, el destino!

Suddenly realize we both have so much vested in our projects. Sean's bookstore, with all his array of 3,000 books. My writings & painting, Shaun's photography. Our little worlds which could implode, and leave us without a center.

Red goes across the street to the hotel grocery store to get a snack. Kapitalism, you can't escape it. Eating meat; eating up the pain of all the suffering animals.

Aw my gawd! Sound of a skateboard roars up. Young man Alex flings the wheel-board aside, collapses into window seat. His overheated body smells of cologne, AGGAH! —His new $100 shirt is ripped! "I was flying down the hill on my skateboard and caught a tree, I rubbed my shoulder against the tree bark, and it ripped!" Alex is mildly upset. $100 for a fucken' shirt and it rips in 2 days! Surrounded by 3,000 books about materialism, corporate greed, built-in-obsolescence that make no difference to him! For the young man will not abandon his habit of mega clothes consumerism easy. Saw pricetag on young Alex's jeans—*designer bluejeans*--$278.00. *--*
$278.00! Yes, that's right!

He has his saving grace when he says:

Red you are a dashing man.
--Alex.

AM Wednesday April 9
Ultramarine Blue background for painting, —yet untitled, (acrylic).

Dear Children: let this book be a prayer to encourage you to do your painting!

Prey, hope… A hope is a prayer. A prayer is a stronger prayer!

Cranked out new posters @ KKK; am now up to 11, including the new ones, The Blue Dog, and Student/Golden Pot—for sale, $20! And postcards cheep--$2 apiece. S. mentions he might put them in the store.

He felt rather low the other day, -- was mightily inspired by a Hogarth print. Found in a Catalogue Masterpieces Of English Painting, from the Art Institute of Chicago show of October/December 1946. Just 3 years after Transman's birth. —Sitting listlessly at his desk, Transman Red fingered his bible, and then turned to this dusty brown covered used book. Saw some works* --Marriage a la Mode, O the Roast Beef of Old England. -- of this renegade revolutionary, a social commentator just like him! An outsider looking in on the world in horror, determined to get it right—thru oil painting!

     *

Ah! Reincarnation, sister! Brother! I remember you; 100,000 years ago when we were still back in Africa swinging on the tree of evolution, running down the DNA trail of the human race. Uhh, another note pops up for SEDNA! Beginning at last? That long-promised 4th Sci-fi!?

PM Wednesday April 9
Back in the 1940's, '50's, when I was a child use to be a saying among colored/black people; 'he/she's doing credit to the race.' They've achieved, are without blemish. They comport themselves in the private sector, they comport themselves in the public sector. They have a gift to bring to society; white people eat them up in appreciation; black people eat them up in pride; they are a shining star —doing credit for the race. Au contraire, the other expression:

    --That boy set the race back 50 years!

    --What you say! That nigga settin' the race back *100 years!*

This individual was so bad a person, they alone offset all the steps forward a thousand colored school teachers, diligent postal workers, bus drivers, black doctors and educators had made—they had set the whole dadgum race back 100 years worth of progress!

AM Thursday April 10

Thus said; a sister who has excelled, who we of color are all mightily proud of—Opra Winfrey. She is the daughter of sharecroppers, raised in the most abject poverty. She has made it up so high, and now helps others. She has issued books on how the human race should be tolerant of each other—of gays, other races, and such. She has captured the nation's eye on her Television program The Opra Show! And champions many good causes there-on —such as Global Warming, and the situation of women in the Middle East. She has become one of the worlds top multi-millionaires. By comparison, Transman was a child of the bourgeoisie & in a basic sense, always took money for granted—he was informed by some kind of informal knowing that it would always be there, —which thus enabled him to go out into far reaches of art with only an afterthought about financial matters; he always assumed money would come to him eventually after a life of hard work, and it in itself, money, was not a goal. *I'd give all my money away.*' Thought the old man, bitterly, on noticing the Worlds Dire Condition.

The Shrink plays Social Worker; helps Red fill out his Social Security papers; she remarks:

> It's an endless loop. All these papers government spits out, and meaningless paperwork, it goes on and on and on for years upon years.

Some poor people sold their children out. Bewildered young black-brown faces ride the po' folks bus thru the tore-down ghetto which use to be their stomping grounds; their homes; most are demolished. A tenement stands here and there, alone on a block; stark reminder to once was a congested community; houses shoulder to shoulder spilling with black tan faces; the rest rubble brick—broke. This once was the ghetto—white takeover, a secret blueprint for demolition, black removal crafted decades ago—a half century past. Old black men, jet black hands with pink palms lined and creased; calloused from hard work clutch giant ransacks of their belongings... they were

307

sold out. At one point, fifty years ago, even 30, if they'd made a Herculean effort to form coalitions among themselves—to purchase housing, many would still be here today, but they didn't. Couldn't.

Early AM Friday April 11
The forthcoming RETROSPECT had ignited the fires of hope of success in old TG Red's feeble heart, as he sat in the window seat of Babylon Falling, watching the young proprietors long white fingers pluck out the keys to the computer navigating the intrinsic mathematical formulas necessary to set up the book on Photo POD, Blurb; and, inspired he thought to himself:

> I just want an equal chance at the marketplace. To be seen, between those big sellers with million dollar ad campaigns. I want the public to see my works—then make the decision for themselves if I've got something they want!

He also knew; I must fight now! Struggle now! While there was still enough strength left in his slowly crippling 64-year old body.
What happens to the poor, the old, the not-famous, those weak in family connections, or social groups—they step off into a closet & eventually die.

Seniors @ Grace, Thursday AM.

You Have To Roll With The Punches
You can't give up.
You can't give in.
You can't give out.
--Black woman @ Seniors Day.

After the group discussion, 20-or so seniors seated in a large circle, a Chinese woman exhibited her promising drawings—faded papers curled at edges, date in corner, 1975.

Have thrown my left shoulder out again, am in great pain. Was this from dragging that heavy cart behind me, combined with Ti-Chi class at Seniors?

Friday PM.
Well, for all my dreams of glory, saving the world, Babylon falling, etc, preaching to the masses about cessation of rent, of war-for-profit,

destruction of environment not to mention racism sexism and homophobia, --its still hard work which is the artists forte. Application. The continuum, day after day. No matter how inspiring the Jimi Hendrix music one plays while painting/writing, etc, they cannot self-combust with sheer energy, must take the practical view, channeling energy thru technique—while letting imaginations soar as wild and free as it is able—and all this, under **God(ess).**

Today, returned to the Lost Dog Shelter for the first time in... 3 weeks? Asked to see my former charge. The white & black 3-legged pitbull shortly was let in to the conference room to meet me. He only acknowledged a mild hello via cold wet-nose sniff, lackadaisical tail wag, then, as the attendant left, shutting the door on us, the dog went to sit beside the door—expectantly for it to open again, so he could go back wherever he'd been. Yes. Reverend turned his back on me. Such is the fickle short-term remembrance of the lower-brained canine! Well, Transman resolved to himself, somewhat grimly; my visits were for the beast's sake, and now that he does not need me—he has new friends here at the shelter—its all for the best. Knowing anyway he'd have more time for art. Shrugged; and, pulling his cart behind him, turned and left for the last time.

If you talked about his work you might call it The Life Of A Stranger. He was outcasted from practically everything.

Back at the bookstore, SV said something interesting today—
> I'm not Indian, raised in Singapore, I'm outside. I don't belong anywhere.

My sentiments exactly—expressed by another human.

More about the most detested outcasts of many centuries—us men-women/women-men; trannys. Something you must know about transsexuals. We are hormone-bound. That is a medical treatment for our trans-status (us being midway between the sexes). The other day so much running around to do from dawn to dark, believe I stressed myself, and was at the very end of my 2-week hormone injection cycle. Too weary to take my shot at the beginning of the window of 1 day to give the 100-milligram shot, decided I'd take it near the end of that window—12 hours later. Well such a rotten day I had all that morning! Got into 3-arguments. Was snappish @ bookstore, patience got worn very thin with the young proprietor. This is because that stressful day pushed me over the edge of where the hormones just gave out. If I'd been mindful I would have given myself the shot early, rather then late. Live & learn, so they say.

Oh, here is a tasty bit of an erotic story, in the style of my earlier work, PASSAGE:

> The young kept mistress of a wealthy physician a very attractive black complexioned lady of a bisexual nature found upon her doorstep one day a transsexual man—a recent cross-over from the lesbian community—accompanying the mistresses black stud lover. The threesome spent a pleasant afternoon together, in which Mademoiselle was soon taken by his charms, letting her glance slide across the room often to admire his young, handsome, strong face; his facile hands. She decided she'd try to top the handsome transsexual man. As a cleaver courtesan who had worked wealthy white males for a fortune over the last 18 years, (having the lavish apartment adorned with unnecessary brick-a-brac to prove it) she thought she recognized the key to this young man's fancy. The following day the transsexual man arrived at Mademoiselle's door after being summoned there on a pretext. He was greeted by a gruff handsome black male, short, about the complexion of Mademoiselle—he could have been her brother, or her twin. A few words were exchanged between them, during which the short, strongly built male pierced the languid Transman with fiery eyes. He drew closer, taking the man's pale hand in his dark one. Drawing him to the divan, the two sat together, while the dark black male caressed the transman's neck, on the pretext of 'giving a massage', then dug deep down into his shoulders, while slowly unbuttoning his manly shirt—and soon was stroking the place where his breasts had once been as a woman; stroking and squeezing his chest as if his once full voluptuous breasts still there. This being a most un-talked about erogenous zone, still fully in operation, sans breasts. In only a matter of moments the Transman had surrendered to the mysterious black man's charms. He mounted her. "I'll set you straight young lady." He said, as he fucked her. And fucked her well with precision thrusts of his 7" thick peter with its sensuous, articulated dickhead. It was only after his disguise was removed that the Transman saw—to his embarrassment— Mademoiselle herself slowly appear from under the fake moustaches and tight pantaloons.

Saturday, CCSF, April 13
Men's Drumming circle. Group support of male survivors of trauma.
Anger, disempowerment by the world, step back take overview, breath deeply, get into self, re-empower.

> Passive no good.
> Anger not productive.
> Assertive—yes!

@ Men's drumming circle, we see each other's humanity.

@ Bookstore told the guys about the awful food giveaway in East Oakland, a long time ago. How for very little cash we were given 50 pounds of chicken, 50 pounds of rice & 100 of beans. Little did we know the beans came in one huge 100-pound sack. There was a man standing among the crowd of poor people with an American Flyer wagon—a child's wagon. Had noticed him going back and forth with loads of food away around the block, then return, and go elsewhere. I stared at my bag, astounded, and asked him could I borrow this wagon for about 5 minutes to carry this sack out of the church to the trunk of my car—parked at the curb outside. He replied that he charged $3 to transport sacks for people. I told him I'd do it myself. No. Came the mans cold reply. I was so shit awful mad, I lifted that fucken' 100 pound sack, held onto it with it with all my might and staggered out of the dusty courtyard down the sidewalk across to my car. I was furious! Sean states: people don't help other people; feel they have no investment in them. *'I don't know this person, their not going to be here a few days from now. They're just traveling thru.'* Well, I says, all humans got to get to the point that it dawns on us, we are all the human family; no matter where we go on earth, and it is the prime directive that we help those in need as much as possible, no matter who they are!

This neighborhood, the Tender Nob is a morphing of Tenderloin slum, and Nob Hill, rich; how it has changed over the years, since the old hippy days of the 1960's; condos spring up everywhere silver and glass and steel—and expensive. It is a new world superimposed on the old.

It is a world, which has forgotten how to see each other's humanity.

311

It's hot now, but the wind will be picking up…

Those many summer days, Red sat in his humble throne at the window seat, to pass time, recounting to Sean, the youthful owner many odd tales of his checkered past, to which he states 'you should write that in one of your books':

About the time his transwoman friend Kitty Kastro, (died, 2006; auto accident, barely 32 years old) worked in a sex arcade; part of her job upon closing her shift—the establishment was open round-the-clock, 24 hours—was to go around and clean up all the stalls in back, put things back in order on the shelves, and so forth. One evening a man rushes in, throws down $3 to go in back in the private video booths; then, breathlessly asks 'do you have any inflatable dolls?' "Yes', Kitty points them out at one of the display racks. He purchases this big sex doll, $80, at the time; it's wrapped up in a package; and with the package under his arm, the man heads determinedly for the back. About half hour later he comes out, more relaxed, sweaty, stinking of pheromones, and embarrassedly exits, fast. That evening, Kitty is vacuuming the plush red carpets, while her replacement on the graveyard shift counts out his money trey. When she goes in back to clean up, there is package wrapping all over outside one of the stalls, and when she opens the door, inside the cubical is the sex doll sprawled on the floor. It had been used—its orifices squirted with cum. The guy had just had his session then threw the damn doll away. Also his $80. So there, I put in the scene of the inflatable sex doll left in the sex arcade. Next the tale of the man, who fell out of the booth stark naked. Another friend, a straight white male, (also now dead, from a heart attack at middle age) worked as a clerk in a sex arcade in Berkeley. There was this regular customer who'd come in every Friday and muse down the shelves, making his selections, then afterawhile purchase $100 worth of videos. $100-of sex videos every week. He required variety. Afterward he'd go in one of the sex video booths, spend a half hour or so, then leave with his purchases, to return the following Friday. One time my friend is busy behind the cashier's desk, and hears this noise, a bumping & thumping—louder then the usual grunts and moans. He looks up, just in time to see the door to the stall where the man is fly open, it's lock broken, and the man, stark naked in just his socks and shoes falls out onto the floor! He lay there dazed, red-faced, and a big fat hard-on. *Ha ha ha! Jagoff!*

The cronies at the bookstore. Like buildings built side by side, we stand shoulder to shoulder.

Do the demons get together down in hell & discuss how they wrecked one human project after another? For whatever reason, Sean is in a vile mood today, we get in at least 5 verbal altercations about a variety of stupid stuff. Later when Red confronts him: "Are you sure you're not on the rag?" He replies. "Yes I'm having a man period." And later admits—"all my life I've been on a man period."

Are you friendless? Make connections where you can in the greater society. So he tried—over a lifetime. *I remember it like it was yesterday...* Attempting to bond with people, to find his niche, in one group after another here and there, over 3 states & cities of the plane..

> I'm tired of waiting, being served 2nd hand, last mentioned. Is this because of the not-white color of my skin? Because I'm short? Not as assertive as a bio born male would be?

It is when challenging moments of daily livings social interactions would arise, that Transman Red, self-consciously inspected his behavior as if under a microscope. The bio-males were having a heated discussion, and nobody was listening to him!

> Is my voice too high? Not powerful enough? Am I too short? Or just too old!

Not quite up to push himself into be included in the conversation, so his mind floated. He is nothing. A meaningless blob. He stands there rhythmically rocking back & forth on 2 feet.

> I don't fit in anywhere! Not here! Not even here in this bookstore! So the only way to go is up.

> Well, the Lord(ess) has told me I'm great—therefore I am.

Sometime people get angry because under great pressure they don't want to compromise their true feelings. They don't have enough skills to get their human rights, to be assertive, to speak the language the master understands—so they lash out in anger. Feeling this is better then being walked all over in defeat. This explains the bottled up rage, which incrementally exploded out of Red and other poor citizens, disfranchised like he was, who increasingly day by day found themselves at odds with the growing monstrous affluence of the city.

Grumbling, he stumbled around alone. There, on Polk Strassa, saw another Open House sandwich board, red white & blue lettering with an arrow pointing to a building nearby, spiffy new modern steel & glass half million dollar condo.

On his way to Babylon Failing that bright unnaturally sunny Sunday morning passed by a studio for rent, manager sat in the doorway on a chair, clipboard in hand, studio $1,600, a one-bedroom $2,800. Yet all along Bush Street are more and more vacancies. Two spots with free stuff out in the street; people moving out—and away, out of the city, out of the state, and out of danger! It's a change-over. A change-over!

He picks up a flyer from one of the monolithic property management agencies. Studios are now priced more then his own; $1,025 was the cheapest, the only one less was an efficiency; and the rest were $1,100 on up to 1,600, 1,700, 1,800 for a simple studio!
Studio prices:
    $1,025
    1,095
    1,150
    1,150
    1,195
    1,250
    1,295
    1,300
    1,350
    1,395
    1,425

AM Monday April 14
Oh I've reconciled myself to the thought that I may have to leave this place—just like everybody else has done. City now too expensive—if I am ever dislodged from my domicile—the Studio—there is nothing in this price range I can afford. $1,200, $1400, even $1,600 for a

place similar to mine! Plus, on my income ($1,000 per month) will not past the qualification income to get another unit.

> You can go anywhere with the gifts I have given you;
> first/foremost, you have love in your heart.
> --Hashem, the Eternal.

An interesting thing. In setting up the Lulu POD file for the last book in the Rondo –Joy/Simca! I have a title page, verso, blank dedication page, blank page, then the first chapter of the book set up with a paragraph pertinent to it, then-the set up end with the city and time where the work will be complete. The numbering mechanism is set in place—and there is a 5-page book! A beginning, and end squished together with no substance.

This is the life then of those who unfortunately die in childhood. And, the life of those who go on-and-on feeling nothing. Doing nothing to speak of. A beginning, no middle, then, it is finished.

People at synagogue are busily starting new families—all their energy goes in this direction; you'd never see a tiny child trying to go home alone in a big city; but seniors are people too—no energy is being put into them. Its culturally built-in obsolescence, viewing the elderly as worthless & the glorification of youth; see an oldster woman trying to make her way home alone, bent over, carrying a sack of food from oneg for her and her ancient husband who is worse off even the she is, I hope she can make it, where are the kind friends who'd walk a senior home and make sure they get into their living space ok? I pass her, limping along with my cane, carrying a too-heavy pack. *Could use a helping hand myself.*

Seniors are forgotten. And so will I be—unless I get rich.

Is that the passion, which drives so many, with their sights aimed towards the top, no matter how many people they step on?

See an old person shuffling along, hands clutched to their person, greedily like claws, face twisted bitter, hatefully, a nauseous green expression on their face, you might think—what a cruel old bastard! But this is incorrect. The person is not mean at all, only suffering! This person was young once, had the use and activity of their body,

315

and now they may be enduring a torturous old age. They have seen thru time, so much pain in the world, *so much pain in my body;* and so beaten down—tho they continue on—that their footsteps can barely pick themselves up over the sidewalk, thus they shuffle along. *Pain in the body. Pain in the soul.*

It seems spring has come, and left me behind! Lovely day to go to the beach—with friends; have a picnic—with a group of compatriots; well, this is not happening for me!

Loud shouting in the street, arguments; sudden change to hot summer heat from a long cold spell, the bustling discomforts of spring; its agitating humanbeings, causes them to yell, and do unpleasant minor stuff.

The cat leaps off of the bed with a soft 4-point thud of its paws; his eyes glistening red, luminance fire. Time for Jasmin to call draws close. Paintbrush in hand, studiously Red studied a small canvas (19 ¾" x 19 ¾") Along the Watchtower (?)

Artist! Don't be disappointed! Continue! As may of the other Greats have done before you! Each brush stroke! Each written word! Each on-point ballet step! The Great Dance Of Life must continue! Must have you! When discouraged, listen to the others who have gone up this rough, stark mountainside before!

You think, you think! You should not think, you should paint! You want to do things 'the right way' Van Gough didn't do things 'the right way!' Pablo Picasso did not do things 'the right way'! They painted! They painted their way! These people who think and ponder & worry 'am I doing things the right way?' —that is their problem right there!

My dear friends; I just want to reassure you, this is a hell of a life! A hell of a life! For my kind, and perhaps for yours also! So what else is there a person to do—but to continue on down their life's path—as if their life depended on it!

This world—you have no control over the things that are important— like length of life, or love.

The painting—from where do you think it comes from? From every days hard work.

Van Gogh studied other artists in the museums of London. He admired the great masters of the past, of whom he preferred:

> Rembrandt, Hals, Ruysdael, and the leaders of the British school.
> --Van Gough Exhibition, Art Institute Of Chicago, 1949.

Ultimately when he began to paint, he couldn't do what Hals could do, but *he did what Van Gough could do!*

AM Thursday April 17
You stand at the canvas, paintbrush in hand. You're depressed. You have no friends. You have no lover but you know you're a good artist. You're great! Your hands pick up brushes; begin application of multicolor to the waiting canvas—you have hope for the future!

PM Tuesday April 15
The Transman was basically a lonely man, and didn't have a family, and few friends, if he had been like others he might not have dallied where he dallied, and hung around where he hung out—*those kind of places.* Which were havens for fallen souls, broken women and men. Before he went out he crossed the small studio room (in 5 steps) sat down on the high chair beside his computer & wrote himself a short poem about a homeless woman:

> This lady is victim of a fallen love.
> He left her with bric-a-brac of a house.

April 17 AM Thursday
People are outcasted in one generation & accepted in the next. Many examples of this: the Chinese Exclusion Act which forbid the immigration of Chinese women—resulting in thousands of elderly, lonely bachelors who never had wives or family; only to be succeeded by a later generation of Chinese men and women who freely married and did have families. The next are severely handicapped individuals. In the 1960's there was a news report: The Home ForIncurables, where wheelchair bound people with physical deformities were kept, secluded from the world, living half-lives in an institution. The report was complete with stark photographs of one woman, now

317

middleaged, her body twisted in deformity, tied into a wheelchair, who sat day after day on the rusty iron balcony of the institute; on her face a horrible smile. She had lived there since birth. Only ten years later the advent of independent living allowed these same people to live as normally as others, having their own apartments with attendant care; wheelchairs access to public sidewalks, ramps up to buildings accommodating them, public busses with wheelchair lifts, for transport. Instead of secluded lives as seldom-viewed freaks, they became part of the social population. The third are transsexuals. The evolution of society's knowledge of us; how we stood yesterday. How we stand today. And hope for complete understanding and inclusion of us in the very near future.

To help others. This is what I was saying in that quote:

> ---- I see in a dream (about Daughters Of Courage) that the most important thing in building a religious movement is to strengthen the human circle. The human links. That is the original purpose of our mortal race—since the cave people days, nothing new about it! When people sit around in a circle together to tighten bonds, to make family.

And to mention, Art is not enough! When I get famous must add my stand to the voices for justice!

Today is L.'s wedding day, resplendent in a tux, pops in Bookstore to say hello, now on to the wedding feast at a restaurant. Sadly Transman Red has not been invited.

I am at the top of my game; 80-books; retrospect of fine arts paintings… Whenever he got depressed he'd tell himself this, and, *remember, good things are coming in my future…*

When things aren't going well in the world; boring places; plans fall thru, you can turn to your self, retire home --return to art. Bowed over a desk painstaking marking one fine line after another--China ink etchings; bent over a meticulous acrylics political arts statement… minor carpentry, and paste together cloth collage assemblages… Doing this uses up huge gaps of time spent in a positive fashion, which saves one from depression, insanity, and gives a feeling of purposefulness.

Emory Douglass at Babylon Falling today seeking help for his new laptop computer programs. Joked about the line in the Federal Building, Red mentioned at a facility where he was there was a small group screaming into the free phone trying to get a hookup to the tax clinic where they fill your taxes out for free; and one screams "I GOT AN APPOINTMENT FOR TOMORROW –THE LAST ONE!" And the other begs, "*Can I go with you? Maybe they'll have time for me too!*"

Emory told us how he'd seen all the hypes, pimps 'hos, winos—folks ain't worked in 20 years all lined up to get their taxes filed. Emory described it as a sort of mini riot. Usually go in there there's a couple of benches full, today there was lines up and down, a line out the door one man staggering in could barely hold himself up---all to get that free $300 tax refund. Free money.

Sean, however darkly thought maybe it was a more diabolical scheme on the part of our increasingly paranoid U$ government—to be able to track all citizens, catch up everybody in a gigantic net, who might have slipped thru the system before. To which Red countered: Yeah, well they send me my social security every month, but now they do know a little more about me, then before.

Odd how Shaun's store stocks over 3,500 books, yet up approaching a year, not a single writer reading for his monthly shows; nothing but a procession of artists of various medias. Incidentally, involving sources of artistic inspiration Transman Red states:

> I was surrounded by art in my new SF location. Art galleries. First itching of my inspiration after 38 years non-painting, to discover a fellow artist back in Oakland—an industrious, tho not great artist who lived nearby. We worked at the same telemarketing survey office. This guy had a hundred canvasses he'd painted, and lived with them alone in a one-room hotel.

Art comes from places high & low. Legitimate, and tainted. Patrick Sequi, artist comes in; he spoke of how Kindisnsky, Paul Klee and others were in the habit of visiting mental institutions to examine the works of the mad, to sketch copies or take home the originals to their studios & copy the ideas; so I myself appropriated for my novels dialogues overheard in the city in common streets, ho strolls, dope

319

dens, bum havens, street corner cliques, where in can be found the apostles of Ripple wine; women's apartments of ill-repute; as well as fresh sprung from my own mind, my own life. He went on to talk about artists who of mid 17th century who'd go thru the streets, and pay little children for their crayon drawings—maybe give them some candy—then take home these brilliant fresh ideas from their little minds, steal them, make copies on their own canvasses.

AM Wednesday April 16
Concentration is most important for an artist. Muster up as much of it as you can.

Unroll canvas, lay out pre-formed stretcher bars, measure, pencil in guidelines for cutting, cut out sections, pull canvas taunt as you can with pliers; staple each to its frame. This progressed over the last several weekends. Now he had 12 canvasses prepared. Plain white canvas sections cut out, partially stapled onto each set of stretcher bars. Red's oeuvre for the next 1-year? Object is to fill them with colorful paintings.

Something, which makes my arts extra interesting—it is drawn directly from imagination. All art is, but some begins as a concept during which ideas flow & are jotted down in sketches in a notepad, then, in a 3rd translation re rendered onto canvas in paint, —these stages, first from the idea, to the mental reworking, sketching, planning, and finally the product committed into canvas or paper. Like some others, I do all this process at once, facing the blank canvas and begin to throw up lines of energy, wild shapes, blobs of brilliant color here and there—and from then, allow my imagination to work out the vision, which slowly emerges—like a diver from the deep sea bringing up strange sea fruits of imagination. The picture emerges! Or like a photograph from the murky chemical bath of a developer's trey in the darkroom, becomes clear.

Some differences in my old age—34 years having past since last touched brush to canvas except for that aborted attempt in 1998: use to hold in left hand a dozen brushes pigment-laden in its own color, while right hand painting fast, pausing for a split second to select out one brush, then replacing that, with another—out of my left hand. Now, arthritis, Carpo Tunnel nerve inflammation, has crept over my aging body. Am aware of muscle stress. Must set each individual brush down. I'm wearing glasses now, which must take off/put on as sit near, or distance myself from canvass to gain perspective. Fans going in both windows—much more aware of toxicity; use latex gloves on hands to avoid contact with pigment on skin. Back at age 20's, would finish a session hands laden with colors, which then washed off in a bath of stinky turpentine. *I remember it like it was yesterday*...

AM Friday April 18
Sometimes I wonder how immediately God is involved in human affairs... These were his thoughts as Red paused to examine a piece of scrap paper before he tossed into the trash. On its back were current notes, recently entered into his journal, JOURNEY and the back had a scene from CARNIVALLA his fabulous play about a transsexual woman. I wonder if and when this tragic, great, often funny play will ever come alive on the boards of theatre!

Scene 10.
Campgrounds. Red holds hose, watering the Elephant's drinking tub. The Pachyderm is not shown if this is a theatre production... 2 Clowns, Hugo & Carnivalla walk past. Carnivalla stops to talk.

Red: Aren't we ridiculous Carney?

Carnivalla: Yes. Ridiculous.

Red: I got a crush on you since forever but also I got a red-hot jones for the Arial Trapeze Woman Klara Von Darling! Dare Devil of the High Wire, and the most Beautiful Woman in the circus! (Said with a flourish.)

Carnivalla: Oh, that's what you meant. I thought you meant we're ridiculous for being human on this God-forsaken planet.

Red: I guess Klara Von Darling can't see doin' no romance with me, but she's got a crush on you! I guess you know that! You're so dense sometimes Carney. So wrapped up in a world of your own!

Carnivalla. I know she does.

Red: I'm not enough man for you Carney.... and too much female for Klara Von Darling.

Carnivalla: Huh.

Red: You can't see me or her as a lover... That Boris comes in to visit every night. Klara don't want him either. So we all just sit up there in her trailer mooning at each other..... Pining like lovesick Polecats.

321

Carnivalla: (Flouncing.) Really Red! I'm just busy trying to be a woman! Something both you and Klara take for granted! Being born—at least in your case—a female, and her actually having become one! It's full time work being a woman! That circus doctor is prescribing me some hormones.

Red: What kind?

Carnivalla: Well Estrogen I hope!

Red: That's all you think about—how female you present! All you been talking about since we first met, when you were a boy who entered the drag contest!

Carnivalla: (Applying some cosmetic part of her Clown face.) And so what about it!

Red: I'm thinking about **love.**

Carnivalla: Love? Forgot the meaning of the word.

Red: A pain like something inside of me is on fire burning & I can't reach in to put it out. My love for Klara Von Darling… And, for you.

Carnivalla: As much as Klara?

Red: Different from Klara.

End Scene.

Scene 11.
Lobos has gained entry to Klara Von Darlings trailer and is beating her. Carnivalla is walking nearby and hears the screams.

Lobos: YOU TOOK MY MONEY TO FIX YOUR TRAILER WHEN IT BROKE DOWN ON THE HIGHWAY THRU UTAH! YOU MADE ME A PROMISE! YOU WERE MY LOVE KLARA!

Klara: HELP! HELP SOMEBODY! LOBOS STOP! STOP LOBOS YOUR HURTING ME!

Lobos: KLARA COME BACK TO ME AND BE MY LADY OR I'LL KILL YOU!

Klara: NO! **NO!**

Lobos presses her up against wall of trailer.

Lobos: Let me take you Klara! Every man in this Carnival has had you! You let me… 2 years ago! Come on! I know how you like sex!

Klara: **NO! NO! NO! LET ME GO LOBOS! HELP SOMEBODY HELP!**

Enter Carnivalla.

Lobos: WHAT THE HELL DO YOU WANT CLOWN!

Carnivalla says nothing. She comes up and stands beside Klara, silent, in her absurd clown face smile.

Lobos: DO YOU WANT A BEATING TOO? I'LL WHIP YOU BOTH!

Lobos begins to reign blows down on Klara, she screams.

Klara: AHHGIGHHGGGLGLAGHAHUHH!

Carnivalla steps in-between the two, turns, sheltering Klara in her arms; Lobos hesitates then begins to strike Carnivalla's back.

Lobos: ALRIGHT! ALRIGHT! I'LL BEAT YOU TOO SISSY CLOWN! GODDAMN IT TURN AROUND AND FIGHT YOU BIG WIMP! TURN AROUND YOU FAGGOT QUEER! FIGHT LIKE A MAN YOU BITCH CLOWN!

Suddenly circus Security Guard bursts into doorway, followed by 2nd Roustabout.

Guard: ALRIGHT LOBOS, BACK OFF OF 'EM! BACK OFF! DO WHAT I SAY OR WE'LL BEAT THE SHIT OUT OF YOU!

2nd Roustabout: He means it Lobos!

Guard produces long club, prods Lobos violently in the back.

Guard: STAND OFF LOBOS! STAND OFF! DON'T LET ME HAVE TO CALL THE SHERIFF!

Lobo acquiesces. Hands down at his side, defeated.

Lobos: This fuckin' faggot here.... This two-bit clown.... It's his fault...he…

Klara: **GET OUT LOBOS! DON'T EVER CROSS THAT DOORWAY AGAIN!**

Guard: Yeah, yeah, I know Lobos. It's all the Clowns fault. Yeah, sure. Wise decision to come along Lobos. (He begins to lead Lobos out of the trailer.) Yuh know any time we gotta call in the town Sheriff they use it as an excuse to revoke our license and run us out of town. You wouldn't want the whole crew hatin' yuh. That's right... Go on down the steps... go on down the steps... go on now… Don't let me catch you in here again, or I'm gonna tell Big Boss Sands! —If he ain't already got the news. —He might give yuh yer' walkin' papers over this shit!

129.

> Homeless people are the warning.
> Living on the sidewalks
> of San Francisco
> Laid out under an Indian death blanket.
> Poisoned by Smallpox from society.
> Egyptian mummy's, embalmed by
> mental sickness, confined in the coffin

323

of a world which hates
the voices in their heads.
Homeless people are the warning.
on the streets of San Francisco,
Reminding every one of us—
without respect to person;
You could be next.

Many political arguments—those evenings @ Babylon Falling. To pass the time, to vent the angst within. Once Red told them this, (he had to impress this clarification upon them, regarding patriotism): "My Grandparents were established Negro citizens, who worked over their lifetime and bought a 2-story flat in a bourgeoisie sector of the black district. They hung out the American flag every 4th of July, and Memorial Day. They were patriots, but hated the status quo in America—which was segregation. They talked with bitterness, resignation, sparks of hope, but mainly mistrust & dislike about: The White People—but not the US Government!"

We speak of Revolutionary change. Save the elephants, the chimpanzees, our human species! Hashem's answer to us is, to begin with our neighbors, cooperation, love, forgiveness—and working together! *This must be! If you want the thing done.*

Thus says God, the Most High. If I have a high power work to do—it must be—to help foreword the good cause. And is part of why I put on the dedication page of this book:

> ---- I see in a dream (about Daughters Of Courage) that the most important thing in building a religious movement is to strengthen the human circle.

Just a little more about myself, how important my life's work—Art— has been to me! My goal, for it to achieve recognition and fame; however, it is possible that all my high-power production will not be simply for people to enjoy but for one additional thing, —to call attention—that this world must bring peace and wholeness –*Shalom*-- to all its inhabitants, including the animal species and lower life forms.

PS: Sometimes an artist thinks of their work—in comparison to the stars in heaven, and as in finality, rendered by time-- as meaningless trash!

> Dec 13, 1943
> I cleaned the shelves of the filing cabinet I once used for my own printed articles and pieces. How proud I was as it filled up between 1905 and 1912. I believed these established my name. Wastepaper!
> --V. Kempterer; The War Diary's.

AM Saturday April 19, 2008
I've given you fire says the Lord(ess). That *fire!*

Sold a The Blue Dog! To Matt, photographer from the bookstore! First sales of a new painting print, which makes me happy. The Blue Dog has passed his test. Well, must exercise today, contend with second-hand cigarette poison from troll in basement who is also home on Saturday, and do some painting. Seder tonight at Avraham's house.

PM Saturday April 19, 2008
Sedar @ Avrahams, quite satisfying. 12-of us. Grape juice, matzo, parsley, salt water, beets (instead of lamb shank) Saphardic & Ashkenazi bitter herbs, white horseradish, asparagus, two African dishes, and song. Went to stand and gaze out his balcony window, which overlooks the city, to see a streets & buildings in a grid below; above, a round moon in the black sky—the full moon of the Hebrew lunar calendar—bringing in the peasa celebration.

One third of us here are converted Jews—not born. When you stare up at the black heavens and silver stars, when you allow your fixed mind to go wandering in wonder, you realize many things. The ordinary world is too simplistic. Yet we see how intricate creation is—the construct of animal, plant, & environmental living things and how all of this is so entwined. Right down to our DNA code, the balance so refined at the smallest, and, at the most vast, how the stars are set in heaven in a grid of magnetic distances. Here, one can see— the hand of Creator at work. So can we see how diversity is also in people wither these be men or women, or men-women, or women men? Wither these be people of mixed faith beliefs and practices—or mixed-race love; all of it is valid! All of it is necessary for creation to be whole!

Soon home. Hope to soon get a lift from Hugo in his red truck to pick up materials for second loft—a smaller one, 6' tall by 6' long, but only 2.5' wide; this exclusively to hold finished canvasses—maybe a few extra boxes, a few not done canvasses. The Art Machine is ready to rumble!

Things change fast in the Trans Community. People, Faces, Names, and places. Opening scene, violin plays while camera pans to inside of 5-cheep hotel rooms of trans, & gay kids: one in a fancy upscale hotel, the others, living on welfare in poverty. A transwoman, ebony complexion, lovely, emerges, she is 7 feet tall in spike leather heels, jet black naked flesh clothed only sparsely by a black SM brassiere and silver-studded mini skirt. In a golden honey accent she corroborates her story that she was born in Africa. Once married to a bio woman, and the parent of a child—whom she hasn't seen for 15 years—gives the bisexual listener an amorous swell of desire that she might be a functional switch. What a delicious dish—and so sweet in temperament, --when she is at peace, and not challenged, which sadly is so often. This is her dark side. Grace is often accosted & harassed on the streets because of being an obvious transsexual, which has caused so much hell for her life it has helped bring about the disorganization of her mind, subsequently to try to 'fix' that, a pattern of unfortunate drug use and other incidents common to a destitute person—who is unemployable because society considers us freaks. Now here is the News Bulletin:

> One of our own, dear 'Miss Africa', incarcerated since November, has since gone to trial and has received a 2-year sentence in the Federal Penitentiary for men. The photo of her shows a fat, short crew-cut individual—how photographs lie! Evidently this is what jail life has done for the girl over the last 8 months. Having gone from her trim physique and lovely feminine hairstyles of only a year ago, when she was last seen in the TL. The sad fact about this story is that she was arrested for stabbing two men who assaulted her. Yes. Grace was walking home late one evening, hurriedly, minding her own business when several men from a group of 8 Hispanics who had been drinking began disrespecting her with loud heckles of 'puta, maricon, juto' and the like. Meaning faggot, whore.

Somehow physicality became involved, and when she found herself being beaten by two of this gang of men, pulled out a knife she carries for protection and stabbed both of them—sending one to visit the General (hospital) for a week. Her attackers were not tried nor jailed. What in the hell justice is this!

All of which brings to mind these poignant words from act III of my CARNIVELLA:

Scene 17.
The RED SHUTTERS. Bartender wiping glasses. The 3 girls seated at a booth. Enter Carnivalla and Red, thru doorway. Red carrying two heavy pieces of luggage.

1st Girl: LOOK WHO'S BACK IN TOWN!

2nd Girl: AMBERST! With that little butch dike.

3rd Girl: MISS VIRGINIA! YOO HOO! (Waves frantically.) Uh.... no. Miss Circus?

1st Girl: Well, well, well. Look who the cat dragged in! Miss Circus is back in town. Hello there Red. (To Carnivalla.) Well *hello* Troglodyna.

Red: Hi girl.

Carnivalla: (To 1st Girl) Hisssssssttt! (Makes cats face & claws.)

2nd Girl: Circus....

3rd Girl: Oh ! MISS CARNIVALLA! (The two hug.)

1st Girl: (To Red.) Still hanging out with bad company huh?

Red: Don't be so catty, we came all the way back from across the country to see you girls! —Back in this lovely RED SHUDDERS! (Indicates bar with a gesture of disdain.)

1st Girl: OH! (To others.) THEY'VE BEEN ON HOLLIDAY! AWAY FROM MISMO! (Indicates with even grander gesture, the town around them.) And all this time I thought you were in lock up! Yo' Miss Thing! Holding court down at the jail!

2nd Girl: Miss Carnivalla you make this poor little man carry all you alls luggage! You should carry your luggage and he carry his!

Red: It's all hers! I don't have any.

1st Girl: WHAT!

Carnivalla: She's got to prove how tough she is, I mean him; the big butch, so I let him carry it. He FORCED me to.

These following 3 lines are said almost simultaneously as the two seat themselves:

Red: How's things around this dump?

327

2nd Girl: Whatever in the world have you two been up to?

3rd Girl: What foreign cities have you been traveling to?

1st Girl: (Leaning over table clandestinely.) The ships docked honey. Our paychecks have been restored.

3rd Girl: Yeah, Navy is in town. We're worken' 'em girl.

2nd Girl: There's a seafood buffet here every night.

3rd Girl: Guess you don't need to do that no more... work the men.... huh.... since you... been accepted. Accepted by the straight world, huh? Carnivalla?

1st Girl: Accepted as a **CLOWN!**

All laugh.

All: HA HA HA HA HA HA!

Carnivalla: I stopped the life of a workin' girl when I went on to better opportunities--- under the Big Top.

3rd Girl: I want to be like you Carnivalla! I want to be like you! I want to break out of this tired town Mismo too! I always admired you girl! You know that! I was your friend, wasn't I!

Carnivalla: I remember girl. You were my only friend... Besides Red.

3rd Girl: Take me with you when you leave! Take me along two! (Grabs both of their arms.) You and Red! Let me come with you! I gotta get out of Mismo! I got to get out of the RED SHUTTERS! I gotta change my life! It's killin' me girl! Killen' me!

Well, I have told you this story, Dear Children, as I would to my own child—if I had any.

This writing is a prayer to the Most High!

Now you've been shown, Dear Children, God(ess) is the author of all things!

God, in Whom I trust.

Peoples souls like the root of a plant, exposed; some have red curling roots, angry clutching, having eaten metal, drawn from the bile of a bitter earth, others have long roots that grow deep, deep, ignoring the

328

poison, the hate of the top soil seeking the true good earth, seeking, persistent.

Only God! Only God!

Only life!

Now, all this is written down, everything in regards to my re-beginning fine arts painting after 38 years. I believe not one bit of information has been omitted, by accident or on purpose. This, being for use by other artists; and would-be artists during their struggles… With time… with encouragement or lack of… With material entities… And for the love of, or avoiding, God.

Peace to you and all living creatures.

Flashing bulbs, lights, think of what this human race is doing to itself… *An ocean of bells clanging, wheels spinning, time racing, lights flashing….*

And what have you got? Your work! Your works! Your work stands after you!

Red Jordan Arobateau
April 19, 2008
6:00 AM Pacific Standard Time
San Francisco, CA
USA

JOY/SIMCA!

Journey Vol. 10

2008

Artist! Don't be disappointed! Continue! As many of the other Greats have done before you! Each brush stroke! Each written word! Each on-point ballet step! The Great Dance Of Life must continue! Must have you! When discouraged, listen to the others who have gone up this rough, stark mountainside before!

--THE PASSION OF ART

130.

The RETROSPECT is finished! It's in my hands! Joy! I hope to be saying these words soon. & in the meantime head onward to complete 2 new works; one that unfinished picture on easel on the books cover, The Raiment Of Love. The other, All Along The Watchtower, a song by Bob Dylan redone by Jimi Hendrix. See the chessboard, the chess pieces, human slaves caught up in the game of coins & dollars. The rook on fire! Babylon Falling!

Must say this—that my hurry to get the paintings into print, and the book—RETROSPECT--- is because so much of my formative years as an artist was spent in the hopelessness of ever connecting my work with an audience in the greater world. After so much effort purchasing stamps, addressing letters sent to publishers around the globe, and receiving **NO** for an answer, finally my thought was to rely on self and self alone to preserve my stuff until such a time it might be discovered— wither before or after my death. So that was another motivating factor—beside the doing and love of it. So RETROSPECT will help locate my art into the world—in my own mind at least, as well as broadcast my paintings to the few souls who stumble across it.

Monday AM April 28
You will encounter over time, many people offering services, a book review, an art showing, et al, shows, collaborations, projects they wish to include you in, etc., I have found that if someone offers you ten such deals and only one of them ever materializes just be happy for the one—which has advanced you further. I don't take stock in promises any more after being so devastated by earlier ones which failed. Now I say OK, fine, scan that book for me, arrange that showing, interview me for your anthology, and if I never hear from them again, I just proceed faithfully on with my end of the bargain which after everything else is said and done, is far more vital--to create more art! That is the rock bottom product upon which all else is based; all the showings, all the reviews, all the inclusions, and luckily it is the one thing which can be done, independent of all others; it is the one thing I am masterful at.

Tonight went thru boxes of old stuff, weeding out, tossing away, consolidating boxes, making more space in the studio; came across copies of old reviews, & fan letters of which I was so proud had made extra copies to show them to people to help sell my books—an idea which didn't really work. Well that moment in time has passed, 15 years later, after the publication of LUCY & MICKEY I'm tossing them out, the Bancroft has a copy or two, I save the original; the rest if one-sided is saved in a scrap pile to write notes on.

Transman had been Spring-cleaning. He threw away approximately 3 boxes of crap and duplicate printings, unnecessary shit, combined large gangling boxes down into smaller banker boxes which were now packed tightly and efficient, and then threw out 4 piles of trash-filled cardboard boxes. Also the hideous metal contraption, which had held the stuff ceiling-high, known as a *storage shelf* in politer circles; suddenly his studio took on much more space and airiness. After 4 days of dragging and pulling and lifting, his hands were sore, his upper body ached; a mass of old age pain, and his hand shaky. But he must continue painting irregardless!

AM Sunday April 20
The big art machine continues to roll along! Took down box of spines for a very special order of his books, AGE OF OM and THE IRON WOMAN, which sit, unbound in storage dating from the time when he had access to free copy machine prints in volume. Jasmin has requested his poetic collection to thumb thru them for an entry to the Dancing Poetry contest—in which, if the two are selected, she will dance, while Red reads the poetic work. After that removed from loft 1970's paintings, The Madman, The Poolshooters, & Flash On The Hustler, and moved them to the site of where the new, paintings-only-loft will be, in main room of studio; however he seemed to recall—now that the Flash! painting has it's caption embossed on posters, and is set up to go into the RETROSPECT, --that long ago he had named it The Players; back in that condemned building in Western Addition—not many blocks from where he now resides—area of blight which was being re-gentrified by the city. Then on to the setting up for final book of rondo, this JOY/SIMCA!

Must tell you one last story before departing for Babylon Falling. First will preface it with this observation: when you are called by

God, the Most High, --touched in your heart, or mind about the existing of Hashem (God)—you must not depart from doing the good works you are currently involved in, believing this is not what S/He wants you to do. The tasks you are doing which are meaningful work must not be abandoned, simply to be involved in the workings of a church/ synagogue/mosque –such as ushering the congregation, leafleting, working as a cook for outings—and the like,—because you believe it is these things by which you will serve God better, since they are direct involvements with a religious organization. Nothing could be further from the truth! If you are a medical student, and are called, a leader in political organizing when you get the Word, a fine arts painter, a diligent civil servant working their way towards future security in order to provide for self & family—it just might be this fact, of your current involvement, that is the reason you've been called from the beginning! Now the story:

> When I first heard the Call, upon the death of my father, desperate with grief, and still dully wanting a girlfriend—and followed that high-yella sister into a small Christian congregation in East Oakland, which was newly forming, I soon discovered God, although the love affair didn't happen, and began to alter the structure of my life. Kept writing, and continued to carry around – in a move thru 3 different houses which I owned, then sold sequentially --- the tools of a fine arts painter; I remember the paint stained metal tripod flimsy, only used early in my career age 16-21, before I'd started constructing the wooden giants which passed as easels for large canvasses; the canvass pliers, a green metal box, rusted, found, very heavy, crammed full of oil paint tubes all of them bent, squished and twisted, their caps dried on by their own substance; crimson red, alizarin red, ultramarine blues; the brushes some stiff with paint, not useable---this equipment. I recall staring at it, then setting it aside for a few weeks, then throwing it out! Into the garbage! Thank God I did not also throw away the 11 oil paintings done from 1969-'70, which now compose the heart of RETROSPECT. The call to God was strong, and had totally occupied my mind for several years when this occurred.

> Now I believe Hashem wanted me to continue painting—and guess what! After retiring on Social Security income, and laboring furiously over the printed word, churning out 10 new volumes of novels, plays, and Journals in this newly released spare time, the call to art hits me, and I must obey! This is what our Great God has

given me to do! Paint! As well as the writing! It is better then only going diligently to Torah studies, Church services, and the other variety of church/synagogue activities—where I was putting myself into the religious world exclusively, while neglecting a very important gift I've been given!

At bookstore, reading an art book, Transman saw a last will & testament, and so he said, to no one in particular; *my descendents, spiritual inheritors, listen to this, it is my wishes also:*

> He also cedes all his copyrights post mortem—as well as those of Freda Kahlo to the trust; that it may then contribute to the maintenance of the museums. He also donates his collection of pre-Hispanic sculptures, his collection of paintings and drawings, his furniture, etc., so that they may remain on display in said museums, but which maybe exhibited temporarily in other museums or galleries by agreement of the technical committee.
> --From Freda Kahlo, The Metamorphosis Of The Image by Nadia Ugalde Gomez, & Juan Rafael Colonel Rivera.

Yes I want a trust! To give longevity to my life's labor!

The back room of BF holds things reminiscent of his own studio—books; wrapping from mailing books—rolled up prints of artists works. Sean has this quote hanging on the wall. Pay close attention to it Dear Children:

> If you want a picture of the future, imagine a boot stamping on a human face—forever.
> --George Orewell, 1984.

There is someplace beyond the future:

> The food we eat in heaven is more delicious (licks pink tongue) then anything on earth.
> --Husky, Red's deceased dog.

Monday AM April 21
The artist has important tasks to do—as well as the construction of art. One sees a painter with 2,000 paintings; a writer with a large collection of his or her own books. It took time, dedication—and isolation. Removal from the daily world, and its pressing needs for such an interval of time, minimum, to engage in the creative process.

The hours spent result in your product. In the meantime, outside the studio door, a great commotion! Bills must be paid; time must be spent in work benefiting someone else for a salary. Meals to be cooked, friends, or relatives to be entertained—because social fun is also a human necessary. Other Things intrude. The baby needs shoes, the baby always needs shoes, then all the older children want new shoes! -- There's always going to be a reason—a very compelling reason at some point—to be distracted from your calling. So realize you must put everything aside, no matter how important, for art to supercede, to Get The Thing Done, otherwise it will not be done!

Push other things, thoughts, needs, aside!

An hour every day! A little bit each time! This is how to get the thing done!

Depressed? Feel lifeless & blue? —Think on higher thoughts a moment, soon the artist is relocated in their forte; the painter at easel, the writer at her desk, the sculptor, chisel at hand industriously sets out upon the scaffold; the dancer stretching sore muscles warms up, to arabesque, and pirouette on point across the boards.

AM Tuesday April 22
Transman sat at his desk, writing in his Journal. Hot breath of a little green parrot blasted rhythmically into his ear; Arial sat chortling in repose on his shoulder as he worked, typing thus: Just for the record, I believe that old oil painting that is now being labeled Flash On The Hustler should be called Players. The Players? I believe that is its original name—1970. The main character set foremost on canvass, in a ghostly white cowboy hat resembles my old friend from Chatham High School, South Side Chicago, who later stars in several works as Alexander d'Oro. But the painting will be relabeled in the future books as Players. This reminiscent of my book RODEO SEX about two homeless bag ladies who become lesbians having sex together, which was mislabeled after a first brief inspiration of something about Rodeos, and the barbaric sport of bull riding, turned into that wonderful HOBO SEX, which was even indorsed by one of the rad feminist bookstore owners of the old Mama Bears; but for a time on

336

all the Internet book lists Rodeo kept coming up as well—as if it was an additional book.

PM.
In his minds eye, Transman saw the end of the world! A big pit of red fiery hell, bubbling over with molten lava; scorching.

> Behold I'm digging a big pit for them—they have dug it for themselves.
> --God Almighty.

Will God wipe us of the face of the map? All this hell people have made of our Garden of Eden once the human birthright?

All Along The Watchtower is a political piece. Karl Marx would approve, also Emma Goldman; the question is, is it Art? Does it have mastery? Would Picasso approve? Van Gogh? I think yes to this too. All Along The Watchtower, 4-2008. Acrylic on Canvas, 20"X 20".

DIRECTIONS
All the arrows point one way
Back to the human heart.

**
Go upon the river of broken glass.
Up the dry creek bed
glistening sharp stones that
cut the soles of human feet.

How much better
 to lay upon the warm fertile breast of
Creator in peace, & joy.

How are things going?
Terrible? (Horrible.)
People are learning mans slaveries.
Only the whisper of morality.
Little by little the wreckage
piles high up in evidence
of a great undoing.
I have no pleasure in telling you
it is very near the end

337

of the human stay.
We are of the last in line of the prophecy
 God will send the Fire next time.
The whole civilization, wiped away
off the rim of the solar system.
Our societies cool and fail
like an orange/red sun collapsing
into a black hole sucking space
whose fuel has run out.
Just enough hydrogen left
to shine in one last violent outburst.
Yes friend, the highway stops here.

131.

Things now change around this neighborhood so fast; the old edifices
torn down & new million dollar condos replacing—T didn't recognize
the streets anymore, and thus was libel to be further upon his
destination then he thought, assuming it to be one street, when it was
actually the next.

Lazy upper class bum saunters down street smoking--- poisonous
cigarette dangling casually in his hand, blowing smoke back into
Transman face, who flinched with disgust, promptly holding his
breath thru pinched nostrils until he was far enough past the fool to
breath 'clean' air once more.

The streets belong to every one—Rich disembarking from taxicabs,
average appearing to increasingly up-scale increasing locals now
inhabit this area; —then there are the old poor, the few mad, no where
to stop, no coins to spend; who go shuffling, mumbling in their
insanity.

These bare testimony to the pitfalls ahead. Worst thing you can do is
to get addicted or ensnared, the next is to bankrupt yourself
financially. Life is like chess game & the opponent is very tricky—
you can't see him—until he plays his final hand at the end.

History is fascinated; the unfolding of the present even more exciting;
life is sure a mystery to unfold; & Hashem holds all the cards!

Mine! The future is Mine! Says Hashem. Who would know the future or control it? It is the province of the Most High God.

Make use of every spare scrap of time.

We are here for a purpose. Hashem allowed us to be born—set up down here for a specific reason. Some of us will accomplish what is to be done, others won't.

You know how it says God loves us with an everlasting love? Well I *hate* KKK (Kinko's Korporate Kopy center) with an unearthly hate! Nasty attitude price-shifters! For all I know they've Googled me & found out I'm trans! And as revenge are jerking me around on a string—messing up my job, making me come back 3 different times to pick it up, so on and so forth. & now the colors ain't true on Poolshooters.

Interesting; Klemperer quotes wife Eva "does not like to hear me talk about Hitler"; his reply; "I'm intensively concerned with him as a cancer researcher is with cancer." So my own thoughts reading informal study of WW II is causes of origin, the Nazis, etc., and how something like it might rise up in the future--and not some pathological draw to it's power & superficial trappings of grandeur.

Friday April 25
Read some of the poetic politicos—Aimee Cesaire—who won the Paris State Award for his Island of Martinique in the Caribbean. Did you know the first successful black slave revolt was on the Isle of Haiti, Toussaint d'la Overture was its hero. The French colonialists were forced to withdraw—but they drove a stiff bargain—demanding the impoverished ex-slaves pay for the damages they'd cost the French *on their own island!* The French money-grabbers then proceeded to set up sanctions against the Haitians, much as the U$, our own country, has done against the island of Cuba today. All this wrecked the poor Haitians even more. Today, it remains one of the poorest nations on earth.

Babylon Falling. Sean plays the same two songs one right after another, reggae, and Red dances in place. The wry proprietor quips to the Transman that he is dancing to the tunes of the most homophobic of any Rasta rocker alive.

Every so often in queer community will see an interesting phenomenon—specific to an older generation. A very dikeish woman and her companion—a faggotish man together, posing as a couple. They'd be in the gay men's club side by side, as well as having the ability to go to straight locales, where they passed themselves off as being heterosexuals. In the old days we laughed & joked about the dike & fag who got married and bought two houses—side by side— for all the neighbors to see they'd come up the walk together, arm in arm and go in one of the doors—but once in side the man would run over to his side of the house—where in awaited his male lover, the woman did likewise having on her side, her own lesbian lover.

So glad painting is going so regularly now must finish my third rondo—OBEDIENCE TO THE CALL OF ART, the binding up of the five chapbooks, with this one, JOY/SIMCA then a break from Journaling, and on to SEDNA! The 4th sci-fi.

If you go to a film series at some church or religious or scholastic institutions, and see movies set in a religious theme, or a intellectual theme, these movies will be about men, women, white, black/brown native, about gay, straight; after 4 or 5 months of a series meeting weekly, eventually you will get down to movies about whites, and nobody else, and finally white men only—because of having seen all the others in that genre earlier when the series began and you have run out of them—because of their scarcity. The master class reproduces itself. This is natural. All human do it! Me, me, me! I, I, I; I am interested in me! I want everybody to see more about Me! Everybody wants to make movies and tell stories about people who look like them—who *are* them. Who have struggled with their same specific problems—but the problem is when the smaller groups, or less funded, those with far less resources, i.e. women, persons of color, native people, people of variant gender, try to do the same, they run into a lack of resources, their potential talent is sapped, contravened, they give up and go to work for the system—that oppresses them--- in order to have a decent life with a decent standard of living & subsequently their stories are seldom told.

A black lesbian filmmaker was making a documentary about butch dikes and FTM's and had shot the first footage 7 years ago, including a 45-minute interview with Red done at Mills college in the Oakland Hills, as a backdrop—years later came several meetings in which clips from its progress were shown to an audience, yet as of date the film was still not completed. Lack of financial backing, and people-support was the number one reason.

Where Transman was industriously putting elements of his painting together on canvas like a jigsaw puzzle—idea, color, shape, dimension, perspective, flow, energy, rhythm, focus, human rendering, symbolism etc., translating his and Hashem's dream into a practical object for household use--a painting!

I am like a fighter, slugging with left hook then right jab, one punch after another right left right left right left; non stop. There is a few others of us who are both writers and painters in history—outside of de Vinci, Henry Miller, Van Gogh (letters), Tennessee Williams, Adolus Huxley, William Butler Yeats, Lawrence Ferlenghetti, that beatnik lady, the other minor names.

PM.
The old Transman thought morosely:

> They forgot about me—people always forget about me.

Well like I said—Transman was a very lonely person:

> As a child I remember being aware that I had a very large family— cousins, an aunt, uncles, the Jordan's. That Jordan's, was a very large, established clan. But my section of it's gone awry, dashed against the rocks of disaster over time, by the family breakup.

Thank you Hashem—for my stay on this earth--as hideous as it has sometimes been.

> I been up the rough side of the mountain.
> --Old blax saying

& I tell you and you, and you and you... I have found great joy in my life's work.

341

Babylon Falling. A modern, colorful bookstore, shelves fully packed with 3,000 books. In the background the young proprietor hunched over his computer return its silvery glare with an evil stare, long white fingers flying furiously over the keyboard, one-handed gyrating the mouse, while he intones: "Ok, ok, getting closer... closer... almost there... almost... almost... almost got it"; like a semi-potent lover attempting orgasm.

132.
CAW! CAW! CAW! Scolds a big ole crow, jet black satiny feathered. Where there is one there's always 2. Where there's a couple, there's sometimes 4.

All this beauty, all this truth.

Went to dance performance w/Jasmin & L. Dance is Jasmin's medium, thru which she flows inside life.

The couple gave Red a lift back to Babylon Falling to pick up a carton of used books he'd forgot, then on to his studio to pick up a rolling cart of books waiting, already packed, then off, cart and all to Aardvark used bookstore. He received $25 in buy backs. Promptly wheeled the still ¾ full cart of books they couldn't use out the door, rolled the heavy burden into the warm sun of Church street, down the block and stopped by a garbage receptacle. There was another abandon carton of used books, so he set his cardboard box there, lightning his load. Rolled it across Market Street and discarded the remainder neatly against the cement wall outside the supermarket parking lot. Then with a lightened pack got on the F line flashing his expired transfer & handicapped pass and rode downtown to Jones Street. Thereupon he climbed the incline, up to Bush. Here is the support housing for the poor, the soup kitchen, the crash pad for homeless men; a facility where you can get off the street and sit in a chair and watch TV. The poor. Where the poor line up for daily dinners at Saint Anthony's Soup kitchen. Swell the population of the ranks in a depression. Damaged children grow into worse adults. God, Guide us with your love! Guide us with your love!

Swan Lake was playing via computer at Babylon Falling. Lithe, long-legged Leonora, dancer, often to be found on-point on the boards listens to her music.

I wish to repeat that I believe in the service of the Lord(ess); to attend services regularly, to pray in a congregation, to study Torah.
However there are points in a person's life when they don't have time. The work they have been appointed to by God is the service—and they need to be about that work!

The last several weeks my synagogue/church going has slowed down considerably—come to a grinding halt, if it were not for the Senior's program which offers one chapel per month (with Communion) and the Seder I attended for Paseo. One might hope my synagogue going would increase thus my spelling and knowledge of the holy Hebrew words, but; *Service* is God's commandment—which must come first! Forgo the starting up of Hebrew Language 102 this Sunday 11AM after prayer to Hashem in which this above commandment was reeducated into my mind—least it go dim and the comfort of routine, of repetition and habit reinstall itself as paramount into my schedule. Hashem has instructed me to go out into new territories! I must follow! Instead today (after awakening just before 11---at which timeslot both the language study and services @ Grace were simotaneously beginning 10 blocks apart, saw me continuing to ready the studio for next weeks onslaught of art. for Monday to be ready to put brush to canvas.

Saturday night cleared off top of large kitchen loft of canvases, stray articles like garbage cans unused for 7 years, etc., foam for spare fold-a-bed off, shifted boxes into place moved all heavy boxes repacked all week up on top, set them neatly in order, then put canvasses back up and proceeded to make a new throw-away pile in the unused Rubbermaid garbage can. It is in excellent shape and valuable—but space too is valuable! The rule, if you haven't used it for a significant amount of time OUT IT GOES! Today, Sunday am stretching canvas I bought with the now dwindling windfall of cash on the found stretcher bars (4 years ago) and removing rolled up prints of my Fine Arts Paintings out of tubes to lay them flat again inside the new

343

Museum Storage box, --acid free… Will save the tubes to give to people to carry their prints home in.

PS Hope Sean will be able to have finished for me the RETROSPECT when we meet again next Tuesday, which was the deadline he gave to himself.

Oh, am one-third thru editing of chapbook THE PASSION OF ART and hope to have this ready to enter via Sean's bookstore computer to my POD, by Tuesday.

It's always important to have greater love. Greater love means to take a superior vision of circumstances, above and beyond what is worldly apparent. We are instructed by Christ to Love each other. We see the individual fallen down on the sidewalk, love compels us to stop (according to the scriptures first found in torah) and give this person a helping hand. However, when we rush to their side to help, we discover the noxious fumes of alcohol—the individual is not sick, but drunk. This is when greater love in required. What is the sad story behind this fallen soul? Picture them as a child growing up with no care, no affection and worse maybe abuse instead of nothing. A diet of it. This is when Greater Love asks us to try to get the individual to their feet, find a place and sit with them awhile—if possible, and not to our grave danger—and become a listening ear. Remember, the Word of God never goes out in vain!

Had occasion today to cut away a found canvas from its stretcher boards to discard, and reuse the very valuable reinforced bars frame. Octagon shape reinforced. The canvas was too thickly laden with paints, didn't want to risk gessoing & painting over it for fear my work would more easily chip off in time & damage. Used very sharp found metal utility knife with all kinds of saw blades on it. Works well—threw it into the utility drawer. Thus the wonders of sorting thru ones stuff to discard/save every few years, finding great stuff you forgot you had. Most canvasses I find in the streets have already been divested of their artistic endeavors, but not this one, and another, which is thinly painted (in acrylic?). So believe I will gesso over it and just make sure to paint on this one in acrylics—as the procedure, oil painted over acrylic is not advised, whereas one can paint acrylic over either oil or another acrylic.

Monday PM April 21

Just destroyed master of IN DEFENSE OF LUCY & MICKEY so I guess that will make it rare. Only distributed 10 copies of that blue pamphlet stapled book. Momma Bears Bookstore, an old feminist relic from the 1980's, had several copies and I believe that's how it made its way into Bolerium books and other collectors on line sites. The Bancroft got theirs, I might have an actual copy elsewhere, but will make no more prints! Cleaning continues with happy zeal—so glad to get rid of stuff, boxes condensed; 4 bagsful of crap thrown out…Into the trash an envelope of info on transsexually--dated 1994, handsome photos of Transman wining contest—one who doesn't use hormones but masquerades easily--- did I have an inclination then? More then one, but was afraid to even think about the subject—ate my heart out whoever I now saw butches appearing more masculine then myself—aided by the irrefutable evidence of male testosterone shots, and top surgery. Their flat chests killed me! Stuck jab of needle into my soul—how long I'd wanted to get rid of mine! –4 short years later it would happen. I transitioned—in '98. Into the garbage with these physical mementos of history—time marches on—I want a clean slate--- I want to travel light! Large bulky boxes slimmed down to uniform, trim banker's boxes. Going down into history. Ironic that I am making manuscripts rare by tossing out the masters. Breaking the mold as it were. All packaged in those old Spectator magazine envelopes 8" x 11" with dedicated notes such as Mafia Dikes, or Wheelchair Momma, or Bang Bang Baby! The Spectator was a sex magazine which came out weekly—in which several reviews of Red's stuff and photos of him and his shows had been printed, plus the fabulous article he had done about Valeria Solanas; one of very few non-fiction pieces he'd done. Weekly he received his free subscription as a contributor, saved all the envelopes, (them being so poor) and used them to catalogue his writing. Now they are being tossed out. Ah memory!

A mass-mailing from now deceased feminist photographer Tee Corinne who visited Red in his East Oakland house in the 80' and took pictures out in his backyard with chickens. And here comes the swimming pool, spa brochures, the patio doors, awnings, green house—sales brochures with which he occupied his time while working double duty shifts at office (during his 11 year hiatus from writing or art of any kind); then the pamphlets on raising dairy goats, chickens. Out it all goes, into the trash! From that home in East Oakland, working so franticly to build a kind of paradise in the ghetto. Their house amid its seething ghetto problems which constantly encroached upon them. It was kind of a relief to give up the place, as the two packed up Jasmin's mustard colored van, and they moved out. A black girl scowling at them from the low-income project across the street—her eyes piercing raw hate, it was good to drive off and leave that behind. She is trapped, by her skin color, her class, yes; but most, by the low ceiling of her mind; we, thank God, are not, as much.

He found in dusty envelopes inside boxes, correspondence from the famous chicken hatchery Murray McMurray; even a goldfish book. Then, a shiny old binder of Nurses Aid notes---from the mandatory course s/he took while working 2-years as in the health care industry, as the lowest level orderly—and flunked.

Joy! Divesting myself of this crap carried around with me since that house back at Lyon Avenue, in the 1980's. If anybody asked him— and they might, (he had a few friends) he was a social being—he was doing Spring Cleaning.

 *

Nicole, an attractive black transwoman at the drop in center cooks every Monday, in her class for those without kitchens—a learning class, in which those housed in a 1 room SRO hotel, having only a sink, can cook efficient, healthy meals on a variety of purchased appliances; small, portable refrigerator, hotplate, toaster oven, microwave, small convection oven, crock pot. Transman said upon returning to bookstore from the event, *I went to trans space for dinner & found only an argument instead.* This altercation was already in progress. T was not involved. He only stared at his shoes on the carpet, sadly. Luke, FTM boss, over at the center blasts Red with a spray from a Tranny Be Calm atomizer; a unique scent concocted by his herbalist girlfriend, a wry smile upon his face.

I remember gay 1950's isolation. Today, we older trans must be pioneers all over again. Trans, it's a different kind of isolation. Thus

346

we need places like the Center. When he returned home that evening, a message awaited him on answering machine:

> Hi Red this is Dominique your partner in crime, in art, music, poetry, and revolution! Was riding the bus the other day, saw you sitting in the window at Babylon so you must be a permanent fixture like the cat that sits in the bookstore window! Give me a call! Peace to you and all beings.
> --Dominique Leslie.

Dominique, as you will recall from my journal PASSAGE, was co-producer for that fun, fabulous, fractious, fouled; finally foiled, failed play of mine PORTRAITS OF A GHETTOIZED POPULATION. It was 4 months of fun, then 5 weeks of disaster so severe my heart jumped up out of my chest to palpitate inside my throat—from all the arguing, screaming, hair pulling!

Trannys sold us out on the advertising to our first and only production of the show—the staged reading at the GLBT Center—they didn't sent out their accustom mailing list as they'd done for every one of their events for 3 years running—we had counted on that. Nobody came. 5 people stumbled in accidentally; a few came because they were friends of the cast. The videotography of it by Jasmin sits @ Bancroft.

Not many years later came the sorry disaster of my group! —In which I was kicked out of my ownself's group, hard worked for for 4.5 years!

Have heard it said that if you get whipped in battles, one after another—maybe its time to get out of the war. So many tranny disasters, the other horror stories I've seen my sisters & brothers involved in just reemphasizes this. Some of us dare no longer to stick our necks out on the chopping block! In the trans community, No Good Deed Goes Unpunished! Also, other trans youth come along, full of energy, crowding their way to the forefront, hogging the spotlight—they have no idea! Us old queers, of our struggle back in the criminal past. They also have absolutely no idea the pain and trouble, which awaits them like gaping pitfalls here and there along their little journeys. Good! It will serve them right for hogging all the attention---on the very stages built by the previous generation's blood, sweat, and tears. Anyhoo, it's time to leave this battlefield!

Transman Red had been hanging out mostly with straight people for the last year, since the sorrowful demise of his group—rather, *his forced departure from his own group!*

133.
I'm a spontaneous painter in execution; but a methodical one in scheduling & dedication.

Must thank Richard Politowski again; he gave me a really big lift back into fine arts painting—one hurdle which had grown up in T's mind was the notorious fact of societies continuous ignorance of his work. In his teenage years he'd gone around town hollering about how he was a writer and painter, but nobody heard. Nobody wanted to publish him. Many hundreds of submissions he'd mailed out to various magazines—and success was never his until age 50, when his first book was published. One great obstacle to picking up brush and color once more was *'what will become of it? It's probably not going to go anywhere—just like it didn't 40-years ago.'* But in providing Red with a disc of his work, he was able to print out posters of his paintings, and by now had sold over 20 of these to various individuals in the last several years. Paintings, the actual canvasses too worn to show now, impossible to go anywhere—but this disk gave the whole project a whole new life.

Sunday night- Monday night:
Moving all boxes out of the way. For Tuesday; to be ready to put brush to canvas. Babylonia she be a fallen' and I'm travelen' light!

Tuesday AM April 29
Miles Davis, Coltrane, Handel, Beethoven, Devork, Bartok; this is genius—it speaks—*hey! Wait a minute! This is speaking to me! It's saying something to my soul!*

April 30, Wednesday AM
All Along The Watchtower or The Watchtower, is done! It sits drying, along beside the yet unfinished Raiment Of Love; while a whole new canvass 36" x "31 is begun, in acrylics—The Crucifixion?

My goal now is to fill up all my walls with paintings!

Common arts; exchanged on the public market daily—a jet stream of it—TV popularity; runway fashion, whose life is short. Big money. I'm in Fine Arts. It's a much more difficult, arduous path up, and its longevity endures.

Any time somebody puts money first there will be a problem with them. People, not profits! Its no wonder the leftwing radical activists have this as one of their slogans—time has born this axiom out to be true—Ayn Rand irregardless! (That great inspiration of my teenage—16-17, whose Atlas Shrugged kept me up allnight until morning, reading.)

PM
@ Babylon Falling; long--legged ballet dancer Lenora spoke of the dance program she has done in two locations this Saturday. We speak of art; me studying paintings in a book, Dalai; then Anton Brenton; and somewhere on this earth a madman is making bombs to blow us all up.

> I say without hesitation that some painters who set out with high-purposes are today being tracked on their path by a vile, stinking beast named money. It is only too possible that after years of disinterested effort and the winning of general esteem they may find themselves attacked by this creature. I am not talking about those who rush into its jaws. But in the guise of that monstrous thing, success, which will come to anyone who waits long enough, the beast will literally hurl itself on its reluctant victims. Poets have been preserved, from time immemorial; from this encounter, but painters know only too well the shape of what they are bound to meet up with one day or another.
> --Andre Breton; Surrealisms And Painting, 1965; Paris.

So time rushes past—in the days @ Babylon Falling.

Thursday AM April
One reminiscence I might share—when I was young I was a tomboy, and many of those I ran around with were boys. I think some of them didn't even realize I wasn't a male-born boy. Most of my closest companions were girls, and one deaf boy, the neighbor, who I was friends with, and we devised our own hand-signals to communicate.

349

At the age of puberty this might have become a problem. However my father and I escaped the neighborhood where we had lived all of my life, because of my mothers abuse, and my grandmothers 'condoning' of her daughter right or wrong. So I didn't have to go thru this pubescent breaking away from the boyhood gang.

Often in my life as a trans-male have found myself associating with male 'gangs' by this I mean not gangstas', but circles of men artists, poets, or would-be artists. There would be no females in these groups, and I was the only butch, tomboy or what have you.

There is a song Sean played in Babylon Falling, 'Back In the Day' might be its title, where the singer reminiscence about his youth, when we were young back in the day, conjures up remembrances of summer backyards us playing in the dirt, hiding behind houses running up the alley screaming in fun. Back In the Day, which is so nostalgic.

Thursday AM May 1
Joy—What do 'dat mean? From where does it spring? Success? Maybe it will happen to me! Success at last! --And Joy about it! My Works released from their prison of confinement—of a public unaware of me! Unaware of my art— to pick it or to discard it for better or worse —but at least having the exposure to the fine eye of others! Success! Joy! Maybe one day very—very soon, I will write the above words in my JOURNEY!

Dear Lord Hashem, it's been a hard life! I'm sorry for my mistakes. (Red's black-clothed figure kneels down on bended knees, bows head.)

If you've led a good life—the dark night of the soul will come to you. If you've been evil, the dark night of the soul will find you. High or low. All must reckon with it.

If you have a real talent, you aren't going to be jealous of those more successful, but you might be resentful, because they have been more highly placed then yourself economically, or scholastically or depending on who they know—be able to attain the golden diploma of success from the world; you wont be jealous because you got your

350

own; your own style, work, but you resent the unfair playing field tipped in their favor.

Some are born to an easier life. You see two children at play side by side in the sandlot—and looking at them you know one will have a life of ease, the other will have to walk up the rough side of the mountain—which is brambly, thorny, straight up, and cold, forbidding, yet we will make it thru children, we will, as so many others of us have before!

Jazz music—Miles, kinda' blue—music notes liquid beauty drips into my room fills the air with invisible media, sound.

> Notes like birds released from horns.
> Music soars heaven-bound.

Oh must repeat from the last complete book (LAMENTATIONS) that any quotes not accredited like the one on this page, are my own! That is from some long-ago poem I wrote I the 1950's or '60's.

From the insistence of Jimi Hendrix to mellow jazz. --- Combo of inspirational music, my faith in the future, an my energy expended kilowatts of sweat-- all have lifted my spirits today, soon will go forth into the world...

Playing, experimenting, technical study, in paints.

Via Apian, Redeux—shall be title of my newest acrylic (formerly The Crucifixion—if that gives yuh a clue). However am questioning my technical ability to portray this central figure the way I'd like— muscles in the back, arms…

Whoops! Kaint' just paint, must struggle with the thing, just as I did before! *38 years!*

One mark of greatness is the message delivered thru the painting. One will say, my work both paintings and written word, certainly has a political message, but not exactly 'message' that would be too crude a definition—sometimes the method is simply the beauty; the message is the raw energy; the emotion which the work elicits.

Let me tell you what happened today—first must explain my 'easel' is an 8' x 4' foot standard size CDX board, structured up by 2" by 2" lumber around its edges. Have vise clamped a long 2/3 board across horizontally (from dead futon Hugo gave me when first moved back to SF, had no bed and was sleeping on floor on a pile of blankets and shirts.) This serves as a resting place to set the canvas on the CDX board; which is tipped at an angle against the wall. Luckily the only sunlight usable to station an easel shines right on this wall—although am using 4 lamps to light my canvass including the tripod mounted one. Well today drilled holes in the sides of the CDX frame; a pair on each side, to accommodate the canvas resting board, thus can change different heights according to the dimension of the canvas; small, large, medium; and drilled holes at both ends of the cross board, stuck 4" bolt thru and now can adjust it. Put the vise clamps into storage. Swept/mopped floor of curled wood bore chips, took my never-fired rifle purchased after the LA Riots, and during the OJ Simpson trial, when it was feared again riots would break out if this black football player went to prison for the murder of his white wife; stuck this behind this plywood easel, then, pushed it back to the wall at its slant again. Well was tired after —had 2.5 more hours until time to go out to socialize—(Babylon Falling is closed today for a mini-vacation ((Sean is taking more & more of these mini holidays, is that saying something?)) and was so tired, wanted to jerk off thinking about a certain transwoman whose name I cannot repeat; wanted to sleep, at most just wanted to sit at computer, but the Good Lord(ess) encouraged my heart somehow, and found myself painting on Via Appian Redux for several hours and it is coming along. Now I feel refreshed, and satisfied with this daily adventure upon the high seas of Art, my voyage for the day. A few last masterstrokes with brush, then prepare to leave. Uncover noisy birds so they can catch the last rays of sunlight.

Every day make some progress!! Artist, Keep On!

Saturday AM May 3
Called Hugo to see when he may be thinking of coming over for coffee—or/and lift to lumber yard, I said, *'well maybe you've been busy out in the country—maybe you've been in the next state'*; then laughed about this; *'well I meant the next state **over**—New Mexico—*

352

*the next **geographic state**, not the next state of **spiritual evolution** or **mental regression'** or something stupid.*

In the '90's or thereabout the expression 'he/she's a survivor' came into fashion. Some years later when Red was first, casually labeled 'a survivor' by a well-meaning associate, it did not make him happy:

> I want to be known as a winner, a victor! Not a survivor who scrapes along the bottom, licking up sustenance out of the bottom from other peoples pots and pans, eating the leftovers to keep themselves alive.

My father, he made it over. He made it over to the Promised Land. Transman thought this. He too wanted desperately to live a good life on a bad earth. To keep his soul intact right up until the moment of his death. To not sell out to the forces of darkness. To not get lost in alcohol, drugs, or sex debaucheries. Nor bitterness, isolation and Hate. The hate. The *hate!* --Now to live inside hate, is the true meaning of darkness.

AM Monday May 5

I expect a long life. I expect it because I need it. I need it for what I'm doing—Gods work, art—which is pleasing in Gods sight. All the pain and loneliness suffered will just have to be withstood—I prey for my life to get better, but good or worse, I'm thankful—I bow down to the one high holy God, thank You! I submit my will to God and God's Great Good. And now continue to Work!

The old man thought:

> The difference between my painting now & my painting then. Hands verge on shaking. Strain at the impossible reaches upward to paint top section of a large canvas because my shoulder hurts terrifically. Both shoulders ache all the time. –Advancing arthritis? The other night when put those newly-stretched canvasses away on top of my loft, thought my body was going to fail, and the pile was all going to come Tumbling back down on metumbling back down on me.

34.

I was in a strange village, in a strange country. Caught underneath the wheel of this machine... Across the street came these junior plutocrats—would be rich—young men in their 20's; dressed in black

353

suit, tie, white shirt, conformist uniform; they were clean shaven, short hair; they walked past me, unseeing; doing what the system dictates.

Transman saw this kapitalist army, felt how they looked right thru him—as if he was a ghost; dead to their world, because he looked poor & scruffy and was rolling a cart; and he felt his days in this city were numbered fewer.

He saw the young adult humans billing/cooing in the streets—arms linked, bodies touching, holding hands… And then he was lonelier Then ever.then ever.

> I was dancing with this guy but I think he was bi.
> --Young yuppie woman, overheard on SF streets.

Two artsy appearing men loiter on the corner, one holds a shopping bag from a designer store; he wears tight black pants—the punk look—and striped shirt in style of the old frigate ship sailors of the 1700'rds. They are soon joined by 3-very showy girls; glam, model styled in tall high heels, much makeup, evening dresses, glitter, hair do's piled high. Off they walk, the 2 men leading the way, the 3 pretty girls behind trailing cigarette smoke. —They reek of Show Biz, minor success; easy money. Although artists like Red, they are another type of young plutocrat, to whom this city is a piece of cake; whose finances they navigate easily. But at least their glance lingers on the little man, picking him out of the crowd---sensing a kindred spirit.

Must say am holding off from Internet dating—being my career is so important currently; gathering material resources, & building an artistic stockpile—because I don't know what the future holds. Sense how important it is for me to try to 'get it together' as it were, not yet ready to take on the intrigue of dating, go thru the changes of adding another intimate person to my life—relationship; especially the kind that doesn't work out.

> Not enough friends
> Not enough good times
> Not enough good food to eat!

This was Transman's mantra, but it was often broken by a rainbow of fun, and a golden pot of friendship. Call from Jasmin Sunday morning—to come over to view their new house!

The old man hastily wiped his hands on a towel, left load of wash dripping over sink. Pull open curtain. (He had strung a green sheet, which has hung across the two studio windows for 8 years—but had been washed now 3 times). A row of plants in pots; birds in the sunlight. & rushed out to the subway entrance, headed towards Dalora's new house. Wind blowing. Take breaths of it fresh clean air.

At the underground transit entrance a huge flock of pigeons lives. This morning a sea of pigeons grey/white dine, tails in air, undulating small feathery bodies—nearly 100; they bob and dip, wallowing in an ocean of birds, peck & swallow—some kind heart person has endowed them with an entire package of potato chips.

The three had a lovely outing at their new small 2-bedroom house, w/yard! Transman walked joyously between room to room opening closets, examining sliding glass mirrored doors, picture windows, gazing upward at ceiling to marvel at two skylights, one in bathroom, (thru which Jasmin fears satellite tracking can view her naked arse) the other in kitchen; while their small dog followed. Red stood in the yard in a patch of sun—his boots on the good earth. He was happy as if it were his own house! And it didn't even actually belong to the couple, but to an out-of-state women; it's been in her family for a generation.

Later they met with a friend who is suicidal—his name must not be mentioned. A young gay man, no longer bright, bushy tailed, but sad eyed; he formerly was one of the regiment of the uniform people who must work for the system to earn mega money, encased in suit & tie, but his suicidal condition has made his participation in this game no longer possible. We all dined on Thai food, and had a wonderful time.

Scored a victory! Dalora was driving me home and on Van Ness spied a new wooden canvas stretcher bars. Quite large; with a carpenter's expert bracing. The sad eyed young man leapt out to retrieve it. L encouraged me to put it in the car, which we did; it just fit.

Tuesday AM May 5

Yesterday was out in the newer, cleaner part of SF, mostly single-family houses w/yards; today, downtown; the old, decrepit, original hub out from which all growth has spread. Ancient edifices. Brick tenements of 6th stories. Demolition row marches up Market Street with FOR SALE/Brokerage Sign's, one after another on the squat 2, to 6th floor old commercial buildings made of time-corrupted stone; old porn palaces, the Strand Theatre-- closed; where play-cousin Angelo went to watch dirty movies, just to have his solemn, secret, serious masturbations interrupted by constant intrusion, jabbering of dopefiends, sex perverts, tricks-for-hire soliciting him & each other, in a fetid little incestuous pool of dwindling degeneracy; the video arcade where T had gone to jerk off @ 5pm during his lunch break from work—he thought those times would never end.

Down here in the gutter, out of their accustom place, he spies two residents of upper Tendernob—and due to their shady reputation, his suspicion is that they are here to buy drugs. Gossipy Transman stuck this information into the back of his brain for future scandal mongering. After his dentist appointment he climbs the hill towards home.

Top of the hill. Another TV commercial is being filmed on Jones @ Bush Street. Crew setting up the props in advance. Inside the open lip of a theatre moving van sits a fake fire hydrant, red; when was the last time you saw a red fire hydrant? It's a thing of the past in San Francisco—all hydrants have been painted & re-painted white for years.

AM Tuesday May 6
I always knew B. was a good writer, some of his stuff was great, but he didn't have a lot of writing it seemed, maybe he wasn't dedicated? Did he spend days on the bottle, or lost in day dreams like some artists (including my early teens) and thus there was little production? Did he have actually a ton of writing, but just did not show it? When I heard he had an excellent job, with benefits, —8 hours a day—I knew that was trouble. That is the death of an artist—a good job! The best defense an artist has is to make a bunch of money at the job quickly—before this job sets in, then QUIT! Get out of it! Before due to comforts and material prosperity it subsumes your entire life! To repeat: The first thing an artist must do when s/he gets a good job—is to QUIT THAT JOB!!!!!!

PM

Heard Rachmananof's Moonlight Sonata last night; it was so beautiful I almost cried. Can you see why artists abandon security for the unknown; what makes a starving composer sit at piano and design beauty thru headaches, insanity, and un-appreciation; dredge it up out of their soul into notes and measures; the poet building a rhyme out of the depths of their mind. I know what struggle they went thru because I went thru it staring at a blank sheet forcing the fountain of creativity to flow up out of me up into reality on the printed page.

There's some people's job it is to tend the fires of the synagogue, church, mosque—to keep the holy institution running' constantly; 24 -7 forever, and others to come by dip their soul into the well as needed, as fuel for their daily journey—which Hashem also has ordained, all for the benefit of Her/His Creation. Thus I am an artist, duly painting, writing, and no longer can attend each and every holy service of the week as I was before (Fri., Sat. Shabbat/ Sunday, Thursday Church service/ Monday Bible study/ Tuesday Hebrew class; Saturday Torah study—not to mention occasional midweek Marieve service, midweek church Eucharist, et al).

I started at the tender age of 15—16. My motivation was definitely not money, it was beauty; it was art. Painting, the smell of turp & oils got immediately into my blood. At my desk under a small light stand, a sheaf of blue-lined paper; the poetry of bairds swimming in my mind.

A visceral love of the tools. The student feasts their eyes over tubes of paints, brushes, canvas rolls. Hues! Color! One response to Shaun Roberts website, about his photographs of Transman's studio, featuring a close-up of his hands holding brushes, paints, pallet; one inspired viewer wrote in agreement; "Id rather go without eating—to buy a tube of paint."

Later, revisited as much older adult I think being a 'multiple artist'-- as my old friend David use to call it-- is to the economic advantage, and each discipline is good advertising for the other. I recounted the deceased photographer Tee Corinne, 'going into book writing to finance her photography career'. Being a multiple artist can't be bad for business.

I always consider writing my duty on earth.
--Jack Kerouac

I was given a very good background as a child, in painting and in reading. I had the freedom to pursue my desires—art. I have the talent. The energy. The physical stamina. Can hear, and see. I met others who understood art, and were gifted artists themselves, who encouraged me. I was a failure in a social setting—at which case I had to flee back into the arms of art. Art is a world I carry around with me, like a snail its shell. I had nowhere else to go but art!

Transman Red was perpetually interested in the details of the lives of other artists, no matter how mundane. Saw Kottie Poloma's website, after Shaun Roberts did a photo interview of him. He lives in a studio apartment (these are essentially 1 room) in a worse part of town. Liked two of his art pieces in particular, in which was painted over and over:

```
Art is killing my life.  Art is killing my life.  Art
is killing my life.  Art is killing my life.
```

And the other, following:

```
    I hate art.  I hate art.  I hate art.
```

AM Wednesday May 7

Last night's medical appointment, Dr. Martinez says the trouble Transman has is due to bursitis, not some deadly sickness rotting his shoulders out of their sockets as he'd feared. —A brief exam in which she holds his shoulders with her firm small tan hands; has him raise both arms above his head, then hold them at half mast. After this she proclaims: "Bursitis! --In both shoulders." Explaining, "The muscle pads of both shoulders are inflamed." Probably due to old age plus carrying the incessant back pack for 20 years, and now, irritated even by pulling his rolling cart up & down hill.

One of the biggest ways to make enemies in this town is to do something. —Some project, show; social organization; political group. That is an afterthought, upon remembering my past involvement in the trans community. My social center and home away from the studio these days are straight places. The synagogue, the church, the bookstore. Tuesday's Tranny Clinic is one of the few trans connections he now had.

@ Babylon Falling; this discussion; how there was a revolution in France and the way France was governed changed forever. --- From a monarchy, to a democracy. There was a revolution in India—that took 100 years—but brought independence for the Indian people from under the British yoke. A revolution in Russia; in Haiti; when their peoples reached starvation level. It won't be a band of radicals doing all the work of change today, revolution won't happen until all the population together decides they've had enough—and overthrow the corrupt system, and start something different.

Enter youngman Alex, just having returned from the high-end youth fashion store down the street. Carries crisp, new shopping bag. Sans skateboard because of a bad spill last week, still recovering. He is exhausted by his job & shopping. Collapses on bench, removes his hat, and turns it over and over in his hand, studying the label inside.

Red (Suspiciously): How much was that hat?

Alex: $70.

Red (Simultaneous as Sean): $70?

Sean (Simultaneous as Red): *$70!*

Alex (Fingering his new, bluejeans): Yeah $300 jeans; $70 hat… I look fresh, huh!

Red: $70!

Sean: $70! For a *hat!* That's shocking to me! I never knew the store'd get that wild with that thing—Charging $70 –for a hat, that's a supreme low!

Red left that night, right after Sean 'pulled his drawbridge up,'(set out the iron burglar bars) at closing. Walking the 3-blocks back to his studio. The wind pried its fingers & lifted his black derby right off of his head.

135.
AM Thursday May 8
Once a police officer puts on his or her uniform, they become part of a very elite family—the police family; they must have loyalty to one another, because their life may depend on their partner, or on other members of the force. At the same time they become walking targets

of the hate of a few of societies most disfranchised who've experienced hard times from authority figures. When doing their job the police are engaged in a battle. It can be like a chess game—you take one of ours, we take one of yours; but it should be you kill one of our officers, *'we take the guilty party who actually committed the crime'* because that is what the police enforcement is suppose to be—law enforcement!

The daily news has seen several occasions when one of their own are murdered, the police just seam to grab whoever was on the crime scene —to pay for the death of a fallen officer *wither or not it was the guilty person!* The case of a white woman in Colorado whose Aryan Nation Nazi boyfriend killed a police officer—then turned the gun on himself. Since they could not capture him—he had committed suicide—the police instead took in his girlfriend of just 24 hours, and put her in jail. She remained in prison for 7 years until a public figure, writer Hunter S. Thompson was active in a program of honesty and fact-finding—and the shoddy conviction was overturned by public outcry. Asatta Shakur is a similar case.

As a person who practices Christianity & Judaism, and believes in the Ten Commandments, of which Thou Shall Not Lie is one; something must be mentioned; it is called The Truth. Which transcends all political human bullshit, *on both sides*. About the case of Asatta Shakur, I want to know the *Truth.* And nothing more, or less. Having heard all the political cries for justice from what is essentially 'my side'—the left wing radical--- and of course the stale, tired, old normal everyday bullshit whitewashing which is the customary trash of via media, the newspapers of the day. At this point, I want to know nothing political, or reactionary—just simply *did Asatta Shakur shoot that State Trooper?* And if not why is she still being hunted –like the old slave bounty hunters did back in the 1800rds—why is there a U$ 1 million dollar bounty on her head?

The medical evidence is that she was unable to have pulled the trigger to kill the Trooper:

> Neuro-surgeon Dr. Arthur Tanner Davidson Associate Professor of surgery at Albert Einstein College of Medicine has stated that the wounds in her upper arms, armpit & chest and severed median nerves that instantly paralyzed her right arm, would only have been caused if both arms were raised & that to sustain such injuries while

crouching & firing a weapon Would bewould be anatomically impossible.
--Wikipedia; *The Free Encyclopedia*, Internet.

PS, help for this situation is technology. In both incidents, plus the Mummia incident in Philadelphia, if the law-enforcement cars had all been outfitted with high tech surveillance video equipment, which feeds into a central information bank, accessible to the public—the whole incident might easily have been captured on film! And we would know who the true killers were! Maybe its somebody living free in the world, and not even a suspect, while people who actually did not commit the crime are going thru the hell of jail, court systems, etc.! Neither police, nor criminal, nor public could then concoct some false story!

What must make it increasingly difficult for the law enforcement is that they are targets; stress is growing in our ill-social system and detection is not always what we would like. Criminals are committing crimes against other citizens---murder, rape battery, theft, and getting away with it all the time. This an aggravation—and embarrassment to the cops. Naturally the police are frustrated when one of their own is gunned down, when there is no killer caught, and no solution in sight! But to take that step over the line and haul in anybody they don't like to prosecute—wither or not they are guilty— is a step over the line into fascism! Remember the saying from the Roman Empire thousands of years past; *Where are the guards to watch those who guard us?*

As a poor person who has lived in not-so nice neighborhoods, I believe in law and order for the average citizen who works and then retires and wants to live their life in peace! And have often been the one who calls the cops because of hoodlums! There was a mistake on the part of the left wing back in the 70's (which they since have recognized) in assuming all law-breakers were oppressed citizens, thus potential revolutionaries—when in fact after the day was done, many of these idiots out to be just what they had been labeled by the cops—thugs! There was a movement in the 70's to free all those convicted of thuggery as oppressed minorities etc. A sad mistake! The inheritance of this wrong-thinking is to polarize the two sides against each other—the underclass public and the cops *who are civil servants of the people!*

361

Saturday AM May 10

    Mine. I set the time. Says Hashem. I set the time for all things.

Oh, s/he has talent! They say. -- If you are given a gift, its simple, you just keep working. God will manifest the work.

The writing and the art are progressing, each, at their own pace. One is not waiting for the other, nor dependent on the other. The deadlines, goals etc; art goals, or writing goals, separately, are this: to have 5 or 7 paintings done to take to Richard Politowski for photographing; and to finish this chapbook—Joy/Simca! For POD publishing, then combine it into the 3rd rondo, the larger OBEDIENCE TO THE CALL --. Two different pets in one house. One a cat, one a dog. Similar, but individual!

PM Friday May 9

People can look at a painting and take it all in, in a few minutes. They can say if they like it or not quickly. A book is not so obvious or so simple.

AM Sunday May 11

My picture Via Appia is interesting—yes, it's a picture about suicide. Along the Appian Way the Roman soldiers nailed up thousands of crucifixions; which was empire's means of execution of their prisoners, both criminals and political. Many, many were crucified by this method. Usually tied by the wrists to a single wooden beam, vertical, stuck into the earth—not all of them had the familiar crossbeam… Hung there until they died, maybe with a spear thrust to the ribs to rush the process along. Some, as was our Savior Jesus Christ, nailed to a crossbeam with a nail in each palm, and a single nail thru both feet together. Many thousands died this way. Well, this suicide in Via Appia is being hounded by the evil dark powers of a fascist state; he/she has stepped down onto the via—or road—which is also the crossbeam of the Cross, and voluntarily is stepping over it, out, off into oblivion—just as a fierce sun rises up over the horizon, maddening, energy packed, gold/red whirling out of the clutches of night's blue depression. Inside the bowed head of this prisoner of defeat, this captive of the dark force of the 'blues' is the face of his-her mother, who mourns after her child has departed from this earth. Also the low, barbaric face of self, and selfishness. Via Apia. Acrylic on canvas. Almost completed.

Was very depressed? Saturday night—or I think that's what it was, maybe simply the effects of a diet (lost 3 pounds). Laying on my bed an inordinate 10 hours of sleep, began speaking in tongues, and immediately the meaning came to me, Holy Name. Holy Name. Holy Name. I called upon the Holy Name of Jesus.

I'm not going to church and synagogue like before, can't, it's too much to be both painter, and writer daily. Need to rest! So, am not getting the positive powerful punch of faith that going to a religious temple brings! I called upon the Holy Name of Jesus, however. All we learn from the old & new testaments is accessible to us, anywhere we are! You don't have to be sitting in the pews of temple! Prey— and so I did, and momentarily was uplifted again, remaining so until the dawns light, upon which I entered the day with a variant plan—to release the birds from cage to sit upon my shoulders, which never do in daylight--- and edit the 3rd Rondo (OBEDIENCE) then work on this JOURNEY, @ 11AM Sunday when ordinarily this was a task for the night before.

Blue night of the souls heartbreak—a fierce yellow/red dawn arises out of it! Hope comes to solicit me again!

136.
 The Buddha. Serenity.

Continue work on Via Appia; small figures huddled under the cross. You are speaking in symbolism; you are talking without words.

  *

Ever since the Lulu edition first peeked itself out over Internet a few books had sold—POD. After a god-awful dry spell, BARRIO BLUES sold awhile ago—in a computer download—and he was glad:

> An amazing stoppage of Internet sales over Amazon. Is it due to tax season? Or, the housing crunch; accompanying that, our nations rapid descent into a depression? Or, is it because so much of the Arobateau reading material now accessible *free* thru the Google Book Search*? Have I made a mistake shipping 15 more of my self-published novels to them to scan and put up for free viewing to the public, to go along with the ten or so already released to them by Lulu?*--A service whereas up to 20% of the contents of a current book in print can be read at no charge. Plus the entirety of the Old Masters.

When I was just writing and thinking about painting I attended synagogue religiously for about 1 & 2/3rds years. Came in to that congregation around or before Sukat—the harvest festival -- went thru two Yom Kippurs—high holidays; then, suddenly about 2 months ago, the painting got steaming along, I dropped out—so that I go one time per month—divided between 2 different temples; seniors at Grace has its service once per month—I climb the high hill for that, but Sunday worship has stopped. Must attend to my own spiritually, by calling upon the Most High, since am not in a service for it to do this for me. Am tired, does the loneliness make greater blue depression, and weight me down? Well, it might be my diet—no carbohydrates — and am loosing weight! Just 2 pounds over the lowest I was before the setback of Jasmin's *raw food diet*—upon which I'd immediately gained 6 pounds; and once again, back in Jan. of '07, when had gotten off my rigorous diet because of eating free candy for the regular New Years in lieu of food, neglected my diet, weight started creeping slowly back up and up once more, so that I had to go back on rigorous diet and lost 15 pounds—to get to where I am now! Am 2 pounds shy of being where I was at around Dec. 2006! OK already! Got to continue! In 2 more pounds will be once again able to fit comfortably into those size smaller black trousers donated by L. Either that, or switch back to the giant clown size pants of my former weight, a size 40's which are ragged and frayed and indicative of the slowly murderous disease--obesity.

Not much energy on a sugarless, carbohydrate-free diet. Must loose weight; that's most important. Eating beef, sausage with onion, green pepper—maybe tomato paste as a treat mixed in-- and raw juiced up greens (the one surviving gift of that raw foods diet—daily… Seniors day set me back a days weight loss—actually gained about 1 pound—sandwiches & salty meat, plus a rich potato salad. Forgo the yogurt with sweeteners, and cakes & cookies, but white bread, potatoes, & mayo add up.

One last thing, have stopped eating fruit once more. Am taking 1,000-milligram vitamin C supplement in powered form. Fruit is fattening!

There you have it my friends! Fellow dieters of the universe!

One day, people may thank me for going into the details of diet, along with encouragement for the artist! To do art one must be alive! Dear Friends, let us be reasonable! -- No matter how driven, how mad, how artistic, one must have a modicum of health! Do not neglect eating your greens!

137.
A transsexual's world is an exceedingly difficult space to inhabit. Today, retuning from his solitary haunts in this fend-for-yourself society, old Transman spied a queer couple staggering up Bush Street; both masculine, Asian, the one, effeminate, w/earring adorning 1 ear, appeared to be a transsexual, tho in male drab, his partner was drunk; due no doubt to the severity of this world against their love. The transsexual shored his partner up, hands under his armpits, alternately grabbed him around the waist; they were of equal size and the butch outweighed him by maybe 40 pounds; he kept slipping out of his lovers arms and went careening into things—sides of buildings, potted plants outside of glitzy upscale image hotels. Old Transman saw these kindred spirits, and he knew, *he knew*. And, as if to spread the circle of sadness even wider, this couple sadly served the old guy only to remind him of his lovelorn status. When he got home, the Troll in the basement had well-polluted the hallway of this upstairs floor, and poisonous fumes were in the courtyard—thus T. must dare not run his ventilation fan, for fear of sucking the smoke indoors into his humble little studio. He thought: *What a life. What a trap!*

AM Monday May 12
At a current event @ bookstore. Hum of people in the background. Pleasant. Red sits off in a corner, reading shyly. Having little in common with those here tonight. T glances up from his book; attention briefly focused on an out-of-town photographer snapping photographs with expertise acquired from years. He looked like a ghost that death had claimed already.

> Suppose I live to be 90—then there's 25 years left. 25 years of joy. 25-more years of love.

This was Red's hope, tho not his present reality. Seated in the window seat, now darkened and chill by night. He lowered his face back into the diary.

365

VK, like myself persists:

> Frau J—began to weep and asked Eva for a handkerchief.
> Afterwards, Eva said to me. "What wretched times. I am not going
> to iron my handkerchiefs anymore".

A few days ago it was just us regulars clustered around the cashiers
desk; Matt, photog says:

> I'm rotting at my job like a spoiled strawberry.

Jasmin is sick of her job; can't wait to go back to processing medical
claims at home. Sean grumbles over his bookshelves. His girlfriend
Kensey Lamb is going to quit her job in 2 months. None are happy,
much less T.

Feel a little depressed from no sales for months. Chainsmoker killing
the air from down in the basement. Along the avenue of commerce
no sales either, but all the taverns and the grocery store thrives. Of
course rent moguls reap huge bags of gold. It is hard times for the
poor. Luckily there are churches and synagogues about—I need to go
back regularly, miss it. And… again, standing at easel, sitting at
writing desk, alone with his thoughts, he wondered:

> Again, again, the artist calls out for placement how high have I gone
> in the art world?

138.
*Times in your life all the popular melodies on the airways ring
familiar…* The ghetto makes its way into upscale white/Asian coffee
shop---thru music. Amid safety of their lap-top computers, young
affluent sip lattés; they have nice clothes/cars; listen to this music not
marred by the rotgut history of segregation and poverty from whence
this music orignated --that's all filtered out, now just the mellow tones
of Billy Holliday remain, these well-to-do people can't hear the drugs
and disillusionment, only majestic overtures, from the soul of Miles
Davis, John Coletrane; not knowing of suicidal loneliness in rot-gut
cheap hotels where drugs were the angel of salvation. They tap their
toes to the beat of dead gangsta rappers.

Those familiar songs ran a groove into Transman's brain; it made him reminisce back about good times. He remembered 'their music'---songs that provided backdrop for the individual acts each performer did in the shows of long ago. Each run of shows had been pulled together by a unique person. Many entrepreneurs had provided so much fun and meaning for so many over his life. Mentally, with tan fingers enumerating on table he began to list some:

Rainbeau's Cabaret held at the now dead Kimo's, on Polk, before that Lilly's @ Market Street. Rainbeau, ex-stripper cum hairdresser ran her show for a year, or two; featuring herself, others, and Jasmin, bellydancer/actress, with Red as a minor roustabout/carrier of his then-wife's costume bags. The next series of shows the couple both starred in, was held in the Redstone Building, same venue, different floor, as Theatre Rhinoceros, the smaller stage, Lunacy Theatre. The show envisioned & created by Miriam Kronenberg. Jasmin twirled & dipped in multicolor veils, above her head wielded frightening silver swords, as she performed her sword dance, Red took the spotlight, attired in black, his prop, a single chair; read from his trashy, freshly New York City published books---LUCY & MICKEY, DIRTY PICTURES, BOYS NIGHT OUT. By the time their house had been foreclosed Hashem had protectively guided them to a warehouse space near downtown Oakland, and, waiting for them--in lights on a theatre marquee-- here was fabulous transsexual-transvestite, show Queen Ruby Tuesday's Klubstitiute, where they performed in a series of events held at various venues SOMA. Jasmin, a starr, beautiful, danced, Red did minor supportive bits. And now Sean with his bookstore... Companionship for lonely days; bi-monthly shows of artists; Transman's books on a shelf, the RETROSPECT and his posters soon to be sold there; already 5 books put up on POD, 4 of them on the Global Account—computer support courtesy of the Proprietor. None of the collection of artists knew when Babylon Falling would fall too... These bygone enterprises of bygone days.... All gone now... memories fade... news clippings yellow in an archive box... You can just say it was a lot of fun.

139.
Culture informs religion. The power of religion—caught up in human nerve endings, superstitions, dreams; group thinking, urged on via peer pressure of a congregation fashions the outsider into a demon.

Suspect at least. At worst it criminalizes all those behaviors not customary to its tribe. Makes parents turn against child, drives the body into a frenzy of gossip, hate, backbiting, until they cross the line and break the Golden Rule, against their own beliefs—tho its ironic they never see it as such, justifying themselves as being citadels of holiness, pure, and nary a wrong bone in their bodies having set themselves up into such a mode of defense purportedly of the same Golden Rule they study. All this against the lonely stranger!

It is detrimental for an activist—ones like myself with a very important agenda of self-survival—which involves our gender issues, race, or the class we are from—to participate fully and whole heartedly in the struggle for some other group without them realizing the full extent of what we are. What happens to the compassionate doctor who gives their services for free in a famine-struck land, a land, which is simultaneously caught up in frenzy-struck persecution to the extreme such as death by machete hacking --against its homosexuals—and this compassionate doctor is gay? Or the writer, dearly beloved by his race, who eventually discloses all? It was about this very subject that Red and Sean differed, having heated arguments. The very straight young man sees no point at all in Queer Rights—he just doesn't understand, and is pissed that some East Coast queers are speaking of organizing a boycott of consumer travel to Jamaica—a true bastion of anti-queer hate, his native land.

May 12 Monday AM/PM

> Do not talk falsely now, the hour is getting late
> --Bob Dylan.

So many artists have technical ability to render perfectly human, animal anatomy to express in symbolism any concept. Many use this fine backdrop then mar it with a cartoon figure—meaninglessly taking the center, the prominence of it. To some this is an expression of modern day life's meaninglessness, its deathlike commercialism. A cartoon figure imposed on such a magnificently done background berates common people in their lust for ordinary amusements; the message is clear. I wish to go further, yes life is shit, society has constructed meaningless cities, it is obvious, the stupidity of so many common people who shun & mock what is genius while they rush to lick up the mundane—yet to end at just mockery of them, or a slap in its face is not sufficient. To me its greater to reach to a higher goal, to portray an alternative to all of it—to push art higher *in its meaning!* To even give alternatives to the current disaster!

PM Tuesday May 13
I have no judge. I have no mentions, no reviews. Who is my vox populous? I am nowhere!

Duly Transman entered the hallowed vaults of the Bancroft Library. Rolling the silver cart, now full of boxes of his latest material. * Well, he thought, satisfied, 'I'm glad my work is *here.*' He'd checked in, asking for Bonnie Beardon, Librarian, and had only seated himself when he was treated to a sight. An archivist resembling a ferret clutching 3 museum boxes of rare manuscripts rushes past, headed towards the Bancroft's inner sanctum; bent over his hoard, arms clutching them with desperate attraction. The archivist is professorially attired; green pullover sweater, suit coat jacket with suede arm patches, a plaid *scarf,* in this clement Berkeley weather. (Even T has removed his coat, & the black derby hat, which is usually firmly affixed to his head indoors and out.) This librarian, like the others—has a purpose! A supreme motivation! His eyes are bright; his moustache twitches. Hastily he is let thru the locked door by a buzz-switch on his own recognition! His comrades gloat at this returning worker bee with antique honey dripping from his wings. Their eyes feast on the sight of this rare assemblage in his arms. T notes all this from his vantage point in a chair, and is satisfied. With librarians like this his collection is safe.

Archivists, --do they live in the past? Don't they collect stuff that is dusty? Time is their media. —They tamper with time by saving it in an acid-free box. Hooray for archivists! They help pay my rent by their acquisitions of the Arobateau Files! They save me for a historical future—in which fame might yet be found—tho it is not so at the present.

I love painting he thought, sitting in his chair @ the Acquisition Library-- & now, in the new millennium, he had a small income, was free to do it. In addition that he had this small outlet for it—via pushing his hand-sold posters, plus posters soon to be sold on his website—& was not so god-damn frustrating as his early years when

369

all his art and writing was bottled up & nobody wanted it, nor paid it any attention.

*Contents of Red's delivery to the archival library:
        For Bancroft Library May 13, 2008
        From Red Jordan Arobateau
        Obedience To The Call Of Art/God --Journey Vol. 8. $100.
        The Passion Of Art—Journey Vol. 9   100.
        Obedience To The Call Of Art/God Lulu Edition   25.
        MERCY Journey Vol. 7. Lulu Edition   25.
        Leader of The Pack, Lulu Edition w/ new author intro. 50.
        3-Color Print/Posters, Red's art paintings 11" x 17"   325.
        Artist in his studio, photo by Shaun Roberts   300.
        Miscellaneous papers & photos; including photo of
        Red, Shaun & Le Bijoutier by Shaun Roberts   55.
        GRAND TOTAL   **$ 980.00**

Red visited his mailbox back in Oaktown on his jaunt to the East Bay. He was now surrounded by many more black/brown faces, then in SF. In this environment his memory stirred. The ghetto. —A black garrison. My daddy lived his whole life in it, and he wasn't even black. —Latin. If my mom died when the Ancestor Search on Internet says—at age 72—giving her last known address on Chicago's North Side—was it still a white neighborhood then? Then she may have escaped the jaws which had held down her mother & father, and all her ancestors since slavery—and my dad. Dad could have escaped but for decades did not, because of being connected there by me; by his then-wife, by his friends, and everything he knew; later, he was still living in the ghetto because of it's cheap housing. At his job nobody knew his deep black secret. Otherwise all Ted would have to do was pack a suitcase, drive his car out to a white neighbored, find a white motel, check-in as a new resident & he'd be gone.

My own identity as a colored person—who arose in the African-American community has always been on shaky ground (outside of my own relatives) due to the lightness of my skin; Hispanics are seen in my eyes as celebrating who and what they are; bound by a common language, appearance, custom. So now, the racial heat to this presidential election process, which so dominates the news is disturbing the murky waters of my mind---as it does the nation. What seems now to be defeat of a woman president with 90% blacks voting for a visible black man Obama, does make me sad. Pitting a (black) man vs. a (white) woman. —That old gender 'superiority' stuff. I have told my thoughts to you Dear Diary. Problem is that what *I am* is not celebrated! It is ignored, scorned, overlooked---I am a statistic shuffled around from category to category! Is he white? Black? He's got to be one or the other! Hispanic? What is he? Whites finally have come around to our side! —After 400 years. So now whites want a *black* person to win the awards. Naturally blacks want a black *person* who looks like them! I'm a stranger in my own land.

See images of the dominant race, which is not your race etched on the lense of the inner eye.

One ray of hope—I realize there are a lot of people just like me! Not just the standard pre-1950's black/white, but Latin, Indian, Eskimo, European, Asian, Chinese, Islanders & all mixtures of the above and much more! But also ones who are a mixture of race. People raised within their own homelands who never felt secure. Never fitted into the comfortable, imprisoning confines of a stereotype.

*

Paint, write every day—or it will slip away from you. What will happen is—you become so certain of your craft, you so love to write & and look forward to paint… To paint, satisfied with the outcome —but certain projects you will procrastination from doing because you know from experience once you begin the momentum of this work you will be embroiled, wrestling with it a long arduous time, until its done. For instance that very thick novel, the gigantic triplich So, the anticipating of all that work makes one stall, hesitate, pencil on lip, sheaf of papers in front of you—which then shove away, to do 'another time'.

Also, beware of collaborations. Am reminded of Ms. M, who did book reviews, taught a writing class, and was the editor of a newspaper as a means to earn a living, but always complained she was so busy looking over other peoples manuscripts to edit for anthologies, and poetry submissions, while her own stories sat in a dusty pile; she never had time to put them into shape to make a book she'd always wanted.

Artists must not be sidetracked by doing extraneous art projects such as book reviews, secretarial functions at writing academies, teacher at how to write paint classes, etc., chiefly one falls into this around issues of money-making—to earn a living –and mistakenly feel it would be smart to be employed in the field relative to their art, --tho not exactly doing the art you love itself. This is a common error. To go astray from the genius of your own passion, to lower yourself into mundane, secondary positions--such as an art teacher, or working in the Rhetoric department of university. Or being on the staff of a publishing house. It saps the most imaginative, it pollutes the well spring of creativity; siphons it out of you drop by drop unwittingly, into a class room, into a brawling discussion in the department, into tutoring, editorial, writing nonsense in the guise of a critique of someone's else's published work for $25 a column, when your own manuscripts still sit unfinished; dusty in a drawer; your own paintings undone, unhung. So that the art vision becomes defused; you are so worn out by doing this stuff you cannot concentrate on the raw art, of applying paintbrush to canvas and creating something out of a blank space or sitting down to a naked tablet and writing lines of prose upon it—few others can do this! Many, many others can teach, edit, editorialize, review; so let them do it! To the ture artist it is a waste of energy! So much artistic energy is used up in commonplace 'art jobs' that when it comes to your own work you aren't at it long enough to progress in style and scope. All Transman's life he had sought out the street life, the bar life, the night life; by day working minimum wage jobs in factories, offices, nursing care homes, a totally different field—so that when he went back to his easel and desk, his mind was fresh, with ideas! Bursting with inspiration!

Those who visit bookstores, search for the current edition, 2007, 2008, of the Writers Digest, rush home to their desk over coffee to peruse it avidly for places they can tailor-make articles for, to earn $5 here $10 there, are writers yes, but not artists! They are twins to the paint-by-number painters—who also are not artists! Even tho they wear big hats, smocks and carry round pallets like Rembrandt. Better to work in a factory (hotbed of great ideas, conversations overheard; backdrop for revolutionary dramas, scenes of romantic intrigue) so as to return to the writing table fresh!

So this is what made him write, write & paint as if it was all he had, ---it was his drop of water in a desert drought, his last morsel of food on a long arduous journey—his very last hope left in the universe! He took it so seriously, his passion! It was not a hobby! Nor a casual thing!

10AM Thursday
Senior Day @ Grace; bible study commences with Cannon Lampen's interpretation of scripture (Psalms):

> For those who don't know Gods law; to uphold the highest standard one is able to know. The instinctive knowledge of right, and wrong. This is the judgment of God. God will judge a woman and a man according to what they know & what they have had a chance to know. God condemns evil wherever it exists.
> --Canon Lampen

Later, in the dining room, over coffee, fruit, salad & sandwiches, Andre comments how one food bank gave everybody a case of cranberries every time they came, for 3 weeks running. No meat, no dairy; no other vegetables. *Canned cranberries*. For 3 weeks! The poor people only trudged home with a bag full of little red berries in syrup. Canned cranberries are something people eat just twice a year—one can for Thanksgiving 1 can for Christmas. It turned out some high ranking government official's father, a huge mega-corporate farmer, had a bumper crop of cranberries he couldn't unload on the public market, so the his son pulled strings for him in Washington DC, and the government bought all the damn cranberries—stacks and stacks in warehouses full, and dolled them out to the food banks of America. Andre quips drolly: *Poor people are given the by-products of big business surplus.*

AM Wednesday May 14
By filling in the large blue planes with more solidly applied pigment Via Appia has now acquired an eerie stillness. The probable-suicide, head bowed in defeat, arms outstretched approaches empty space; right foot, ghostlike, in suggestion hovering off the side of the Crucifix's cross beam, reaching into destruction. A blue ocean below with tumbling black wave crests. Maybe I'm a better writer then painter and should only suggest these paintings via the printed word- and not try to paint them (tee-hee!). I fill the paintings up with imagination.

Whoops, back to holding 4 brushes in one hand, detail features of the mourner in Appian----must work fast; light blue, white, dark blue, yellow!

*

Let us talk for a moment. Forget this Allah, this God, this Eloheim, this Yahweh, for a minute—these confusing Names, these Names above all other names, each competing with each other for attention in the human mind. There is this Great Force, this Divine Intelligence— meaning great, genius, and always Good. Holy. People worshiping this Force by dancing, waving palm fronds, whatever the ritual or discipline may seem strange to us in more advanced civilizations then our accustom rendering of the Divine Force, but all methods of praise speak to one thing—this is God we're talking about. And it is this God, which cannot, must not be left out of any endeavor! Hashem must be incorporated into everything we do, create, think, or feel— and so much better goes our lives and our work! And let the people say----Blessed Be!

A Feminist Lecture: So first the Divine Creator made the heavens, earths, seas, and air. Then put down upon the rocky firmament, trees, plants, animals. Finally, in Creators crowning achievement—a human being--an exact replica of Creators self was made; what better design then to perpetuate this species? A woman, capable of bearing forth more just like herself, and to nurture and care for them way beyond even the time that they matured into adults. But she was lonely, this woman. Wanting companionship, and then man was created—a dismal facsimile of the original mold, woman—but exceptionally handy at some things! (Wink-wink!) In addition some transsexuals—that is a part of both the women and man all wrapped up on one body-- became apparent. The different colors, races, heights weights appeared. This was life. So in this style the human race has lumbered on right out of the Garden of Eden, into the present hell! Addendum: And as a queer/transsexual I've been called disgusting.

Dear Children; don't forget your lessons of a political nature: (Does anyone in the following quote sound familiar?)

> Fully 64 percent of the Russian radicals in the years 1855-1869 were from the nobility. A mere 8 percent came from the lower

middle class, the lower class, and the peasantry combined. Poverty
did not fuel activism, and poorer students mostly did what they
could just to scrape by. Privilege alone gave young people the time
& energy to devote to radical causes. Sixty's radicalism was not
born of oppression, but was nurtured in privilege. It grew in places
the Russian regime never suspected: in elite boarding schools and
private high schools, in military academies and clerical seminaries.
There, the sons and daughters of Russia's most elite citizens became
passionate anti-state activists, disclaiming the very class that bred
them.
-- Ana Siljak; Angel Of Vengeance

OBEDIENCE is pounding down to the finish, pounding like
keystrokes on a computer; pounding like hooves of horses on which
Transman lost money betting @ racetrack in his youth. Worse, where
looser horses were put to death.

PM--You learn lessons when you're old that you could never, ever
learn when you're young. You can read about it, but never really
know. The things you take pride in, one day come to realize they
were just a gift from God, as age slowly, inexorably strips them away.
Transman for many years after conversion took pride in a rigorous
service to God, being able rise for every scripture reading; to stand all
thru length sermons, now he sees it to be foolishness ---if you're old
and legs are weak. Once thought he could stay up all night doing art--
-forever—assuming it was simply a matter of willpower, that all
lesser artists were slackers; lazy; and now he knows that is not true.
Talents one attributes to self, set afire, impassioned arise not just from
self, but are temporary gifts from God, and they are on loan!

All will praise Creator! The strongest, the most lame. An invalid
gives thanks for the barest squeak of life left! God You Are Holy and
Your Mercy endures to all generations. Have mercy on me!

Am sitting in newly acquired Starfucks acquisition, for years an
Italian coffee shop (the chain 'bought it 3 weeks' ago chirps the
friendly lady busperson); spent $1.85 on tall coffee w/cream &
matching cup of ice. Left 15 cents tip. Came here for the air
conditioning. Its hot; 97% out. Body can no longer process it. When
he was a young boygirl of 20, he used to go to sit at the beach Lake
Michigan in 102% weather. Thus deepening his skin color to a brown

375

tan. Surreptitiously pulling down the straps of his bathing suit—this was before having breast removal surgery-- lay face down on his towel over the sand to hide his chest. And bake for several hours in enjoyment. No more. The extra layers of fat aren't helping! Must sincerely get down to 165 pounds—then determine if must I continue on. (On meaning losing more weight, not *on with life*—such a dismal life without no food treats; damn!) Have had very little to eat today. Heatwave. There he sat @ table, looking over his life's work—which was completely enclosed in a cellophane baggie of medium size. His 80-book catalogue, and a small green photo album of 13-postcard size prints. What am I going to do with my life?

> I'm so happy I'm in here! Testifies a young worker, its 90% outside!

Referring to their cool air conditioning to another worker from the hotel down the street, attired in a colorful red uniform with heavy gold brocade, who must stand in the street in the hot sun opening hotel doors for tourists again & again.

T sat, listening to Billy Holliday riff In My Solitude. *We are souls passing thru the universe...* Stooped over a coffee on ice mixed with cream, brooding upon his curriculum vita contained in the cellophane envelope; the voice of God told him:

> Come Alive Red Jordan!

A black man stands on the corner begging; proffering an empty cup; a white tourist passing stuffs some green cash into it—I feel nothing but conspiratorial gratitude for him, feeling so good myself—now—being rescued by caffeine.

Dear Hashem—thank you for restoring my life. —Suddenly feel that one day I will no longer be alone. If I live to be a very old TS man-woman living in a very nice room(s) in a very nice building in a very nice neighborhood, preferably right here in this upwardly mobile city of great culture; that I will have many, many friends. And if one area current in my life disappoints me there will be 5 other areas likewise vital, to compensate!

Hashem ! Hashem! I've done my best to do the work you have appointed! God! Lord! Hashem! *It's been so long* ---11 years since he'd sat down @ café over coffee, gloating, with a review copy of his newest NYC published book just received @ mailbox in his hands; rereading avidly the covers, back/front, other extraneous materiel inside which a publisher puts in, outside of his text with which he is well familiar. *Hurry!*

140.

 She was better off then the other girls who carried their belongings in a paper sack, she carried a purse.

They were on their way to Trans Space, the nefarious Transgender center where many destitute transwoman and a few challenged men come to get resources.

As he approached Trans Space he saw Miss B. round, female attired in a barmaid kind of way; quite flouncy with enormous self-grown tits, coming down the hill thru the hot summer afternoon leading her little piece of trade she carried on a string; --a string of kink. As a young boygirl, Miss B. had been loved by her poor but decent poor white family, who desperately attempted to put her into male drab, for her own good. As she matured she was sent to their public school's counselor. However not even a host of Psychiatrists of the Ivy League could change the girls mind. She was in good company with her trade, who after many sex dates had become a friend. Even at middleage this dismal straight man was not sure of his sexual orientation. All the madams of the world could not help this poor boy. Nor all the dominatrix sex therapists, of all the sex dens, of all the Babylons' in the belly of the beast. He wore supreme drab, his face was bland, to mask his secret identity. Beside him Miss B is a star! She switches, she poses, she wears the highest fashion a thrift store allows; she is *woman* herself! Miss B. has pushed her ture identity to the limit! She has lived her life to the hilt! She played her hand of cards to the fullest, and tipped her whole hand to the world for it to see! Miss B grinned, because she knew what the two of them were going to do that evening back in bed, in his motel—she was going to give it to him good with her 8" strap-on flesh colored peter; a necessity, as years of feminizing hormones had made her own cock flaccid; non-functioning.

Greeting them a moment, the short, aging Transman then continues on his pilgrimage to Trans Mecca—the Center. Those dizzy, crazy, girls, carren down its stairs in high heels. Inside, divas diving into the second hand close closet emerge with new, donated frocks. He is not there for 5-minutes, using free copy service on the photocopy machine, where, just beyond the door to an inner office the girls had got to laughing & every so often, and a baritone *GUFFAW!* issued out; there were a chorus of *tee hee's* and *ho ho ho's* bellowed uproariously, at some twisted joke, when suddenly the door came bursting open and there appeared Miss K. Hers too was a story of interest. She was a de facto sex predator. Which means she was not a real sex fiend, the dangerous, and bad kind; but an innocent child who had been lumped into this criminal class thru sheer misfortune. One evening feeling quite jolly, and drunk, Miss K. had Exposed Her Breast on a public street—was arrested by the police under Megan's Law—as a sex predator.

The reason for this arrest was given by the officer-in-charge:

Well, children could have seen it.

So now the poor dizzy child has a record under Megan's Law---as a sex offender! She will never get a job working for the school system----even as janitress. All for showing her firm, bronze body to the sun! And promptly a blue uniform arm of the gendarmes whisked her off in the patrol wagon.

Now, as two destitute dikes grumble over food hoarded in their soiled backpacks, a beautiful, emaciated Asian T., spills out her story in butterfly falsetto, of discrimination back in Arizona; toilet issues—her job *forced this beautiful lady to use the men's restroom!* A very dangerous idea.

Don't be without understanding, part of every transsexual is very much the opposite sex then their genitalia would indicate to the traditional world. We are born with this, and no manner of coaxing, denial, psychiatry, torture, or ostracism will change it!

He wanted a dominatrix but I'm not a dominatrix, I'm a sub. In the streets I'm dominant, in the bed I'm submissive all the way.
--Overheard; TS Girl about her Miss-adventure @ The Power Exchange

378

God's little vagabond children. Since the beginning of Transman's street life starting at 15, 16, there had been some little shack where we all met, together, to escape the harsh investigating light of straights, us queers.

Ever since the sandlots sunny of South Side Chicago, since I took up the tools of an adult, would I have thought, while running with brown/tan shorties thru the alleys screaming in fun under hot summer sun, that'd I'd mature to be an artist? And leave that place; travel across continent; to live here, on the oceans coast—the Wild West of miners 49rs Gold Rush; in Mark Twain's city of murmurings of revolution; beatniks, hippies; although I was very sure I was a boy; nor again did I know I'd be habituating low-down dirty dives of deviates & divas…

141.
PM Friday May 16
Down a stones throw from the bookstore, at Self Fashion Design, a 3rd year anniversary party. Music, dance—long legged Lenora does the Borea, on ballet tiptoes over Scott's worn carpet. Music spun on old recorder turntable by John (Gatsby). Things come alive on this street!

Reading Siljacks Angel of Vengeance it occurs to me some of my readers might wish me to comment on revolutionary prophecy.—That is the view that God has ordained revolution necessary—a concept expressed in my fine works LAMENTATIONS IN THE COOL OF THE EVENING. And EMPIRE! This is advocating change in a political system, overthrowal of its killing chains of avarice & it being in alignment with the Word of God—hence, prophecy. —I quote: **I Am a Just God**. & it is in matters of justice—true and complete justice--- that a revolutionary is concerned.

Now am going to reference the book What Is To Be Done written by Nikolai Chernghevski, circa 1860.

As Transman Red read by the dim bookstore light, that late evening, a particular passage jogs his dim mind as to the purpose—perhaps—to which he was sent; he who had lived so much persecution, &

379

experienced the depth of injustice by a multitude of ways---racial, gender, wise, class wise:

> Young educated Russians of the 1860's did not merely read this novel. (What Is To Be Done) They perused it obsessively, memorized it, quoted passages from it like a catechism and carried it around like a prayer book.
> --Ana Siljack; Angel of Vengeance

Shades of Mao's little Red Book which every of my socialist/commie pals of the 1970's had in their homes, in their purses, their duffle bags, & the I-Ching, a decade before this, carried, along with the 3 necessary coins for tossing the I-Ching, of bearded, beaded, long granny dresses, sandaled hippies with flowers in their hair.

> If you don't want a revolution in America you better be quiet about your wealth
> --ABC News May 16, '08

A TV Special interviews an immigrant from India, earning 1 billion dollars a year. He gives 2-3% to charity.

You work & you work. When its hot. When its cold. When your body is twisted out of shape. When you are in pain—you can't miss a day for fear of getting behind. You go to work when you been up at the hospital allnight with a sick loved one. When there are problems at home you must still tear yourself away to go to work. T did it for 40 years. Now, in his lonely impoverished retirement, his art continued to chug along the same track it had first headed into at age 10 or 11.

Yet here is a man who has never had to work at all. He inherits. He masses great wealth from the capital given to him at birth.

We have fallen away from the laws of God, which plainly tell us to share with each other—and not to rob; not to rob until each sequential generation becomes more immired in haplessness then the one preceding it. We have forgotten—tho we pray, bow knee in church/ashram; say the barcu in synagogue—we have somehow pushed aside what the scriptures really say. That it is untenable for a few—1% of the world's population--- to hoard such an amazing pile of filthy blood-drenched wealth, while others are starving to death, and most others live a life of wage slavery. The Commandments God has given thru the prophets are instruction for the holistic living of the society of humankind. We forget what they say! We have pretended that mere church going, donating cash in the proffered golden collection plate, being a $10,000 per year member to Temple; and regularly attending services, that we have fulfilled all that we need do. Many attend bible/torah studies rigorously—reading over and over with each cyclical year each and every word from the mouth of God, davananing about justice, and God's mercy; and God's wrath, and yadda yadda yadda, yet cannot pull it together that Creator has plainly instructed us to share the wealth! Not to steal more and more!

That God—God the Most high is calling for revolution—because this mess humans are making is so untenable, so corrupt, so backwards & vile.

Finally, these days, there's a hint of it in the air. Of revolution catching afire. It can be overheard, subrosa, subliminal on the airways songs; in poetry, movies, plays, street guerrilla theatre, graffiti writers, poetry slam, all are calling for this world-capitalistic system to fall. When this rumor becomes a mantra in every worker & senior's brain, then change will easily fall into place!

Violin soars, Bella Bartok. The high ranges of intellect.

Red Jordan, what will you say to the world (as if it is my hearts last truth)? Dear Children:

> Love each other.
> Find a quiet moment.
> Reach out when possible.
> Have fortitude.
> Never abandon hope.
> Care & make care manifest.
> --Red; 4:15pm Peet's Coffee Shop

An artistic collaboration it's like a graft, putting a transfusion of your own self into this mutual work. There are others working along beside us, tho we don't see them, each in their private rooms. Right now we bide our time. Soon day, all will be seen in full, all will be

381

revealed in the light of day. The streets will echo with our jubilant shouts, running side by side along the corridors to victory.

Transman thought: if I see one more dental school waiting room… As he looked in at the pristine white, modern fixtures … Knowing the prolonged treatment which lay ahead. I had to fight for every last stinking fucking thing I got. Everything. Food, housing, love, friends, fame. But I thank God I didn't have to fight to get my art. I was born with an artistic expression, a talent. Yes I had to fight to *do* my art. Isn't it odd that many were born with the reverse problem! Having every material necessity in place, being loved, and sociable, and amidst family and pals—yet having not one bit of talent at all! Ha ha ha! The genius's revenge!

Outdoors it was like a furnace had been opened---blasts of heat came in waves across his face and body but soon a wind went flowing along the building fronts and was slowly blowing the temperature down out of the 90s to the 80s out of the 80s to the 70s. Ah, San Francisco.

The old man had little faith in the world. Grumbling, he returned again to the comfort of his paints. Of earthy pigments, color, substance, odor, meaning, expression thru imagination. He had partial faith in God, and feared the future as does everyone, applying brush to canvas, listening to Higher Love.

PM Saturday May 17
People in heaven will be far more sophisticated since they now *see* whereas before they saw imperfectly. The old grey drab weather creased face redneck wife and husband of earth will be sitting down with the gay attired queer—dining on their favorite foods together in heaven, in friendship:

> A great understanding shall come to pass.
> --Hashem to the Prophet, Red.

Transman industriously pulled boxes of books aside, to make way for the next shipment of Goods, in his studio storage shelves. (RETROSPECT.) Periodically one has to build up ones inventory— then over time the books/or print sell off, you regroup your money— tho far from the initial date of the expenditure; and due to inflation at that later date, and increased price of the volumes, in the inside mind you are satisfied that, you are gaining not losing—but not by much!

AM Sunday May 18
Transman thought about Flash On The Hustler—or The Players as it was originally called; he thought about the pennies, jewels, and bags of cash in all Along The Watchtower. He thought: *I have a message*.

AM Sunday May 18
In little ways the guys from the bookstore are like my art baby sitters—each day I get there asking me did I paint, and what I painted and these type of questions, which adds fuel to the motion of returning to the easel again.

Being Jewish in adopted faith, I have found my self upon occasion to be somewhere strange to me. Foreign to me as a queer. Dangerous to the person of-color. To the alternative gendered. Rural or suburban areas of mono-racial tone in which outsiders suddenly realize they are strangers dropped down into a strange place--out there in the land of the unforgiving hell. I've found little twists of this, during my life. Anti-Semitism being chief on top of the list. Blacks (by a different epitaph, a racial slur) next. Queers are right up there at the top. So far Mexicans & other Latin's are ignored—because the white Aryans Nazi types notice they are doing all the work (picking fruit, gardening, restaurant help, construction labor.) —so they let them pass.

To a believer, to an avid worshiper of The Almighty, one of the greatest times is when they've finally got to haul themselves up out of bed on a Saturday morning, or Sunday morning, put their clean clothes on and got down to the holy place, seat themselves on a pew (or mat) settling next to others of their clan, faces expectant. It is a poor persons refuge, the holy place, for The Compassionate One gives us hope. It is a place to be with little or no money, it is a refuge from the storm of their lives—wither this storm be economic, or emotional, or spiritual.

I know a young man who is very selfish. He is suicidal. —Seriously in pain, and a detriment to his own well-being economically, and physically. *He is very selfish*—Transman privately had always held this opinion. 'Me me, everything is centered around me'; no matter the affect it has on others. He himself has said he is selfish. It goes without saying that to have interest in others and to help them along life's way a bit, does take your mind off of your own pain; but self-centered people cannot do that. I have seen this quite a few times in people who later committed suicide, and now believe this 'selfishness' is just an indicator of something far greater within them churning like a dynamo, bothering them so greatly, so that it just appears to be an extreme-self centeredness on the surface. This dear young man, was on my mind, in part while doing Via Appia.

The artist also may be selfish—highly so—but somewhere in our minds realization that we are devoting a huge amount of our life's energy to the creation of a product to *give* back to the human race. Which is in its special way *a very highly unselfish act.*

Blues settles into a poolhall in the evening—I believe this will be my latest work, beginning strokes in acrylic on canvas Sunday morning while signing the Kaddish de-Rabbanan:

> Yit barach ve yish ta bach
> veyit paar ve yit romam ve yit na sei
> ye yit hadar veyit a leh ve yit halal
> shemei de kudsha
> brich hu.
>
> May it be blessed and honored
> And beautified and exalted and extolled
> And glorified and raisied up and praised
> Gods holy name,
> Blessed be God.

You, the artist, is doing a self-portrait of your soul.

Blues Settles Into The Poolhall For The Evening. (?) Acrylic on gesso over (acrylic?); 30" x 24" on found-canvas worst part of Market Street, @ 6th leaning up against garbage can at 10pm.

Oh, RETROSPECT has been finished thru much sweat, effort of Sean vulture-posed over computer; 2 copies ordered by me to approve, then it goes up for sale online over Blurb POD, and at bookstore.

Every word an artist writes, every word a painter paints, --they fought for that! Back up your files on computer! Make copy discs, set in a separate place-in case your computer crashes, Artist, try to photograph each of your paintings before it leaves your studio! There is an art book I recently saw in which a *photograph* is shown of a painting by a well-known artist which bares the caption: this is a photograph of picture stolen.

If/when I ever write my book OBEDIENCE TO THE CALL OF REVOLUTION al la Das Kapital, The Communist Manifesto, et al, it will include this chapter: The Cooperation Of The Rich In Their Own Overthrowal. Every so often one hears some rich person admit they are uncomfortable just going up and up in income, while others are falling lower, but if they gave away all their money it would only be engulfed in hoard of penury cash-grabbing, and spread out over the earth, their vast fortunes would amount to only a few do-nothing pennies in the hands of each individual.

It is the system itself, which must be changed.

Think, how if the peoples of the world were to study their own predicament; to analyize it diligently and come to realize, that they if in company with each other, would lay down on their jobs and no longer continue to be cogs in the wheel of fascist kapitalism, the whole thing would fall apart by itself, in days, weeks… dissolve into the mass of impure garbage fit to be swept away by diligent brooms of the new order; the system would fall and the new order arise in its place, one more humane, less controlling, more just and all this could be accomplished without a shot being fired!

Police, military are just tools of the people. They do what they are ordered to do. Overnight, suddenly they would find themselves working for the New Order, and would enforce that—so there could be no opposition—*if,* all people of earth were cooperative in this overthrowal!

There must be complete and simultaneous meltdown of the United States & other super powers as it's imperative that no one be overthrown before the other, least the one surviving be conquers and the archaic system of master or slaves perpetuate itself.

PM Sunday May 18

Peoples' houses foreclosed. Peoples brand new appliances don't
work; furniture promised, never even delivered; they go back to the
store that sold them, bill of sales in hand to find the place has gone
out of business; their doors locked.

Current economic news of the USA people loosing their houses in
every state; —God this is horrible. J. moves out of her condo, arms
carry boxes; along with half of the nations 'home' buyers; the great
economic loss sweeping the united state economic market into a
severe depression.

Moving a load of boxes out of the condo, in the elevator J. & Red turn
to look at each other: *'well how many times have we been thru this—
flying by night.'* J only smiles sweetly, chagrined, droll, at the
supreme irony of the thing as the modern elevator silver panel lets us
gently down, and the modern electronic beam high tech door
smoothly slides open to let us out—out the door into the cold night!
Literally this is the 4 or 5th time we have gone thru this. Her and me,
and now her and----. Ah life!

AM Monday May 19

> Friend, I have a terrible story
> I wish to relate.
> Its as if I've come thru a terrible storm
> Not in what has happened to me
> But to a person I've witnessed.
> I can tell you this.
>
> Some human lives
> Are put down on earth
> & they just don't work out so well.
> Creator is saddened by it.
>
> For some of us
> Life is so simple.
> Work hard,
> Have a *cause.*
> Preoccupy yourself
> Do something meaningful.

Be unselfish.

We try to cheer them up
In our own way
But they can't
Or don't.-
Their condition
Its' more serious
Then we think

We can't reach them.

I have known 3 now, directly;
Two own condos,
The other owned a house.
All had been able to access the top
Of middle class society
  Just using their brain power,
Achieving better jobs.
Yet that could not save them.

Yes friend
I have a terrible story
I wish to relate.
It's as if
I've come thru a terrible storm.
I wanted to die
But couldn't
 Didn't.

I am a survivor.

Another point about artists, must tell you, they push things all the way
to the end, and never abandon the mission. This is all-important.
Both people have the same saint like compassions. Both weep at the
sight of an abandon cat. Both go to try to save the cat. The one,
however falls away after much opposition. 'its just a cat, after all.'
They say, dismissing the problem from their mind. The other says;
'oh the poor cat!' and continues to rescue it with all their might.

The one is the average compassionate. An empath. But the other is a
Mother Teresa. Both share deep feelings for others. One helps
mightily. The other devotes their entire life to the heart of the subject.

And so the great artist, and the minor one—and all the little, forgotten ones. It is the level of commitment which is key to the equation. How far do they push their art? A decade? Two? Three? Then give it up for just simply living? Or all the way to the end?

My lecture to you, thru JOURNEY, for I must self-encourage. And these reminants, these leavings, these scribbles, these Notes; are left for you Dear Children, to muse upon. To davain upon together in synagogue/church religiously, & in political study groups politically; and above all, as encouragement to the artist.

AM Tuesday May 20
For all practical purposes, Transman had had a dehumanizing life. So he exhibited some disassociation from the natural world. Both by choice, as many of us, and also in as underlying mental illness, which actually prevented him from being accepted into society groups, easily; having their suspicions because of his stiff, unnatural behavior; and highly agitated nervous state.

> Why 'kain't those days, come back no mo'? Why 'kain't those days come back no mo'?
> --Blax pop hit, '70's

Will say this again. Then, there comes the fork in the road. —The choice. The decision. Artists will be glad he/she chose the road of his art and not mundane, meaningless ways of the common world, which build things that do not last.

His mind busy w/daydreams—by the time Transman had tucked himself into bed with his little cat, at dawn, he'd been awarded the Nobel Prize & received Academy Awards for Best Book used in a making of a Motion Picture.

AM
T stood at easel, brush in hand, minuet detailing; making a poolhall scene happen. Evening Descends In The Poolhall. (?) Busy painting, writing, and doing the physical tasks that accompany art. Setting up for shows, building canvases, washing brushes, trekking to the store to buy supplies, assembling paraphernalia, etc.

T stood, struggling over Evening Descends on The Poolhall. Had to learn how acrylic *acts*.

Red has access to tools, Van Gogh didn't. He had abstract art. The validity of this school which had come before him, but after Van Gogh. So it opened up a door to extend out of natural rendering, into extraordinary. Figures montage upon the pool table itself, instead of their normal placement at the pooltables edge.

PM
Like lost, frightened animals, wandering the maize of this modern civilized landscape—finding refuge in stray nooks, basements, side alleys; the places uninhabited; unconformable and inaccessible; the human lost wander down here along the homeless quarter. ---The TL. Here a derelict woman pushes a baby carriage her 'baby' is a bundle of blankets & a radio, tied down to prevent theft, playing into the stale days air of maliferous aromas from wino gutters and tenement garbage cans.

And this familiar; male of an Islander descent, stocky, thick greasy black hair, brown thick features, late 30's; see him smoking on Hyde & Ellis early, 3pm, pushing the homeless persons vehicle, the shopping cart, laden with black garbage sacks wrapped in bundles laboriously, but without comment, gesture nor grimace, up the gradually increasing incline; now here he is; night fallen, 9pm, chill, pushing, his eternal shopping cart, pausing slowly up the incline on Bush towards Leavenworth—doing penance for the world.

> I knew him when he was clean & sober & had a job.
> --Overheard, TL.

Had taken it upon himself to rescue stray animals who'd fallen down into the cracks of civilization and were lost. Life sure is busy in the life of a compassionate—who carry their caring as far as they can.

To make a long story short, the cat spied hiding under cars in the parking lot had worked its way into Transman's conscious.
Was so tired, making his cat-care rounds & painting, AM's, and writing PM's; his wallet was now sprinkled with red & blue BART tickets.

In this big, cold, crazy city is there compassion enough for 1 lost cat?

Things are going from one disaster to the next. Life like a net closing in, problems everywhere.

So afraid he began to imagine all kinds of things; some zealous official will give me a huge fine for 'cat feeding' for loitering. Thoughts racing. Head spinning. Heart pounding. So much stress. Some really don't understand why I'm doing this to try to save this cat:

> Compassion is all-important on my list.
> --Hashem The Eternal

Day 1; Sunday. Saw cat; left dog food morsels in water & cooked shrimp, with help from Jasmin. Cat ate.

Day 2; Monday. Searched for, and found cat. Cat ate.

Day 3; Tuesday. God! What a relief! This cat has done me a great favor by being in the same place at the same time as before! So tiered, can think of little else.

Day #4. Success partially. Cat is waiting in the exact spot last fed. Fast turn around... flipped a can over left food there, popped tell tale can away this time left no water. Threw can into a waiting bag, wiped hands of smelly cat food with alcohol swabs, tossed bag into garbage. That's for tomorrow's run will leave water. Mission accomplished; back on train by 2 pm.

Day 5; Wednesday. No cat.

Suddenly a slew of things had come to rock the old man's schedule. I must hang onto my painting time tenaciously he thought, worriedly, bustling about the studio, paintbrushes in hand.

Day 6; Thursday. No cat. He started noticing things over time—for instance, car mufflers from a distance resemble a crouched cat sitting underneath the vehicle.

So the higher question is, one pertaining to all the world is, how can we have a compassionate revolution with kindness, gentleness &

inclusion of all beasts, & not, instead end it all in the fiery orange/red ball of x-ray, nuclear holocaust?

It's the only possible thing if the two can come together—revolution, and the heart of compassion; the (Christian) religion, meaning of agape and not the enforcement of some religious hierarchy or doctrine or papistry; the idea to end suffering on earth of its peoples, animals and the environment—the thing to be worked for; by scientists, doctors, writers, poets, dancers, musicians, soldiers, peace keepers; taking radical action.

The compassion of an empathic: —serious.

Finally, by nightfall when he'd come to rest @ Babylon Falling finding himself with a distorted grin pasted on his face, heckling some inane statement along with the cronies he must ask: 'Why am I laughing when my heart is breaking over this lost cat. Is my mind false? Is it listening to my heart? Or, too preoccupied, wheels spinning on crazy ideas. Did mother Teresa laugh so loud, so often, so falsely & tell bad jokes. Did St. Francais of Assisi? What is real and important in my life?'

Well the heart compels you above & beyond politics:

> Revolutionary passion practiced-----is to be employed with cold calculation.
> --Sergi Nechaev, Catechism Of A Revolutionary

So this is where me, and a 'true revolutionist' differ. After struggle all an artistic life, all political desire; all eyes will lift their eyes to God.

AM May 21, Wednesday
History repeats itself; all thru time there's been this growth phenomenon. An individual opens a salon, café, tavern, bookstore, and a group of persons of great future fame begin to draft towards its light, beckoning thru the dim drab silent storms of ordinary life. Gertrude Steins salon where Hemingway, Picasso, gathered; the great migrations of artists to Paris, musicians to Berlin; Babylon Falling had entered the theatre of Transman Red life—to this point he had come.

I had painted ten years since about age 16 thru 23 or so with dips and dabs after that. In this time learned the craft of oil painting and some acrylic. Had spent from age15 to 18 drawing wild slashings of pencil mark across large drawing tables with spiral binding, carrying one always thru the classrooms of public high school torment so when I returned to SF in 2001, I was prepared with a distant background in the craft. In this new spot, as previously I have said, found myself engulfed in a galaxy of small art galleries and a non-stop acquisition art college which was growing exponentially by importing foreign students with a desire to 'study in the USA' who chose this college which was easier then for them to endure, than some technical or medical school. This art school owner was busily acquiring more and more properties, stocking them with these students, and adding more classrooms, more school adjuncts so as between the time I retuned here from cheaper living in the East Bay until now (2008) had doubled, no, tripled the torrent of young art school students walking to and fro in front of my apartment with paint kits, canvasses upon which were school class assignments, easels, drawing boards, art portfolios etc. All the paraphernalia of the fine artist, an occasional clay bust on a board—went parading, careening thru the streets at a dizzying pace. If this wasn't enough for our great Hashem to give me the *Nudge* with His/Her elbow, to awaken my painting spirit, I don't know what! Adrift in a sea of art! Then---came the catalyst. A direct touch. Babylon Falling opened its doors June of '07, proprietor Sean Steward, young white man, from Jamaica, stood proudly in his doorway as the carpenter put finishing touches on the bookshelves, which were later crooked. I came in a week or so later, introduced myself as a writer—Red Jordan Arobateau. Brought back some books for him to see, showed him my website (thus outing myself as trans/queer) and immediately ensconced myself in the window seat as the Lion Who Sits Beside the Door—like one of those two magnificent bronze lions who sit on either side of the palatial Art Institute of Chicago on Michigan avenue. *Inside the artist come and go, speaking of Michelangelo.* Well more like invoking the name of David Chung Lee, Frank Kosik and others. Met Grey, a young art student, and soon we were all talking art, and I became involved. Swept up. The paints began to assemble in my studio. I resurrected all my supplies and set up the painting section, awaiting me to *start*. A sudden windfall of money (which isn't the first time amazing sums have been imported to me just when I need them; miracle?) so I'm discussing toxicity with the others, and began buying acrylics, aqua oils; oh had found a box full of oils paints discarded by an erstwhile student who had graduated/flunked out and no longer wanted them, plus about 15 discarded canvases. Then on Jan 1, 2008, I stepped over the bridge. The gulf of 40-years absence of my craft.

142.

Steps on the bus are getting higher & higher. I feel a bigger gulf from the common world. My mind tells me one thing, my heart tells me something else, all this; Holy God, the world madness, these superficialities, lost in it all, where's your heart? *My whole body is coming apart in pieces.* T. told himself. His left knee, his right foot, both shoulders. Pain. My life is in a hole artistically—still anonymous & nobody knows my name. I'm hoping my art will dig my way out of this hole into prominence recognizing for my life long work.

In events which happened last night all illustrates I have absolutely no rights & this city.

I was locked out of the front door of this $1,000 per month apartment; and the Japanese nasty restaurant owner next door wouldn't let me in thru his establishment to the common basement we share, so I could let myself in. The front door stayed broken with a bunch of people milling around in the entranceway, non-working keys in hands fussing/fuming, and having to let each other in. Once inside, have to contend with the bi-polar mental patient in the basement's second hand cigarette smoke permeating the kitchen of my studio. Sometimes fantasize of getting a windfall of money and pooling my money with----, but don't trust them enough to really go in with them in buying a house.

Awoke to The Arab vibrating with color, which hung over his head— no longer upon wooden stretchers. Color as clear & true as if it was painted yesterday. White, reds, orange, turquoise, brilliant yellow; stripes of his/her holy coat of many colored holy coat.

I will paint a picture; My Peace I Give To You:
> I come with healing, I come with peace, I come with ease of discomfort with remission of pain I come with resurrection I come with life, I come with hope; I come with the answer to all things. I'm coming back. I come with compassion!

Compassion! Compassion! One hears so little of it in this ordinary time. Hard, proud, vain world. Compassion ! Compassion! How little one sees of it! The very word hardly ever spoken! Compassion.

393

Bow deeply to God; ask for the things God wants you to have.

He felt agitated that morning. Afraid. Was his mother perusing him? Over time and years, --about 50, half a century to *get him*, once more? Corner him in the bathroom and do to him nefarious acts—which adults pay good money to have done to themselves in dungeons of the dominatrix? *'I pray for peace Hashem. Give me peace today'.* Was the small guys prayer, while fervently he applied brush to canvas—as if his life depended on it, and indeed the life of his soul and mind did depend on it, if not his actual physical life. It was the events that had transpired the night before which had rocked his boat. It is difficult to be an artist when surrounded by brutes. By self-serving, unfeeling, — and dishonest, inhuman beings. But more, like the wash or backdrop of a painting, already there, it was the ongoing strain of tending for the stray cat, daily coming and going there, plus feeling sorry for the creature—who was too afraid to come to him for salvation.

> Have faith, I will work all things out to My satisfaction. Says the Lord(ess).

There's foreign money pouring into this city. There's Japanese money, Chinese money, Arabic money, a lot of little scrabbling Latins, each small amount of hard-working businesses, all amounting together as money on a large scale; there's white money; some left over Italian money, but no black money. Less then .01% black money. Yet it is my ancestors, black people, who built the foundations of this nation thru their slave labor. There is no Native American Indian money in this city—yet this continent is their land.

There is gay money, Jewish money, tourist money, political money, French, German money, and Russian money, small and dabbling, plus, big money beginning to pour in along with the Russian mafia being laundered into businesses & realestate here. But no money for me and no money for you!

Thus this is the city, it is, and always has been this way—corrupt. Greedy. Feelingless; and outside of a few Do-Gooders, Saints, life would be total hell. What passes for love; lonely allies in a barroom killing the nights cracking jokes, exchanging gossip & cigarettes in quiet desperation; drinking themselves to sleep, awaking to look foreword to their job another morning. Each, in their own slot, or frame. Each in their own bare room shivering in terror, until a fitfully sleep comes over them. 8-hours later, coffee, awake, go to work at a detested job, go home to their slot again and disappear from sight.

Damn this system that cheats me out of every penny.

They cheat and steal.

No, this is not thugs I'm speaking off, the common robber wielding gun or knife in the street, but owners, bosses, landlord, rulers; those over us, the common person. Dylan Thomas speaks of *the thief who stole your heart away* which is an emotion, a state of mind. This is a material nature I'm speaking of---but it influences the heart, it helps set up the conditions which break the heart and which destroy love. Which destroy all the finer sentiments, of beauty, grace, art, patience, ---these thieves of the material plane.

You got to be pretty damn tough to survive in this world, or else your just a doormat or somebody who hops skips and jumps all over the place in attempts to avoid trouble or spend their life laying low to avoid confrontations. Like people too afraid to say anything for fear of being called a fool. When you take risks you will confront yourself. You will see yourself.

Don't give up; don't give in! —Which is why an artist paints; a writer writes! A dancer dances!

There is something I want to tell you---there is something I'm afraid of. Its name is the future. Now I'm not simply afraid of death but of this future & all the probably inescapable pain it brings. Only faith in God maintains thru this & from this God will deliver us. *I will bring you thru.* But my faith is not great enough. Yet this is the answer. There is no other.

The Holy Spirit gives instruction anywhere and everywhere.

*

Those might wonder, as T lived 2 & one-half blocks from a grant writing place, The Foundation; why he didn't stop, take the time & learn how to write himself a grant. – You dare not pause for the mundane duties, because you are doing the all-important, creating new art.

143.
Joy! At Last! Can say I am very pleased! RETROSPECT is in my hands!! Gave thanks to Creator. Actually kissed the book. A mutual giving thanks to God, while simultaneously knowing---how much of my own labor went into this—the blood, sweat and tears stuff! And give credit to the others who helped. Richard Politowski, Sean Stewart, Shawn Roberts, Jasmin, & Laura.

AM Saturday May 24
Joy! Simca! Transman went around his studio with a mighty smile on his face. A constant smile of his mouth stretched ear to ear, a smile which did not melt as the evening went on, so happy was he.

Periodically, doing his nightly tasks he stopped—he smiled. Still smiling he clapped his hands in joy! He Danced!

The old man was dancing! Dancing around his studio!

The old man danced in place in his worn black trousers and shirt, his new brown boots, he lifted the soles of his feet ever so slightly off the hardwood floor, bobbed and bounced in one spot, shaking and weaving his body rhythmically to his joy without music, in blasts of energy. His constant motion served to move him slowly around, thus he went from the main room into the little entrance way, back, thru the main room into he small kitchen, danced there, turned around bobbing, jogging; upon occasion when an exceptionally strong burst of joy hit him, clapped his hands. Moved back into the studio, bobbing, weaving; rocking on the balls of his feet.

RETROSPECT is so important to me—a milestone. My paintings are now concretized. Before they were nowhere. This colorful book serves to remind me of my job—to create more of them! Get them photographed. Turn them into posters at first, and when enough are assembled, another retrospect. The text is flowing along as usual—like a blue river.

Must give thanks to Hashem for locating me here in a major city. So many resources have been drawn from it to make this book. Geographic proximity to art supply stores, to have the fortune to meet up with Richard, a photographer with a photo lab at his service, to meat Sean in his bookstore, whose technical abilities sent the book to press. To live near competing cheaper photocopy shops by which the text of the JOURNEY journals was drawn for the public to share… all this technological stuff, this material stuff, down to the free Internet computer time I begged, borrowed and stole here and there---all of this possible in a large city, and little of it could be done in a town, or rural habitat.

> A brief addendum; a memorandum about change: I remember when I use to hang out on the ho' stroll (1972-'73) we'd stand there, the hustlers of all varieties busy on their jobs, drug sellers, hot clothes men, fences, gun runners, loansharks, users & chumps; the pimps and so-forth driving by to check on their ho's; sometimes lame young boy-men hobbled by low-slung trousers, teenagers fresh dropouts from high school, growing up amid constant crime which overran their neighborhood; see these slick players who they would secretly emulate, but as of then as teenagers, 'these boys, they wasn't hitten' on nothin' empty pockets, & no game in dem'. Red and some of the oldtime, retired players would talk about other ho' strolls in Chicago, New York, St. Louis, Kansas, places down South; and say how you weren't going to see many more of these spots because the police were gonna shut 'em all down, however the truth is this, these kind of pimp-ho hustlers, un-reformed parolees and street drugs thugs lives thrive in a world rapidly disappearing. They need a cosmopolitan area to thrive and this acreage is increasingly becoming prime turf for realestate—even the once wore down, tore down ghetto—the inner cities--- are being gentrified so all the crime action is being displaced—is pushed out; it's going to the lesser towns and countryside.

Would his long-ago mentally insane mother be proud of him now; as he held his gaily colorful package, RETROSPECT in hand—after all her tutelage in the fine arts; brining home portfolios of Picasso, Van Gogh, Rembrandt prints from the public library?

Yes I am.
--Red's long-dead mother in heaven.

After transfiguration our Savior saw his wounds with joy—it was the marks of love for the human species. We too are covered with red marks of the effects of our love. Bites and scratches of small animals. Bleeding calluses of hard labor to feed loved ones. My paintings should be hung with an accompanying text-pertinent, as this above statement for the Raiment of Love, also others regarding the subject.

AM Monday May 26

I'm not an ordinary person. And wouldn't be in the manner of young Russian Revolutionists of the 1800rds who went out into the Russian countryside, attempting to bring their salvation of Socialism Communism & Revolution to the former serfs; who put on workers clothing, caps and kerchiefs—but were easily seen thru as being from a privileged class. I am not an ordinary person, nor was I raised as one of the 'regulars' of this world, and this difference always shows up, no matter where I am, from skid-row food line, to factory floor, to small support group for the disadvantaged. I do have a message to bring to everybody, to the 'regulars'—the world's modern day peasants, as well as to the establishment itself and its privileged pampered children.... It is something familiar, and all have heard it in one form or another, that red-hot message of *change*—revolution which especially in these troubled times of global unrest, U$ financial crisis, as the old order slides down into a Great Depression of length and breadth never seen before in Amerikkka; today this message might awaken a new interest. Some of my paintings reflect my stance on radical ideas, and reflection on the inequity of laboring vs. owner classes. The Pig and its meaning are easily observed---once I point this out. The Pig is round; well fed, massive; he is attired in a blue uniform of totalitarian authority. He sits at a bar, one might conjecture, of a tavern. A drink sits in a translucent glass before him. His mighty right fist, powerful, is crushing out blood from a wad of green dollars. Blood of the people. His left 'hand' is actually a foot, and it is upraised ordering one more. One More. One more human soul for him to squeeze the blood, sweat & labor out of, to feed his gargantuan body. —His smug face smiles. He is a no-neck person, round head engulfed in his massive fat/muscles. As Sean Stewart pointed out, which even me, the artist hadn't noticed, The Pigs right eye is twinkling in an obscene wink. The lecher is winking at us all in his debauched power. It is these kind of accompanying texts I will use for the 2nd retrospect. Using a duplicate photo of paintings from the first RETROSPECT—in small thumbnail shots, with these explanations to accompany. All new paintings will be in full-size page, each one to its own page. Haven't decided will I put the accompanying details for these as well, along with the regular text in the 3rd book, or wait to explain them in some future book. More notes on the young Ruskies of 18th century. Culled from Ana Siljack's book, about young female assassin Vera Zasulich. The radicals attempted to work the factories along with common folk, and till the soil under the hot sun, pretending this is the labor they'd known all their lives, when in fact they'd been raised in mansions of privilege with many former surfs—destitute, the lowest cast of society-- to wait on them—great orchards dripping in fruit and large meadows to play in as girls and boys… Upon adolescence they'd been shipped off to the finest schools of 1800rds for education in at least 3 foreign language—French, English, Greek, or Latin; all the current sciences & knowledge. Their manners were well-rounded, befitting their class status. Once out in the hot fields laboring tirelessly from dawn until sunset, these young aristocrats soon wilted and could not go on. In the factories amid unbearable din, dizzying pace, long 17-hour day shifts, ill food to eat—black bread, weak soup with no meat—the children of the aristocrats soon were forced to abandon their pose. Their guise as 'peasants' was quickly seen thru, the peasants became suspicious of them—and hence their message of liberation too was suspect.

I myself have worked the factories, the hospitals, the kitchens and the homes and offices of the world for 40-years. And know the drill well. But one thing about me seems to be different. Having been raised in a home where art was predominated, and work not mentioned—outside of schoolwork. Where time was given to me freely—time to play with my scientific lab kit, my builder's set, my toy soldiers, and my books; my wonder was honed, my dreams were nourished. These have never left me as an adult. While my more practical playground friends became hardened, disciplined, adopted an adult-appointed work schedule; cut out art, books, wonder, from their lives as unpractical and superfluous to survival—in fact detrimental to their survival. In them art shriveled and died. Was killed by parents who forced adult chores on them by necessity. Hard, adult work commencing at an early age. In me, time was allowed. And I have used it well. Producing all that I am able. Must repeat: Red was raised in a house, an ordinary house; 2 story 2 flat building like almost all the other houses on the block, it just that he was not raised in an ordinary way.

Dear Journal. You are going to think I am *absolutely insane* that the realization has just now hit me—at age 64---*after all these years...* That a reason for my mother's incessant torture may have been my transgender appearance as a child! Without words—never expressing a thought about this subject by hardly any snide remarks... was she trying to force-feminize me? One thing she did say, I remember— what my grandmother also would declare upon occasion, always in a foreboding sad, sonorous and fateful tone of voice:

> A whistling woman and a crowing hen never do come to a very good end.
> --Old folklore proverb.

It was proof of T's great mental block against his tortured childhood, that he never had thought until this day—nearly 60 years removed— that his mother, back in 1945, observing her tomboy child, clothing himself in bluejeans, plaid shirt, oxford shoes, may have found him so male like, it brought out the extra wrath she bestowed on him—as hatred of the man who had abused her, the boys grandfather; and as a warning to the child that he must break down, conform to the standards of being a girl...

Now, holding the RETROSPECT in his hands, face sober, he stared into space, remembering... that might have been one of the triggers of her schizophrenic rage... And he hadn't thought of it until now.

Sunday AM May 25
Day #6; Came up to meet Dalora at BART; did casual walk thru while waiting to see sky blue car/wagon pull up in front of parking garage; went down then up on interior under cement grey 3-story structure, just turning off to go back outside to the street—there was cat. Scruffy has black and white patches, ruffled fur from outdoors living. Fed him; again we exchanged looks. Cat seems bigger, more active. A success—am helping keep him alive. Hope he will find himself a

safe house, as he is feral and runs when I approach under the 8-foot distance margin.

PM May 25, Sunday

> Back down here on earth, I gotta get sales.
> --Sean, Babylon Falling, after lengthy political debate.

Sunny, but cold afternoon, bright light streams in upon the figure in the window seat. The young proprietor spoke with the old man about RETROSPECT, which the latter had painted & written over a 40-year period of his life; and the former had produced via modern-day technology of photography discs, & Internet POD. He informed Red:

> I like this, the writing compliments the painting, and visa versa. This will really catch people. It will speak to struggling artists. They will especially want this book.

The old guy thought:

> The kinds of images that are in my soul, people are going to want to see & read about; unlike a contented happy person whose smiling figures, albeit in brilliant, eye-catching Technicolor, occupy 200 picture frames, in their well-accomplished oeuvre; some art lovers in pain themselves will be attracted to tortured extreme of visual limits pushed by Van Gogh, stark revenge of (woman painter who cut off the head of her teacher); not placid water lily's of a wonderful Matise, yet still not as hideous as an Albrecht; ala The Portrait of Dorian Grey (homosexual subtext) by Oscar Wilde. They will see & buy my stuff, because it scours out the bottom of ones soul & returns, pronouncing some undeniable truth to the viewer.

AM Early Monday May 26, Memorial Day
7pm last night closed down bookstore w/Sean waiting while he put up his drawbridge for the night (the metal burglar bars) walked past new Starfucks, but didn't see tranny girl at work; thus did not go in. Went home. Jerked off, buzz clipped hair, trimmed beard. Slept. Awoke to work on the finishing touches of JOY/SIMCA! And thus the finale of the rondo; masterwork, OBEDIENCE TO THE CALL OF ART. Decided would use Student At The Golden Pot for its cover, Dr. Sam bought a copy of that print last night. Took me to dinner as sushi joint, for me, Beef Udo. Over Starfucks coffee we discussed the painting. He was especially pleased to discover insider info that underneath the golden pot in the picture from which the student draws

both paints and prose, was genitalia—female--- of the student, who is, in suggestion seated cross-legged with multicolor green/yellow backdrop, grass of a meadow or lawn masking his-her legs. Sam declared that in his most depressed hours, just knowing that genitalia lay right underneath the Golden Pot would cheer him greatly.

Also discussed the vagina in blue/red pubic hairs, of THE POOLSHOOTER's primary character, Sam saying he thought the rest of the figure looked like a man, to which I responded: *well yeah! It's a butch dike shooting pool!* One just like we were. Sean mentioned again the following day; that blue/red haired vagina was the first thing he'd noticed about the whole picture. My pictures have many layers...

I think of my friends who are gone—some in heaven. Others I have lost here on earth.

Dear Lord(ess) what ever I do, it must be to furtherance of my career—Your Art--- and to provide for my and animals and loved ones survival & to help this planet wherever possible.

The sun peeks out momentarily from behind 2 skyscrapers & the dark storm clouds of evening; with a brilliant gold light, then, vanishes once more. He sat there in Starfucks, the sun winking on/off; studying Hebrew—then went back to his cheerless rooms to lift weights, work on JOURNEY & to be the human for his cat & birds. Pages of ancient aleph-bet pushed aside, he began to write:

> For explanation, symbolism, let us go thru the RETROSPECT page by page.
>
> Ho's Bath. Gold high-heeled boot, her big feet centerground, will soon pull on these boots as she begins to walk the streets. Large hand taking off/putting on wig. Bar of soap masturbatorily placed, exposed electric light bulb suggests the shoddy hotel where the working girl must live—backdrop shadows/squares indicatory of the cold streets where she will go strolling. PS: *Ho's bath* is a slang expression of the working girls trade once taught to me by friend Natashia who sex-worked Chinatown once per month when the old men got their pensions; this is what she did:
>> Afterwords honey, you squat down over a basin of warm water, reach up inside you with two fingers and that stuff just comes right out, it spirals down into the basin.

Watermelon Eaters. —Note; 's', plural. Yes, 3 hands. Two of them delicately hold watermelon slice, a horse face being in background. Champaign glass; foreground. Face laughing, surreal, sinister, diabolical, skull like, merry.

Oyster Eater. Discoloration on forehead must be repaired. It is the soaking thru of a faux color and not intentional. Red hairnet, which Dr. Sam mistook for red hair. Simple figure—self-explanatory--solemnly eating oysters off a half shell prying them open with a knife. Bottle of vinegar sits on table. Red himself had so fond memories of clams on half shell at Nathan's in Coney Island w/friends in poverty ($1. per plate; cheap!) at age 16, 17, when he'd run away to Greenwich Village to be gay; however was first introduced to them by grandmother and her sister—his aunt, Anna, who lived in Bedford-Styvesant, Brooklyn-- on a family jaunt to Coney Island when he was young. He loved this dish—raw clams on half shell, so they may look like clams but picture is entitled Oysters, but was thinking of those good times. When it was painted in '69.

Lost Dog. Dog. Thrown ball. Figure top searches for dog, hand shading eyes its face being also a dogs face.

The Howl. Yelling face, fingers of hands spread, framing the head, encouraging it's scream. A second mouth, surreal to the side, also howls. Inside the centermost howling face lurks another strange face, mute, not howling, dumb.

La Suena. Surreal in background, left top, the dreamer dreams the scenes, its right hand embracing the canvas in which a series of characters frolic. A black man strides out of the canvas with a jaunty air, a rotund black woman behind; a couple embraces from the waist up—they are a single figure from the waist down, symbolizing androgyny. Several other figures walk into the canvas, one carrying a white lunch pail. To the right, another suggested figures, ghostly, one whiteface embracing a black one.

The Madman. Obvious theme. A deranged black man wields a knife or razor, he is a murderer. What is strange about this, is, I recall after painting it, some days or weeks, hearing about an identical murder in the Mission district, a black male knifing to death one or more persons. This painting was a premonition.

The Poolshooters. The shooter in addition to his-her previously discussed genitals, is centermost. Behind him to the left, an abstract figure whose predominate hand indicates the score, which he yells out of an open mouth. A third, ghostly figure, barely seen in dark blue background space between them.

The Players. It was too late to rename this—which I recall was its title back in 1970. In RETROSPECT, and on my posters it's Flash On The Hustler. The predominant chocolate brown figure is a hustler, street man, but very sensitive as the face indicates, and his ghostly white hat players hat does not sit well on his head. His crony a jive nigga in a yellow pimp suit, whose big balls and indication of a dick are suggested, laughs uproariously while pointing a scornful finger---his face is a grotesque caricature of brutal jest, he is half human, because of lacking a heart. Another massive blue figure with a crimson, blood red head looms behind him. Disaster waiting to take both men out? Oh, the finger of scorn is colored by skin identical to the sensitive player, and not his darker companion; it could be the extension of the arm of the mysterious massive blue figure behind them, and at the same time, a turn about of the main 'Player'—the sensitive one's--own karma. His own scorn and bad deeds returning to condemn him?

The Arab. I believe photog Suzanne de Young first labeled this painting the A-rab (pron.). He/she is androgynous. Third-estate, mixed race. Wears Jacobs Coat Of Many Colors. S/he stands on an unearthly plane—the planet earth can be seen at its horizon. A foreign object is sweeping down at him—or, moving away. Is it troubles descending upon his head? When doing the Sci-Fi trilogy Unity of Utopia, I used this picture for the 3rd book, Acts Against The Powers Of Authority, because I had a dream upon waking up, that this picture (purposely unfinished in 1969) had found its completion now—the object being a spaceship taking off in the background, and many silver white stars dotted the other side of the yellow sky---this I rudimentary painted in, in the canvas hanging on wall of my studio, circa 2007.

Student At The Golden Pot. The student wears the talleet—a Hebrew holy prayer shawl, given to me in a vision @ synagogue by God—the vision, drawing me to it's holiness, to holiness, and to God. The student wears a yarmulke, also stripped blue/white like a talleet. This rabbinical type being is drawing inspiration from the golden pot, which expands by suggestion in ever widening concentric circles. Both a painter's brush, and a writer's pen dip into the pot. It covers genitalia previously discussed—no longer visible. The knees—suggested of the student--- grip the pot from both sides. In the background, a schoolhouse; steeple of a church? Figures approaching, studying, learning and following the Students example. The smile on the Student's face is enigmatic. The brilliant orange/red sun breaks directly onto his head.

The Blue Dog. The figure, centermost wears the tallees-striped headgear in the fashion of Mother Teresa's holy garment, who the figure resembles; yet the face is not well defined, a blur; and this figure makes the holy sign with two fingers, yet its other hand is a dogs paw, colored blue—the same color as the dog, whose face is pronounced, maybe griming with a red tongue apparent, its eyes steady gazing out at the viewer, for it is the dog in fact who is the primary subject; it is the dog whose paw, upheld is actually a hand, this hand gives the Benediction! The holy blessing!

I am developing a slight smoker's cough from the madman who lives in the basement, who nobody knows, nor wants to know, his name. I know Hashem is my guide, has given me Her/His Purpose, and will deliver me by His/Her Hand.

I think painters of the future will wish all artists had described their work so carefully—to be an inspiration, an instruction, and to clarify any mystery. We are in an age that this is possible, unlike the historic periods of art, when even a biography written after an artists demise was unheard of, and, as usual women, and 3rd estate persons were undocumented altogether.

Regarding matters of revolution, I leave you with this, from Ana Siljak, Angel Of Vengeance:

> We must pay attention to the particular characteristics of the moral nature of crimes against the state. The physiognomy of such crimes is often quite variable. That which yesterday was considered a crime aginst the state, today or tomorrow, becomes a highly respected act of civic courage. State crimes are often just the untimely expressions of a doctrine of premature reform, the preaching of that which is not yet ripe and whose time has not yet come.
> --Peter Alexandrov's summation, trial of Vera Zasulich.

I leave you with another vision! Transman goes nearby to attend the opening of a trendy, upscale shop, on the common block, following on the heels some better dressed cronies from bookstore—but is denied admittance! Blocked at the doorway, and told; Go Away!   I leave you with the sight of black clad old man shouting into the empty air! About injustice! Unfairness! Him knowing all the things which have been, and seeing the dreadful stuff the future foretells!

     Justice! Justice tempered with mercy.

I hope this collection of Volumes 6-10 of my journal; JOURNEY, OBEDIENCE TO THE CALL OF ART will be a blessing for you all!

Red Jordan Arobateau
May 27, 2008
12:00 AM Pacific Standard Time
San Francisco, CA
USA

www.ingramcontent.com/pod-product-compliance
Lightning Source LLC
Chambersburg PA
CBHW020722180526
45163CB00001B/68